CW01496510

Pit-folk and Peers
The Remarkable History
of the People of Fryston

Volume 2 — Diamonds and Rust (1909-2023)

David P. Waddington

route

First published by Route in 2025
Pontefract, UK
info@route-online.com
www.route-online.com

ISBN: 978-1901927-94-8

First Edition

David P. Waddington asserts his moral
right to be identified as the author of this book

Cover Design:
John Sellards

Typeset in Bembo by Route

Printed & bound in Great Britain by TJ Books

All rights reserved
No reproduction of this text without written permission

In loving memory of Edith and Samuel Holmes
and all their beloved sons and daughters.

Foreword

This second volume of the 'remarkable history' of the 'pit-folk and peers' of Fryston, Castleford, deliberately concludes in 2023. That year marked the 150th anniversary of the ceremonial occasion on which the future Lord Crewe dug out the 'first sod' in the sinking of the new Fryston Colliery in the grounds of his father's Fryston Hall estate.

I am proud to add that this date also marks the centenary of my father's arrival as the new general practitioner for Fryston and neighbouring Airedale, from Lurgan in Northern Ireland. This was the start of a long and mutually cherished relationship between my own family and the people of Fryston, which has endured to this day.

I feel equally proud (and humbled) by the way in which David Waddington refers to my father on these pages as 'the beloved Dr Sloan', in describing the kindly, unpatronising and egalitarian manner by which he related to his patients. I know that he consciously under-charged his patients, accepted payment 'in kind' (in the form of a loaf of bread, perhaps) or waived his fee entirely in those austere decades predating the NHS. These selfless and compassionate values were consistent with local sensibilities. Not surprisingly, he was universally regarded as a friend.

It was, perhaps, inevitable that the harsh industrial environment in which my father practiced proved progressively intolerable for his first wife and my three half-siblings, and hastened the breakdown of his marriage. His second wife, my mother, Gerda, subsequently arrived (as a newly qualified doctor) in Fryston during World War II, having fled from Nazi Germany, and married my father soon afterwards. It never ceases to amaze me that the people of the village befriended her so readily. She was cut from the same cloth as my father; and, following the inception of the new health service, they were both regularly rebuked by the medical authorities for constantly prescribing only the best available medication for their patients.

My post-war upbringing was a far cry from that of my village-born contemporaries. While they mostly lived in modest terraced homes with outside toilets, we resided in a five-bedroom property known as 'Tieve Tara' (the Gaelic term for 'house on the hill'), well beyond the village boundary. Ours was one of five large houses located on the relatively secluded Airedale Drive, all with beautiful, well-kept gardens. The first house was the manager's and his was one of two properties also boasting a tennis court. My parents employed a housekeeper and a gardener, while I also enjoyed the company of a live-in nanny. I was stridently discouraged from playing or consorting with the village lads, who were considered too physically robust for me to contend with.

Yet, for all that, after completing my medical studies and working down south for several years, I eventually yielded to an irresistible inner yearning by returning to live in Tieve Tara and re-opening the adjoining surgery. I gradually built up a thriving new practice – thanks, no doubt, to my family name. I remained in that role from 1978 until retiring in 2005. During that time, I witnessed, first-hand, the impact of the miners' strike and resulting deindustrialisation. I like to think that I consistently stayed true to my parents' working values and treated my patients accordingly. My continuing relationship with local people and their reminiscences about my parents constantly remind me that David's two-part history of Fryston is something that greatly underscores my own identity.

David's personal roots in Fryston stretch back to 1901, when his maternal grandfather, Sam Holmes, arrived as an eight-year-old with his large family from his native Shropshire, via a brief stay in the Nottinghamshire coalfield. Sam and his wife, the Whitwood-born Edith Bairstow, eventually settled in the house on Brook Street that both David's mother and he, too, were born in.

I was first introduced to David in the late 1980s, when he interviewed me at great length about my parents' backgrounds and working relationship with the people of Fryston, and also questioned me about my own upbringing and subsequent experience as the village doctor. It gave me enormous pleasure to talk to him. We have remained good friends since then, and I am delighted to see that many quotes and insights deriving from those interviews have now been included in this book.

David and I had both been aware when we first met that an earlier connection had already been forged between our two families. This was due to the fact that David's Auntie Elsie had served as a housemaid for my father and his first wife in the 1930s, and remained a good friend of the family long after his remarriage. In slightly more tenuous vein, Elsie's younger sister, Dora, occupied the similar role of housekeeper for our one-time next-door neighbour, the charismatic ex-Fryston pit boss, Jim Bullock, who features prominently in this volume.

The woman who David affectionately refers to as 'Our Dor' died, as coincidence would have it, just short of her 101st birthday in January 2023. She would undoubtedly have taken pride in what her nephew has accomplished on these pages.

For David Waddington has compiled this truly remarkable history with the kind of empathy and respect that comes from such a close emotional connection to his subject matter, but also with the rigour and self-discipline of a professional sociologist and historian.

He also writes with an open-minded appreciation of the philanthropic and humanitarian traditions of Fryston's land-owning aristocracy and their illustrious descendants (the 'Peers', referred to in the title), and of their impressive contributions to British cultural and political history.

As such, these two volumes are a testament to the rich and enviable social heritage belonging, not simply to the people – whether past or present – of Fryston, to residents of the wider town of Castleford, or to former mining communities more generally, but to all members of an island nation that was historically built on coal.

Dr Richard Sloan, MBE, PhD, FRCGP
Author of:
The English Doctor
Tieve Tara
A Journey of Friendships: Cherished Bonds Woven Through Time

Chapter One

Crewe Road Revisited

The Road Not Taken

A short, tree-lined road in Castleford, West Yorkshire, flanked on either side by a diverse array of privately-owned houses, provides a handy conduit between the large Airedale and Ferry Fryston housing estates to its north and the streets of Townville to its south. It takes a mere three minutes for the pedestrian – and scarcely seconds for the motorist – to travel the full distance of this aptly named 'Poplar Avenue', as it extends upwards from Sheepwalk Lane and terminates at its junction with the longer Crewe Road, Airedale.

By taking a right turn onto Crewe Road, walkers or drivers find themselves only 30 to 40 metres away from the entrance to the Airedale Academy state secondary school. It was under its former name of Castleford Technical High that I joined this institution as a pupil in September 1968. The school was renamed Airedale High, following its amalgamation with the Airedale and Ferry Fryston secondary modern establishments in the transition to comprehensive education three years later. I stayed on to complete my GCSE O- and A-level studies before entering university in 1975. *

On first joining 'Cas Tech', pupils like me were assigned to one of four 'houses', each named after a distinguished scientist, inventor, technological innovator or social reformer (all of whom were male). These were: Sir Humphry Davy, the Cornish chemist and inventor of the miners' safety lamp; Sir Michael Faraday, the Surrey-born scientist, famous for his contributions to the fields of electromagnetism and electrochemistry; John Smeaton, a civil engineer from Austhorpe, Yorkshire, who built a variety of bridges and canals, along with the third Eddystone Lighthouse; and Richard Oastler, the Leeds-born Tory politician who campaigned for shorter working hours.

Somewhat perplexingly, we were never taught the origins or significance of the street name on which our school was built. It seems inexplicable in hindsight that each of our houses was named in honour of a 'role model' of dubious significance to our lives – rather than in recognition of seemingly more relevant figures, such as: Lord Crewe (in whose honour the road is called); his illustrious father, Richard Monckton Milnes; or Crewe's eminent sister, the writer, Florence Henniker. The fact remains that we were taught nothing whatsoever about these distinguished one-time occupants of the now derelict, nearby Fryston Hall mansion or, for that matter, their many celebrated descendants, illustrious visitors or associates.

Within easy reach of the Airedale Academy is 'The Square', a local shopping hub and bus terminus. Perched directly opposite to this is the imposing Holy Cross Church. These two landmarks are situated on either side of another T-junction formed by Crewe Road, this time with the mile-long Fryston Road – the backbone of the 1920s Airedale council house estate. The lower half mile of the latter thoroughfare runs steeply downhill before arriving at another road junction, heading left along Wheldon Road into the nearby Castleford town centre, or right into the close-lying village of New Fryston (colloquially referred to simply as 'Fryston').

Only six streets remain of this former mining community (including the small, isolated row of four 'Smith Cottages') out of the twelve rows of terraces existing in its heyday. The pithead winding gear, colliery buildings and surrounding land has been supplanted by a new housing estate, similar in design to a slightly less recent property development standing on the outskirts of the village, a few metres away from the railway bridge which constitutes the only route into, and out of, Fryston.

The street names of the new estate, which is located downhill from what remains of the original village, suggest a closer affinity to such natural landmarks as the River Aire and the nearby Fairburn Ings nature reserve than to Fryston's longstanding association with coal. Occupants of Starling Way, Linnet Drive, Swift Way, Dunnock Way and Mallard Close overlook the departure point of the recently conceived Fryston Country Trail.

These new and original settlements are physically separated by a centrally located 'village green' and play area, containing some of the last vestiges of Fryston's mining heritage: an almost obligatory half-sunken pit wheel and a specially commissioned cairn sculpture (a finger-like construction of three stones, piled up on top of each other), whose symbolism is lost on most observers. Proudly attached to the supportive brickwork structure underlying the railway bridge is a three-dimensional wall mural, comprising two adjacent images: one of Fryston miners installing pit props underground; the other depicting four young miners and two greyhounds, variously leaning against, or perched on top of, a brick-built garden wall.

Halfway across the few acres of fields and woodland separating Fryston from nearby Ferrybridge lies a derelict stable and a handful of equally rundown outbuildings – all that remains of the once majestic Fryston Hall, the former ancestral seat of Monckton Milnes and, subsequently, Lord Crewe. To witness further local manifestations of Fryston's aristocratic and mining heritages, it is necessary to retrace one's footsteps to the Airedale Holy Cross.

Built in 1932 by local miners and their families, this church represents a fusion of Fryston's socially elitist and proletarian pasts. Nothing exemplifies this more succinctly than three symbols in particular: the porticos of the church, which once dominated the entrance to Fryston Hall; the church altar, which is built on stone extracted from Fryston's Beeston seam; and a miner's Davy Lamp (donated by Fryston Colliery) which still hangs by the aumbry – the small steel safe in which the 'Sacrament of Christ's Body and Blood' is reserved for special Communion.[1]

These physical landmarks (the church, the remaining streets of Fryston, its play area and wall mural, and the decaying outbuildings of Fryston Hall) constitute the only tangible local reminders of the area's aristocratic and industrial heritage. Also available, however, is a vast trove of literary and archival evidence, capable of providing a compelling insight into Fryston's otherwise vanishing past. Elements of this resource were employed in Volume 1 to document the seminal period in Fryston's history running from 1809 to 1908. This second volume now utilises similar materials, in conjunction with face-to-face interviews with former village residents, to present a corresponding narrative of the more contemporary historical era stretching from 1909 to 2023.

The first component of our two-part study[2] – 'Echoes of Fryston

13

Hall' — concentrated primarily on the exploits, friendships and accomplishments of Richard Monckton Milnes (the first Lord Houghton) of Fryston Hall, and, to a lesser extent, the early lives and careers of two of his three children: the above-mentioned Florence Ellen Hungerford Henniker (nee Milnes) and Robert Offley Ashburton Crewe-Milnes (latterly, Lord Crewe).

This earlier instalment emphasised how Milnes was one of the most ubiquitous and socially extravagant individuals of his day. His Fryston Hall mansion and London salon ranked among the main hubs of Victorian society. He counted scores of the brightest political and cultural personalities of the era among his close friends and acquaintances — exemplified by the fact that he almost married the immortal Florence Nightingale. Milnes was a far more estimable individual than the flippantly mischievous and libertine character he was sometimes portrayed as. There is incontrovertible evidence to show that he was an immensely committed and greatly renowned political reformer and philanthropist, as well as a first-rate poet and biographer.

'Echoes of Fryston Hall' also charted the flourishing literary career of the younger of Milnes's two daughters, Florence, showing how she not only achieved acclaim as the author of a fine series of novels, but also became the protégé, muse and romantic obsession of the great British writer, Thomas Hardy. Just like her father before her, Henniker was roundly praised for her humanitarian and charitable preoccupations, including sustained attempts to relieve the terrible plight of military horses. This was a commitment she shared both with Hardy and her husband, Arthur, a cavalry officer whose heroism in the Boer War was widely recognised. It remains indisputable that both Florence and her father contributed widely and with great distinction to the British social, political, literary and cultural life of the nineteenth century.

The first volume dwelled with relative brevity on the early ambassadorial career of Milnes's son, Robert (most notably, his two-year tenure as Viceroy of Ireland), portraying him as a somewhat staid, aloof and uninspiring individual, scarred by the emotionally debilitating loss of his young wife, Sibyl. Yet, evidence was already emerging of the solid judgement and adroit strategic skills he would subsequently deploy during a lengthy and distinguished political career.

Correspondingly, Volume 1 also focussed (again, quite briefly) on the early origins and development of Fryston village, paying particular attention to the industrial relations activity (most notably the Wheldale-Fryston strike of 1902-04) and associated migratory patterns, which gave rise to its distinctive demographic profile. In addition to outlining further developments in the lives of Lord Crewe, his wife, sister (Florence) and the most prominent of his descendants, the present volume continues to trace the evolution of the community and its colliery from the late Edwardian era to the commemorative year of 2023, which marked the 150th anniversary of the inaugural sinking of the mine.

Equivalent amounts of energy are therefore devoted to describing the fundamentally disparate (though often converging) experience of both the 'pit-folk' and 'peers' alluded to in the main title of each volume. The following two sections of this introductory chapter pave the way for such discussion by: (i) highlighting those individuals within each social stratum whose exploits were of especial historical significance; and (ii) signposting the key events and developments on which we shall primarily focus our attention. The first of these sections focuses on those members of the 'Milnes-Crewe dynasty' (see Figure 1) whose lives will be most closely scrutinised in subsequent chapters.

Roots and Branches
It was the renowned chronicler of British mining history, Robert Page Arnot, who noted how the 'splendour and fair seeming of peace and prosperity' marking the first decade of the twentieth century endured right up to the death of Edward VII in May 1910.

> But from 1910 onwards the storm clouds were gathering. The epoch of monopoly capitalism, coincident with the twentieth century, was now made visible by many signs and tokens. The growing rivalry of the Great Powers had taken shape in the two armed camps: the Triple Alliance headed by Germany and the Triple Entente headed by Great Britain. [...] At home there were signs of a new epoch in the militant suffragettes resorting to violence, in the House of Lords rejecting the Lloyd George Budget and so bringing on a 'constitutional crisis,' in the threat from Northern Ireland that Home Rule legislation would be met by armed rebellion.[3]

Figure 1:
The Milnes–Crewe Dynasty

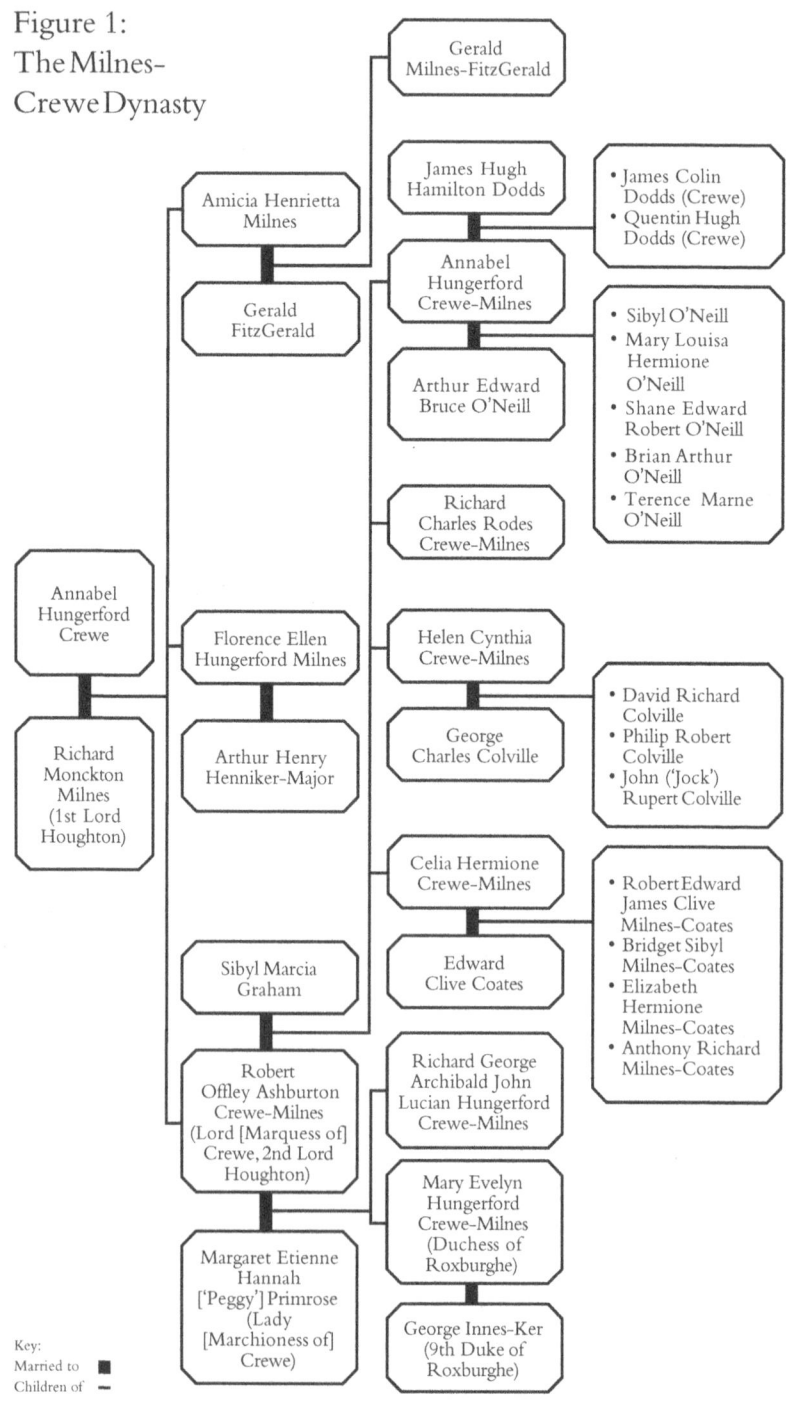

Key:
Married to ■
Children of ▬

This 'new turbulence' was accompanied by the numerical growth and organisational development of British trade unionism (including the Miners' Federation of Great Britain), which proved more ready to strike in response to higher costs of living. It was amidst these increasingly challenging circumstances that Lord Crewe first embarked on his long ministerial career.

By the onset of this new era, Lord and Lady Crewe had already relocated to Crewe Hall, Cheshire, having sold off their two Yorkshire estates, Bawtry Hall (Doncaster) and Fryston Hall in 1904. The latter had originally been leased by Sir John Austin, erstwhile MP for Osgoldcross, who ran local breweries in Castleford, Wakefield and his native Kippax. Austin bought the Hall outright in 1906, but died in the same year, following a long illness spent at his seaside retreat in Scarborough.[4] After his death, ownership of the Hall was passed on to his company, Austin Brothers Limited, which was run by his two sons, William and Joseph. The building was briefly occupied by the former, who soon left it, abandoned and neglected, while allowing the surrounding land to be utilised by a local horse breeder.[5]

As of 12 April 1908, Lord Crewe had been appointed Secretary of State for the Colonies; and, soon afterwards he succeeded Lord Ripon, both as Liberal Leader of the House of Lords, and as Lord Privy Seal. Sometimes referred to more formally as The Lord Keeper of the Privy Seal, the last-mentioned role invested him with the responsibility for 'the organisation of government business in the House, providing assistance to all Lords and offering advice on procedure', and for expressing 'the collective feelings of the House on formal occasions, such as motions of thanks or congratulations'.[6]

Crewe's rapid elevation to these positions provided the initial momentum for a remarkably influential political and (latterly) diplomatic career that extended into the early 1930s. His brief tenure at the Colonial Office (1908 to 1910) was followed by a slightly longer spell as Secretary of State for India (1910 to 1915), and then as member of the Coalition Government's War Council during the global conflict of 1914-1918. He continued to serve for this entire period as Liberal leader of the Lord's, only vacating this position in 1923, by which time he had become the British Ambassador to France, a role in which he remained until 1928. We shall see in the following chapters how, for the best part of these two decades, Crewe would become significantly embroiled, whether domestically, within the colonies and on the wider world stage, in some of the era's most controversial and momentous political and diplomatic developments.

By 1909, Crewe's wife, Peggy, had become well established as the patron and/or figurehead of a wide variety of charitable and educational institutions. She was an active fundraiser, for example, both for the pioneering Bedford Women's College within London University, and the Women's Free-Trade Union. Her sister-in-law, Florence Henniker, continued, in the meantime, to enjoy a close friendship with the great writer, Thomas Hardy, who strove, assiduously as ever, to help promote her literary career. On one occasion (in 1907), for example, he thanked her for presenting him with a copy of the newly-published novel, *Our Fatal Shadows*, which he regarded as 'a great advance' upon anything she had previously written.[7]

Lord Crewe's three surviving children (Annabel, Celia and Cynthia) had all entered married life by this stage, having long departed from their childhood home of Fryston Hall. The first to do so was the eldest sister, Annabel, who was married in 1902 to the 'A' Squadron 2nd Life Guards Captain and future MP for Mid-Antrim, Arthur O'Neill (one of two brothers and three sisters from a prominent aristocratic Irish family). Annabel and her husband were destined to have five children together (three sons and two daughters) and spend much of their married life at the O'Neill's ancestral seat of Shane's Castle in Northern Ireland and, to a lesser extent, at their second home in London.

One of Lord Crewe's twin daughters, Celia, had been introduced to her future husband while staying with Lord and Lady Aberdeen at Dublin Castle. Captain Edward Clive Coates was serving there as Master of the Horse on the Vice-Regal Staff, having recently returned home from military duties in India. It was only when Celia returned to Dublin a year later that she and Edward were first engaged and then married (on 8 October 1906), eventually having two sons and two daughters together between September 1907 and March 1920.

The second twin, Cynthia, was married to George Charles Colville on 21 January 1908 at St. Margaret's Church, Westminster. The couple had first met while indulging in their shared passion for sailing, boat-racing and other aquatic sports while on holiday on the Isle of Wight. At seventeen years Cynthia's senior, 'Geordie' Colville was the latest in a long family line of army or naval officers. He and Cynthia would remain happily married for 34 years, producing three sons together.

Of Lord Crewe's three daughters, it was Cynthia who would go on to achieve greatest public prominence, due partly to her much-acclaimed work on behalf of women and children in the deprived London Borough of Shoreditch, but also on account of her role as Woman of the Bedchamber to Queen Mary. Her twin sister, Celia, generally steered well clear of any public attention, while the older Annabel was destined to experience the tragic loss of her first husband – the first MP to be killed in the First World War – before raising two more sons as part of her second marriage to the diplomat, Hugh Dodds.

This second volume reviews all such developments in the lives of these former residents of Fryston Hall. Additionally, it also traces the activities and achievements of three of Lord Crewe's grandsons, each of whom became exceedingly famous in his own right: Cynthia's youngest son (Jock Colville); Annabel's earliest child from her marriage to Arthur (Terence O'Neill); and Quentin, the younger of the two boys produced by Annabel and Hugh Dodds.

Jock could claim the distinction of having served as private secretary to three successive British Prime Ministers and the future Queen Elizabeth II. A second such spell with Winston Churchill saw Colville acting secretively and unconstitutionally to offset a potential national crisis. No less momentous was the period spent by Terence as Prime Minister of Northern Ireland, which was accompanied by unprecedented levels of sectarian conflict. It was the youngest of these three grandsons, Quentin, who managed to overcome severe physical disability in cultivating a considerable cultural reputation (mirroring that of his great grandfather, Richard Monckton Milnes) as a writer, debonair socialite and member of royal circles.

The final member of the Milnes-Crewe dynasty to figure prominently in forthcoming chapters is Mary, the only daughter of Lord Crewe and his second wife. Similar in age to her nephews, Jock and Terence, Mary is chiefly remembered for the notorious circumstances surrounding her divorce from a well-known Scottish aristocrat. Following the deaths of both her parents, she inherited her mother's Surrey mansion, whose contents included the remaining artistic and literary legacies of Fryston Hall. The subsequent bequest she made to her godson – a well-known historian and television presenter – and donation of books to a high-ranking British university would determine the final resting place of these rare surviving artefacts.

Diamonds and Rust

Not to be overshadowed in this narrative is the story of the second of our featured sections of society. On 21 May 1853, an article called 'Coal – Our Black Diamonds' appeared in the influential *Scientific American* magazine.[8] This essay emphasised the growing importance of coal to the world economy. It claimed that it had been the unrivalled capacity of two nations in particular – Great Britain and the United States of America – to harness this crucial resource with such effectiveness that had given them both a vast economic and industrial advantage over international competitors. This theme was repeated in the wartime Britain of 1915 by the British Minister of Munitions (and Prime Minister in waiting), David Lloyd George, who asserted to an audience of coal-owners, colliery managers and miners that:

> In peace and in war King Coal is the paramount lord of industry. It enters into every article of consumption and utility. It is our real international coinage. When we buy goods, food and raw material abroad, we pay not in gold but in coal. We pay in diamonds, except that they are black, and not in gold. Coal brings meat and bread, say, from the Argentine, and brings it all the way. It does more. It pays across the counter there for it out of its own pocket. We cannot do without coal. In war time it is life for us and death for our foes. Coal is the most terrible of enemies and the most potent of friends.[9]

It was, of course, the escalating demand for this then-precious resource which gave Fryston its principal raison d'être.

In 2005, the freelance journalist, Stephen McClarence, provided a potted history of the village's rise and fall in a regional newspaper article.[10] McClarence informed his readers that the village was initially constructed in 1887 to accommodate workers at the newly developed Fryston Colliery.

In its prime years (extending from the early 1930s to the mid-1950s), the village's population numbered between 1,500 and 2000 people, while the colliery itself employed a workforce of approximately 1,300 men.

The article revealed that, in addition to its twelve terraced streets, the village was self-sufficient in possessing its own educational, religious, retail, leisure, health and legal facilities, as well as a thriving informal economy. Due, no doubt, to its physical isolation and social and occupational homogeneity, the community was characterised by a rare spirit of independence and togetherness.

McClarence explained how this distinctive social ethos had been captivatingly illustrated over a 60-year period in the photographs of a local miner-cum-hairdresser, Jack Hulme. This community stalwart had continued taking pictures as the village entered a steep decline in the 1970s and 1980s, accelerated by the miners' strike of 1984-85 and the closure of Fryston Pit shortly afterwards.

> Three years before he died in 1990, Hulme brought his legacy full-circle by photographing the demolition of the recently-closed pit. At the time, the demolition seemed like Fryston's last rites; the pit was its only reason for being there. Many of the terraces were boarded-up or bulldozed; the bus service was cut back; prairies of dereliction stretched out. With most of the shops already closed, the community shrank to 150. The atmosphere was listless, with a sense of time suspended. It was eerily quiet. Redundant miners walked their dogs or scrambled over slag heaps, picking for coal, as though the 1930s had never gone away. As a final symbolic farewell to the old days, the corrugated iron chapel that hosted Jack Hulme's funeral was demolished and its graveyard left bleak and overgrown. The blue plaque marking Hulme's former home was a rare splash of colour.[11]

The cumulative neglect and deterioration of the local housing stock, the out-migration of younger residents, and the fact that coal was being supplanted by rival forms of energy, consigned Fryston to the growing 'rust belt' of the declining Yorkshire coalfield. Here was a term initially applied to the once-prosperous but now decaying, steel-making and coal-producing heartlands of the United States,[12] although it clearly resonates with the corresponding British experience.[13]

McClarence explained how, by 2005, the village had entered a period of renewal and reconsolidation, epitomised by the grassing over of its former slag heaps. 'There were still no shops,' he wrote, 'but a regular bus service resumed and many of the houses were spruced up.'[14] The 200 people now living in Fryston constituted a 'fiercely rooted community'.[15] Attempts were also underway by national and local regeneration agencies – most notably the charitable Castleford Heritage Trust (CHT) – to socially and economically regalvanise Fryston and restore a sense of pride in its lengthy mining tradition.[16]

The most high-profile of such activities was the creation of a local village green by an acclaimed American architectural designer, which was partly commissioned by Channel Four and featured in its *Kevin McLoud's Big Town Plan* series of television programmes. McClarence remarked that, insofar as regeneration experts were concerned, the green now represented 'a stylish community space', variously lauded as 'dynamic', 'exciting' and 'stunning'. He was personally more sceptical of its value to local residents. It constituted, he ventured, 'an unlikely adornment for a former pit village'. All told, he went on, 'it suggests something between a sculpture park, an adventure playground and a post-modern garden of remembrance'.[17]

Other developments followed in its wake. A second commemorative feature appearing in 2011 was the previously mentioned 'wall sculpture' (commissioned by the CHT) by the former Fryston miner-turned-artist, Harry Malkin. The images featured in this casting were reproductions of much earlier photographs taken by Jack Hulme. At this juncture, the village had been reduced to only six of its twelve original terraced streets, two of which were soon to be given a substantial makeover. By 2019, the former colliery buildings had been supplanted by the new housing estate, also referred to earlier.

A second strand of our two-part history of Fryston continues to trace this progressive development, followed by the eventual near demise, of the village and its mine. This narrative will incorporate comprehensive overviews of Fryston's most prosperous period (from the 1920s to the mid-1950s), via its threatened extinction of the 1980s and 1990s, onto more recent attempts to ensure its long-term viability. It will thus comprise a longitudinal insight into a former British industrial way of life already in danger of being forgotten. Central to our discussion are recurring glimpses, authenticated by the accounts of former residents, of the various ways in which local miners and their families 'culturally adapted'[18] to and therefore coped with the arduous, often dangerous and exploitative circumstances of their everyday existence.[19]

This aspect of our study includes first-hand, local perspectives on what it was like to live through such key historical events as the two World Wars (of 1914-1918 and 1939-1945), the General Strike of 1926, the nationalisation of the mines and introduction of the National Health Service (in 1947 and 1948, respectively), and the year-long miners' strike of 1984-1985.

Also conspicuous in this narrative are numerous high-profile local activities and achievements (e.g. the construction by Fryston villagers of their own welfare hall, sports stadium and place of worship, and an especially daring underground rescue which earned one local pit deputy the highest possible civilian decoration for bravery). The exploits of the colliery's much-vaunted association football team – most especially, its unflagging attempts to win the coveted West Riding County FA Challenge Cup (WRCC Cup) – provided an additional reason for Fryston to be persistently featured in the media.

A ubiquitous presence within this historical account is that of Jim Bullock, whose journey from pony boy to colliery manager, landowner, and founder member (and, ultimately, national president) of a managerial trade union provides a unifying thread for many of the following chapters.

In the concluding chapter of Volume 1, anticipatory references were made to individuals and families already residing in Fryston in the early 1900s who were likewise destined to figure prominently in the events of subsequent decades. Included here were members of the Soar, Whetton, Kriens and Holmes families, all of whom served with distinction in the Great War of 1914-18; and the charismatic barber-cum-musician-cum-amateur photographer, Jack Hulme, already alluded to above. Further significant and frequently mentioned contributions to Fryston's history were made by scores of other village stalwarts: e.g. a selfless local midwife; a beloved village doctor and his refugee Jewish wife; a cantankerous butcher who saved the village from starvation; an inspirational parish priest who oversaw the building of the Holy Cross; and two young sweethearts separated by global conflict, but romantically reunited afterwards. The exploits of all these and more are celebrated in coming chapters.

Emotional Regeneration

The task of highlighting the nature, achievements and significance of our two juxtaposing sections of society in the period from 1909 to 2023 is attempted with continuing reference to a diverse range of biographical and autobiographical accounts, archival sources (including relevant documentation and media coverage) and face-to-face interviews with 60 current and former residents of Fryston (and/or people who worked at the colliery) undertaken in 1986 and 1987, shortly after the closure of the mine.[20] A full list of these respondents appears in the Appendix. The widespread use of interview material underlines a commitment to prioritising the lived experience and recollections of relevant actors over more arid 'statements of fact'. Patience will be required of the reader as the focus of our discussion repeatedly shifts back and forth from one of the two featured class strata onto the other.

There is a growing desire among members of former mining areas to reclaim, preserve and reassert their industrial heritage – not least, for the benefit of current and future generations. This trend is epitomised by the inception of the New Herrington Miners' Banner Partnership of County Durham.[21] Following a period of mourning and retrospection in the wake of the miners' strike, the Partnership achieved fruition in 1999, when a core group of community activists (including the former NUM Lodge Official) set out to 're-establish the old collective identity lost following the closure of the mine, around which a new sense of community could coalesce'.[22]

As its name suggests, the Partnership was initially intent on creating a substitute pit banner for the one rendered obsolete by pit closure. This artefact was sure to embody profound symbolic and emotional significance:

> For them the Banner was now a physical representation of a unique way of life that had been destroyed. It was carried now in a celebration of, and commitment to, the maintenance of a social order and occupational identity that underpinned all that they were. It was no less than a defiant and iconic emblem upon which their lives and the life of their community were represented.[23]

In due course, the newly resurrected New Herrington banner became the centrepiece of a wider touring exhibition which included a diverse range of accompanying items, such as mining tools, books and photographs. Eventually, the Partnership accepted an offer to house a permanent exhibition of memorabilia within the community's YMCA building.

Wray describes this as an act of 'cultural or emotional regeneration'. He refers, by way of illustration, to the assertion by the Partnership's treasurer that he and his colleagues were striving to see 'a proper history written, a people's history; the truth' – one that will 'tell the kids what our lives were about and how those lives have changed' and 'give them some pride in who they are'.[24] People like this treasurer saw themselves as 'guardians of a collective memory of occupation, trade union and community that they are determined to pass on to a generation that, in these social excluded communities, will never be able to achieve for themselves'.[25]

I announced in Volume 1 that the present study harbours a similar ambition to that stated by the New Herrington Partnership, insofar as it sets out to 'reclaim' and 'celebrate' the 'unique heritage of a village whose identity and raison d'être have otherwise been erased'.[26] Its focus extends more widely than this, however, due to its commitment to presenting a history of the Fryston proletariat alongside a corresponding overview of that of its aristocratic counterparts. It will become apparent that the aggregated histories of these class factions constitute an unrivalled local heritage capable of providing positive social identity and enhanced self-esteem as an antidote to sustained industrial decline. In the next two chapters, we start to outline this argument by redirecting our attention back onto the early career of the fundamentally significant figure of Lord Crewe.

Chapter Two
A Mahatma, a Mad Mullah, Concubines and Kings

'Neither Bold nor Revolutionary'
Our narrative resumes in 1909, one year into Lord Crewe's brief stint as Colonial Secretary, a period not generally considered the most auspicious of his career:

> Crewe's reign at the Colonial Office was stamped by common sense and dignity. It was neither bold nor revolutionary, and though certain major policy decisions were taken during his two years' tenure of the office he cannot be classed among the very few great Secretaries of State who have had our very great Colonial Empire in their charge.[27]

Pope-Hennessy maintains that public concern in Britain at this time was 'as languid as it has always been on imperial or colonial matters'.[28] It was only when relevant issues were highlighted by sensationalist media commentary that they briefly aroused public attention. There were three such examples in this era, all of which proved problematic from Crewe's perspective.

By the time he entered office, the unification of the South African colonies into one self-governing nation had largely been accomplished. A constitution was agreed in February 1909 and formally established in May of the following year.[29] A related issue, involving the newly emerging South African government's restrictive attitude to Indian migration, had still not been resolved. This latter controversy brought Crewe into direct contact with one of the most exalted and estimable figures of the twentieth century, Mohandas Karamchand (later, 'Mahatma') Gandhi.

It is evident with hindsight that the Colonial Secretary's dismissive attitude to Gandhi's pleas for Indian migrants to be treated more equitably had a transformative effect on the latter's approach to British domination of his country. Crewe fared no more admirably, and with similarly unfortunate consequences, in his handling of the two other major crises of this era: the rebellious behaviour of a religious leader in the British Protectorate of Somaliland; and a moral panic concerning sexual relationships between British officers and 'native' women in the colonies. These three infamous episodes are closely considered in this chapter.

Pope-Hennessy balanced his somewhat reticent evaluation of his subject's period in office by observing that, in every sphere of politics, the Liberal Prime Minister, H.H. Asquith, 'could count upon the intimate support of Crewe, who proved from the outset to be a steadying and moderating influence'.[30] This was exemplified by Crewe's 'firm, sagacious attitude through the Parliament Bill controversy, which highlighted his character at its best'.[31] Centrally significant in this regard were Crewe's close and extremely confiding relationships, firstly with King Edward VII, and then with his successor, George V. As we shall see here and in Chapter 3, it was Crewe's skilful behind-the-scenes exchanges with his monarchs which eventually helped pave the way for an historical House of Lords reform, restricting the 'upper' House's powers of veto over decision-making in the 'lower' House of Commons.

Crewe and Mahatma Gandhi
The first of these contentious issues originated from as long ago as 1860, when the South African colony of Natal opened its doors to hundreds of indentured Indian labourers, who had been brought in to work the newly introduced sugar cane plantations for a fixed ten-year period (beyond which they were eligible for free passage home or could opt to stay on as labourers or domestic servants). Those returning home in 1870 and 1871 complained to their own government of physical maltreatment by the South African authorities, prompting Indian administrators to block any further such migration.[32]

Being thus deprived of this essential labour supply, the Natal government hurriedly set up a 'Coolie Commission' in 1872 to investigate the living conditions of Indian workers. This resulted in a recommendation to allocate land to those Indians located near Durban, thus promising them a greater stake in South African society.[33] A resulting resurgence of inward migration in the 1880s was accompanied by an influx of Muslim 'Passenger Indians', who arrived at their own expense from Gujarat with the intention of establishing themselves in the South African commercial and retail sectors.[34] These enclaves eventually extended into Transvaal and the Orange Free State.[35]

Growing opposition to this trend arose among those South Africans said to be repulsed by the allegedly 'dirty' living conditions of working-class Indians, and resentful and/or afraid of the competition posed by their 'more respectable' middle-class counterparts. Numerous mechanisms were introduced in the next two decades to deter further migration, e.g. making entry conditional on the ability to speak a European language, and by ensuring that existing Indian migrants were made to feel as unwelcome as possible (by insisting, for example, that all business documentation be written up in English, and depriving them of the franchise in local and national elections).

Not surprisingly therefore,

> The Indian community in Natal was clearly in need of a champion, and in 1893 he arrived in the unlikely figure of a man small in stature, primly dressed in European garb, who had just finished his law training in London. This man was Mohandas K. Gandhi, who was destined to spend some twenty-one years in South Africa and develop there a dramatic new philosophy of revolution.[36]

Gandhi's initial contribution was limited to representing Indians in legal cases and organising petitions to the British and Indian governments. His avowedly pro-British orientation at this time was exemplified by his successful attempt to raise an ambulance corps during the Boer War, consisting of 1,100 fellow Indians.[37] By 1908, however, the introduction of a series of ordinances and statutes, requiring Indians to be fingerprinted and produce registration documentation immediately on demand, saw Gandhi organising various forms of protest, ranging from marches to passive resistance, which occasionally led to his imprisonment.[38]

A climax was reached that year when, just as the four South African colonies were about to merge into a single Republic, three bills were introduced in Natal, with the objectives of: blocking any further allocation of trade licences to Indians after 31 December 1908; abolishing such licenses altogether by no later than 1918; and preventing any further introduction of Indian indentured labour after 30 June 1911.[39]

Meanwhile, General Jan Christian Smuts, the Colonial Secretary of the Transvaal Government, had coined new restrictive legislation, permitting only six 'educated' Indian migrants per year to take up permanent residence in his colony.[40]

In June 1909, Smuts travelled to London along with the future first premier of the dominion, General Louis Botha, to witness the debating of the Union of South Africa Bill — the legal platform for unification. Delegations were also sent on behalf of the more oppositional African and Coloured populations, and of the Natal and Transvaal Indian communities, the last named being represented by Gandhi, who was especially dismayed by the Bill's failure to make any reference to the Indian migrants. 'The Act will unite all the Colonies,' he protested beforehand, 'But the respective laws of the Colonies will remain intact.'[41]

Eager to establish some sort of political leverage, Gandhi wrote to Lord Crewe on 20 July 1909, explaining that he and his co-delegate were keen to achieve progress via *private*, rather than publicly aired, discussion. Gandhi diplomatically added that: 'We shall, therefore, be deeply grateful to His Lordship if he will be pleased to grant us a private interview.'[42]

Crewe agreed to this request, and he and Gandhi met up in person on 12 August, when the latter argued in favour of reversing the planned abolition of trading licenses, and presented the case for granting *permanent* residence to Indian labourers hitherto employed only temporarily (i.e. on an indentured basis). Gandhi also advocated that Smuts's proposed limitation on migrant numbers be urgently reconsidered: he advocated that this should be a matter of discretion for the Governor of the Transvaal, rather than a process rigidly inscribed in law.[43] Things initially looked promising: 'Crewe made agreeable noises; Gandhi's hopes were briefly aroused,' one academic stated. 'He even cabled back to Johannesburg: "GOVERNMENT AGREE REPEAL".'[44]

This euphoria waned somewhat when the Bill gained House of Commons approval on 19 August 1909, but Gandhi remained sufficiently optimistic to stay on in London with a view to wringing out the raft of concessions he firmly had in mind. A setback occurred when, later that month, the Natal delegation wrote a letter to the Viceroy of India, calling on the British to support a suspension of any further recruitment of indentured labourers 'if our trading rights are not respected'.[45] The delegates received a reply, not, as might have been anticipated, from the Viceroy himself, but from Lord Crewe, who pointedly 'did not give an undertaking to write to the Natal government about trading licences, nor did he say anything about the demand to stop indentured migration'.[46] This outcome was described by Gandhi as 'very disappointing'.[47]

Crewe and Gandhi eventually met again on 16 September, when discussion focused on Smuts's highly contentious stipulation that any future migration would be limited to the 'six educated Indians' per annum. Gandhi indignantly protested that this reference to the intellectual status of his compatriots was a ghastly discriminatory slur ('a racial taint on the Statute-book') which must therefore be expunged in the name of 'theoretical equality'. Crewe rather feebly replied that: 'What you say is just and proper, but General Smuts is not an Englishman and, therefore, does not like the idea even of theoretical equality.'[48] Furthermore,

> Crewe said he had already spoken to Smuts of the wider repercussions, but the General felt that 'if theoretical equality were kept up, it might be used for fresh agitation in order to increase the demands'. Gandhi clarified that if the principle of right was conceded, 'we should not raise any further agitation'. Crewe said, in closing, that he would discuss the question again with Smuts.[49]

Gandhi stayed on in London for more than two weeks longer, still confident in the expectation that Crewe would succeed in persuading Smuts to amend his immigration policy.

> He waited in vain until the Colonial Office informed him on 3 November that only Smuts' proposals could be accepted, that is, there would be no legal equality for Indians, but six educated Indians would be allowed entry each year. Gandhi replied to Lord Crewe that the failure to secure 'recognition of theoretical equality as to immigration' was a matter of 'very deep regret' as this alone 'can justify the holding together of different peoples of the world under the same sovereignty'.[50]

With his optimism now depleted, Gandhi spoke passionately at a public meeting in London on 12 November 1909, just before returning to South Africa. He emphasised to his audience that: 'It would be impossible for him and his countrymen to owe allegiance to an Empire in which they were not accepted, even in theory, as equals.'[51] As he sailed home on the SS *Kildonan Castle*, he wrote up *Hind Swaraj* ('Indian Home Rule'), thereby abandoning 'the very core of the kind of respectability and loyalism that in an earlier incarnation he had embraced'.[52]

Crewe and the 'Mad Mullah' of Somaliland

A second major substantive issue that Crewe was called upon to resolve concerned the enduring problems posed by the Mullah, Muhammad Abdullah Hassan of Somalia (the legendary 'Mad Mullah'), who was embarked on a longstanding mission to overthrow British rule over its Somaliland protectorate:

> In the eyes of the British, ['Abdullah'] was an outlaw, a madman, a profligate, and a libertine. But, grudgingly, the British acknowledged the power he had over his followers and his extraordinary tenacity of purpose in facing a European power with whom he never compromised himself or came to terms.[53]

Although he had been born in British Somaliland in 1856, Abdullah spent his boyhood in Aden, where he became familiar with the precepts of Islamic law and customs. He was increasingly exposed to the teachings of the more puritanical Islamic religious reformers and often made pilgrimages to Mecca, 'earning for himself the honorific of "Hajj", and gradually established a reputation as a holy man and sheikh'.[54] On returning to British Somaliland in 1895, Abdullah set up a doctrinaire school, but initially gained few converts to his philosophy. His preaching quickly began to resonate, however, among the Darod tribes of Ethiopia and British and Italian Somalia. His reputation and prowess as a mullah (a Muslim leader and learned authority who is often hostile towards other religions) also grew exponentially.[55]

With hundreds of followers under his command, Abdullah declared a 'jihad' (holy war) on all infidels. This was initially directed at those Somalis most resistant to his religious principles, but he eventually turned his ire onto the Ethiopians and British. From 1900 to 1905, these two nations collaborated in 'a series of futile expeditions' against the Mullah and his converts.[56] A respite occurred in March 1905 when the Mullah negotiated a deal with the Italians, allowing him to establish a coastal town in the assigned territory of the Nogal. The British respected this agreement and also granted the Mullah and his followers access to pastures inside the British protectorate throughout the dry season.[57]

Inter-tribal conflict persisted, though, as the Mullah pursued his expansionist designs and opposing tribal leaders combined in turn in a bid to crush him: 'There followed a series of battles, now won, now lost by the Mullah. [...] The nominal protectorate was a contradiction in terms, and Italy appeared to be sovereign over north-eastern Somalia only upon sufferance of the local rulers.'[58]

A critical conjuncture was reached when a 'trusted friend and adviser' of the Mullah, Abdullah Shahari, defected from his ranks because the Mullah had raised a religious objection to the former's choice of wife. Shahari took off immediately to Mecca — where, in an audience with a highly eminent Muslim cleric, he set out 'accusations against the conduct and religious orthodoxy of the Mullah'.[59] This resulted in the Mullah's excommunication. Sensing a weakening of his prestige, influence and personal ambition, the British sought a negotiated settlement capable of terminating the ongoing conflict.

The kernel of a British 'solution' to the problem posed by the Mullah had first been mooted just before Winston Churchill — by this time a 33-year-old Parliamentary Under Secretary of State for the Colonies — set sail for Berbera (on 20 October 1907) aboard the HMS Venus. Two days after landing, he dispatched a memorandum to the Colonial Office, dated 28 October, outlining what he considered the 'only two secure alternatives' — namely: to occupy the country with the help of the Italians and seize all its major wells in the process; or to withdraw to the coast in line with the precedent established by the Italians. While dismissing the first of these two options as impractical, Churchill declared a personal preference for the second.[60]

Among those invited to comment on Churchill's memorandum was Captain Harry Edward Spiller Cordeaux, Commissioner of the Protectorate. Cordeaux was clearly unimpressed. Uppermost among his many objections was the fact that such a plan represented an abrogation of treaty obligations to other parties, notably the Abyssinians.

Adopting Churchill's preferred approach would inevitably 'precipitate a state of affairs in Somaliland which we have already spent several millions in averting'.[61]

It was not until the winter of 1908 that Lord Crewe became centrally involved in his role of Colonial Secretary. On 8 December, he circulated Cordeaux's reply among his Cabinet colleagues, while adding the important caveat that he (Crewe) was in close agreement with Churchill. 'We must face the possibility of our being confined to the coast towns,' Crewe stated, 'but even this might be the less[er] of two evils.' The situation at hand made it absolutely essential that the Government become 'all the more anxious to devise some method of winning the Mullah by a subsidy, difficult though it may be to do so'.[62]

Britain's possible departure from Somaliland was debated in parliamentary committee on 9 March 1909. The former Prime Minister and Opposition Leader, Arthur Balfour, was among those who warned impassionedly of the consequences of withdrawal for those tribes – especially the coastal ones – who would be left, dangerously exposed, to the Mullah's predatory behaviour. Otherwise,

> The general tenor of the debate was that an expedition was too expensive […] and abandonment immoral and dangerous to British prestige, particularly in the Sudan. However, when total abandonment was opposed, it was sometimes only because the coast was felt to be important to British interests.[63]

Crewe turned for further advice to Sir Reginald Wingate, the Governor of the Sudan, and Sirdar (Commander) of the Egyptian army. The Colonial Secretary spelled out as follows two highly contrasting alternatives for Wingate to choose between:

> Faced with the difficulties of the situation as a whole, tired of having to remain indefinitely on the defensive, weary of holding a worthless country at great civil and military cost, a great body of opinion is tending more and more to incline with favour towards a policy of complete evacuation, or, as an alternative, to a withdrawal to certain positions on the coast. Evacuation or such a withdrawal would in themselves be satisfactory to His Majesty's Government if, after consideration of the pros and

cons, you could recommend one or [the] other of these lines of action.[64]

Crewe also invited Wingate to consider the possibility of offering Abdullah a financial inducement, even though such a strategy risked enhancing the Mullah's local prestige and influence.[65]

Wingate responded with a 124-page report which totally rejected Crewe's preferred position. It fundamentally objected to the idea of a 'coastal concentration', fearing that the Mullah might be provoked into wreaking savage vengeance on those tribes now thrown onto his mercy. Wingate reminded Crewe and others that, because these tribes had stood alongside the British in previous campaigns against the Mullah, His Majesty's Government was under an obligation to continue safeguarding their security.[66] The report was never actually published, and the decision-making process was short-circuited when the Prime Minister wrote to Crewe, requiring him to contact Cordeaux with the following directive:

> Tell the tribes that as the Mullah continues to attack them and has broken off negotiations with us they must take whatever measures they think proper to protect themselves. It must be understood further that we do not undertake any responsibility for consequences of action taken by them.[67]

It did not matter that Cordeaux had no stomach for this policy. In October 1909, the Cabinet authorised the British withdrawal to three towns on the coast. This operation was kept secret from the tribes until it had been successfully completed. In the meantime, Crewe redeployed Cordeaux into the role of Governor of Uganda – on the basis that it would have been unfair to expect him to implement a policy to which he was fundamentally opposed.[68] Disastrous consequences inevitably arose from this:

> The British now undid whatever good might have been accomplished by the Mullah's excommunication. By their evacuation of the interior they left the door open for the dervishes to return to Somaliland, while the prospects for expansion out of the narrow Nogal valley allowed the Mullah to rally his remaining followers with the promise of earthly success.[69]

Yet another unenviable task awaiting Crewe's arrival at the Colonial Office involved the contentious issue of 'concubinage' (the keeping of 'native woman' by officers serving in the British colonies to satisfy their sexual desires). Prior to Crewe's period in office, concubinage had become 'a well-established informal institution' throughout the British Empire. The practice was not merely tolerated, but *actively encouraged* by colonial governments and businesses alike.[70] The Colonial Office also turned a blind eye, taking the view that whatever officers and officials did in private was of no concern as long as it remained devoid of public scandal. Moreover, concubinage was held to incorporate the hidden advantage of enabling administrative personnel to use their native 'lovers' as 'sleeping dictionaries' — i.e. sources of information beneficial to controlling the masses.

Attitudes suddenly changed when, in 1908, Hubert Silberrad, an assistant district commissioner in Nyeri, Kenya, brought the practice into serious disrepute. Silberrad had purchased a pair of young Kenyan girls, not yet in their teens, for 40 goats apiece from a colleague who had been promoted into a position outside of the area.

> When, three years later, Silberrad attempted to acquire a third mistress (of similar age) and one of his own policemen objected, Silberrad locked him up for the night, on grounds of insubordination. Two white neighbours, a Mr and Mrs Scoresby Routledge, came to express their outrage and then Mr Routledge rode four days through the rain to complain to the Governor in Nairobi. The Governor ordered a private investigation, which concluded that Silberrad had brought the administration into disrepute by 'poaching'.[71]

The Governor personally recommended that Silberrad (who currently topped the list of possible candidates for promotion to a higher grade) should be relegated to the bottom of this pile. The case progressed to the Legal and General Department of the Colonial Office. Senior officials acknowledged the distasteful nature of Silberrad's conduct, and decreed that, in order to put a stop to concubinage, a general circular should be issued, appealing to officers' 'sense of propriety and good conduct', without necessarily threatening them with sanctions.[72]

Routledge had ominously declared that, were he to remain dissatisfied with the way his complaint was being handled, he would then draw the matter to the attention of the British Parliament and national press. Problematically, however,

> The [Colonial] Office was thoroughly indignant at this threat, especially since it was now known that Routledge had himself almost certainly followed local custom and had intercourse with African girls before his marriage. It was also obvious that Routledge had a grudge against Silberrad, who had taken official action against him on liquor charges involving his Masai workers and porters. Routledge's importunate demands were counterproductive. The fact that he was 'disposed to be nasty' in public was probably one of the considerations which led [Lord] Crewe not to adopt the governor's tough punishment proposals, but to accept instead the Executive Council's more moderate recommendations that Silberrad should lose one year's seniority (from April 1908), and not be put in charge of a district for two years.[73]

Crewe's seemingly dismissive attitude ultimately proved costly. Routledge angrily concluded that Silberrad was getting off scot-free, and reacted, as promised, by writing to *The Times*. His letter published on 3 December 1908 stridently condemned the Government 'for not acting severely enough to check the "abuses" in Kenya and to stop the "demoralisation" of African women by British officials'.[74] The case was then discussed in Parliament, with the result that pressure was exerted on Crewe to rescue the Government from further scandal while also appeasing Routledge.

His solution to the problem was to issue two variations of a 'Concubine Circular': 'Circular A' was to be issued to all British officers 'who in future enter the service of any of the Colonies or Protectorates'; and 'Circular B' to all those officers already serving in those domains.[75] The former was deliberately intended by its author (Crewe) to act as a stark warning to new recruits of the dangers associated with engaging in concubinage:

> Gravely improper conduct of this nature has at times been the cause of serious trouble among native populations, and must be strenuously condemned on that account; but an objection even

more serious from the standpoint of the Government lies in the fact that it is not possible for any member of the administration to countenance such practices without lowering himself in the eyes of the natives, and diminishing his authority to an extent which will seriously impair his capacity for useful work in the Service in which it is his duty to strive to set an honourable example to all with whom he comes in contact.[76]

As a softening device designed to obviate any resulting indignation, Crewe added that the purpose of the circular was not to cast aspersions on the character of anyone entering such an 'honourable profession'. Rather, its intention was 'simply to advise those who enter the service of a danger in their path, and to warn them of the disgrace and official ruin which will certainly follow from any dereliction of duty in this respect'.[77]

The briefer Circular B was even softer in tone, exhorting already established officers to 'do the right thing' by not only abstaining from acts of concubinage, but also registering their disapproval of such conduct by others:

Their admirable work and excellent conduct are fully appreciated by His Majesty's Government, and I feel sure that this Circular will be accepted by the Service as an appeal for loyal co-operation in vigorously reprobating and officially condemning all such cases of concubinage between Civil Servants and native women whenever and wherever they are detected.[78]

Crewe's circular thus placed an onus on senior officers to use their own discretion in deciding whether to administer more serious warnings to those officers flouting the required code of conduct. Similar discretion would also be applied when determining the nature and severity of any 'summary punishment' deemed necessary for extreme or persistent cases of noncompliance.[79]

It was widely acknowledged thereafter, not least of all by the Colonial Office itself, that the circular had constituted 'a piece of panic legislation'.[80] During the two decades following its initial publication, it was allowed to 'quietly die away'. This reflected a growing perception that, far from helping to 'shore up British colonial authority', it had unfortunately done the opposite:

In the years following its release, when it had the most visibility, the circular had been used by Africans to accomplish a range of different goals: addressing workplace grievances by disclosing to authorities that a European officer was in violation of the circular; using it as a tool to extort money; blackmailing officers in order to prevent them from bringing an end to an arrangement of concubinage, et cetera. And when European officers used the circular against one another these results were no better.[81]

On His Majesties' Service

A far more rewarding feature of this period of Crewe's political career was the mutually respectful and affectionate relationship he enjoyed with his monarch, King Edward VII. The two men were socially well-suited: it was evident from Edward's visit to Fryston in 1896, for example, that he and Crewe harboured mutual passions for shooting and horse racing. The King and Queen were occasional guests at Crewe House. In turn, Lord and Lady Crewe were frequently entertained at Windsor and Balmoral castles.[82] It was only with regard to their *political beliefs* that the two men did not see eye to eye: 'King Edward was fundamentally as reactionary as his mother had been — a somewhat natural tendency in monarchs.'[83] The King was nonetheless apt to call on Crewe (both as a friend but also in his capacity as Lord Privy Seal) whenever he sought to 'express disapproval' of the comments or behaviour of members of the Cabinet. He also relied on Crewe to keep him up to speed on salient political matters. This included regular briefings on any progress towards the possible reform of the House of Lords.[84]

The Liberal Government's longstanding commitment to reforming the 'Second Chamber' (by restricting its power to veto decisions arrived at in the 'Lower House') became even more resolute when the Lords invoked its power to stymie the progress of David Lloyd-George's controversial 'People's Budget' of 29 April 1909, which sought to employ tax rises and welfare reforms 'to wage implacable warfare against poverty and squalidness'.[85] The Liberals responded to this 'constitutional crisis' by calling a general election in January 1910, with the objective of securing a public mandate for the budget. The outcome was a hung parliament in which the Liberals, while not commanding an overall majority of MPs, were able to remain in office with the support of the Irish Parliamentary Party. The House of Lords followed a long-established informal convention requiring them to cede to the will of the electorate by endorsing the People's Budget on 28 April 1910, but the wider question of possible reform went unresolved for much of the remaining year.[86]

Crewe's daughter, Cynthia Colville, recollected in her memoirs that the period extending from the obstruction of the People's Budget to the eventual passage of the Parliament Act 1911 was one in which her father was transformed by some Conservative peers into a social pariah: 'Old friends with whom my father used regularly to shoot wrote to suggest,' she said, 'that it might be better if he did not come that year.'[87] It was, nonetheless, apparent that:

> Throughout this difficult, tempestuous episode the Prime Minister took care to keep in step with Crewe, and would in fact seem to have relied upon him to expound the Cabinet's view to Edward VII and to help him to persuade that King's successor to give the pledges which they felt they must demand.[88]

It was in the nine-day period immediately preceding the Lords' final approval of the budget that Crewe explicitly raised the possibility of Edward being called upon to personally intervene in the event of a constitutional deadlock of this nature. This took the 'time-honoured unofficial form' of a memorandum to the King (dated 19 April 1910), sent to him via Edward's Private Secretary, Lord Knollys. In referring to the growing public anger, impatience, and despondency permeating the nation, Crewe added that: 'If nothing is going to happen our supporters may ask what is the use of returning a majority in Parliament.'[89]

One possible solution, Crewe tentatively ventured, would be for the King to help break the deadlock by using his royal prerogative to create sufficient additional peers to overturn the existing Conservative majority in opposition to reform. This implied, he continued, that insofar as procedure was concerned:

> If and when the House of Lords rejects the proposals contained in the Resolutions [i.e. contained in the Bill], the Prime Minister must lay the situation before the King and point out the various

possible courses. This is technically 'giving advice' because the Prime Minister cannot tell the House that he will talk the situation over with the Sovereign. If you carefully consider the various possibilities, I think you will agree that the really undesirable situation, that of a Government with a majority (even though composite) in the Commons having to resign because it has asked for something which it cannot get, is less likely to come about in this way than in any other.[90]

Knollys passed on Crewe's sensitively crafted exposition to the King, who happened to be staying at Biarritz. While grateful for this explanation, Edward pressed Crewe into further clarification of his views. Crewe responded, in a second memorandum, dated 27 April, by carefully rephrasing his initial position:

> My answer would be that I can imagine a hypothetical case, of a kind which I trust is likely never to arise, in which, after a definite refusal by the House of Lords to act upon the express desire of the country, the Sovereign might find himself, as the *Spectator* said in a rather interesting article last Saturday, in the position 'of an Institution rather than an individual' (or some such words) and so playing a constitutional part in which his personal view would hardly enter.[91]

The monarch was to play no further part, however, in the resolution of this 'crisis'. Edward's death, a few days later on 6 May 1910, was not entirely unexpected by those who, like Crewe, had been conscious of the monarch's gradually deteriorating health. Lord and Lady Crewe heard of Edward's demise at a dinner party hosted by Mrs George Cornwallis-West. Among others present were the Prime Minister's wife, Margot Asquith, and Winston Churchill. As the former put it in her diary, 'At the end of dinner Winston said: "Let us drink to the health of the new King," to which Lord Crewe answered: "Rather to the memory of the old."'[92] Somewhat significantly,

> On the day of the King's funeral Lady Crewe and Mrs. Asquith were the only women inside Westminster Hall as the funeral cortège moved out into the sunshine of Parliament Square. As it left, Crewe stooped to give a pat to Caesar, the King's wire-haired terrier, led on a leash by a kilted loader from Balmoral.[93]

Crewe's biographer characterised Edward's successor, George V, as a 'modest, sensible and unassuming' 45-year-old of simple ways and proclivities. 'He was the epitome,' Pope-Hennessy maintained, 'of those qualities and tastes, habits, aspirations and points of view which represent the level ideal of the average English family-in-the-street'.[94] It was not long before Crewe was presented with an ideal opportunity 'to study the workings of the new King's mind'.[95]

In his continuing eagerness to secure the desired House of Lords reform, the Prime Minister, H.H. Asquith, suggested to his opposition counterpart, Arthur Balfour, that they host a series of secret talks in an attempt to achieve a possible compromise – the alternative being to call yet another general election. A 'Conference' of this nature (involving Asquith, Crewe, Lloyd George and Birrell for the Government, and Balfour, Landsdowne, Austen Chamberlain and Cawdor for the Conservatives) was instigated in June 1910, and met up on no fewer than 22 occasions.[96] 'By November,' however, 'it had solved nothing, and had merely served to emphasise the differences between the Government and Opposition on many matters besides the House of Lords veto.'[97] The Asquith regime therefore calculated that it was high time they turned to the new monarch in search of much-needed support.

Only two months previously, the Prime Minister had asked Crewe to switch from the Colonial Office and become Secretary of State for India. This required him to start working straight away in close conjunction with the King on a planned visit to India. It was these two major concerns – the royal visit to India and the passage of the Parliament Bill – which would preoccupy Lord Crewe for most of the following year.

Chapter Three
Burning Issues

House of Lords Reform: Act 1

It seemed like a strategy of last resort when, in striving to achieve the hitherto elusive objective of House of Lords reform, the Liberal Prime Minister, H.H. Asquith, obtained permission for Lord Crewe and himself to talk directly to the King.

> This was the famous 'scene in the Royal Closet' over which Opposition peers and Tory newspapers were so indignant. The two men explained to the King in clear terms that they were now under an obligation to hold a second General Election, but that they could not take this step without the King expressing himself willing to create peers if necessary. At the close of the interview the King agreed, in his own words, 'most reluctantly to give the Cabinet a secret understanding that in the event of the Government being returned with a majority at the General Election' he would use his prerogative to create peers.[98]

With this 'insurance policy' now in place, the Liberals predictably called a general election in December 1910, which saw them secure only one seat more than the Conservatives (272 versus 271), and therefore dependent on a combination of Irish and Labour MPs for continuing in office. Nevertheless, the Government now looked set to finally realise its reformist objectives.

It will become evident in this chapter that Lord Crewe not only played a central role in ensuring the difficult passage of the relevant Parliament Act 1911, but also helped manage several other 'burning issues' of the day. This included the controversial visit by King George V and Queen Mary to the Delhi Durbar of 1911 (which saw the reunification of Bengal and the creation of a new seat of government in Delhi) and a prolonged tour afterwards by the same monarchs of Britain's hard-pressed industrial heartlands. Arguably less laudable was

Crewe's handling of two highly contentious issues also brought to his ministerial attention: the recurring matter of Indian citizenship in South Africa; and the central involvement of an exiled Maharaja's daughter in the increasingly conspicuous women's suffrage movement. These, too, are dealt with comprehensively in this chapter.

Crewe was not the only member of his family experiencing major life events or career transitions at this time. A postscript to this chapter therefore dwells on significant developments in the lives of three of Lord Crewe's close relatives. Discussion focuses, more specifically, on work undertaken in an impoverished London borough by Crewe's daughter, Cynthia; on a personal tragedy experienced by his sister, Florence; and on the steps undertaken by Crewe's son-in-law, Arthur O'Neill MP, to organise units of Protestant paramilitaries in opposition to Irish Home Rule.

Such developments occurred while Crewe was not in the best of health. These 'burning issues' were also preceded, as we shall see, by a more literal conflagration: the outbreak of a fire at Crewe House which coincided with the birth of Lord and Lady Crewe's first child – hence the ironic title of this chapter.

Baptism of Fire

A strange and highly disconcerting convergence of events occurred in February 1911, when a large fire broke out in the opulent Crewe House. According to one version of events, local builders had been in the process of creating alterations when, around midnight on 7 February, a 'serious fire' spontaneously broke out: 'Thanks to the efforts of the fire brigade, the blaze was restricted mainly to the second floor; but it resulted in the destruction of most of the roof, as well as causing water and smoke damage to the rooms below; in the clear light of the day the blackened remains presented a most melancholy spectacle.'[99]

The prevailing sense of drama was heightened by the fact that Peggy Crewe had just given birth to a son when the blaze first ignited. She subsequently recalled how it had seemed for one horrible moment that the surrounding trees might catch fire, making it difficult for anyone trapped inside to escape. 'Happily,' she reflected, 'all was subdued and in the early hours of the morning, my child and I were taken in an ambulance to my father's [Lord Rosebery's] house, number 38 Berkeley Square.'[100]

Lord Crewe briefly alluded to the event in a hastily despatched letter to Lord Hardinge, dated 10 February 1911, in which he told the latter:

> On Tuesday night Peggy's boy was born. The event is the greatest possible joy to us, I need not tell you. Then our house caught fire, from the old story, I think, of joists running under a hearthstone, a place which always gets you sooner or later.[101]

Crewe is said to have responded to the partial destruction of his home 'with his customary equanimity'. He was in the process of altering the property in any case, so this comprised an unscheduled opportunity to hasten things along.[102]

Lady Crewe was nonetheless aware that this and other sources of stress were impacting on her husband's physical well-being. Referring to an incident which occurred in March 1911, she insisted that: 'The strain on my husband was great, and it was due no doubt to this and other anxieties that, a short time after, he was brought back unconscious from the Pricking of Sheriffs' Dinner at Claridge's by John Burns, and for a time my father's house became a sort of hospital.'[103]

Pope-Hennessy wrote of this incident in more specific detail. It occurred, he pointed out, just after dinner had been completed:

> Lord Crewe standing by himself before the fireplace, was suddenly seen to sway and fall forwards, hitting his forehead very hard on the floor. Taken home by John Burns, Crewe was found to have sustained concussion of the brain. The doctor insisted on a complete rest from work for eight weeks.[104]

Unfounded rumours proliferated that the overworked Crewe had suffered a stroke, and that 'his career at an end, was likely also to be incapacitated for life'.[105] As spring unfolded, however, an air of normality returned. The christening of Richard George Archibald John Lucian Hungerford Crewe-Milnes took place at the Chapel Royal, St. James's, with King George V acting as chief sponsor. 'Dicky', as he became known within the family, was initially given the title of the third Lord Houghton. He would subsequently assume his father's secondary title of 'Earl of Madeley' when, as we shall see, Lord Crewe was elevated to the status of Marquess in the 1911 Coronation Honours.

Lord Crewe acted contrary to medical advice – not only in returning prematurely to the India Office, but also in throwing himself into the continuing debate on the Parliament Bill, which was introduced into the House of Commons on 21 February 1911 and passed by its members the following spring: 'The Bill was short and simple: it removed from the upper House the right to delay or reject money bills, replaced the Lords' veto over Commons Bill with a suspensory delay of two years and reduced the maximum length of a Parliament from seven years to five.'[106]

In the face of predictably implacable opposition to the Bill in the Conservative-dominated Upper House, Asquith wrote to Balfour on 20 July 1911, informing him of the commitment he had received from the King to overturning the Conservative majority in the Lords by installing the requisite cohort of 'rival' new peers. This letter was immediately published in the press, generating a greatly indignant reaction, including 'Angry letters speculating on "what had passed in the Royal Closet."'[107]

Tempers rose exponentially as the relevant Lords debate 'dragged on' before entering its final stage in August 1911, when a 'sub-tropical' heatwave prevailed outdoors.[108] Though clearly still unwell, Crewe 'toiled ceaselessly' during the first week of that month in a bid to guarantee the Bill's passage. He set his sights on encouraging the helpful interventions in this process of the Archbishop of Canterbury and Lord Cromer of the Unionist Party, 'both of whom were influential supporters of [the] policy of bowing to the inevitable by letting the Bill slip through'.[109]

In the course of secret discussion, the Archbishop assured Crewe that, while he was in no position to act as a 'Whip' by inducing his fellow clerics to vote accordingly, he would, nonetheless, 'help generally as far as he could'.[110] Crewe's similar backstage deliberations with Cromer proved more tortuous and complicated, with the latter eventually committing to delivering the requisite number of Conservatives assenters to the Bill. This was achieved on the strength of a guarantee by Crewe that his government would immediately abandon any intention of creating additional peers. Weston and Kelvin[111] confirm that it was Cromer who occupied the role of leader of the 'Judas group' of opposition peers who helped sway the vote in favour of the Bill's eventual passage.

Crewe's final act of great significance involved the unenviable task of speaking on the Government's behalf during the debate on a Vote of Censure, occurring a mere three days prior to final voting on the Bill. He had the distinction of being one of only three individuals who could personally vouch for what happened in the previous November's audience with the King. He was also someone 'whose word commanded absolute and instantaneous belief on both sides of the House'.[112] Here, then, was an opportunity to set the record straight and, hopefully, quell Unionist indignation concerning accusations of political chicanery. As Crewe therefore stated in addressing his contemporaries:

> The effect of that interview was that we ascertained His Majesty's views. We suggested that if the opinion of the country was plainly ascertained upon the Parliament Bill, in the last resort a creation of peers might be the only way of putting an end to the dispute. His Majesty faced the contingency and entertained the suggestion as a possible one, but with natural and — if I may be permitted to say so — with legitimate reluctance. His Majesty naturally entertained the feeling, which we shared, that if we resigned office having, as we had, a large majority in the House of Commons, the only result would be an immediate dissolution in which it would practically be impossible, however anxious we might be, to keep the Crown out of the controversy. The mixing up of the Crown in a controversy such as that was naturally most distasteful to its illustrious wearer whom we regard as the express guardian of its prestige, but scarcely more distasteful even to His Majesty than to myself and my colleagues. It is altogether inaccurate to state that any time we asked His Majesty for guarantees.[113]

The Government ultimately prevailed by the slender margin of seventeen votes. Buttressing those of its own supporters were the thirteen cast by prelates and 35 more by Conservative peers. It was clear that Crewe's astute backstage manoeuvring had resoundingly succeeded in its aim.[114]

A Passage to India
The definition of the word 'Durbar' has been helpfully explained by Pope-Hennessy. In India, he points out,

It most usually signifies a consultative meeting of chieftains for the purpose of taking administrative decisions; its secondary significance is a ceremonial gathering to pay homage. It was in this latter sense that the word was used to designate the three Imperial Durbars held at the ancient city of Delhi during the brief period of history in which Great Britain possessed and ruled her Indian Empire.[115]

At the first such event in 1877, Queen Victoria was proclaimed Empress of India. The second Durbar of 1903 (which Crewe had personally attended) celebrated the accession to the Imperial throne of Edward VII. This third 'Coronation Durbar' (of 12 December 1911) had been set up with the objective of announcing the Government's intention to transfer the seat of Imperial Government to Delhi.[116]

Back in 1905, Lord Curzon had controversially decided to divide Bengal into two separate provinces. The official reason given for this political manoeuvre, which was stridently opposed by Bengali Hindus, was to ease the administrative burden associated with such a diverse and densely populated province of 85 million people; but, as Johnson points out, 'government correspondence at the time also shows that Curzon's aggressive colonial policy toward Bengal stemmed from his fear of the rising power of western educated Bengalis who called for a greater voice in government. Partition, he hoped, would break this emerging bloc.'[117]

The spur to major reform in India came from the recently crowned George V:

As Prince of Wales, he had visited India in 1905-1906 and had been convinced that the partition of Bengal was a mistake. He now decided that he should return as Emperor to spur the loyalty of his Indian subjects, and he suggested to his ministers that Bengal should be reunited as a grand gesture of Imperial goodwill.[118]

To this end, he summoned Crewe to a meeting on 23 January 1911 and directed him to hatch a reunification plan for unveiling at the Durbar.[119]

Both the Viceroy of India, Lord Hardinge, and the Government of India were initially opposed to the idea, but nonetheless recognised that something of this magnitude was required to transform the King's visit into one of lasting historical impact.

> This question was unanswered for six months until finally in June, 1911, the Home Member, James Jenkins, with a *volte face*, made the dramatic proposal that Bengal should be reunited and the Imperial capital moved from troublesome Calcutta to Delhi. Hardinge was now willing to accept the idea for he had been convinced 'that a grave injustice has been done to the Bengalis, seeing that they are in a minority in both provinces, and this injustice should certainly be rectified'.[120]

Hardinge thus wrote a memo to Lord Crewe in London, commending the idea. On 10 August, Crewe secured the King's approval of the scheme. The Cabinet also endorsed the plan in early November, and final details of the reversal of the partition were ironed out in secret. It was determined that George V would announce the chosen date for reunification (1 April 1912) at a Delhi Durbar on 12 December 1911.[121]

Befitting his meticulous eye for detail, Crewe was centrally involved in all necessary arrangements. This advance planning gave rise to numerous potential problems. Uppermost of these was the question of whether the King should undergo a separate Indian Coronation ceremony; and, if so, which dignitary should be required to do the crowning.

> Lord Crewe, supported by the Cabinet, explained that it would be a dangerous precedent to have a separate Indian Coronation since it might lead, in after years, to the assumption that a King of England was not Emperor of India until he had been crowned at Delhi. [...] 'One's instinct,' wrote Lord Crewe to the Viceroy, Lord Hardinge, 'is to avoid the theatrical, but it does not follow that the instinct is sound, as we have got to impress the people of India, not some more or less cultivated persons over here.' Crewe suggested that the King should at a given moment advance to the front of the arena, receive the crown from the Viceroy who would be holding it up on a velvet cushion, and place it on his own head to the sound of massed bands followed by a general salute. 'The Crown would be brought from here,' Crewe added, 'what Crown it would be is a matter for future decision'.[122]

A final decision was taken to have the King appear before the masses with the crown already placed upon his head; but it then dawned on everyone concerned that it would be illegal to transport the crown outside of the British realm. Crewe therefore coined the solution of having a new 'Indian Crown' created, and then 'taken out to India on the *Medina* passenger ship in a special safe, placed on the King's head in private in his tent and publicly worn by him throughout the Durbar ceremonies'.[123] This 'Crown of India' would ultimately be returned to London and placed for posterity in the Jewel-house inside the Tower of London.[124]

A second potential problem concerned the King's well-publicised desire to go tiger shooting while out in India.

> The trouble here was that the King, having refused to visit the Madras Presidency on the score of lack of time, wished instead to set off six hundred miles from Delhi for a week's shooting. Crewe [...] felt that this would 'give an air of flippancy to the tour' and ill accord with the King-Emperor's role in India as a 'semi-divine figure'. Also, if the King-Emperor went shooting, what was to happen to the Queen-Empress? 'It would hardly do, would it, for her to begin in Calcutta without him?' Crewe asked Hardinge.[125]

As it transpired, Crewe's objection was disregarded by the King.

The 24-person Royal Party duly sailed on the *Medina*, a 650-berth vessel temporarily commissioned by the Royal Navy from the Peninsular and Oriental Company. King George and Queen Mary landed in India in late November and made their way to Delhi on 5 December. The Durbar commenced, as scheduled, seven days later. The unprecedentedly lavish ceremony was attended by a quarter of a million people.[126]

Having stayed for ten days in Delhi, the royal couple temporarily separated – the King ignoring Crewe's advice by leading a shooting expedition in Nepal, while the Queen paid a visit to the Taj Mahal in Agra, followed by a tour of Rajputana. The royal tour was proclaimed a great success, even if the King did emotionally falter while making his farewell speech. The monarch subsequently confided to Crewe how, at that point, it had 'flashed across his mind that he would never see India again, and the thought was too much for him'.[127]

Crewe benefitted greatly from the voyage. It proved, as Pope-Hennessy observed, 'a recuperative experience for a still-delicate man'.[128] Crewe touchingly informed his wife that the King and Queen had watched over him 'with singular care' and constantly insisted that he be seated in their company. In the final stages of the return journey, the King summoned Crewe to his cabin, where he presented him with the Victorian Chain, 'a new, high honour invented by Edward VII', which had only been conferred on five other individuals.[129]

Crewe's work was still not finished: 'Introduced into the House of Lords as soon as possible after the Secretary of State's return home, the Government of India Bill was skilfully designed by Asquith and Crewe to blunt the Opposition's claws' – so much so that the reversal of the partition of Bengal and the transference of the Indian capital to Delhi were soon constitutionally endorsed.[130] Additionally, Crewe was, in his biographer's terms, 'very really and very directly responsible' for successfully pressing the claims of Edwin Landseer Lutyens as the architect responsible for designing the new capital.[131] Crewe's Marquessate was subsequently bestowed in recognition of his key role in the House of Lords debate, and of the part he played in the organisation and prosecution of the Durbar.[132]

A Royal Tour of Duty

The royal party (including Lord Crewe) returned from India into the 'crisis' surrounding the national miners' strike of February to April 1912. According to Edwards,

> The miners were demanding a minimum wage of five shillings a day for men and two shillings a day for boys. Negotiations broke down four weeks after the start of the strike, and Prime Minister, Asquith, using unprecedented dictatorial powers, forced an acceptance of the Minimum Wages Bill over the protests of Parliament. The King gave it his Royal Assent a fortnight later.[133]

It may have surprised some people that, notwithstanding his long association with mining communities like Fryston, Lord Crewe played no part in relevant negotiations. Unlike others of his class, he rejected the opinion that the strike was politically motivated and disputed the accusation that the miners (whom he regarded as 'the best of working men') were behaving callously by depriving the nation of its most vital source of energy.[134]

At least one of the two monarchs Crewe had recently accompanied to India was equally unwilling to blame the miners. 'Fully aware of the discretion required in the Consort of a constitutional monarch, Queen Mary never revealed her political feelings in public,' said Edwards. 'But she did make them known to her husband, and in the coal-strike crisis she adamantly blamed the Government.'[135] Sensing that politicians were out of touch with the needs of working people in the factories and mines, the royal couple undertook, in the post-strike period of 1912 and 1913, a tour of coalfield and other heavily industrialised areas, to see for themselves the type of conditions their subjects were enduring.

The two-year tour began with a three-day visit to South Wales in June 1912. The final day of three was devoted to visiting the coalfield communities of Glamorgan and the Merthyr Valley.[136] Within one such community, Queen Mary famously sat down to tea with a local miner's wife.[137] One month later, the royal couple stayed at Wentworth Woodhouse, seat of the wealthy Fitzwilliam family near Barnsley, South Yorkshire. Their itinerary was dramatically interrupted when, on 9 July, 91 men were killed in an explosion at nearby Cadeby Colliery. On hearing of this tragedy, the King and Queen insisted on being driven immediately to the stricken mine. Soon after their arrival, 'As she talked to the bereaved families at the pit-head, it was observed that the Queen, whose control over her emotions was usually adamantine, had tears pouring down her cheeks.'[138]

In April 1913, the King and Queen followed this newly established precedent by staying with Lord and Lady Crewe at Crewe Hall as part of a royal visit to the Potteries. The regal acceptance of this invitation represented a 'public affirmation' of Lord Crewe's personal friendship with the King.[139] The advance preparations required for the visit proved exceptionally taxing. 'Though it only lasts three days it seems to take almost as much arranging as the Durbar,' Crewe complained in a letter to a friend, shortly before the visit;[140] but all this effort ultimately proved worthwhile:

On this occasion [King George] and the Queen visited the Minton factory at Stoke, the potteries at Fenton and Longton, Wedgwood's Etruria works, the silk mills at Leek, and a colliery at Kidsgrove, as well as railway workshops and orphanages in the town of Crewe. Each evening, they returned exhausted to Crewe Hall, to be revived by the Crewes' superlative food and — in the case of Queen Mary, since the King drank whisky only — wine. Glees were sung in the evening by local choirs, the King planted a tree in the grounds, and on Thursday 24th April, the royal visitors entrained for Euston Station, much gratified, as they wrote, by their stay.[141]

More Indian Unrest

Other issues within Crewe's jurisdiction as Secretary of State for India proved infinitely less rewarding. This was true with regard to the inception of the Union of South Africa in 1910, which ironically reinforced the subjugation of its Indian population by uncoupling the restraining effect of the British government. The newly-formed South African regime reneged on its promise to repeal the 1908 Transvaal Immigration Registration Act, and the Natal Act, requiring all formerly indentured Indians choosing to remain in the dominion to pay a prohibitive annual tax of £3. The Cape Supreme Court then ruled in March 1913 that only Christian marriages were legal in South Africa, and that polygamous marriages endorsed by some Indian religions would now be considered illicit.[142]

It came as the final straw when the passage of the Union Immigrants' Regulation Act of 1913 not only 'effectively barred' any future Indian migration by making entry conditional on an extremely challenging language test, but also prohibited the movement of Indians from one province to another.[143] A campaign of civil disobedience was unleashed, under Mahatma Gandhi's leadership, involving, among other things, ostentatious flouting of the law by hundreds of Indians marching from Natal into the Transvaal.[144]

Crewe refrained from publicly supporting the Indians. Speaking in the House of Lords on 30 July 1913, he somewhat patronisingly emphasised how it was 'altogether impossible for most Indians in India who consider this question or who hear vaguely of it to realise in any degree the difficulties which confront either His Majesty's Government or the Ministers of the

South African Union'. He warned against any attempt to impose on white South Africans 'a policy in regard to another race which they hate and which they only accept because they are obliged'.[145]

Crewe ventured that it would be more advantageous for Indians to accept 'a system of law which may seem in itself to be more severe but which is at any rate kindly and sympathetically administered by those who have charge of it'. He insisted that Botha and Smuts were both sincere in their determination to 'meet the desires of the Indian residents *so far as public opinion in South Africa will let them*' (italics added). The Indians should therefore endeavour to achieve their objectives with due 'patience and moderation'.[146] Crewe then rejected a subsequent appeal by the leader of the Indian Congress, Gopal Krishna Gokhale, for a senior member of the Government of India to formally convey to the South Africans the utter disapproval of all Indians of the 1913 Act. There was a danger, as Crewe saw it, that such an intervention might 'act as an irritant to South African opinion generally'.[147]

A more sympathetic and decisive stance was adopted by the Viceroy of India, Lord Hardinge, who took the bold step, on 27 November 1913, of publicly criticising the South African and British governments' failure to resolve a crisis which had resulted in troops being brought in to put down strikes and other forms of protest, and seen Gandhi sentenced to a nine-month term of imprisonment.[148] Crewe stridently rebuked the Viceroy, emphasising that the King had been 'rather alarmed by one or two of your expressions, and begged me to impress on you the need to keep on good terms with the self-governing Dominions'.[149]

Hardinge's comments nonetheless helped to reinforce the increasingly irresistible pressure being exerted on the South African government from India and abroad. On 18 December, Gandhi and other high-profile protesters were released from prison; and, on 21 January 1914, he and Smuts struck a deal, abolishing the £3 tax on former indentured labourers, recognising the legitimacy of Hindu, Muslim, and Parsi marriages (whether polygamous or not) and allowing some inter-provincial movement by Indians. Gandhi then departed from South Africa in July 'to almost universal acclaim'. With his prestige and influence thus swelling, his attention would now turn to the even greater political priority of liberating India from British rule.[150]

Crewe displayed a similar lack of conviction when asked to participate in events leading up to the arrest of the prominent female activist, Princess Sophia Alexandrovna Duleep Singh, daughter of Maharaja Sir Duleep Singh and goddaughter of Queen Victoria. Sophia had been brought to Britain from India when her father was exiled from his kingdom of Punjab, and had since become an outspoken suffragette. In the latter half of 1913, the princess began selling copies of the Women's Social and Political Union (WSPU) newspaper, *The Suffragette*, outside the gates of Hampton Court Palace, much to the chagrin of the royal family.[151]

Unlike his father (Edward VII) and grandmother (Queen Victoria), King George V was unfamiliar with the princess and regarded her without affection. Acting on the monarch's directive, the royal Keeper of the Purse, William Carrington, cut out an article on Sophia from *The Suffragette*, enclosed it, along with a compliment slip bearing the Buckingham Palace crest, into an envelope, and sent it to Lord Crewe. Adamant that 'He did not think it was up to the India Office to do the King's bidding,'[152] Crewe recommended that Carrington should ask the King to consider threatening Sophia with eviction from her Hampton Court flat, which she occupied by dint of royal patronage.

The King showed no desire to evict his recalcitrant tenant; and, undeterred by the reaction she had generated, the princess continued to sell *The Suffragette*. Sophia was eventually arrested and brought before court in December 1913. As on previous such occasions, she declared herself unwilling to pay any fine imposed on her until 'the women of England are enfranchised and the State acknowledges me as a citizen'.[153] The judge set a deadline of the New Year for Sophia to pay her £12/10s fine. Subsequently,

> A collection of newspaper cuttings about Sophia's day in court found their way to the desk of the Secretary of State for India again. In one from the *Daily Mail*, the princess's words had been underlined in blue pencil. Sighing, Lord Crewe wrote a note to his private secretary: 'Dear Hirtzel, buck Pal [Buckingham Palace] will probably write here again full of rage and grief. They read the Mail assiduously there' […] and with that, he added the papers to Sophia's file.[154]

It seems plausible to assume that Crewe's apparent indifference reflected the fact that he had, in his own words, 'always been unfavourably disposed to the idea of Women's Suffrage', but was reluctant to air his views in public, primarily because 'my Father (in more placid times) was one of those who helped the cause in public and private'.[155] This was a position he would eventually relinquish: Pope-Hennessy reports that, 'It is characteristic of [his] total lack of prejudice that after 1918 he entirely changed his views about female suffrage, on the grounds that the work done by Englishwomen during the four years of war abundantly proved that they deserved, and ought to exercise, the Vote.'[156]

Wider Family Developments

Finally, we may note that this was an era in which notable changes were also occurring in the lives of other members of the Crewe family – namely, his daughter, Cynthia, his sister, Florence, and his son-in-law, Arthur O'Neill.

Following Cynthia's marriage to George (Geordie) Colville, the couple had settled down in Cadogan Place, Chelsea. The former continued working at the Institute of Chartered Accountants in Moorgate Place. Cynthia succumbed, in the meantime, to 'a special lure in the thought of philanthropic endeavour in the famous East End'[157] by becoming a committee member of the COS (Charity Organisation Society) in the hard-pressed East End (of London) Borough of Shoreditch. This gave her the opportunity to develop on-the-job insight into various aspects of social work.[158]

Shoreditch encompassed an area of barely one square mile. It had a population of 110,000 residents, living mostly in slum dwellings. Despite its severe overcrowding, local people seemed invariably upbeat, tended to know each other well and were therefore mutually supportive. The COS urgently sought to improve maternity and child welfare services within the borough. Having rapidly risen to the position of COS Secretary (a role she was to occupy for the next two decades), Cynthia was instrumental in the creation in 1913 of the Shoreditch Infant Welfare Centre. 'The personal familiarity with the circumstances in which a large portion of the community lived left me,' she wrote, 'with a profound admiration for the courage, common sense and kindliness with which countless households faced anxieties, difficulties and privations of many kinds.'[159]

By now, Cynthia's aunt, Florence Henniker, was busily consolidating her longstanding relationship with Thomas Hardy by becoming a firm friend of his future second wife – another Florence by the surname of Dugdale. The three of them had begun attending theatre together; and, in a letter dated 21 April 1912, Hardy wrote of his and Dugdale's great admiration of Henniker's latest novel, *Second Fiddle*.[160]

This letter arrived in the wake of great personal tragedy. On 6 February 1912, the sudden death occurred of Mrs Henniker's husband, Major-General Arthur Henniker, who was a mere 56 years old. The Major-General was now serving in the 1st London Territorial Division. It was while stationed in the capital, that he sustained a broken leg, resulting from a kick by a horse, and died not long afterwards of heart failure while resting up at home.[161]

Florence Henniker responded to her loss by producing a small memorial volume, *A Little Black Book for His Friends*, for Arthur.[162] Among the many tributes it contained was a brief poem by Thomas Hardy. Bearing the simple title of 'A.H., 1855-1912', the last of its three verses exhorted:

> Yet let us not lament. We do not *weep*
> When our best comrade sinks in fitful sleep,
> And why indulge regrets if he should fall
> At once into the sweetest sleep of all.[163]

Another family member with strong army connections was Lord Crewe's son-in-law, Captain Arthur Edward Bruce O'Neill of the Life Guards, who had been seconded on half pay to the House of Commons in 1910 to serve as Unionist MP for Mid Antrim. O'Neill chose in 1913 to defy the pro-Home Rule proclivities of his wife's family by joining those like-minded Northern Irish protestants who had pledged to stand alongside the renowned lawyer, Sir Edward Carson, in resisting (by force, if necessary) the creation of an all-Irish parliament.[164]

This jarred, of course, with the political sensibilities of O'Neill's Liberal father-in-law. According to his biographer, Lord Crewe had left the role of Viceroy of Ireland 'a more convinced Home Ruler than when he had gone there'.[165] He had conspicuously referred since then to the 'odd and hypocritical anomaly' whereby England (the avowed 'champion of oppressed minorities') continued to occupy Ireland by force and denied its claim to separate nationhood.[166]

As Lord Privy Seal, it was Crewe who organised and opened the debate on the Second Reading of the Government of Ireland Bill on 27 January 1913. His preliminary speech was unequivocal: Ireland, he insisted, was currently being ruled by an 'arbitrary Government from the outside'. The country had 'never become an integral part of the United Kingdom because the principle of Irish nationality [had] altogether refused to die'.[167]

It was in this context that that the paramilitary Ulster Volunteer Force (UVF), known colloquially as 'Carson's Army', rose to prominence. The UVF consisted, during its peak period of 1914, of some 100,000 civilian volunteers, equipped with more than 50,000 secretly hidden rifles. Other trappings of a modern, conventional army included a Motor Car Corp of approximately 350 vehicles, and two mounted divisions, one of which (the Ballymena Horse) had been raised, trained up and prepared for action by Arthur O'Neill.[168]

Serious doubts were cast – not least by O'Neill himself – regarding the UVF's numerical potency, its military efficiency and the mobility required to cope with the increasing threat posed by the rival Irish Volunteers.[169] Such capability was not ultimately put to the test. A respite followed the onset of war:

> In September the Cabinet produced their solution, one often regarded as a characteristic Asquithian compromise: the Home Rule Bill would go on the Statute Book but would remain inoperative until after the war. As a further sop to Ulster, Asquith promised to consider amending legislation before the measure went into effect. Of course, neither side was satisfied.[170]

Chapter Four
'Mining Shangri-la'

Fryston: An 'Ideal Type'

From the Industrial Revolution onwards, former coalmining communities like Fryston have been heavily mythologised. The work carried out by miners was hidden from wider society, and the methods they employed scarcely comprehendible to most. Miners therefore belonged 'to a hidden world known and understood only by themselves'.[171] It has been argued that the villages they and their families inhabited long represented 'little more than work camps constructed to house the workers and their families, who were brought in to meet the needs of the mine'.[172] Their geographical isolation reinforced perceptions of their unique distinctiveness (both physical and cultural); and, 'if miners saw themselves as different to outsiders, there is ample evidence that they themselves have historically been seen as different by outsiders looking in'.[173]

One eminent sociologist, M.I.A. Bulmer,[174] famously presented a model of the 'traditional mining community' in the form of an 'ideal type', which was said to exhibit several definitive characteristics:

> In the ideal type, mining communities are both physically isolated and occupationally homogeneous. Arduous and dangerous working conditions promote solidarity amongst miners in opposition to the employer. Gender roles are markedly differentiated, with women leading a home-centred existence spent chiefly in the company of female kin and neighbours. The primary function of the miner's wife is to service the needs of her husband and family. By contrast, male leisure-time is spent in public places, notably the miners' welfare or working men's club, exclusively in the company of other men. Work, leisure, family and neighbourhood relations are therefore close-knit and interlocking (or 'multiplex') in form. Longevity of residence and dense kinship networks reinforce traditions of mutual aid.[175]

Bulmer adds the important corollary that ideal types of this nature would seldom exist in reality: most mining communities would possess at least some, though not all, of these characteristics, albeit to varying degrees.

There is good reason to argue that, perhaps more so than any other community in Yorkshire, it was the small village of Fryston which approximated most closely to Bulmer's ideal type. Fryston was characterised by what the journalist, Stephen McClarence, aptly described as a 'curious geography': it was cut off and isolated on three sides by a river bend and, on its remaining flank, by a railway line. Thus, 'it was, and still is, isolated even by the standards of pit villages, with no through road and just a single-lane bridge to take you in and out'.[176] McClarence observed that most Fryston miners and their families could even see the pit from the vantage point of their own front doors. A second local journalist, Frank Metcalfe, reinforced Fryston's mythical reputation by referring to this self-contained and socially vibrant village as 'a mining Shangri-la'.[177]

Future chapters will focus on the patterns of everyday life which made Fryston such a 'tight knit' and mutually supportive village, marked by a strong sense of local identity, community spiritedness and self-worth. For the present moment, we concentrate on those more tangible features of the village already evident by 1910 – that is: the physical fabric of the housing; the demographic structure of the village; the presence of major institutions (employment, religious, scholastic, retail, sporting and leisure, transport and legal); and those significant individuals who were most closely associated with this era.

Steam-Driven Thing

Seminal industrial developments in Fryston, up to and including this first decade of the twentieth century, are conveniently summarised by Downes.[178] As reported in Volume 1, the first sod of the new colliery was cut by Lord Crewe himself on 20 April 1873. The 180-metres-deep Warren House Seam was reached sixteen months later, followed by the Haigh Moor Seam (lying a further 80 metres below ground) in May 1875. Two shafts were utilised in producing coal from the 48-inch-thick Warren House, which commenced in 1874, and the 54-inch Haigh Moor, which started up four years later:

The No. 1 Shaft was equipped with a steam winding engine attached to four-deck cages, carrying 2 x 10 cwt tubs per deck and was used for coal winding. No. 2 Shaft was also equipped with a steam winding engine attached to single-deck cages and was used for winding men and materials only. [...] Initially, the Colliery was ventilated by natural means until furnace ventilation was introduced in February 1886. The furnace was sited near the Warren House No. 2 Pit Bottom, ventilating the whole of that Seam and part of the Haigh Moor. Furnace ventilation ended in 1895, when a steam-driven Walker Indestructible fan was installed at the top of the No. 2 Shaft.[179]

So as to facilitate the mass transportation of coal, the company built a canal basin in 1894.

Five years later, Fryston merged with Wheldale, thus forming the Wheldale Coal Company Ltd. The former pit's 500-strong workforce was producing up to 4,000 tons of coal per week at this stage from its two existing seams. A decision was implemented in 1900 to sink the two pit shafts to a further depth of over 550 metres, where the 48-inch Beeston Seam was reached. This encouraged the termination of production from the Haigh Moor Seam which was becoming progressively thin. In 1910, work also ceased on the Warren House Seam, due to the vastly superior quality of Beeston coal, which was now being extracted at the impressive rate of 14,000 tons per week.[180]

Bricks and Mortar

The evolving nature of Fryston's streets and houses, circa 1910, was comprehensively described in interview by the local amateur historian, Maud Raftery. There were, as she explained, two chapels (a Wesleyan and 'Primitive' Methodist) within the village; and, standing on its periphery, a church (St Peter's) and local farm. Raftery also pointed to the presence of six cottages, scattered alongside the River Aire within close range of the village pub, the Milnes Arms. Three further 'railway cottages' nestled at the foot of the village entrance. Most functional of all was the lengthy Wheldon Road, which ran from Castleford town centre, crossed the railway bridge into Fryston, and skirted the bottom of the village before terminating at the pit entrance.

On top of this,

> The first houses to be built were Smith, Hope and William Streets
> in 1884 and the 'low buildings', Castle, Oxford and Wellington
> Streets, must have followed shortly after. Brook Street wasn't
> built until 1910 and Smith's [Smith] Cottages and South View
> even later. The village school was established in 1889, hence
> 'School Street', soon after; and St Peter's Church before that in
> 1896. Of the two large houses in the middle of the village, Fryston
> House came first in, what, 1898? And Mount Pleasant, I think,
> in 1907. The village had three worked lime quarries, but there
> were two main ones. One was situated in Fryston village itself.
> It ran from the end of William Street, Smith Street and Hope
> Street and carried on to the river. And there was another one
> situated across from where St Peter's is built. You can still see its
> sides, though it's now exhausted. It was worked with men and
> horses and you could see the actual kilns. It was regarded as very
> healthy to live next to. Anyway, by the second quarry, there was
> the quarry house, for the quarry manager, and three quarry
> cottages. Higher up still, there was another little building that's
> surviving to this day: that's Wheldale Lodge, which was built in
> 1894 as part of the Fryston Hall Estate. (Maud Raftery, 1987)

This Lodge provides a lasting historical connection between the
village and the Fryston Hall estate. Speaking in 1988, its then occupant,
Winifred Wilson, explained how the property came initially to be
built. It was the result, she maintained, of a frosty encounter between
men working on the estate and Lord Crewe's daughters, who were
out riding their horses when they came across a gate which was locked
and barring their further progress.

> When they asked some men who were standing around if they'd
> mind opening the gate, the men were rude to them. When
> they got back, they told their father [Lord Crewe], and he said,
> 'Right! I'll have a lodge built.' And he did: Wheldale Lodge.
> When it was first built, it had two bedrooms, a living room and
> kitchen. Then a gamekeeper came from Scotland, but he had
> a wife and four children and they found that the Lodge wasn't
> quite big enough, so they went back to Scotland until two more
> bedrooms were built on; and that's how it stayed until 1920.
> (Interview, 1987)

Table 1: Origins of Miners Living in Fryston (1891-1911)★

Place Of Birth	Census Year		
	1891	1901	1911
Fryston	0	1	26
Brotherton	1	7	24
Castleford + Pontefract	12	42	50
Elsewhere in Yorkshire	50	85	109
Derbyshire	14	21	30
Lancashire and Cheshire	3	5	23
Leicestershire	26	14	23
Nottinghamshire	15	13	13
Shropshire	2	0	10
Southwest England	29	14	13
Staffordshire	54	42	89
Wales	2	1	16
Other	16	33	21
Total	224	278	447

★Source: National Census for England and Wales, 1891, 1901 and 1911.

Following the death of Sir John Austin in 1906, ownership of the Fryston Hall estate fell into the hands of his registered company, Austin Brothers Limited, which was managed by his two sons, William and Joseph. Sometime in the pre-war period, Fryston Hall estate was sold off as the company went into liquidation. Its new owners were the West Riding Standing Joint Committee, who adapted the building and its immediate environs into police offices and a training college for new recruits. This new venture was short-lived: as early as 1922, the Hall had been vacated and was falling into disrepair.[181]

Flesh and Blood
The 1911 Census returns provide unequivocal evidence of Fryston's occupational homogeneity. Only rarely were male occupants of the village streets employed outside of the mining industry (as in the case of a stone miner and sand quarryman). The raison d'être of two other such workers (a 'boot repairer' and 'shoemaker') was to provide an ancillary service for local miners. The remaining non-mining male residents (three butchers, a store manager and his assistant, the publican and his bar staff, local headmaster and village constable) were all staple to the everyday functioning of the village.

Most female residents were engaged in unpaid housework. Notable exceptions were three teachers (including the headmistress) and a teaching assistant, a midwife, and eight women variously categorised as 'housemaid', 'domestic servant', 'servant' or 'cleaner'. It is likely that these eight were employed in the service of 'elite' members of the local society, such as the pit manager, senior engineers, the headteacher, publican and members of the retail sector. It is also probable that four remaining women in paid work (a milliner, a weaver, and a dressmaker and her apprentice) either serviced the local drapery store or provided clothing items and/or repair work for village residents.

The village was far from monocultural in its origins. As we can see from Table 1, Fryston's population had evolved by 1911 in such a way as to continue to be well represented by Yorkshire-born menfolk (26 of them originating from Fryston itself, 24 more from nearby Brotherton, 50 from the wider Castleford, Pontefract and District, and another 109 from elsewhere in the county). Conspicuous among the remaining male residents are the 89 having originated from Staffordshire.

Considering that there were a supplementary 33 Staffordshire-born women also residing in Fryston, and 209 dependants of one or both of these adults, it is fair to say that this county was significantly represented in this and in subsequent eras.

In the first volume of this study and in a related history of association football in Fryston,[182] I explain how, in the wake of industrial disputes occurring in the late 1880s, 1890s and, especially, the Wheldale-Fryston strike of 1902-04, there had been a steady influx of former Staffordshire miners and their families from such places as Fenton, Burslam and Pelsall. This trend continued throughout the first decade of the twentieth century and well beyond World War I.

One major impact of this trend was that Staffordshire 'migrants' brought with them a predilection for association football which was pivotal to the foundation of a strong sporting culture in Fryston. This was true, for example, of the closely related Foulkes and Astbury families who would figure prominently in footballing exploits of the next four decades. One descendant of these families explained on a Pelsall area website how her forebears had travelled the hard way up to Fryston:

> I estimate that the Astbury's consisted of 20 adults and eighteen children and one wonders how they managed. Presumably they travelled by rail for the major part of the journey but my mother told us that she remembered walking alongside the carts carrying their belongings and that she and her sisters wore straw boaters. [...] By the time of the 1911 Census, thirteen more children had been born to the families. Fryston appears to have been a happy village and no doubt the Pelsall people injected a boost to the life of the village. I believe the locals called the village Little Staffordshire. Fryston Colliery football teams were filled with Pelsall players including a number of the Astbury family and did very well against the local clubs.[183]

Once this core of former Staffordshire men, women and children had been established in the village, it set a pattern for other migrants to head north in search of mining work.

Census figures for 1911 also indicate large numbers of miners residing in nearby villages also nestling by the River Aire, most of whom are likely to have worked at Fryston. In each case, the Staffordshire influence was negligible: of the 124 miners living in Fairburn, only eight originated from the county; in Brotherton it was a mere three out of 228 such workers; while Newton's total of 46 pit employees included none at all. It is therefore safe to assume that Fryston's culture had much in common, but was subtly distinct from, that of even close-lying mining communities.

Houses of the Holy

By 1910, Fryston contained three places of Christian worship, two of which (the chapels) were located within the actual village, and a third (St Peter's Church) just prior to its point of entry:

> There was the [Primitive] Methodist Chapel: as you're coming over the bridge, you go down some steps and the Methodist Chapel was there [...] and the Smalleys were big people at the 'Primitive', a man called Wagstaffe was the organist for years. The Wesleyan chapel was down by the shop on Wheldon Road. Firths were more or less the main people there. Both chapels were built much earlier than St Peter's, which has links with the old Hall. (Fryston woman, 1986)

Methodism established an initial toehold in the mid-1800s, when it was first practised by a small Wesleyan congregation of nine, who gathered in a farmhouse in neighbouring Water Fryston, owned by Mrs Frost, the housekeeper of Fryston Hall. It is possible that this person was instrumental in persuading the first Lord Houghton (Richard Monckton Milnes) to provide this growing religious society with a chapel in the grounds of Fryston Hall. Houghton commissioned the Hall's bricklayer and mason from his own estate to design and erect an appropriate lean-to building, comprising two cottages, work on which was completed in 1851: 'Although seating but forty persons, it was at that time capable of holding the entire population.'[184]

The in-migration of labour following the sinking of Fryston Colliery necessitated an even larger place of worship. Relevant negotiations were conducted with the second Lord Houghton (soon to become Lord Crewe) by a Reverend Aaron Edmon, of the Castleford 'Friends of Methodism'. These talks resulted in the leasing for 99 years of a 300-yard plot of land. The foundation stones of the new chapel were laid on 24 September 1890, with Lord Crewe donating £10 from his own pocket, and the Colliery Company a further £25, towards the eventual completion cost of £650. The building was formally opened on 16 April 1891. As the *Express* reported at the time,

> Outwardly, the chapel is not at all pretentious. Inside it is very plain, but well lighted, comfortable and airy, and providing sitting accommodation for some 300 persons. The furniture is for the most part loose, with a view, no doubt, to the use of the chapel as a schoolroom also. [...] In front of the chapel is a vestibule, and at the rear a large classroom and other conveniences.[185]

The Fryston woman quoted earlier was partially mistaken in assuming that both chapels were built prior to St Peter's Church. The development of Primitive Methodism lagged behind that of its Wesleyan counterpart. Around 1889, local 'Primitives' began worshipping at the Co-operative Stores (see below). Following the shop's temporary closure during the lengthy stoppage of 1887-89, the Fryston School Board allowed the congregation to meet up in one of its classrooms. The chapel commanded a fellowship of 25 by this time. It also provided a Sunday School, attended by some 190 village children.[186]

Further progress was made in August 1901, when the foundation stone for a new chapel building was laid on a site leased for 99 years at nominal rental rate by Queen's College, Oxford. 'The site is near a railway crossing and a big limestone quarry at a corner of a road, and facing William Street,' the *Express* reported on 24 August 1901. The building, it added, 'will have a small porch, a vestry, and a classroom and will be completed in six weeks'.[187]

The completion of this project was predated by the construction of St Peter's Church, which was built by local colliery workmen on five acres of land donated by Lord Crewe. Local folklore maintains that Crewe's benevolence arose in response to a plea by a local miner who wanted to give his recently deceased daughter a 'proper Christian burial'.

> And, of course, the nearest church was St Andrew's, Ferrybridge. So, they set off with this corpse through Fryston Park, which was the quickest route to Ferrybridge at that time. [Lord Crewe] stopped them and asked them where they were going and why. When they told him, he said, 'I'm not having this. I'll build you

a church and I'll give you a cemetery.' And that's how St Peter's came into being in 1896. He also gave £100 for the vicar's stipend. (Ex-Fryston man, 1987)

The plot of land included sufficient space, not only for the church building itself, but also an encircling churchyard. St Peter's was dedicated for full use on the Feast of the Epiphany, 6 January 1896.

Days of the Old Schoolyard
The local village school was erected in 1889, and a new classroom added in 1906. It comprised two separate units: New Fryston Infants (catering for 130 children) and the Public Elementary (Mixed), which accommodated up to 210 pupils. Eunice Fox was headteacher of the infant school, while her husband, William Fox, was head of the elementary.[188] They were both strict disciplinarians:

> Old 'Gaffer' Fox, he had a big beard. He had a daughter that died and we knew where she was buried in Fryston churchyard. He was a wicked old schoolmaster! I was always late 'cos we had all to do: get ready for my mother's baking, do the hearth and everything. And as soon as I ever got to school, old Gaffer Fox would say, 'All hold your hands out.' And he had a long cane and it was murder! It was a blister many a time on your hand. Them was bad days. (Ex-Fryston woman, 1987)

By 1911, the roles of Mr and Mrs Fox had been taken over by another married couple, J.S. Rickaby and his wife. One version of history maintains that Mrs Rickaby started out as a teacher's assistant and became fully qualified shortly afterwards. Her husband wore a distinctive wax moustache and was known to give a little cough as if to warn the pupils of his presence:

> They were a good-hearted couple. The whole of Fryston liked them. Mrs Rickaby tended to dominate him. She was the power behind the scenes as far as the children were concerned, old Rickaby was a real disciplinarian, only he was disciplined himself by Mrs Rickaby. You could see him doing his little walk into Castleford every night for his drink at 'The Ship'. He used to take us for 'reading'. We had a test every month. He'd say, 'Read me this passage. Nine out of

ten!' and then tell you where you'd made your mistakes. She
was a large woman, very much bigger than Mr Rickaby.
(Ex-Fryston man, 1987)

One ex-Fryston man recalled how, having reached his teens, he earned
up to fifteen shillings per year by running errands to the village pub, the
Milnes Arms, and bringing back regular supplies of beer or whisky –
not, as one might suppose, for Mr Rickaby, but rather for his wife.

One major feature of this era was the provision of evening schools
for local women, where an emphasis was placed on needlework and
woodwork. In the first week of April 1911, for example, the school
hosted an exhibition of artefacts, created not only by local boys and
girls, but village women as well. The *Pontefract and Castleford Express*
reported that: 'The needlework, both plain and fancy, reflected great
credit on the girls and women, whilst some specimens of the teacher's
own work gave ample evidence that the students had had a very capable
instructress in Mrs Rickaby.' Similar praise was earned by the boys
and their headmaster on account of the 'exceptionally good' drawings
and models they produced. Most notably of all,

> The woodwork of the girls was a feature of admiration on the
> part of the men and boys, these including towel rollers, key
> racks, brush and bath trays, egg stands, etc. A cot made by girl
> students from an old banana crate, beautified by staining and
> with bedding, daintily made, was deservedly admired.[189]

Spending a Penny
Kelly's West Riding of Yorkshire Directory (1908) indicates that the village
incorporated a local shop, the Co-operative Stores, combining a
grocer's and drapery (run by Henry Curtis) and a butcher's shop,
belonging to George W. Bateson. Such detail was endorsed by one
ex-Fryston woman who vividly recalled how:

> Against the pit baths, where they are today, was the shop. A
> man called Curtis had it, then it was Albert Firth. Next door
> was old 'Cuddy' Bateson who had t' fish shop. He also had a
> butcher's at the top of North Street, but he had a fish shop when
> I was in my teens; you'd get a ha'porth of chips and a penny
> fish. (Interview, 1986)

Absent from this account is any mention of the newsagent's shop, 'The Evening News', situated close to the pit entrance at the end of Wheldon Road, which was initially run by Phil Wagstaffe, before he sold it on to the Brace family.

The one person invariably singled out in interviews was the squarely built and ruddy-faced 'Cuddy Bateson' – a man universally known for his meticulous standards of cleanliness and persistently cantankerous demeanour.

> I remember one day, somebody came in for a quarter of potted meat for tuppence and he said, 'There you are. Here's your potted meat. But you take your tuppence and tell your mam to buy some soap and give your hands a good scrub.' He was like that. Wouldn't allow dogs in and, if you put your fingers on the counter, bang! He'd take your fingers off. His bench that he used to cut his meat on was *absolutely spotless*. He used to scrub and scrub it all the time. (Fryston man, 1986)

This is not to discount another, more endearing dimension of Cuddy's character. One ex-Fryston miner, Wilf Hunter, recollected how, having only recently been married, he was called upon by Cuddy to line out his storage fridge with zinc sheeting and copper nails. The newly married man made such a good job of it that Bateson paid him handsomely in cash but did not leave it there:

> 'Wait on a minute,' he says, and he gets this big, bloody knife and wham! He cuts through this big piece of beef and says, 'Here, take that home to your lass [wife] and ask her to put it in t' pan for thi supper.' (Interview, 1987)

Cuddy's gruff public facade disguised an underlying community spiritedness. An early sign of this was evident in the oblique benevolence he sometimes showed towards the very children he had recently chastised:

> As soon as the kids heard any squealing, they'd shout, 'Cuddy's killing pigs!' and they used to swarm from every direction. His wall had rounded bricks, you see? Tailor-made for jumping up on. I only saw it once, but that was enough for me! Half the reason they gathered was for the pigs' bladders so they could blow them up like balloons. (Ex-Fryston woman, 1986)

This was a decidedly inhumane ritual, involving stunning the pig with a hammer and soaking the beast in a vat of boiling water before gutting it and chopping it up into its constituent parts. 'We'd be waiting for the bladder so we could use it as a football and he'd just chuck it at us,' Jack Hulme recalled. 'It would still be full of pee so we'd nick it with a blade, empty it and it would be good for three or four games of football.'[190]

Also fondly remembered was the early village grocer, the kind and 'gentlemanly' Albert Firth, who arrived in Fryston from Bowers Row, Allerton, just prior to World War I. His son, the equally popular and mild-mannered Reg Firth, was au fait with the relevant village history:

> A man called Curtis had it before him. I think my dad worked for Mr Curtis before moving back to Bowers Row and then came back to Fryston when Mr Curtis died. He [Mr Firth] actually came from Kippax. The whole family came from there. The shop was right by the side of the pit in Wheldon Road, across from the school. It was a grocer's, draper's and post office: it was three shops in a row! My father received the telegrams via the post office during the First World War. When I was very, very young, one of my particular jobs was to sell pints and quarts of paraffin when I got home from school in the evening because there were no electric lights in the village. That trade disappeared when they electrified the village. (Interview, 1986)

Reg Firth spoke of his father with understandable warmth and pride. 'I think he was the most even-tempered man I've ever come across,' he said.

> My mother tended to run the family; she was the disciplinarian! Dad was a superb self-taught musician: a regular chapel man. One of the few people I've met who could sit down and transpose a hymn tune into a higher or lower key. Religiously, he was very open-minded: it didn't matter to him whether people worshipped in this style or that; there was just one God. (Interview, 1988)

Local women remembered 'Firth's' as 'a real old-fashioned shop'. Huge, muslin-covered cheeses were paraded in front of the counter, while practically everything else was arranged in 'old-fashioned containers', an example being 'that lovely dark treacle that used to come in tubs' (Fryston woman, 1986). The shop also functioned as a drapery. Directly above it was a 'Reading Room', and a small premise off to the side where the visiting doctors — initially a Dr Ward from Brotherton, followed by Dr Crispin and Dr Binks, both practitioners in Castleford — held their 'surgeries'. At the rear of the shop was a wooden hut which a peripatetic barber used three times a week in giving local men a haircut.

Sport, Recreation and Leisure
As in most, if not all, of the mining communities of this era, recreation and leisure activity was a largely male preserve, with women engaged in more privatised and organised pursuits of a practical nature, epitomised by the sewing classes. Though officially available to everyone, the Reading Room was primarily a male bastion, replete with a billiards table. This village sanctuary was introduced in April 1903, at which point the *Pontefract and Castleford Express* described how,

> Recently, rooms have been prepared above the Co-operative stores to be used as reading and recreation rooms and library. The Wheldale Colliery Company have furnished the rooms and put in an installation of electric light. The library has been started with about 150 volumes, 100 of which have been purchased by subscriptions and by a grant from the Rebecca Hussey Charity. The other 50 have been obtained through the Yorkshire Union of Village Libraries and will be changed quarterly. There are already 100 members.[191]

Gender differentiation was also a hallmark of the village pub, the Milnes Arms, so-called, in deference, of course, to the local, land-owning gentry:

> It was called the Milnes Arms, but lots of people referred to it as the 'Miners' Arms'. It was right on the riverside below Brook Street, so much so that it was often in flood. They used to bring barges up the river with coal and they used horses to pull them. And they used to tie the boat up at the side of the pub, bring the horses round to the stables to feed, and come in for a pint. (Fryston woman, 1986)

The section of the pub commonly referred to these days as the 'tap room' was known colloquially as the 'pick hole', depicting a male sanctuary where discussions relating to work took place, and weekly wages were distributed. Separated off from that was the 'jug hole' in which women would sit together in private conversation. Every Sunday night, weather permitting, men and women would congregate on the surrounding 'pub hills' and listen to a local band while sipping their drinks.

The *Kelly's West Riding of Yorkshire Directory* (1908) attributes ownership of the pub to George Williamson but this proprietorship shifted soon afterwards to his son, Sam, who then ran it for the next three decades. 'A quiet sort of bloke was Sam. Pleasant enough,' one ex-Fryston man recalled. 'Funny thing was, he didn't smoke or drink. I can remember his wife was a blonde woman' (interview, 1987). According to this interviewee, Sam 'did well out of the miners', often accepting their gold chains and watches as 'down payments' for beer and spirits. 'He had a good few off my father,' he ruefully recalled.

Organised sport was equally male dominated. A local emphasis on association football was paramount. Fryston teams had appeared sporadically in local leagues since the late 1800s. In August 1910, the newly-formed Fryston Colliery Association FC was accepted into the Castleford and District League. Under the presidency of the Colliery Manager, Hezekiah Soar, Fryston swiftly developed into a powerful force in the local amateur game.[192]

Keen to elevate his colliery's prestige, Soar buttressed the considerable local talent by importing players with football league and, in some cases, international experience. In only their second season, Fryston entered the very strong Yorkshire Combination League (which included several reserve teams of professional clubs, like Bradford City, Bradford Park Avenue and Leeds City, and semi-professional clubs, such as Goole Town and Dewsbury's Mirfield United).

The undoubted highlights of the club's first two years of existence (1910-11 and 1911-12) were good runs in pursuit of the much-coveted WRCC Cup. Fryston lost out in both campaigns to the all-conquering Mirfield, who went on to lift the trophy, twice running. The second occasion was a close-run semi-final in which Fryston's star player, the full-back, Harry Millership, was greatly instrumental in limiting their more celebrated opponents to a 1-0 victory,[193] before leaving the club in the close season to join Blackpool of the Football League. The colliery team went one step further in the 1913-14 season by reaching the final of the WRCC Cup, where they were narrowly beaten (1-0) by Horsforth of Leeds.[194]

Going Places

The earliest forms of transportation in and out of Fryston were the horse-drawn carriages belonging to a family firm called Brocklehurst's. These vehicles were quickly supplanted, however, by hard-wheeled, engine-driven waggons, providing a somewhat uncomfortable ride across unmade road surfaces:

> It was a square box on wheels, but it had an engine and, on the front of it behind the driver's cab, they used to have a carriage lamp with a candle in it. The seats face inwards and everybody sat opposite each other. Once you set off, it would go in a hole and the candle would go out. The driver would say, 'Wait a minute while I light the candle!' You didn't know whose lap you were going to fall into! Then they developed from that to Harvey's and Petty's buses. (Ex-Fryston woman, 1986)

Petty's 'charas' (charabancs) quickly cornered this local market, to be eventually displaced in the 1930s by the more modern and monopolistic West Riding buses.

The only way for miners living in Fairburn and Brotherton to gain access to Fryston Colliery was to cross the River Aire by ferry. Workers from these outlying villages were obliged to follow a footpath down to a small hut located on a riverside jetty, alongside the railway line, go down some steps to a jetty and into a hut, where they were charged a halfpenny each per week to travel, eight at a time, in a row-boat across to Fryston. 'We'd hear them many a time if the ferry was on the other side,' one ex-Fryston man explained. 'They'd just stand there and shout, "Boat!" and he used to ferry them across' (interview, 1987).

A similar facility was available for the benefit of those miners living across the Aire in Newton. This second ferry was moored on the riverbank adjacent to the Milnes Arms. It was rumoured, though never satisfactorily confirmed, that the ruins of an old abbey were submerged under that part of the river. Eventually, both ferries were supplanted by a footbridge across the river with steps leading up and down on either side.

Meting Out Rough Justice

Number 1, Brook Street was the 'village Bobby's' house. Its best-known incumbents were 'Bobby' Lofthouse and his immediate successor, 'Bobby' Roebuck. The former's son, John Lofthouse, became a senior policeman, in his own right, as well as a captain in the army. He remembered the precise circumstance in which his father came to Fryston:

> Wakefield born and bred was father. He joined the police force and his first station was Norwood Green. From there, he moved to somewhere near Brighouse and then on again to Thurnscoe. However, he was moved – it would be about 1910 – to Fryston when I was nine months old. We lived in Hope Street; number two or four, something like that. And when Brook Street was built, we moved into number one, overlooking the Milnes Arms. The miners used to have their Sunday pint and then start a 'tossing school' down by the pub. Father used to go plonk himself under an elderberry bush at the top of the rise. Suddenly, he'd just jump up and shout, 'Right lads, that's it!' and off they'd go without stopping to pick their money up! (Interview, 1986)

This was an era in which summary justice was the norm. Village 'bobbies' were familiar with the local population and therefore well-versed in terms of individual reputations, possible hiding places, etc. Each officer carried a lengthy walking stick. Instances of mischief or transgressions of the law were punishable by a whack on the legs or 'clip on the ear' (in other words, a 'short, sharp shock'). It was not only children and youths who Lofthouse dealt with in this fashion:

> He was a well-built fellow. There weren't so many that would get him down. He lived to be 93 – so did my mother! – and he never had much trouble. Mind you, if there was any marital trouble or anything like that, they'd fetch him and he'd go and sort it out. If they really got out of hand, he'd have them in court in Castleford. Not normally, though. He'd give them a well-intentioned slap across the chops and that would be an end to that. He did his own policing. (John Lofthouse, 1986)

In the early 1920s, Lofthouse left Fryston to become Security Officer at Glasshoughton Colliery and Coke Works. The policing tradition was then maintained by his replacement, Bobby Roebuck, whose methods carried a familiar ring.

> There was once a goldfish pond in the pit yard and me and a relative of mine, Eddie Rotherforth, were on our hands and knees trying to catch a fish. Before we knew it, we were both picked up by the scruff of the neck and our heads were banged together. It was Roebuck! Worst of it was, if he hit you, you used to get another when you got home as soon as he told your parents. (Fryston man, 1986)

These, then, were the major village institutions and prominent individuals associated with them at the start of the 114-year period covered in this volume. Little has so far been said about prevailing experiences, relationships and interactions relating to work, family and social life in the early decades of the twentieth century. These relatively stable and enduring aspects of community life are comprehensively discussed in Chapter 9, but not before we have devoted the next three chapters to describing the wartime experience of the pit-folk of Fryston and their aristocratic counterparts.

Chapter Five
A Family at War

Facing the 'Folly of War'

On 28 June 1914, the Austrian Archduke, Franz Ferdinand, and his wife, Sophie, were shot dead by a Serbian assassin, following an earlier, failed attempt to blow up their carriage. The assassination occurred while the royal pair were heading towards a local hospital, where they planned to see the victims of the earlier bomb blast. Austria sought, with the backing of its German neighbours, to hold Serbia responsible for the murder of the heir to the Austro-Hungarian Empire. Serbia's protestation of innocence was supported by its own Russian allies. The dispute swiftly escalated: in the next three weeks, both Germany and Russia mobilised their armies in readiness for possible conflict.[195]

On 1 August, well before any negotiations had taken place, the Germans declared war and, in complying with a mutual protection pact, France mobilised its army in response. A 'domino effect' was activated. French fears that Germany might invade their country via neutral Belgium were quickly vindicated:

> On 2 August, Germany invaded Luxembourg and on the following day formally declared war on France. On 4 August, claiming to be responding to a French attack, the Germans invaded Belgium. Having been one of the guarantors of Belgian neutrality, Britain was now forced to attack. With a massive overseas empire, Britain could not allow international law to be flouted, nor could it allow Germany, the only naval power in the world able to challenge the Royal Navy, to establish itself in the English Channel where, once France was defeated, there would be no barrier to an invasion of England. Conflict was now inevitable and at 11pm on 4 August, Britain declared war on Germany.[196]

In Britain itself, Lord Crewe looked on incredulously at these developments. The Minister for India 'could not, in 1914, seriously believe that the folly of general war would ever again be indulged by the civilised nations of Europe', and that 'the Sarajevo murders could lead to war offended his sense of logic'.[197] Crewe could not accept that Franz Ferdinand was a 'national hero' of such great standing as to arouse a clamorous commitment to avenging his death. He was speaking from recent personal experience, having attended a 'peaceful shooting party' at Windsor, one year earlier, at which the Archduke had been a guest of honour.[198]

Crewe's primary objective following the onset of war was 'to coax the Government of India into agreeing with the despatch of as many trained men as possible to Europe, while simultaneously trying to prevent the War Office, under Kitchener, from depleting India of soldiers'.[199] This formal involvement in the conflict subsequently cut across other relevant roles occupied by Crewe, thus embroiling him in several crucial aspects of decision-making, most of which proved extremely controversial. These activities are described and analysed in Chapter 6. The present chapter comprises a preliminary discussion of the wartime experience of other members of Crewe's nuclear and extended families, both on the 'home front' and on the unforgiving fields of battle. Chapter 7 presents a similar overview of the corresponding activities of residents of Fryston village.

'Well-Meaning and Well-to-Do'

One of the least-publicised aspects of the war effort was the voluntary aid provided by affluent women – including female members of the Crewe family. This assistance took such forms as: collecting money and clothing to relieve the newly unemployed and destitute; and knitting socks and stomach belts, and making shirts for armed service personnel. One such initiative was Queen Mary's Needlework Guild (based in state apartments at St James's Palace), which the monarch set up with a view to encouraging and co-ordinating activities of this nature.[200]

One unfortunate consequence of these voluntary endeavours was that thousands of female factory workers (and those working from home) were being deprived of orders which might otherwise have gone to them, and were consequently being deprived of employment opportunities. Objections were levelled at these efforts of the 'well-meaning and well-to-do' by representatives of the women workers, the most prominent of whom was Mary Macarthur, Secretary of the Women's Trade Union League.[201]

Now aged 34, the Ayrshire-born, middle-class Macarthur was married to the Chair of the Labour Party. Even at this tender age, Macarthur was the 'recognised champion, indeed the saviour, of the exploited working women of Great Britain'.[202] She employed an irresistible combination of personal dedication, charisma and powers of persuasion in organising women into trade unions, raising levels of pay, reducing working hours, and mobilising industrial action (e.g. that of the striking jam-makers of Bermondsey who 'forced a Select Committee enquiry upon a hitherto reluctant Government'). Generally speaking, Macarthur 'liberated hundreds of thousands of her countrywomen from a life of slavery'.[203]

This 'delicate and critical' situation was put before the Workers' War Emergency Committee, of which Macarthur was also a member. The body had been set up by the Labour Party at the outbreak of the war with the objective of safeguarding the interests of ordinary workers while conflict was in progress.[204] The committee first raised this issue on 10 August 1914, and reconvened three days later to plot a specific course of action. A sub-committee (chaired by Mary Macarthur) was duly formed and charged with asking Queen Mary for her co-operation and support.

This approach proved to be superfluous, for the monarch was already seeking to instigate appropriate pre-emptive action of her own. As Woodward further explained, 'Among the people who rendered invaluable help at this extremely difficult time was the Marchioness of Crewe, whom Queen Mary had summoned to Buckingham Palace.'[205] One of the pivotal 'first fruits of their cogitations' was a letter, dated 17 August, from Queen Mary to the Emergency Committee, asking them to nominate four or five working women to sit on a small sub-committee, which would be responsible for administering a proposed 'Queen's Fund' – an initiative dedicated to sponsoring alternative work for unemployed women.[206]

This invitation was immediately accepted. The monarch adopted the pre-emptive approach of talking to Mary Macarthur directly. As Pope-Hennessy maintains, 'This brilliant firebrand was not the kind of woman with whom the Queen had ever come into direct personal touch.'[207] Macarthur was escorted to Buckingham Palace by Lady Crewe. The meeting proved highly successful: the two Marys 'recognised each other's qualities instinctively, and on her side the Queen further realised not only how she and Mary Macarthur could help the cause they had at heart, but how much she, personally, could learn from her'.[208]

By working in close co-operation, Queen Mary, Mary Macarthur and Peggy Crewe quickly established a Central Committee on Women's Employment, responsible for directing the Queen's Work for Women Fund.

> The Central Committee, in its capacity both Advisory and Executive in this great effort, initiated by Queen Mary to keep trade where possible in the ordinary channels, to open up new trades for women, to start model workrooms in London to absorb women who were unemployed and, in connection with its central work, to advise mayoral and citizen committees which were being organised all over the country, how to conduct their work and to control them by grants from the Queen's Fund, represented Her Majesty's first contact with a definitely political organisation.[209]

The all-woman committee was politically variegated, placing members of the aristocratic elite alongside trade union and Labour Party supporters. The committee began sitting at Wimborne House 'under the adroit chairmanship of Lord Crewe's young wife', and with Macarthur occupying the role of Honorary Secretary.[210] Between 1914 and 1916, the committee met no fewer than 111 times. These were occasions on which 'high Tory notions' were often disputed by the more 'pugnacious' Labour representatives.[211] It was therefore fortunate for all concerned, that the Chair and Hon. Secretary operated according to such a 'close and splendid friendship':

> Miss Gertrude Tuckwell, one of the most intimate friends of Mary Macarthur, told me once: 'Not long before Mary died she was reviewing to me her various friends and what each had meant to her in life. She came to Lady Crewe and of Lady Crewe she said, with rapt face: 'Ah! She has been such a precious and exquisite jewel in my life!'[212]

Lady Crewe's stepdaughter, Cynthia Colville, was just as eager to make a personal contribution to the war effort. In January 1915, Cynthia joined the Men's Clothing Branch of the Officers' Families Fund. This charity occupied the drawing rooms of a spacious London house belonging to a friend of Lady Rosebery's. Parts of this property were transformed into showrooms and fitting-rooms for items of clothing (suits, overcoats, shoes, socks, etc.) donated for the benefit of male 'customers' during times of acute shortage and austerity. Cynthia subsequently spent an eighteen-month period working as a temporary correspondence clerk for the Ministry of Pensions. She was totally unaccustomed to this type of work, which involved writing some 40, relatively straightforward letters a day, many of which could be dealt with by simply returning the appropriate official form.

> Nevertheless, there would be several that required serious thought, clear exposition, and the detached judgement that is demanded from a Government Department. I have always felt that I owed a great deal to this year and a half's experience; it gave me an insight into the responsibilities of official administration, and was a valuable lesson in the necessity for clear thinking and intelligible explanation.[213]

The Democracy of Death

'Privileged or poor, public personality or private individual, it really didn't matter. The First World War was democratic in its delivery of death.' These were the first spoken words of a radio broadcast featured on Ireland's RTÉ Radio One's *The History Show* on 2 November 2014. The aim of this programme was to commemorate the death in action at Ypres on 6 November 1914 of Lord Crewe's son-in-law, the Hon. Arthur O'Neill, who was the first British Member of Parliament to be killed in the First World War. As the writer of the broadcast, Mark Duncan, noted, the historical significance of O'Neill's death would only become apparent many decades later:

> Arthur O'Neill's involvement in that war lasted only three weeks and his death, aged 38, robbed a wife of her husband and five children of their father. The youngest of those children, a boy, was only two months old in November 1914. His name was Terence, who, on growing up, would follow the father he never

knew into the political life. In time, Terence O'Neill would become the Prime Minister of Northern Ireland, a state that had hardly been imagined let alone realised at the time of his father's death.[214]

Captain O'Neill had suspended his parliamentary duties as Unionist MP for Mid Antrim to rejoin his Life Guards regiment in France in October 1914, where he served as commander of 'A' Squadron. A mere one month later, he was reported 'missing in action'. Great uncertainty still surrounds the precise circumstances of his death, let alone the exact location where his body lies buried.[215] It is generally accepted, though, that O'Neill was killed in action at Klein Zillebeke Ridge in Belgium during a bayonet charge in which his squadron was rushing to support the 1st Irish Guards and 2nd Grenadier Guards, who had suddenly become exposed following a retreat by French troops on their flank. As Thornton notes, however, 'The exact circumstances in which O'Neill met his death vary depending on the source.'[216]

Thornton refers in substantiation of these comments to an article in the *Ballymena Observer* (20 November 1914), in which one eye-witness reported that O'Neill and two fellow commanding officers (2nd Lt. W.S. Petersen and Major Dawnay) were shot dead after they had each 'dismounted and advanced under heavy rifle fire on the village, which was charged at the point of the bayonet'. This is slightly contradicted by a second account (by a member of the Household Cavalry), insisting that O'Neill was mounted at the time of his demise. Arguably more plausible is the following, comprehensive version of events:

> According to a letter received by O'Neill's family, he was shot together with another officer while providing covering fire as his men retired. After being wounded, he continued to give covering fire that allowed his comrade to be rescued. The Germans then came upon O'Neill and, as he lay wounded, an enemy officer stood over him and put three bullets into him at point blank range.[217]

One expert source maintains that, whilst there is no official recognition of the whereabouts of O'Neill's place of burial, accounts submitted in

1914 suggest that one of the unidentified graves in Zillebeke churchyard is almost certainly his.[218] One such testimonial — by a Trooper in the 2nd Life Guards — maintains how: 'I know they recovered his body after several days and buried him, as I remember the three crosses with the names on them, one for his grave and the others for Major Downey's and Mr. Mr. Peterson's [sic].'[219]

News of his son-in-law's death, and of thousands of other fatalities occurring in the early months of war, had a predictably sobering effect on Lord Crewe: 'The daily news of fresh losses, and the dulling sense that this holocaust might well go on for many years, worked powerfully on Crewe's imagination,' said Pope-Hennessy.[220] He therefore did not hesitate when asked by the schoolboy editor of *The Harrovian* if he might contribute to a special edition of the magazine, which paid tribute to Harrow 'old boys' who had perished in the conflict. Crewe's personal sentiments were poignantly exposed in a poem called 'A Harrow Grave in Flanders':

> Here in the marshland, past the battered bridge,
> One of a hundred grains untimely sown,
> Here with his comrades of the hard-won ridge,
> He rests unknown.
>
> His horoscope had seemed so plainly drawn, —
> School triumphs, earned apace in work and play;
> Friendships at will; then love's delightful dawn
> And mellowing day;
>
> Home fostering hope; some service to the State;
> Benignant age; then the long tryst to keep
> There in the yew-tree shadow congregate
> His fathers sleep.
>
> Was here the one thing needful to distil
> From life's alembic, through this holier fate,
> The man's essential soul, the hero will?
> We ask; and wait.[221]

Contrary to popular assumptions that the poem had been written with his son-in-law specifically in mind, Crewe subsequently revealed that he had been thinking more generically of a recent school-leaver who had been robbed of a life full of promise.[222] It is impossible to decide whether the family drew some consolation from the fact that, as mentioned above, a son was born to Arthur O'Neill, a mere two months before his death, and a nephew shortly afterwards.

Two Little Boys

Arthur's son, Terence Marne O'Neill, was born on 10 September 1914 at the family home of 29 Ennismore Gardens, which was within close reach of London's Hyde Park. He was the fifth child in a family of two girls and three boys. His unusual middle name recalls a Protestant success in Northern Ireland's sectarian conflict. 'It was thought that the first name went well with the surname of O'Neill,' he explained in his autobiography, while the second 'was in gratitude for the recent victory at the battle of the Marne'.[223] He had no recollection of his father, knowing only that the latter was a 'reluctant MP' and that his political speeches were 'not very exciting'. Terence derived comfort from the fact that Captain O'Neill 'must have been a simple, straightforward and sincere man. I have never met anyone who did not speak highly of him'.[224]

O'Neill's parents had bought their house in Ennismore Gardens for £1,500 in 1910. His nanny and a Swiss governess helped make up a staff of ten people responsible for running the house. O'Neill was especially fond of 'Nanny Barber'. He could still vaguely remember how she shared bags of sweets with him while out walking in Hyde Park. This apart,

> One of my earliest memories of London was of the maroons going off to warn us of an air raid during the First World War. As soon as this took place we all assembled in the drawing room on the first floor. My mother had a theory – widely held at the time – that a bomb would damage the upper floors of these tall London houses. Or alternatively would bury us if we went down into the cellar, but that half-way up we would somehow escape! I also remember another occasion when my nanny held me out of the night nursery window to see a Zeppelin caught in the beams of the searchlights.[225]

The youngest of three brothers, Terence's cousin, John ('Jock') Rupert Colville, was born on 28 January 1915, and spent his early life, including the war years, at Cadogan Place in London. Colville's day-nursery was located on the third floor, overlooking a riding school from which two older brothers rode their ponies over a cobbled street to nearby Hyde Park. Colville constantly played at the time with an army of lead soldiers – often in the company of a nanny who religiously spun 'such stirring records' as 'Belgium put the Kibosh on the Kaiser' and 'Sister Susie Sewing Shirts for the Soldiers'. 'Then there were the air-raids,' Colville recounted in his memoirs.

> It was thrilling to be woken up in haste, swathed in an eider-down, carried downstairs and placed in my pram in the basement. While the rest of the household sat apprehensively in the servants' hall, Nanny wheeled me up and down the basement passage and fed me with Air Raid sweets. They were, I believe, acid drops, but such is the power of psychological persuasion that they tasted quite different from any sweets eaten in daylight and I positively looked forward to air-raids on account of them. The raids, mainly by Zeppelins, were insignificant affairs by comparison with those of a generation later, but there was one exciting night when a bomb fell in Lyall Street, scarcely two hundred yards from where I was contentedly sucking an Air Raid sweet.[226]

Nanny's brother, George, was far away on active service in Flanders. She shared her brother's view that the Germans had risen from Hell and must quickly be returned to it. 'In consequence she disliked dachshunds which we used sometimes to meet in Hyde Park and from which she would avert her eyes in disgust.'[227] She harboured warmer feelings towards the Belgians, but had strong reservations about the French and Russians, and had not forgiven the latter for having murdered the Czar. As Colville therefore explained, 'My early training in foreign affairs was thus somewhat slanted; but I was in no obvious danger of being infected with left-wing views in spite of my mother's [i.e. Cynthia Colville's] strong, Liberal distaste for the Conservative Party.'[228]

Being similar in age, and also due to the fact that they lived so closely together, it was inevitable that Terence and Jock would regularly meet up and play with one another. Terence O'Neill had particular reason to relish these occasions, which continued to take place even when the war was over:

> The nursery bathroom there was stuffed with clockwork boats. Many of them impressive 'men-of-war' and tea there in the winter was agreeable and included making toast in front of a gas fire. This was something unknown to me in the primitive precincts of Ennismore Gardens where coal fires were the only kind of fire we knew.[229]

Defying chronological logic, the two boys were born *prior to* the birth of their half-aunt, Mary, in London on 23 March 1915. This was the second child of Lord and Lady Crewe. Precious little has been written about her early childhood, except for the fact that she was reared amidst the grandeur of Crewe Hall and Crewe House in Mayfair. As we shall see in later chapters, though, Mary was to have an important say in the final location of artefacts once belonging to Fryston Hall.

Return of the Native
The indiscriminating brutality of war was further emphasised when, in September 1915, Lord Crewe's sister, Florence Henniker, learned of the death of Thomas Hardy's second cousin, Frank George, who had been shot dead in action. Only nineteen months earlier, Hardy had written to Henniker, informing her of the surprise news that he had married Florence Dugdale.[230] It is apparent from Hardy's letters to Henniker that any joy or optimism the acclaimed author might have felt on getting married quickly subsided following the onset of war.[231] Hardy revealed in one such letter how he had become increasingly disinclined to travel up to places like London. 'I dislike being there more & more,' he told her, 'especially with the incessant evidence of this ghastly war under ones [sic] eyes everywhere in the streets, & no power to do anything.'[232]

Hardy's personal exposure to the horror of war became more tangible when Frank George – a peacetime barrister who had enlisted in the Dorsetshire regiment – was killed 'during a brave advance' while serving in the Dardanelles. Hardy informed Henniker, in a letter dated 2 September 1915, that, whilst he accepted that the 'death of a "cousin" does not seem a very harrowing matter as a rule,' he nonetheless 'felt distressed' by the tragic loss of his relative.[233] The novelist's decision to write to Henniker underlined the continuing closeness of their relationship:

> Florence Henniker was the first person he told about Frank's death. She was the widow of a professional soldier so could be expected to understand and she also remained probably Hardy's most trusted and intimate friend. He would turn to her when most upset, even though the things he wrote on these occasions were usually understated and overformal.[234]

Hardy and Henniker continued to correspond for the entire duration of the war. In a letter dated 20 May 1917, for example, the former alluded to the increasingly close friendship that was developing between Henniker and Mrs Hardy:

> Florence says I am to tell you that she is looking eagerly forward to the issue of your book. She is hoping to be in London after Whitsuntide, and to call and see you. She still keeps up her reviewing, but will soon drop it; not having sufficient spare time with the household to look after, and the garden also, which she has taken upon herself, much to my relief.[235]

As Hardy and Pinion point out,[236] it is not clear what became of the book in question, although it seems to have gone unpublished; but, as we shall see in later chapters, the friendship between the Hardys and Florence Henniker would remain solid for the remainder of his protégé's life.

Choosing 'The Path to Danger'

Arthur O'Neill's and, for that matter, Frank George's deaths were not the only causes of family suffering. As the war extended into its fourth and final year, the Crewe family experienced further sadness when, on 15 November 1917, the Marquess's 'brilliant brother-in-law', the Rt Hon Neil James Archibald Primrose, second son of Lord Rosebery and Hannah de Rothschild, was killed in action.[237]

The 34-year-old Primrose's wartime political career – as MP for Wisbech Division of Cambridgeshire, Under-Secretary of State for Foreign Affairs, and Parliamentary Secretary for the Treasury – was thrice interrupted by military service. It was announced in June 1916 that he was to receive the Military Cross for the 'gallantry and leadership' he showed while serving with the Buckinghamshire Yeomanry in Palestine. Having subsequently joined the 3rd Cavalry Unit, however, he was tragically shot from his horse while leading a charge against the Turks during the *Third Battle of Gaza*, and died of his wounds shortly after.[238]

Primrose left behind a widow (the Earl of Derby's daughter, whom he had married in February 1915) and the baby girl they had together during the following year. Shortly after Primrose's death, the Prime Minister, David Lloyd George, read out a tribute in which he referred to the former's 'bright and radiant spirit', to the fact that he was 'one of the most loveable men we ever met', and of how he had forsaken the opportunity to occupy 'safer' positions in the political sphere and chosen the 'path to danger' instead.[239]

Chapter Six
For King and Empire

'Devoid of that Touch of Drama'

Lord Crewe's own wartime activities were initially in keeping with his specific responsibilities as Secretary of State for India. Three months after he had relinquished that role (in May 1915), Crewe was appointed by the Liberal Prime Minister, H.H. Asquith, as chair of a War Policy Committee, charged with determining the number of armed personnel likely to be required in 1916, and deciding on the methods of conscription and/or voluntary recruitment required in order to achieve this figure. The committee, which also included such well-known politicians as Winston Churchill and Arthur Henderson, was unable to arrive at an agreed conclusion, thus forcing Asquith to pass on the responsibility to Lord Derby. This enabled Crewe to concentrate on his more enduring role as member of Asquith's War Council.[240]

This chapter describes and evaluates Crewe's involvement in three crucial – and highly contentious – instances of wartime strategy formulation: two infamously disastrous military campaigns (the 'Mesopotamia debacle' and 'Dardanelles fiasco'), both of which proved costly in terms of the loss of human lives; and events leading to the creation of a Palestinian homeland for the Jews. In this latter case, we shall acknowledge the contributory influence of Crewe's wife, Peggy, the Marchioness of Crewe.

It will become evident during this discussion that the wartime conduct of Crewe and Peggy was consistent with their underlying personal characteristics, the nature of which are insightfully described in the meticulously drafted war diaries of the Prime Minister's wife, Margot Asquith.[241] In one especially powerful distillation of her views (the entry for 17 August 1915) Margot not only justifies her almost entirely favourable impression of Peggy, but also alludes to the frustrating dichotomy she observed between Lord Crewe's inherent 'soundness' of judgement and his fundamental indecisiveness. 'She' (Peggy), said Margot, 'is an angel':

> I love her – clever in spite of a certain crudeness, can see very fine shades. She loves Crewe and knows him <u>well</u>. She quite agreed when I said my husband cared more for Crewe's judgement than anyone's, but that action was not her man's strong point. He is to my mind strangely devoid of that touch of drama and quickness which in times of great stress are essential in men at the head of things. He is not very strong either vitally, which accounts for this probably.[242]

This reference to Crewe's wise, methodical but essentially unassertive nature is repeated in a further diary entry (dated 29 December 1915) in which Margot compares him to a second prominent Liberal politician, David Lloyd George – someone whom she clearly regards as lacking principle: 'Crewe an angel, but very slow and without initiative of any kind (*au-fond* conventional and white-blooded), and Ll.G. is a <u>hound</u>.'[243] These aspects of Crewe's and Peggy's essential characters would repeatedly surface during the key wartime episodes alluded to above. We begin by highlighting their relevance to military catastrophe occurring in the western Asian region of Mesopotamia.

The Mesopotamia Debacle

It was whilst he still occupied the role of Secretary of State for India that Lord Crewe received an early wartime boost when, on 14 August 1914, Mahatma Gandhi and other Indian political activists wrote to him with an offer to set up another Indian ambulance corps. 'The one dominant idea guiding us,' they stated in their letter, 'was that the British would see it as an earnest desire to share the responsibilities of membership of this great Empire, if we would share its privileges.'[244] There was no disputing that 'we were slaves and they were masters,' Gandhi explained in subsequent correspondence, while also acknowledging that it was 'the duty of the slave, seeking to be free, to make his master's need his opportunity' during times of crisis.[245] Crewe thanked Gandhi and his colleagues warmly for this gesture, and the first 50 recruits duly arrived at Eastcote near London on 2 October 1914.

Also around this time, the Minister became embroiled in a more complicated and demanding issue in which 'lengthy and often acrimonious correspondence' was exchanged between Crewe, the War Secretary, Lord Kitchener, and the Viceroy of India, Lord Hardinge, regarding the number of Indian soldiers to be devoted to the war effort.[246] Crewe was required in this instance to 'act as the "honest broker" between the Empire's most famous soldier and a viceroy who was easily ruffled, with, as he wrote, "the possibility of receiving a black eye from either, or even from both"'.[247] With Crewe's prompting, Hardinge eventually swallowed his initial reservations by agreeing to redeploy some 210,000 Indian and 80,000 British troops.[248]

The significance of this issue was nothing compared to that of the crisis that emerged, shortly after open war had materialised, when Turkish activity around the Persian Gulf and in Mesopotamia – an area encompassing present-day Iraq, and parts of what we now know as the countries of Iran (formerly, Persia), Kuwait, Syria and Turkey – was generating growing concern: 'The Admiralty, worried about the safety of their oil installations on Abadan Island and the pipe-line along the Karun river into Persia, were among the first to favour action, which was also supported by the India Office.'[249] Crewe heeded Hardinge's advice by agreeing to despatch a brigade of Indian troops to Bahrain.

This operation gained momentum following the declaration of war on Turkey on 5 November 1914:

> On 21 November 1914 two infantry brigades of Indian Expeditionary Force 'D' captured and occupied the port city of Basra on the Shatt al Arab river. This small-scale military operation secured for the British and Indian Armies an important strategic position at the head of the Persian Gulf, ensured the security of the Anglo-Persian Oil Company's installations at Abadan in Persia, and confirmed the loyalty of the local Arab notables and tribal leaders in Basra and its hinterland.[250]

Ulrichsen emphasises that the operation had the 'limited initial objectives' at this stage of safeguarding the nation's strategic and commercial interests, and had no ambition to seize Baghdad.[251]

In fact, Crewe urged caution in the face of growing political pressure to appropriate additional Persian territory. 'In the absence of extensive power to reinforce,' he wrote, 'we must not cut more cake than we can eat.'[252] He granted the small concession of allowing Indian troops to advance the short distance into the nearby town of Kurna on the Tigris, which was taken on 9 December 1914, but refused to sanction a more penetrating incursion.[253]

Competing pressure continued to mount. Having visited the Gulf at the start of 1915, Lord Hardinge was now convinced that 'Basra needed to be protected against Turkish raiders, troublesome Arabs, and the unsettling effect of rumour, and that this could best be accomplished by the capture of Nasiriya on the Euphrates and Amara on the Tigris.'[254] Support for Hardinge's preferred course of action increased when, in April 1915, the cautiously minded General Barrett retired through illness and was replaced as commander-in-chief of the Expeditionary 'Force D' by the more ebullient General Sir John Nixon.[255]

It soon became apparent that Nixon was intent on marching into Baghdad, even though the city lay a daunting 300 miles further up the river. To this end, he requested of Crewe another two separate brigades of infantry and cavalry. Crewe responded with characteristic reticence:

> No advance beyond the present theater of operations will be sanctioned [but] an advance to Amara with the objective of controlling the tribes between there and the Karun River might be supported because it adds to the safety of the pipeline. Our present position is strategically a sound one, and we cannot afford to take risks by extending it unduly. In Mesopotamia a safe game must be played.[256]

According to Skelly, Crewe's telegram constituted 'sage operational advice'. The word 'safe', Skelly argued, has a different meaning when employed in a military, rather than civilian, context. Thus,

> He did not mean fighting in a cautious or timid manner; no, far from it. The word must be understood in its military context. 'Safe' signifies a methodical, well planned, fully resourced, prudent course of action — combined, naturally, with ferocity, audacity and élan on the battlefield. It implies correlating strategic ends with the logistical means to achieve them, ensuring that

military objectives do not outrun their communication and supply lines. This is one of the fundamental principles of warfare. Matching ends to means is the proper path leading to the objective of all military operations, namely, victory.[257]

Skelly asserts that it was, ultimately, Nixon's failure to comply with Crewe's 'sage advice' which led directly to the disastrous British assault on Baghdad.

There had, in fact, been one interim occasion on which Crewe re-emphasised the need for Nixon to show greater circumspection. The latter had been straining to follow up the defeat of Basra by taking on the Turks at Amara. This objective had Hardinge's full backing, based on the view that Amara constituted an ideal location from which to keep indigenous tribesman in check, thus bolstering the security of local oilfields. On 23 May, Hardinge cabled Crewe, informing him that, while Dixon proposed mounting an assault further up the Tigris, he would not progress beyond Amara without seeking the Secretary of State's permission to do so. Crewe wired back, grumpily insisting that he was only prepared to grant permission,

> On the clear understanding that the General officer commanding Force 'D' is satisfied that he can concentrate a sufficient force at Amara to defy any attack from Baghdad during the summer [...] we can send him no more troops and he must clearly understand that his action must be guided by this fact. Arrangements for this move must have been made some time back and I am of the opinion that General Nixon should have submitted his proposals before the last moment.[258]

Crewe's suspicions were well founded. Several weeks earlier, General Harry Beauchamp-Duff (commander-in-chief of the Indian Army) had exhorted Nixon to establish a strategy for advancing on Baghdad. Barker is convinced that Crewe was unaware of this directive. For,

> If he had known, he can hardly have failed to realize that the safety of the oil wells had become subsidiary to the control of the whole Basra region – the Basra vilayet, as it was known – and he might have been expected to have issued sharp instructions to the Indian Government for an adjustment of Nixon's priorities. As it was, the secretary of state's telegram was merely

forwarded to Nixon with the advice that he should use his own discretion as to coping with the threat to the oil.[259]

Knowing of this inherent contradiction between Crewe's cautious directive and instructions he received directly from the Indian Army, Nixon turned for clarification to the Indian Government. He learned in reply that 'his orders and the British Government's policy were not really conflicting; it was merely that the Secretary of State wanted to emphasize that no reinforcements would be forthcoming'.[260] Feeling appropriately reassured, Nixon ordered his troops to begin marching on Baghdad.

Within days of tentatively authorising Nixon's advance on Amara (though not on Baghdad), Crewe's involvement in this episode was abruptly terminated, following the sudden dissolution that month (May 1915) of the last-ever Liberal government in British history, and creation by Asquith of a Coalition Regime. Crewe was succeeded at the India Office by the Conservative Austen Chamberlain while he was reappointed to the post of Lord President of the Council, which he had formerly occupied from 1905 to 1908.[261]

Nixon's campaign had meanwhile started promisingly enough with the taking (in September 1915) of the town of Kut, located 100 miles down the Tigris River from Baghdad. All that stood between his forces and Baghdad was a Turkish encampment at Ctesiphon, 20 miles south of the capital. The assault on Ctesiphon commenced on 15 November. Though fighting was evenly contested to begin with, the Indian Expeditionary Force D gradually exhausted its supply lines and made an enforced retreat back into Kut. The town was besieged and eventually overcome by the Turks, resulting in the surrender of 13,000 British and Indian troops and the resignation of Austen Chamberlain.[262]

According to Skelly, the Indian Government in New Delhi must bear the blame for the Mesopotamian debacle, primarily because:

> It did not insist that Lieutenant General Nixon follow Lord Crewe's principle of playing it 'safe' in Mesopotamia. That is, the Indian government failed to correlate ends to means. The primary logistical train ran directly from India to Mesopotamia, but the campaign there was underfunded, undermanned and undersupplied from the start, which proved deadly when India Expeditionary Force 'D' outran its support system at Ctesiphon.[263]

Crewe had clearly been opposed to the initiative since it had first been mooted; but it remains plausible to argue that a more assertive and authoritative individual in his position could possibly have done far more to prevent the eventual debacle from unfolding in the way that it did.

The Dardanelles Fiasco

A second controversial military campaign, in which Crewe eventually became embroiled, had already been evolving in the meantime. The 'Dardanelles fiasco' originated in July 1914, when Winston Churchill, then First Lord of the Admiralty, prevented Turkey from collecting two British-manufactured battleships:

> The Turks had paid £3.7 million for the two ships, the *Reshadiye* and *Sultan Osman*, and a crew of 500 was already preparing to sail into Constantinople. British sailors boarded the vessels to prevent the hoisting of the Turkish flag, and despite official protests the ships were requisitioned by the Admiralty without compensation.[264]

The stakes grew higher in mid-August, when two German ships, the *Goeben* and the *Breslau*, fled into the Turkish Straits with the British Mediterranean fleet in hot pursuit. War conventions forbade enemy ships from remaining in neutral waters for more than 24 hours, but the German Ambassador in Constantinople ingeniously flouted this obligation by declaring that the ships had been sold to the Turks. Churchill's frustration was held in check by Cabinet colleagues – notably, Lord Crewe and Lord Kitchener (who was now at the War Office). Thus, as the Prime Minister, Asquith, explained:

> Winston, in his most bellicose mood, is all for sending a torpedo flotilla through the Dardanelles to threaten if necessary to sink the *Goeben* and her consort. Crewe and Kitchener were very much against it. In the interests of the Mussulmans in India and Egypt they are against our doing anything at all which could be interpreted as meaning that we are taking the initiative against Turkey. She ought to be compelled to strike the first blow. I agreed to this.[265]

Further tension arose in September 1914 when Turkey decided to close off access to the Straits. Later that month, a British warship patrolling the Mediterranean acted on Churchill's authorisation by stopping and searching a Turkish vessel, thereby ensuring that 'naval breach between the British and Turkish empires was complete'.[266]

A crucial juncture was reached on 2 January 1915, when Kitchener learned via the Foreign Office of an urgent appeal from Grand Duke Nicholas, head of the Russian Army, calling on the British to create a 'naval or military demonstration' capable of diverting Turkish forces from the Caucasus, where the Russians were critically under pressure. Kitchener referred the matter to Churchill, whereupon the former advised that, although all army personnel were desperately required on the national front, a naval demonstration was still operationally viable. On 3 January, Kitchener wired the Grand Duke to confirm that the requisite 'demonstration' had been sanctioned. Churchill contacted Vice-Admiral Carden (Commander of the Mediterranean Fleet), one day later, to confirm whether he, too, might consider this a 'practicable operation'. The First Lord attached the ominous proviso that 'Importance of results would justify severe loss'.[267]

Carden responded cautiously. 'I do not think that the Dardanelles can be rushed,' he told Churchill while adding, 'but they might be forced by extended operations with a large number of ships.'[268] Churchill nonetheless rushed him into designing a plan of action, which recommended 'the bombarding of the outer and inner forts of the Gallipoli peninsula and then, once the minesweepers had done their job, advancing through the narrows to the sea of Marmara'.[269]

Thereafter, Churchill presented to the War Council an unstintingly over-optimistic and, as events soon proved, *unrealistic* prognosis of the operation's chances of success. Virtually all Carden's colleagues in the Admiralty stated emphatically − often to Churchill's face − that the plan was a disaster in the making. Yet, Churchill remained adamant throughout that 'all the senior officers at the Admiralty enthusiastically supported Carden's plan for a naval attack from the outset' and 'seems to have studiously avoided, or ignored, all the negative opinion towards his scheme at this time'.[270]

Churchill was invariably accompanied to subsequent War Council meetings by Admiral Sir Arthur Wilson and The First Sea Lord, Lord

Fisher, both of whom seemed constrained and/or inhibited from mentioning to assembled Cabinet Ministers that naval gunfire (with its typically flat trajectory) would inevitably prove ineffectual when directed at land-based Turkish targets. Consequently,

> Churchill persuaded his Cabinet colleagues to sanction his naval attack 'by ships alone', at the 28 January War Council meeting. Expectations were high, with the Royal Navy about to enter the war on a grand scale for the first time. Lord Fisher's and Admiral Wilson's silence throughout merely signified their concurrence in Churchill's bold scheme. Or so the Councillors believed, as Asquith later told the Dardanelles Commission. Victory, Churchill told his audience, would not come easy, but it could be achieved, with the destruction of the forts at the Narrows.[271]

The campaign proved utterly disastrous. The naval assault begun by British and French warships on 19 February started to unravel with the early sinking of two British vessels. Other ships fell foul of deadly Turkish landmines. When fighting continued for longer than anticipated, thousands of allied troops were landed (on 25 April) on the Gallipoli peninsular; but poor planning and coordination, allied to the positional advantage enjoyed by Turkish troops, ensured that thousands perished in the process. As if to rub salt into British wounds, the huge warship, *Goliath*, was sunk on 13 May with a loss of 600 crew members. Each fresh attempt to regain the upper hand resulted in predictable setback, until, in mid-January 1916, British forces were withdrawn and the campaign ignominiously abandoned. It was at this point that Lord Fisher tendered his resignation and Asquith's Liberal government was dissolved in favour of a wartime coalition.[272]

It has been speculated that the remarkably quiescent attitude of Crewe and others towards Churchill's plan was driven by a growing anxiety within the Cabinet that the spiralling wartime cost of food might ultimately result in social unrest. Indeed,

> The forecasts were so dire and the political implications deemed so serious that Asquith formed a secret food prices committee and – remarkably – appointed himself chairman. [...] [W]ithin days both Asquith and Lord Crewe [...] came to believe that there were powerful domestic political reasons – namely, the

hope that opening the route to Russian grain would reduce food prices at home — to reopening the Dardanelles.[273]

Such was their desire to see the operation introduced that relevant ministers 'eschewed debate of long-term considerations'.[274]

During the subsequent formal inquiry into the fiasco (the 'Dardanelles Commission'), Churchill doggedly maintained that, each time he addressed the War Council, he was faithfully representing the collective view arrived at in a daily meeting with senior Admiralty officers. The First Sea Lord and Sir Arthur Wilson were two friends and colleagues who, he maintained, 'had the right, the knowledge, and the power at any moment to correct me or dissent from what I said, and who were fully cognisant of their rights'.[275]

Lord Fisher complained to the Commission that, even though he fundamentally disagreed with Churchill, the only options open to him were 'either silence or resignation, since it would have been inappropriate to contradict his political chief at the Council table'.[276] It would have been unseemly, in his view, for Wilson or himself to have contradicted or quarrelled with members of the War Council: 'We were experts there who were to open our mouths only when told to,' he maintained, while adding that Churchill knew full well that 'I was dead against the Naval operation alone, because I knew it must be a failure.'[277]

The Commission heard that, during one War Council meeting, Fisher had departed from the table and spoken separately to Kitchener — presumably with a view to registering his personal reservations. The only Council members who could recall Fisher's departure were Churchill and Crewe, 'although the latter maintained that he had not known at the time why Fisher left the table'.[278]

Crewe acknowledged under questioning that 'the political members of the Committee did too much of the talking and the expert members as a rule too little'.[279] The resulting absence of dissent was taken by Crewe and his colleagues as a sign of 'assent or at any rate acquiescence'.[280] Crewe was adamant that, had Kitchener or Fisher raised 'technical objections' to the Dardanelles operation, the mission would never have been sanctioned:

I should be very sorry indeed to state what the effect would have been on our minds if Lord Fisher had made a full statement of his actual objections from the naval point of view, speaking as First Sea Lord. Of course, the Government would have had to consider whether the political advantages were worth the risk. I cannot say what the ultimate decision would have been, but I have not the least doubt that it would have altered the form and manner of our consideration of the whole subject to a great extent.[281]

The Dardanelles Commission concluded that, while Lord Fisher and Sir Arthur Wilson each favoured a *joint* naval and military attack (rather than a naval operation alone), they failed to express this opinion with sufficient clarity to the War Council; but neither were they explicitly invited to do so.[282] The blame for the fiasco was therefore evenly spread amongst the key protagonists:

We think that there was an obligation first on the First Lord, secondly on the Prime Minister and thirdly on the other members of the War Council to see that the views of the Naval Advisers were clearly put before the Council; we also think that the Naval Advisers should have expressed their views to the Council, whether asked or not, if they considered that the project which the Council was about to adopt was impracticable from a naval point of view.[283]

It would therefore be unreasonable to apportion too much blame for the fiasco to Crewe alone. It nonetheless remains apparent that his characteristic reticence may have prevented him from striving to engage the naval chiefs in more thoroughgoing discussion. There are reasonable grounds for suspecting that his own strategic predilection was predicated on the typically pragmatic calculation that any failure to undertake military action might have dire consequences for British supplies of food.

The Balfour Declaration
The 'Balfour Declaration' of November 1917 was embodied in a letter sent by Arthur Balfour to Lord Rothschild on behalf of the British Government, committing the nation to supporting the establishment of

a permanent Palestinian homeland for the Jews. The Cabinet decision of 31 October to endorse this statement has been widely interpreted as a product, at least in part, of the moral and political conviction of politicians like the Prime Minister, David Lloyd George, who were sensitive to the need to atone for the historical persecution of the Jews.[284]

Complementary academic analyses maintain that governmental attempts to promote these Zionist aspirations were largely driven by the strategic notion that the creation of such a 'Jewish state' was consistent with British imperial interests. Proponents of this viewpoint considered it desirable to establish 'a grateful, loyal, developmental European settler community close to the exposed eastern flank of the [Suez] Canal'.[285] This was inextricably related to British fears that whoever controlled this part of Palestine might pose a threat to British interests in India.

> Germany had caused much alarm by its ambitious Berlin-to-Baghdad railway project, commencing in 1903, and its eagerness to stir jihadi unrest among Britain's Muslim subjects in Asia. Turkish-German forces had been able to march from southern Palestine across the open spaces of Sinai to attack the Suez Canal, albeit unsuccessfully, in February 1915 and May 1916. British commanders and politicians alike concurred that the best guarantee for Suez, and therefore Indian, security now lay, by simple equation, in pre-emptive strikes to the east across Sinai with the ultimate goal of seizing from the Turks their departure base in the strategically vital Judean hills around Beersheba. The issue was regularly before the War Cabinet in its deliberations of 1916 and 1917.[286]

A third, but closely related, motive for creating a Jewish homeland was linked to a growing British perception that, so as to secure and maintain US involvement in the war, it was first necessary to gain the support of influential American Jews, many of whom appeared neutral or, worse still, pro-German in orientation. This would have the additional advantage of helping to 'sell' the idea of a British-administered territory to key strategic nations, notably, the French and Russians.[287]

Highly conspicuous in most narratives of the genesis of the Balfour Declaration is the name of Chaim Weizmann, leader of the so-called Democratic Fraction of Zionists, whose assiduous lobbying of Lloyd

George and other strategically important politicians was key to achieving British support. The charismatic, Russian-born Weizmann embarked on an academic career in chemistry which took him, via the universities of Freiburg and Geneva to Manchester University, in 1904, where he qualified as a British citizen six years later. As Mathew points out, 'Weizmann was to prove a hugely persistent and persuasive campaigner, unabashed in his approaches to the most influential people in the land.'[288]

By 1915, Weizmann had developed close connections with the British Government — partly by virtue of his role as Technical Advisor to the Admiralty, but due also to the celebrity and gratitude he had earned by inventing a process for producing synthetic acetone, a vital ingredient in the manufacture of naval guns. It is significant that, at this stage of the proceedings, Lloyd George was in charge of the Ministry of Munitions and Arthur Balfour was soon to become First Lord of the Admiralty. This had important ramifications:

> It was natural that, in the context of an increasingly close relationship with Lloyd George, marked by numerous private meetings, Weizmann found common cause with the imperialist prime minister in the objective of establishing a national home in a future British Palestine — where, adjoining the strategically crucial Suez Canal, there would ideally emerge a European community indebted and obliging to its imperial protector. A Jewish entity could become, Weizmann astutely suggested, 'the Asiatic Belgium,' a buffer 'separating the Suez Canal' from any hostile forces to the north.[289]

There is no doubt that Weizmann was supported in the pursuit of his Zionist objectives by crucial networking and behind-the-scenes processes facilitated by Lord Crewe, his wife, Peggy, and other members of her extended Rothschild family.

Historically, this incredibly wealthy and supremely influential European banking dynasty had been resolutely opposed to the Zionist agenda: 'Through their own self-invention, religious reforms, civil rights campaigns and institutions such as the Jews' Free School, the family had for generations encouraged the Anglicisation of immigrant Jews, and attempted to carve out a space for them in the civic and cultural life of Britain.'[290] This tide began to turn following Weizmann's pre-war visit to Paris, where he attempted to win the backing of Baron Edmond de Rothschild for a Hebrew university in Jerusalem. In quick succession, Weizmann was introduced to Edmond's son, James (who was soon to enlist in the French army), and James's English wife, Dorothy, both of whom were both quickly converted to his viewpoint.[291]

By November 2014, James had gone to war, but Dorothy had also since spoken with Charles Rothschild, the second son of the influential Nathan ('Natty') Rothschild, his Hungarian wife, Rózsika, and Lord Crewe, each of whom had responded sympathetically to Weizmann's idea of a Jewish homeland. Crewe is said to have commented that 'our compatriots would not be unwelcome in Palestine [...] if by some chance it became British'.[292] It was, however, the reputedly 'headstrong' Rózsika who seemed most enthused by her new acquaintance's 'zealous and uncompromising approach'.[293] She wasted no time in introducing Weizmann to such useful future allies as Robert Cecil, a parliamentary under-secretary of state for foreign affairs, and cousin of Arthur Balfour, and C.P. Scott, editor of the Liberal *Manchester Guardian*, who confessed to having been persuaded by Weizmann's 'clear conception of a future Jewish nationalism'.[294]

Far less convinced on the basis of her first meeting with Weizmann, was Peggy Crewe, who had initially been 'alarmed' by 'the man's unrelenting focus on bloody, antisemitic violence'.[295] It did not take long, however, for her, too, to become converted to Weizmann's idealistic ambition. This transformation proved pivotal to his eventual success:

> Peggy was precisely the sort of political hostess who could help Weizmann win over the political establishment. With Dolly and Rózsika, she subsequently set up an unofficial three-woman advisory group to coach Weizmann on his lobbying technique – so as to avoid the tactical mistakes he had made on his first approach to her. Under the women's tutelage, Weizmann learned the intricacies and mores of lobbying among London's political class: who would be susceptible to his ideas, and who would be resistant; what kind of story was suitable for the dinner table, and what for the drawing room. He learnt to tone down his *folks-mensch* image in a way that would make him and his cause more palatable to the conservative political tastes of Anglo-Jewry. Less than a year after Peggy had recoiled from

Weizmann's first approach, her salon at Curzon Street had become the unofficial headquarters of his insurgent campaign.[296]

Weizmann's 'campaign' was still not home and dry: fierce counter-lobbying was now being implemented by an influential anti-Zionist, Lucien Wolf, the director of the Conjoint Foreign Committee of British Jews, who was averse to the idea of Jewish nationalism: 'Jews could assimilate in an adopted homeland without losing their cultural distinctiveness, he believed, if only their hosts were sufficiently enlightened, which is to say sufficiently liberal.'[297]

Wolf was exhorted by the French to develop a formula to guarantee a secure place for the Jews in post-war Palestine which would prove palatable to the American Jewry. This reflected French concern that the Germans were now lobbying to an ever-increasing extent for Jewish backing in the war. It was in this context that, on 3 March 1916, Wolf sent the following formula to Robert Cecil, which stopped short of advocating an exclusive Jewish enclave:

> In the event of Palestine coming within the sphere of influence of Great Britain or France in the close of the war, the Governments of these Powers will not fail to take account of the historic interest that country possesses for the Jewish community. The Jewish population will be secured in the enjoyment of civil and religious liberty, equal political rights with the rest of the population, reasonable facilities for immigration and colonization and such municipal privileges in the towns and colonies inhabited by them as may be shown to be necessary.[298]

Wolf told the Foreign Office that, subject to their acceptance, he would announce the formula to a mass meeting of Jews in London's East End on Sunday, 12 March. The Foreign Office objected that they needed more time for comprehensive consideration. Two of Weizmann's sympathetic contacts duly intervened. Lord Crewe, who was acting Foreign Secretary in the absence of Sir Edward Grey, asserted that 'Mr. L. Wolf cannot be taken as the spokesman of the whole [Jewish] community,' while Robert Cecil wrote 'that if and when we are allowed by our allies to say anything worth saying to the Jews it should not be left to Mr. Lucien Wolf to say it?'[299] As Schneer explains,

Already Britain contemplated extending Wolf's 'formula' in a direction that would please the Zionists. Crewe informed the British ambassadors to Russia and America that if the Allies did agree to court Jewish opinion, part of the inducement could be that 'when in the course of time the Jewish colonists in Palestine grow strong enough to cope with the Arab population they may be allowed to take the management of the internal affairs of Palestine (with the exception of Jerusalem and the Holy Places) into their own hands.' Weizmann could have asked for little more.[300]

This successful attempt to help steer political opinion in favour of a Palestinian homeland for the Jews was Crewe's final wartime act of any significance in government. His parliamentary political career ended abruptly in December 1916, when David Lloyd George, 'taking advantage of Unionist dissatisfaction with Asquith's lack of a more vigorous war policy, supplanted him as leader of the Coalition Government'.[301] Crewe predictably resigned out of loyalty to Asquith.

Ironically, Lloyd George accession as prime minister helped shift the balance of political power firmly in favour of Zionism. By now, he and other key members of the cabinet (such as Balfour and the Minister Without Portfolio, Lord Milner) had been decidedly won over to Weizmann's way of thinking. On 2 November 1917, James Balfour wrote to Lord Rothschild, setting out a 'declaration of sympathy with Jewish Zionist aspirations' from the British Government in which they promised to 'use their best endeavours' to establish a 'national home for the Jewish people' (the 'Balfour Declaration').[302]

A huge demonstration of gratitude was staged at the London Opera House on 2 December, when thousands of attendees, constituting 'all sections of Anglo-Jewry', gathered to express their appreciation. Among those present were Lord Rothschild, Weizmann and Robert Cecil. Rothschild read out numerous messages from absentee well-wishers, one of whom was Lord Crewe, who stated that he had 'long hoped that it would be possible to make such a Declaration; and it is now pronounced in terms that should be equally welcome to those Jews who have found happy homes on friendly shores, and to those who have longed for the re-establishment of their race, in the ancient land'.[303]

With his political career now behind him, Crewe had decided to accept the 'honorific post' of chairman of the London County Council (LCC). During the same year (1917), he was elected Chancellor of Sheffield University, in replacement of the recently deceased 15th Duke of Norfolk.[304] Crewe and his wife, Peggy, had reserved one final contribution to the war effort until the last year of the conflict.

Displaying 'characteristic public spirit', the two of them placed Crewe House at the disposal of a new 'propaganda unit' under the direction of the newspaper tycoon, Viscount Northcliffe:

> There he [Northcliffe] built up an organisation staffed by military and foreign office officials, academics and others all deeply versed in foreign politics, with an understanding of the different enemy countries. Their aim was to reveal to the enemy the hopelessness of his cause and the inevitability of the Allied victory and thus to undermine his moral resistance.[305]

Propaganda literature, such as leaflets, were scattered by aeroplanes and balloons over enemy lines, or distributed via civic networks within oppositional territories.[306] The Germans generally conceded that the British propaganda effort was vastly superior to theirs. Crewe House therefore became deserving of lasting renown: 'Its unique role in 1918, and the coordination of the propaganda activities carried on within its walls to the Allied Victories gave the house a distinctive niche in modern English history'.[307]

Chapter Seven

For King and Country

A Patriotic Ardour

The academic historian, Carolyn Baylies, observes that the Yorkshire Miners' Association (YMA) responded to the prospect of war with 'a mixture of caution and cynicism'.[308] The YMA Council formally demanded that the Government do everything in its power to restore peace and avoid 'embroil[ing] the people of this country in an international quarrel which can lead only to the advantage of the ruling classes of the countries concerned, and can bring nothing but ruin and privation to the workers'.[309]

Thousands of Yorkshire miners were galvanised by feelings of patriotism into signing up 'with the same selflessness apparent in their readiness to assist in rescue efforts following an explosion in the pit'.[310] By the end of 1914, 15,000 of the county's mineworkers had enlisted. The total of 27,000 Yorkshire miners who had joined up by the end of 1915 represented a quarter of the YMA's membership.[311]

Unskilled labour was brought in to compensate for the loss of experienced miners, but shortages of personnel led to a marked drop in output. Faced with the dilemma of ensuring sufficient recruitment for the war front and enough coal to fuel the war effort, the Government issued contradictory directives to the coal industry, 'at some points workers being combed out and at others being prevented from joining the forces'.[312]

Governmental recruitment drives were launched intermittently, the most pertinent involving a request to the West Yorkshire Coal Owners' Association to raise a miners' battalion. The War Office also asked the YCOA to meet the costs of housing, feeding and training the new battalion to the tune of £22,000. A height limit of five-feet-two-inches was waived and the War Office agreed to provide all arms, ammunition and equipment. By late December 1914, a 'Miners' Battalion' (initially called the 'Pontefract Battalion') was being trained up at Farnley, near Leeds.[313]

This Miners' Battalion was subsequently renamed the 12th (Pioneer) Battalion of the King's Own Yorkshire Light Infantry. As Ede England emphasises, the work of the 12th KOYLI closely corresponded to their quintessentially peacetime form of employment:

> Static warfare required suitable road and rail links between the rear supply depots and the artillery and infantry at the front. As both sides increasingly used heavy artillery to destroy their opponent's defensive trench systems there grew a need for deeper trenches and underground bunkers, and who better to construct these than experienced miners. They were skilled in the use of explosives underground, in the laying of roads and narrow gauge rail tracks, in the laying of water pipes and, should the need arise, they knew how to react when an emergency occurred. Also, in the event of an explosion underground they instinctively knew how to work as a team and were familiar with escaping gas, the rescue of buried workmates and some had basic ambulance training.[314]

Although most working-class Britons failed to see any relevance to their lives of the murder of an obscure archduke, years of anti-German propaganda had hardened their patriotic ardour and belief in an impending threat to the homeland.[315] It was this commitment to 'King and country' that motivated Fryston miners to join the armed services, even though they belonged to a 'reserved occupation', and for those remaining home to support the war effort as assiduously as possible. This chapter outlines the nature of everyday wartime activity occurring in Fryston village itself, and of the courageous deeds of those local miners enlisted in the forces.

The Home Front

The principal way in which working-class women contributed to the war effort was by taking on jobs more traditionally associated with their menfolk. Long and arduous shifts were endured in the huge munitions complex at Barnbow, near Leeds, whose 16,000 workers included women from Fryston and neighbouring villages, who travelled there and back by charabanc. These local women worked at least six days per week. Eight-hour shifts, commencing variously at 6am, 2pm and 10pm, were completed in the company of female counterparts from as far afield as Harrogate, Selby and York.[316]

Attempts to sustain the physical and emotional well-being of Fryston's military personnel were led by local chapel committees. On 30 June 1916, the *Pontefract and Castleford Express* reported that numerous letters of gratitude had been received from Fryston soldiers by Messrs A.J. Firth and G. Teal, secretaries of the Fryston Wesleyan Soldiers' Comforts Fund. Among those specifically referred to were those of Sergeant. E. Latham, 'who states that the parcel contained things that every soldier on active service needed'; and Sapper J. Whetton, who commented: 'Yours is a good work, and you are doing your bit to cheer up the boys out here. […] Our one aim is a victory for us and our brave allies, which we hope will soon be fulfilled.'

Less savoury examples of social behaviour were directed by Castleford residents against individuals misguidedly presumed sympathetic to the enemy. This was especially true of anti-German riots in response to the sinking, in May 1915, of the armed British merchant vessel, RMS *Lusitania*. This ship had been entering the final stage of its journey from New York to Liverpool when it was hit, off the coast of southern Ireland, by a single torpedo fired by a German U-boat, which detonated the huge stock of ammunition on board and resulted in the deaths of 1,191 passengers and crew.

> In Britain, the sinking of the *Lusitania* was the final straw. The atrocity stories that had come out of Belgium at the start of the war, the attack on Scarborough and the east coast in December, the bombing of Great Yarmouth by Zeppelin in January and the use of poison gas the previous month had all created in the public eye an image of the Germans as barbaric Huns who no longer deserved to be treated as human beings.[317]

Within a week, attacks on German-born traders occurred in Pontefract, and soon afterwards in Castleford, where, at approximately 9:30pm on Saturday, 15 May, a crowd shattered the windows of a shop on Carlton Street belonging to Charles Farber. Assailants seemed oblivious to – or simply ignored – the fact that the German-born Farber had been a Castleford resident for 25 years and a naturalised citizen since 1900.[318] At roughly 10:30pm, the crowd turned its attention onto Alexander Stein's butcher's shop, located on the same street. His windows were also caved in. It proved immaterial that

Stein's nephews were currently enlisted in the British Army.[319] It is not clear whether members of Fryston village participated in the riot, though at least one well-known village character *was* centrally involved:

> Stein's, the pork butchers in Carlton Street [Castleford], were obviously of German origin and the people got a bit out of hand and smashed all their windows in. I know Bobby Lofthouse was one of those called in to help them quell the riot. (Ex-Fryston man, 1986)

The most tangible threat to the safety of Fryston residents was posed by the dreaded German Zeppelins. As Lynch points out, these aircraft 'created panic and alarm wherever known to be flying overhead: factory production stopped and pit winding gear was stilled'.[320] Fryston villagers knew that the Germans had specific targets in mind:

> German Zeppelins used to come up the Humber and the River Aire looking for either Barnbow, the ordnance place where they were making all the munitions, or the Prince of Wales or Glasshoughton collieries, because the coking company at Glasshoughton was built by Germans and they'd a fair idea where it was. (Ex-Fryston man, 1986)

The slow pace at which the Zeppelins floated menacingly above ensured that sightings were seldom greeted with outright panic:

> When the Zeppelins used to come over, there was quite a lot of time to warn people. There was no such thing as 'blackouts' and we'd only lamps to put out. Out of South View, at any rate, they used to go into the field and assemble by the river. My mother would get so upset with me because I was laughing every step of the way. 'Shut up! Shut up!' she used to say, 'Or else they'll have you!' (Ex-Fryston man, 1986)

There were few local examples of bombs being dropped by Zeppelins. One major exception occurred on Monday, 27 November 1916, when the Germans focused their attention on Pontefract.[321] According to one ex-Fryston man:

They were over one night when a man from Pontefract lit up a lot of lamps in Pontefract Park to divert them from the works. They did actually drop bombs in Pontefract Park because there was a crater there for years afterwards. (Interview, 1986)

Ungentlemanly Conduct

Many aspects of everyday work and leisure continued undisturbed, but the outbreak of global conflict did force local amateur football teams to adopt a more parochial outlook. Fryston was therefore entered in the Leeds Senior League. The team enjoyed wins against Rothwell Parish Church and Calverley in the English Cup, before coming a cropper against South Kirkby. They enjoyed the compensation of winning both the Leeds Workpeople's Hospital Cup, beating Clarence Ironworks 4-2 in the final; and Goole, 2-0, in the final of the Castleford and District trophy.[322] Having beaten the likes of Preston White Rose and Huddersfield Town in the early rounds of the WRCC Cup, Fryston earned the right to play Goole Town's full Midland League side in the final at Wheldon Road, Castleford.[323]

The Fryston team was strengthened by the return of three army personnel, but the game still proved overwhelmingly one-sided, with Goole winning 2-0 despite missing three first-half penalties – all symptomatic of the roughhouse tactics repeatedly employed by Fryston defenders.[324] Indeed, later that month, the West Riding Football Association Executive committee met up to investigate complaints by the Goole Town officials and referee of 'ungentlemanly conduct', both during and after the game, by Fryston players and their club secretary. Deemed guilty as charged, the team was duly suspended from playing league football for the entire next season, and two of its players banned *sine die* for their part in the proceedings.[325]

Fire Down Below

Working life in mines like Fryston was accompanied by ever-present danger. On 11 June 1915, the *Pontefract and Castleford Express* reported the occurrence of an unprecedentedly serious underground fire at Fryston which resulted in the 'lamentable deaths of an aged deputy and a pony driver', the 65-year-old widower, Theophilus Smith (popularly known as 'Topsy') and Ben Alfred Addy, the 15-year-old son of Albert Addy, another local miner. Around 150 men were working down the mine when the fire broke out at approximately 3:30am; but, with the exception of the two deceased, all were brought safely to the surface. The arrival of the Altofts Rescue Brigade was calamitously delayed until 8:30am when its fire engine collided with a coal cart in Castleford town centre. A car had to be flagged down to transport the firemen and their equipment into Fryston.[326]

The Altofts brigade was preceded underground by a local response crew, including Colliery Manager, Mr Soar, which was eventually joined by a delegation of officials, including the company director, Percy Greaves, the Divisional Inspector of Mines and his deputy. Eventually,

> The rescue party came up at 4 o'clock [...] and reported that they had made considerable progress in combating the fire by the use of water and sand, but held out little hope of the two entombed men being found alive, as the heat of the fire was intense and it gave off suffocating fumes and smoke. Many more hours elapsed before the fire was overcome, and the dead bodies of the two workers were found. Relatives of both kept anxious vigil near the pit mouth throughout the day.[327]

The inquest into the causes of deaths was held in the Reading Room on the following Monday afternoon. In addition to the coroner, Major Arundel, and a jury of fifteen members, the meeting was attended by a variety of colliery directors and agents, mine inspectors, police officers, a representative of the YMA, and a solicitor acting on behalf of the coal company. Formal identification of the victims was provided by Smith's stepdaughter and Ben Addy's father.

Among those called on to give evidence was the Colliery Manager, who provided general details of the accident and of his own role in the attempted rescue:

> Hezekiah G. Soar, manager, said that he was in bed when he was first informed that the pit was on fire, and was down the pit in ten minutes. There was no fire to be seen but a lot of gas and smoke was drifting towards the shaft. He short-circuited the ventilation immediately to prevent the fire spreading. By means of brattice-sheets, sand and water the fire was got out by

Saturday noon. There was no getting to the two deceased, who were on the other side of the fire. The body of Smith was found about 4 o'clock on Saturday morning among the overcast in the return airway. He would die shortly after the fire started. The body of Addy was found half-an-hour sooner, about 80 yards beyond the seat of the fire. His clothing was not burnt but the body was slightly charred. The heat was intense and in the place where they found the bodies they could scarcely breathe.[328]

Soar maintained that, although he sent word to the Altofts Rescue Brigade around 7am, he already felt pessimistic about the chances of anyone surviving in such a temperature.

The precise cause of the initial explosion was controversially disputed. According to Charles Swansbury, an underground 'rope-rider', a 'corve catch' used to prevent coal tubs from running backwards was somehow rendered inoperative, thus allowing them to run freely downhill and collide into an auxiliary motor. Swansbury maintained that the danger catch was already 'broken and fastened down' – dependent on a makeshift combination of dirt and mud to hold it in place – prior to the accident.[329]

Soar disputed this version of reality, asserting that: 'The catch was alright about 9 o'clock on Friday morning. It has not been touched that I am aware of, only cleaned out. The other catch was only clogged with dirt.'[330] It was hypothetically possible, Soar maintained, for a catch to suddenly become defective in the space of a single shift, in which case, the problem should have been reported to a deputy – in this case, Theophilus Smith. The coroner then addressed Soar directly: 'You seem to be throwing the blame on Swansbury for this,' he said. 'That is rather an important thing to know,' he added. 'You say it could easily get out of order. You did not say so before'.[331]

Dr Crispin of Brotherton pointed out that the bodies were too decomposed to allow for an adequate post-mortem examination. External appearances suggested that Smith had died of asphyxiation by carbon monoxide gas, and Addy due to shock resulting from the severe scorching of his body. Verdicts of 'Accidental Death' were returned in each case. One of the colliery directors was quick to emphasise that this was a rare stain on an otherwise exemplary safety record.[332]

The funerals of Addy and Smith were conducted at St Peter's Church on the following Monday evening, before a large congregation which included several soldiers in uniform. Copies of a letter of commiseration from Lord Crewe to the Chair of the company were passed on by Percy Greaves to the families of each victim. 'I am grateful to you for your full account of the Fryston mishap,' Crewe wrote in the letter, 'and feel very strongly how fortunate it was you could be on the spot so promptly, both for the general steps to take and especially in the matter of the wind current.'[333] Crewe asked that the Chair 'give my sincere sympathy to the families of those who lost their lives,' adding: 'There is something very touching in the contrast of the ages of the two, the lad entering on life, and the man past most of his.'[334]

Miners Under Fire

Away from the mine, Fryston men had enlisted by the dozen. It was not long before *Pontefract and Castleford Express* reports of their experiences at the front begun highlighting the harsh reality of war. The paper's 6 November 1914 edition quoted from a letter, dated 1 November, from Private A. Hewitt of the 2nd Battalion of the York and Lancaster Regiment to his wife. Currently convalescing in a military hospital in Weybridge, Surrey, Hewitt confessed that he felt worn out but lucky to be alive:

> If I had been turned a little more, I should have been killed instantly, for the bullet came across my breast into my right arm, just above the elbow. It has gone straight through the muscle, and it is very sore at present. [...] Thousands have gone, most in the same battle – Lille. It has been seven days' hard fighting, and the villages and towns are all burnt down to the ground, and the homes of the poor children and women are all gone. [...] It is a treat to get shut of the lice and to get some clean clothes on, plenty of something to eat, and a good bed to lie on. [...] I have done my duty as a soldier, and if I have to go out again, I will go with the same heart as before.

Fryston recruits were drawn from various strata of the village 'social structure'. In November 1915, a Fryston schoolteacher, Thomas Dodgson, joined up, having only left teaching college earlier that summer.[335] Arthur Wilson had turned eighteen only four months before war broke out in late July 1914. Due to the fact that he was a trained engineer, the colliery did their best to prevent him from going to the front. He stood repeatedly before tribunals until he was eventually conscripted into the King's Royal Rifle Corps in Blyth, where he received three months' preliminary training before setting off for France. As his widow, Winnifred, explained, Wilson and his comrades were immediately deployed at the front.

> Of course, it was September, 1916. The war was terrible. The Leeds Pals had just got wiped out in the July and now it was the King's Rifles. My husband said that, when he got there, the Prussian Guards had been over. He said he'd never seen such big men. There was a full moon and he said he'd only ever seen one dead man in his life before and that was a man who died in the pit yard and they'd taken him into his office. The officer said, 'We go over at eight o'clock in the morning.' Again, September, misty morning, and the Germans thought the same: they met in No-Man's-Land and my husband said he was one of eight that came back. (Interview, 1987)

My maternal grandfather, Samuel ('Sam') Holmes, could neither read nor write when he was among those voluntarily recruited into the 12th KOYLI in October 1915. When war broke out, he was living with one of his several older brothers and sister-in-law in Hope Street, Fryston. After a brief spell of training at Farnley Hall, near Otley, Holmes set sail on 7 December with the rest of his Battalion for Egypt, before being redeployed from March 1916 onwards to the frontlines of Belgium and France.

Though illiterate, Holmes was taught a rudimentary form of writing by a former schoolteacher who served alongside him in the trenches. He was therefore able to send occasional letters to his future wife, my grandma, Edith Bairstow, who was lodging with her sister and her husband in Oxford Street, Fryston. Instances of misspelling are evident in the two surviving letters, the earlier of which (dated 2 June 1917) refers, with typical understatement, to conditions in the trenches. 'Wel [sic] Dear,' he wrote, 'I have quite got used to the shells wissing [whizzing] through the air but it's alright as long as they do not hit. And we have desent [decent] billets, plenty of rats to keep us company but we are quite used to them.'

Having left France on 1 July 1917 for Flanders (Belgium), the 12th KOYLI spent four months laying 29 miles of light railway track under heavy enemy fire.

> Many brave deeds were performed by volunteers, who never hesitated to go out and repair the damage [to railway lines] under very heavy shell fire, and many of our brave men went out with the full knowledge that an almost certain and violent death awaited them.[336]

Holmes was one such man. The citation for the Distinguished Conduct Medal he was awarded 'in recognition of gallant conduct during the work on the light railways in Flanders' stated that: 'This man by his steadiness under fire in the front line has been one of the mainstays of his platoon. He has twice volunteered to repair breaks in the line under intense fire and his common sense has had a good influence on the other men.'[337]

Holmes, like other miners of his generation, regarded acts of bravery as too mundane to make a fuss about; but one of his daughters explained in 1986 how village folklore placed an even more valorous interpretation on his exploits. 'Tommy Edwards once told me my dad had saved his life during the war,' she explained:

> He said, 'I wouldn't have been here today if it hadn't been for him.' Jack Winterbottom told my mam that an injured bloke had his head blown off just as my dad was carrying him to safety. Then, one day, they were all running away and my dad manned a machine-gun to give them more time to escape. Mr Rounds said my dad should have had another medal for that, a 'VC' [Victoria Cross], but he wouldn't own up to it. After the war, he should have been presented with a gold watch at the Queen's Theatre, but he didn't turn up for it. Too shy. (Interview, 1986)

Sam Holmes's lack of formal education contrasted with that of another Fryston miner, John Whetton, who was one of thirteen children born locally. Whetton had left school aged thirteen to work alongside his father and two brothers at Fryston Pit, but soon enrolled as a part-time student at Castleford Technical College, with a view to obtaining a mining engineering certificate. His studies were curtailed by the onset of the war. In common with many Yorkshire miners, Whetton immediately enlisted — in his case, as an infantryman with the 8th Battalion King's Own Scottish Borderers.

Few local miners experienced a more central role on some of the most notorious and bloodiest fields of battle.

> In 1915 his battalion lost a third of their men at the Battle of Loos, where chlorine gas was used for the first time to deadly effect. After he was seriously wounded by shrapnel at the Somme in 1916, Lance Sergeant Whetton was sent to officer training school. He transferred to the 6th Battalion Yorkshire Regiment and was back in action in 1917. The horrors he witnessed in the mud of Passchendaele would have been etched on his memory for life.[338]

When war came to an end, Whetton embarked on a controversial expedition with his battalion into the arctic conditions of Murmansk, in northern Russia, where they fought against the Bolsheviks. Whetton was promoted to the rank of acting captain in charge of a mobile ski unit, conducting survey and reconnaissance work. For his part in this operation, Whetton received the Imperial Russian Order of Saint Stanislaus and the Military Cross.[339]

Others did not survive the wounds of battle. Whetton's own brother was among the 36 Fryston men who perished on the battlefield. Two other victims were drawn from one of the two families most closely associated with the above-mentioned fire.

On 3 December 1914, the *Pontefract and Castleford Express* reported on the death of 20-year-old Private Sidney Wright, who had been killed in action while serving with the 8th King's Own Scottish Borderers in France. Wright was the youngest of three Fryston brothers, all miners, who had joined up early in the war. His other siblings (his brother, Henry Wright and step-brother, John Kriens) were serving in France with the West Yorkshire Regiment (Prince of Wales Own). Wright's father had been killed down Fryston pit many years ago, while his stepfather, Theophilus Smith, was the deputy who died in the recent underground conflagration.

The family was further affected when John Kriens was killed during the first Battle of Arras in March, 1918. According to his grandson,

Kriens was born the 'illegitimate' son of Henritta Kriens in London in October 1893, and adopted at an early age by the Wright family, who lived over the river in nearby Newton.[340] A rifleman with the 2nd/7th Battalion 'West Yorkshires', Kriens had enlisted in November 1914, before commencing active service in France on 26 August 1915. He had already been injured twice – firstly in July 1916, and then again in April 1917. His death came in the final year of the war: 'He was stretcher bearing at the time. He was 34 years old. 2/7 battalion was in action around Rossigny [sic] Wood, just East of the village of Hébuterne, SSW of Arras. He fell close to the village of Bucquoy.'[341]

Fryston's Air-born Hero

Other conspicuous acts of heroism were engaged in by a member of Fryston's 'managerial class'. Reginald ('Reggie') Rhys Soar was born in Fryston House on 24 August 1893, the eldest of three brothers raised by the above-mentioned Fryston Colliery Manager, Hezekiah Soar, and his third wife, Catherine. Standing approximately five-feet-seven, Reggie was an engineering student at Leeds University when war broke out. He originally enlisted with the Royal Naval Division (RND), with whom he briefly served as a sub lieutenant in the Belgian trenches. He subsequently transferred into the Air Department and was posted to Royal Naval Air Service (RNAS) Eastbourne on 26 August 1915, where he gained his flying certificate on a Grahame-White biplane.

Soar's incredible aerial exploits, both as a solo 'flying ace' or in co-operation with the highly acclaimed Australian fighter pilot, Robert Alexander Little, have been comprehensively described by Franks,[342] who enjoyed access to the 'descriptive action reports' contained in each man's logbook. The following summary draws heavily from Franks's thoroughgoing distillation of these records.

Reggie Soar's first wartime posting in the RNAS was with No. 3 Wing RNAS in the Dardanelles. A similar brief spell followed with No. 5 Naval Wing at Dunkirk, before he was transferred once more (in October 1916) to 8 Naval Squadron. Soar's first plane was the single-seater Sopwith Pup. Its German rivals, the Fokker and Albatross scouts, boasted two machine guns and larger engines, but the Pup soon became renowned for its ease of handling and slick manoeuvrability.

Its name connoted 'something small, warm and cuddly', but nonetheless 'deadly in reality'.[343] Soar had briefly flown the Sopwith Strutter while serving in the 5 Naval Wing in France, but reverted back to the Pup on joining 8 Naval.

It was in this vehicle that he tasted his initial success (on 20 December 1916) in shooting down the first two of the twelve German aircraft he would eventually account for overall. His logbook recorded his experience as follows:

> Several engagements. I dived on two Halberstadt scouts and got one at close range, the enemy aircraft going down entirely out of control with its engine still on. Later on, picking up the FE 2s, I saw Hervey engaged by a Halberstadt. Hervey dived away. The enemy aircraft did not see me until I was on his tail, and at a very close range I gave him a burst, whereupon he went down absolutely out of control (confirmed by Little). My engine then cut out and Little escorted me back. In the air for two hours and thirty minutes.[344]

Franks observes that these were Soar's only successes while flying the Pup, and that it was during his longer association with the Sopwith Triplane that he graduated into a true 'flying ace'.[345]

The Sopwith Triplane was the only three-winged fighter plane to be deployed by the British air force during World War I. The RNAS's 8 Naval Squadron began using them in February 1917, following the unit's formation four months earlier. The two planes flown by Soar were known by the names of 'Lily' and 'Hilda', the latter so-called in honour of a cousin.[346] He secured his first victory on a Triplane on 23 May 1917, when he shot down a two-seater LVG over La Bassée: 'Having out-climbed it, manoeuvring set in, so I attached it,' he began, 'but on my pretending to come home, it sat under the clouds, near Sainghin, where I dived on it and shot it down out of control.'[347]

Other victories were accumulated in quick succession. On 7 June, for example, Soar reported that,

> Whilst 'Bookie' tackled an Aviatik I tackled his consort and shot him down in a slow spin near Ecourt St Quentin. Returning, we met five more Aviatik two-seaters being 'Archied' near

Gavrelle. Downed one. Landed in St Katherines near Arras. Pilot wounded in head, observer in stomach.[348]

Further success was then achieved in the company of the immortal, Australian-born, but British-trained, Robert Little, who scored 47 air-born victories, prior to being shot down in action in May 1918. On 29 June 1917, for example, Little and Soar each fired repeatedly at a group of enemy planes. 'Little and I attacked the seven scouts and engaged and concentrated on one, which we shot down,' said Soar.[349] His admiration for the Australian bordered on hero worship. Little 'had few equals when it came to air fighting,' Soar maintained, 'and although not a polished pilot, he was one of the most aggressive'.[350]

Soar experienced one of his closest shaves when, on 26 February 1917, he suffered engine trouble and was forced into emergency landing. As one colleague directly observed:

> During the morning Soar took up Sopwith Triplane No 9. This machine was rather tricky on the engine when gliding in, so he could not quite reach the aerodrome. He came down in a ploughed field and the Triplane turned on to its nose, breaking the propeller and inflicting damage on the leading edge of the top plane.[351]

On 11 August 1917, the Supplement to the *London Gazette* confirmed that Soar was being awarded the DSC for his 'courage and skill as a scout pilot'. The *Pontefract and Castleford Express* of 22 February 1918 subsequently reported that he was one of three hundred men 'decorated by His Majesty the King at Buckingham Palace last Saturday'. He suffered great personal tragedy once the war was over when his wife, Kathleen (whom he had married earlier in 1918) suddenly died of 'Spanish Flu'. He was remarried to Laura ('Lily') Smith in 1921.

Unity, Indomitability

The last throes of military conflict coincided with the reemergence of tensions between miners and coal-owners within the Yorkshire coalfield. Events in the later stages of the war and in its immediate aftermath may be interpreted as the prelude to more bitter and prolonged industrial disputes occurring in the mid-1920s. Central to this narrative was the President of the Yorkshire Miners' Association (and future MFGB President), the Glasshoughton-born Herbert Smith. Adored and deferred to in equal measure by his union members, Smith's tough and unyielding style of leadership — much evident in the prolonged Wheldale-Fryston strike of 1902-04 — was sustained by a 'profound belief that the union was the servant of its members and that the members owed a reciprocal obligation of loyalty to the union'.[352]

Such tight discipline and reciprocity between the YMA leadership and its members had been exemplified in 1916, when the YMA agreed to 'no-strike agreements' with the West Yorkshire and South Yorkshire Coal Owners Associations (the WYCOA and SYCOA, respectively).[353] These agreements were rarely violated. One notable exception was the dispute originating at Wheldale in the summer of 1918 over allowances paid out to families of miners enlisted in the armed forces.

> Early in the war, local employers had agreed to pay 5 shillings per week and provide free house coal to help support the families of those miners who chose to enlist, but had set an end date of September 1915 as the cut-off point for volunteering. [...] The National Registration census of October 1915 was the precursor to full conscription and management felt that goodwill payments to volunteers was one thing, but making payments to support men who had come into mining as an alternative to military service who then found themselves conscripted was not something they could support.[354]

This action soon spread to neighbouring collieries, including Glasshoughton, and Fryston. Solidarity paid dividends. The 12,000 strikers were told at a mass meeting held at the Queen's Theatre, Castleford, on 1 July that the coal-owners had now agreed to make payments and provide coal to dependents of *all men* leaving the mining industry to enlist.

The tenuous basis of wartime co-operation between owners and miners was further impaired once the conflict was over. In January 1919, a strike by 150,000 YMA members succeeded, after only 24 hours of having started, in securing a 20-minute 'deadstop' (or lunch break) for all surface workers in the coalfield.[355] A less successful outcome was achieved in July 1919, when striking YMA miners were unable to secure improvements on piece-rate payments and the length of working hours

Here, pump men and winding-enginemen throughout Yorkshire had acted contrary to Smith's advice in joining their fellow miners on strike and exposing all pits to the risk of flooding. The Government's 'Industrial Unrest Committee' responded by despatching 2,500 naval ratings into the coalfield with instructions to pump the mines. They and any potential strike-breakers were promised the support of troops and police personnel. Meanwhile, an ideological onslaught was directed against miners and their leaders by the mass media, likening Smith to 'a menacing Prussian bully', and generally labelling them the 'forces of disorder'.[356] In the last week of July, 3,000 troops armed with machine-guns arrived in Leeds, awaiting re-deployment to mines like Fryston.

Smith toured the coalfield, persistently appealing for calm. The media blamed him for letting his ego get in the way of resolution; but as Ives points out, 'Herbert Smith's support for the strike came not from personal conviction,' but rather because 'the members were loyal to the union, and he did not wish to do anything to damage that loyalty.'[357]

The YMA was destined for defeat. Within one month, hunger and hardship set in. The £370,000 paid out in strike pay (draining funds which had taken 25 years to accumulate) proved woefully insufficient. Herbert Smith was spared from post-strike criticism or recrimination by his members, who registered a vote of confidence in him and other YMA officials. The YMA President had proven indomitable from first to last – despite the 'enormous pressure' he was known to be enduring: 'In between EC meetings, occasional negotiations and an almost constant tour of the mining communities, he was tending his son Ernest who had been wounded at Ypres in March 1918. He died shortly after the strike.'[358]

Chapter Eight
Have Pony, Will Travel

'The Rock From Which He Was Hewn'

It was during the long period in Fryston's history extending from the end of World War I to the mid-1950s that a succession of especially memorable developments occurred. This golden era was synonymous with the presence of Jim Bullock, who lived and worked there for its entire duration. In this chapter, we begin to chart the progress of Bullock's career from that of humble pony boy in his local mine at Bowers Row (Allerton Bywater) to his eventual role as Fryston Colliery Manager.

An article on Bullock appearing in the *Yorkshire Illustrated* magazine of October 1952 was affectionately headlined 'Salt of the Earth'. It dwelled on the fact that Bullock had been the youngest of six brothers and six sisters, and surmised that the death of his oldest brother when Jim was only eight instilled in him a lifelong determination to do everything in his power to make mining a safer occupation. The article emphasised that, even when Bullock was a boy, his brothers and sisters had already earmarked him as someone who saw things more accurately than they did, and who would ultimately forge a far more illustrious career than they could ever aspire to:

> Mining was to them a job. A difficult and dangerous occupation. One that they put out of their minds in their free time. And to have a brother who saw it in its truer perspective was difficult. But all of them knew that this youngster would go far, though they did not know how to say so.[359]

Here, we trace the formative effects on Jim Bullock's character, of his experience within his own family, at the Bowers Row village school, inside his native community, and down the local mine. It will become evident that all such aspects of this experience helped shape his determination to transcend his designated place in society, while remaining true to his class roots – or, in his mother's words, the 'rock from which he was hewn'.

'A Bit of Heaven Below'

Jim Bullock received an early lesson on the nature and significance of class relations on the day that he and one of his sisters were due to have their outstanding scholastic achievements formally recognised. The local village school was built and paid for by the 'Lord of the Manor', Sir Charles Lowther. In 1911, Bullock's father had been elected chairman of the newly-formed School Management Board. It was shortly afterwards that Bullock and his sister each won first prizes as the outstanding boy and girl in their respective years. These awards were due to be presented by Sir Charles himself. It was an auspicious and greatly anticipated occasion: 'All morning,' Bullock recollected, 'I had been taught to salute – and my sister to curtsy – when we received our prizes.'[360]

They were each destined to be sorely disappointed. Even as Bullock, his sister and the remaining school children gathered in front of their teachers and Sir Charles, young Jim already knew from the tell-tale aroma associated with pig-breeding that his father had entered the building. 'I was not mistaken,' said Bullock, 'for as I stepped up to receive my prize and make my salute, in a loud voice he shouted, "Stop".' Immediately afterwards,

> He [his father] walked through the crowded hall and stopped in front of Sir Charles and said, 'When people like you command my admiration and respect then, and only then, will I allow my children to salute or curtsy to you.' Then father turned round to us and said, 'Leave the prizes where they are. We have managed without their charity for quite a long time and we can still manage.'[361]

Bullock would never forget the immense dismay he experienced – especially because the prize he was scheduled to receive was a fabulous looking box kite.[362]

Class differences were further manifested in countless other aspects of village life, none more so than the annual 'Chapel Anniversary', an occasion on which – always assuming their family could afford it –

local children were bought new clothes in anticipation of a grandiose religious service. Bullock recalls how, on one such occurrence when he was twelve years old, several female members of his family constructed a velvet sailor suit for him to wear for the event. It was a hot June day and the village roads were extremely dusty. Bullock was standing outside the chapel, waiting in deference with the rest of his family for the Colliery Manager and his guests to arrive, comfortably seated in their carriage and pair. Just as this vehicle was 'pulling up with a flourish', Bullock's sailor suit became smothered in dust, causing the young man to grumble, angrily under his breath, but within earshot of his dad.[363]

The old man endeavoured to console him by insisting that 'the future of the colliery manager and the coal owners was bleak in the extreme,'[364] but it failed to have the desired effect:

> To me it was the bit in between now and eternity that was beginning to matter. Even then I asked myself was I doomed to spend all my working life at the coalface like my father and my brothers? Were these people really better than me, just because they had more money and were better dressed? I didn't think so, for when occasionally their children went to the same school they were no better at lessons than we were. When they played in our teams at soccer and cricket they were certainly no better. When we fought, they were certainly not as good and the results of our contests quickly proved this.[365]

Contrary to the stance adopted by his father, Bullock's attitude to the owners and managers was not starkly oppositional: 'Why shouldn't I get a bit of their heaven below?' he asked himself. 'And so the idea was born.' This was the start of a lifelong career mission. 'As I grew, it grew with me,' he went on. 'As I developed, so the desire to be something different developed.' Bullock was emphatic in his personal commitment: 'I wanted to do something with my life,' he stated, 'and any talents I possessed for my family, for my people, and for myself.'[366]

That Awful Vigil
On 29 July 1911, Jim Bullock experienced a form of tragedy all too familiar to mining families of that era when his oldest brother, John

Willie, was killed by an underground rockfall. The *Yorkshire Post* of 30 July 1911 reported how, in the early hours of the previous morning, a 'serious fall of roof' had resulted in the deaths of two miners at the Victoria Pit, Bowers Allerton, near Kippax. The victims were 25-year-old Don Farrar of Kippax, who left a widow and two small children; and 33-year-old John William Bullock of Bowers Row, who was leaving a widow and three children. 'Operations were at once commenced to extricate the bodies,' the *Post* reporter soberly explained, 'but despite the most vigorous work seven hours elapsed before the tons of material could be moved away and the bodies reached.'

Jim Bullock subsequently wrote a precise narrative of how the fateful accident had occurred. The tragedy had taken place just before John Willie was due to take young Jim and one of his six sisters on an eagerly anticipated excursion:

> My brother had asked if he could come out of the pit early because he was going to take my sister and me to Scarborough. He had finished his own job and he was actually on his way out of the pit when another miner who was just going to set a girder said, 'Give us a lift, John Willie, will tha?' And John Willie being what he was, immediately took his coat off and was just walking towards the girder when the whole place collapsed. The fall killed him and the man whom he was going to help, instantly, as well as two pit ponies.[367]

John Willie's father heard from the Union Secretary that his son had been involved in an underground accident. Bullock senior set straight off to inform his own wife, the victim's mother, who quickly rose from her bed, hurriedly donned her coat over her nightdress, and ran to the pit top, with the rest of the family in pursuit. It was the start of what Jim Bullock described as 'that awful vigil which, alas, was so common, but a vigil to which we never grew accustomed';[368] but nothing or no-one could have deterred Mrs Bullock from anxiously standing in wait.

> She watched all that day and all the following night. We all tried to persuade her just to come home for a cup of tea, but she would neither speak nor move. She just stood there, immovable, like a statue; a living symbol of real tragic

heartbroken grief. Friendly neighbours kept bringing her cups of tea but there was no conversation, just sympathy of silence that somehow one could feel passing from them to her. Then my brother's body was brought out and she followed the stretcher to his house and bathed his broken body. She cradled it to her breast and kept murmuring, 'Oh Lord help us, help me to bear it, help me to bear it.'[369]

Jim Bullock wrote, some 60 years later, that he could still not forget the feelings of 'misery and distress' that John Willie's death had caused to his family. His older brother's widow received a mere two hundred pounds in compensation, her only 'consolation' being that 'John Willie was a well-loved son, highly respected in the village, and, I am told, his was the biggest funeral the village had ever seen.'[370] His tombstone was poignantly constructed in the form of a loose configuration of stones, cemented together to resemble the rockfall that killed him. A simple inscription read: 'Thy will, not ours, be done.'

Bowers Pony Boy

The First World War broke out while Jim Bullock was still at school. By now, his father was suffering from a chronic illness and his brothers had all enlisted in the armed services. Bullock had passed the County Minor examination, entitling him to attend the local grammar school, but his father's poor health and his brothers' absence compelled him to seek work down the mine, as soon as he was old enough to apply. This would entail the incredibly daunting task of approaching the Colliery Manager *in person* to request that he set him on.

The Bowers manager lived at the top of a lane which stretched, a one-mile distance, to the pit. He invariably left the house on foot at 8am each morning. According to Bullock, 'This stretch of roadway was his interviewing office for each person that wished to see him.'[371] It was with understandable trepidation that young Jim took up his turn in the already lengthy queue, ready to comply with a simple convention: 'He never stopped walking,' said Bullock. 'You walked by the side of him, bare-headed. It is the only conversation that I remember that was measured in yards and not in minutes.'[372] This proved a difficult, though ultimately successful, encounter:

All down the lane, men and boys were spaced at intervals of about thirty yards. That distance was considered long enough by the manager for any request or complaint to be made and to allow time for his answer. Usually his answer was 'Yes' or 'No'. My question was, 'Can I start work Sir?' – 'Who are you?' – 'James Bullock' – 'Alice Bullock's brother?' (Alice was his servant) – 'Yes Sir.' – 'Start tonight at 9pm, report to Harry Whitelaw, the deputy.' It took only ten yards, but that ten yards marked a change in my whole life because I had been changed from a schoolboy to a pit boy.[373]

Bullock's mother reacted with 'subdued excitement' to the news of his appointment. Any pleasure she may have felt was moderated by the fact that she had constantly hoped for something better than the life of a miner for her son. She nonetheless helped prepare him for his first ever shift by equipping him with a 'snap tin' containing six slices of bread and dripping. The teary-eyed woman formed part of a small crowd of well-wishers lining the 100-yard route from his front door to the Victoria Pit (known colloquially as 'The Johnny'). This name was used to distinguish it from 'The Star' – the name given to the Albert Pit, standing a mere 30 yards away. Bullock subsequently recalled how,

> When I went to work that first night, history was repeating itself, for generation after generation of Bullocks had made the same journey. They had all undergone the same experience, but whereas most of them had made their descent in the comforting presence of their father, I went alone.[374]

The ritual of becoming a miner and going underground began in earnest from the moment that Bullock presented a note from the pit manager to the 'lamp man', authorising the provision of a safety lamp. Having received this essential piece of equipment, Bullock took it to a deputy, who tested it for safety by blowing all round it to ensure there were no leakages capable of sparking off an explosion of gases. Young Jim then stood among a group of other men and 'pit lads' awaiting his turn to descend. 'It would be silly to say I was not nervous, but I certainly wasn't frightened,' he maintained.

When it came to my turn to go down I was placed in the middle of the cage with men and boys in front and behind, so I certainly had company. The bells rang, the cages lifted a little and then plunged down into the depths. My heart and stomach seemed to be trying to escape from my body. We went down and down, faster and faster, nobody spoke and a silence came, sort of deadly silence and a queer, stuffy atmosphere filled the cage. Everyone seemed busy with his own thoughts. Our lamps were held in our hands at about knee level, so by the time we reached the pit bottom we were in total darkness. It's difficult to describe the darkness of a pit, the blackest, thickest fog is nothing like it. It's a darkness that can be felt. If you put your hand in front of your eyes you cannot see it. The darkness becomes oppressive. It seems to weigh you down and this horrible blackness, coupled with the awful silence, is enough to staunch the stoutest heart. The silence is only broken when you hear the creaking of the timbers and the slow settling of the strata on packs and roof supports.[375]

Bullock provides an equally vivid and fascinating account of the terrifying nature of working underground. The prevailing atmosphere was, as he described it, one of the deepest darkness, in which the 'flickering oil lamp' carried by each miner casts 'weird shadows which assume all sorts of fantastic shapes' or creates frightening red reflections from the eyes of indigenous mice and rats. On his first night underground, Bullock was temporarily left on his own with nothing but his oil lamp for company:

One thing about that night which I will never cease to remember was that, as soon as the deputy had showed me where I was to work and how many tubs I had got to fill with dust, he said, 'Oh! you'll be interested to know that this is where your John Willie got killed.' I can never, never forget that, because as he went away and I saw his light slowly going into the distance, I was left completely alone. I had John Willie's face in front of me that night, as plain as day. I kept thinking, Good Lord! If he got killed here, what might happen to me[?] I dared not hang my lamp up in case it toppled over, I dared not put it on the floor in case it rolled over, I dared not turn the wick up in case it smoked, I dared not turn it down for fear it went out – oh! it was a hell of a night and I thought that it was never going to finish.[376]

Relief eventually arrived when Bullock suddenly caught sight of a light appearing in the distance. The tapping of a stick confirmed that it was the deputy returning to escort him back to the pit top. Bullock's maiden ascent was a happier experience, with the accompanying laughter and joking forming a welcome contrast to the forbidding silence which had characterised the earlier lowering of the cage.

Young Jim could hardly wait to hand back his pit lamp before rushing home to his mother, who was already cooking breakfast. One day earlier, Bullock had been presented with bread and jam, but his graduation to manhood was now commemorated by a meal of bacon and eggs. Bullock showed off his black legs and body with pride, and refused to wash himself clean until he had paraded himself before his younger friends while they were trudging off to their lessons. 'They were school kids and I was a worker,' he gloated. 'I had arrived. I was important, a contributor to the family exchequer.'[377]

It was not long before Bullock was given his first pony to handle – an obdurate animal called 'Windsor', who was entirely resistant to his authority and control. Bullock suspected that the pony knew he was a novice and exploited it accordingly. Once the new handler had developed the necessary experience and know-how, and the animal's respect for him had grown commensurately, a special understanding was forged between them.

> I had many ponies but the ones I liked best were those that were given to me to train. They came straight from the Welsh hills or the New Forest and, if only you handled them, you taught them in your own way. My favourite pony was called Tim. He would drink water out of my bottle, he'd nuzzle into my pockets and fetch out bits of carrot or sweets I had taken to work for him. He'd follow me like a dog. He would come when I whistled. He'd find me if I hid and he would let me ride on his back on the way to the pit bottom where the roads were high enough to ride.[378]

This 'special relationship' could sometimes be demonstrated to breath-taking effect. Bullock had good reason, in fact, for believing that pit ponies possess 'a sense of danger sometimes superior to the men who drive them'.[379] One day as he was trying to liberate a coal tub which had somehow been lodged into a side of rock, the tub lurched back on him, trapping his body and slowly depriving him of breath.

> Then to my relief I saw a light approaching. It was [another pony lad] Jackie Moulding, who realizing I had not followed him down the road had come back to see if I was all right. He sensed immediately what was wrong and with superhuman strength for a boy he eased the tub off and got me out. We realized that my pony had stood firmly and held the tubs with his back end and this is what saved me from being run over.[380]

Crossing the Bridge

The war ended and, shortly afterwards, Jim Bullock's mother died. The family had gathered around her bedside, awaiting her demise. Before taking her final breath, she beckoned Bullock forward and secretively spoke to him:

> She feebly put her hand on my head and in a whisper murmured, 'Tha seems to have got above thy share of brains. Make sure that whatever you do or whatever you become, never forget the pit from which you were dug or the rock from which you were hewn. Try and use the talents which God has given you to help other people.' Shortly after that she died.[381]

Bullock now harboured an ambition, not only to climb the managerial ladder, but also to use the position attained for the benefit of ordinary mining families. He therefore made a point of closely observing the skills applied by older miners, asked questions of his brothers, and began attending night school. It dawned on him accordingly that it would be necessary to leave Bowers Row in order to fulfil the destiny his mother had prophesised. 'I was beginning to realize that I should never get far in the mining industry if I stayed at the family pit,' he explained. 'The bosses at this pit seemed to be here for ever, and their sons were waiting to take their places when they died.'[382]

An unexpected family precedent was set when Bullock's brother, Dick, became engaged to, and eventually married, the local undermanager's daughter. This was initially regarded as 'a real embarrassment'. It seemed to Bullock that 'this hero' of his had 'sold the pass' and 'crossed over with a vengeance to the other side'.[383] It was not merely that Dick had risen to the rank of pit deputy. Worse still,

> He shaved with scented soap and his father-in-law – the boss – had begun to visit us socially. Dick built the first bridge between *them* and *us* because being a loyal Bullock, even though he had joined *them* he still had to come back to *us*.[384]

Jim Bullock's pursuit of a more challenging career was given further impetus when he was once seen fighting in a football match by a man who spotted his potential to take up professional boxing. For a while thereafter, Bullock entered contests as far afield as Leeds and Newcastle. He boxed without his father's knowledge, using the pseudonym of 'Allen'. The pugilistic novice once sparred with the famous British middleweight champion, Ted 'Kid' Lewis, who was training in Leeds in preparation for a fight.[385]

Misfortune eventually arose when a local policeman saw Bullock fighting in a bout in Keighley, West Yorkshire. Without realising its implications, the officer gave Bullock's father a blow-by-blow account of the fight. The old man 'went raving mad' on discovering that his son had been deceiving him.[386] News of Bullock's clandestine boxing career did not go down too well, either, with the religiously minded Bowers pit management. An offer to start working over at nearby Fryston therefore arrived at a most propitious moment.

> I fell out with the undermanager at Bowers because I was boxing and he didn't like me in any case. And I found that, if I left the house, my father would have to leave because I was the only one at home; but, if I tried to get the sack and got the sack, they couldn't turn my father out. So, I managed to get the sack and I went to Fryston [...] to break their ponies in. You know, the Welsh ponies coming from the Welsh hills. (Interview, 1987)

The potential move also made good practical and financial sense. Fryston was within an easy cycling distance of six miles, and his new job would involve a pay increase of sixpence a day, elevating his wage to the princely sum of five shillings and eight pence per shift. Moreover, 'Because it was a much bigger pit than our family pit it was far more modern, there would be more opportunities, a fresh environment, different people, but above all, away from the family influence and all the local bosses.'[387]

At first, Bullock cycled or walked the daily, twelve-mile round trip from Bowers Row to Fryston. One year later, he left home and moved in with the local Astbury family. He had initially encountered this huge Fryston dynasty in all its glory on the day he first clasped eyes on the village. 'I thought my family was a large one until I met theirs,' Bullock declared:

> We had a basic dozen, plus in-laws, but the Astburys had a score plus in-laws. On my first visit to the village – I was going to be interviewed for my new job – there was a funeral. As I was passing, the coffin was just being taken into the church. As I cycled past it the last mourner had still not left the house, and the house was over a hundred and fifty yards away from the church! All of the funeral train were descendants or in-laws of the old man Astbury, who had died.[388]

According to Bullock, the deceased man had called all his sons after the names of the disciples – with the sole exception of Judas. The sheer size of the funeral procession left a lasting mark. 'That gave me an impression of prolific output,' he stated. 'I thought, "By God, I'm coming to a marvellous pit here!"' (Interview, 1987)

Chapter Nine
Hard Days

The Start of the Bullock Era

Jim Bullock remembered how the Fryston village he joined in 1920 was not only physically isolated but also exceedingly parochial. The facilities and amenities he discovered on arriving remained as rudimentary in design as when first introduced. The local community was fiercely protective of its own and immensely suspicious of outsiders.

> When I first went to Fryston, they had outside toilets. They'd cold water laid on to the house, but no hot and cold water; and a lot of the houses were what we called 'back-to-back': I mean [...] your fire was back-to-back with their fire and, if you wanted to give a message, you used to knock on the fire back. If a stranger came in at the top of the street, they would all knock and, by the time the stranger got to the bottom of that street, everybody knew his business: 'Where's tha going? What does tha want?' (Interview, 1987)

By this time, of course, the village had been 'upgraded' following the introduction of three higher grade terraces (Brook Street, South View and Smith Cottages), each constructed on either side of World War I to accommodate colliery 'overmen' or 'deputies' and their families. Looming just beyond the nearby quarry was the imposing 'boss's house' – which, as Bullock often admitted, 'I always had an ambition that someday I'd live there!' (interview, 1987).

On first arriving in Fryston, Bullock began lodging with one of the male offspring of the recently deceased Astbury patriarch. The present chapter draws on Bullock's early experience of working underground – initially as a pony boy – and his more general immersion in the village as a springboard for discussing the major aspects of everyday life (industrial and domestic work, family, community, sport and leisure) and the health care provided by the indigenous local doctor and equally popular midwife.

Men's Work

Jim Bullock's new pit was a much larger proposition than his previous one. Fryston had recently merged (as of 21 February 1919) with Wheldale and Allerton Bywater to form Airedale Collieries Ltd. Within two years of his having joined, Fryston could boast a workforce of 1,554 underground and 381 surface employees, exclusively working the Beeston Seam. Around this time, the new company conveyed a 100-acre land mass to Pontefract Rural District Council to facilitate the development of an Airedale estate capable of accommodating growing numbers of Fryston and Wheldale miners and their families.[389]

Young Bullock would never forget his first 'shocking' experience of descending in Fryston's pit cage:

> I mean, a big enough shock going down Bowers was to meet the darkness that I'd heard all about, but never anticipated. [...] I'd got used to that but, when I went down this pit, it was two hundred yards deeper. Instead of having two decks on the cages, there were four. When I got to the pit bottom, it just felt as if all hell was let loose. Sixty-odd men had come down the pit at once and sixty-odd were waiting to come out. My old pit was a single-shift pit. Fryston was three shifts. And the minute you arrived at that pit bottom, you thought you were going into Hell itself. I mean, it was absolutely red-hot and the miners were running about with just the briefest of shorts on – some none on, just a pair of clogs. And there was a famous district called 'Fryston Panel' and you used to get what they called 'panel rash'. And [the manager at that time] started sending the water down in tubs that were lined by tiles. And I've seen miners actually jump into these tubs of water. And it was just like being in Hell, I should imagine. It was, for all the world, like a Lancashire boiler, anyway. That was the sort of pit I started out at as a pony driver. (Interview, 1987)

Bullock's comments were endorsed by former Fryston miners and their womenfolk, who vouched for the fact that, during these early inter-war years men worked practically naked (wearing only 'skull caps' and primitive wooden clogs, in the absence of more modern safety helmets and boots). The work itself was excruciatingly demanding: 'You used to go in some places and t' coal were like that brick wall: braying all day to get a tub,' explained David Rutherforth – a man who spent 51 years as a Fryston miner.

> And if you got a bit of muck in your tub when you sent it out of t' pit and they found it, they'd make you 'laik' the next day: you'd to stop at home. They used to call it 'mucked': you'd been mucked. You see, your number used to be on the tub and you got paid by weight – eleven hundredweight in a tub. Well, if it turned out there was too much muck in... (Interview, 1987)

Men steeled themselves against the prospect of injury or disaster by adopting peculiar superstitions, varying according to their coalfield of origin. Some refused to have their backs scrubbed by a woman, as they believed this might increase their vulnerability to spinal injury. Others balked at the prospect of going into work if any female emerged from the bedroom before them. This was regarded as a portent of underground catastrophe.[390]

After two years spent pony driving, Jim Bullock started his mining apprenticeship. He went to the coalface as part of a six-man team consisting of him and the five, Fairburn-born Kelsy brothers. Bullock had never experienced anything remotely so difficult or demanding. The coal seam was only two-feet thick. It had to be hacked away by pick and shovel, and then hurled, fifteen feet backwards, to be loaded into tubs. Bullock had always taken pride in his reputation for working hard.

> Now, however, for the first time, I realized what physical effort was. My back, arms and legs were so stiff that I felt I would never straighten them again. The brothers laughed at me when I complained. 'If you feel you can't straighten them, don't try to until the end of the shift.'[391]

All miners went underground bearing six pints of water in huge canisters dangling from their waistband, but still found it necessary to avail themselves of the barrel-loads of liquid constantly arriving at the coalface. Bullock and the five brothers were paid two shillings and three farthings for every ton of coal they produced during each shift.

'At this price,' he explained, 'miners had to work eight or nine hours, shovelling non-stop, to try and get enough money to pay for the bare essentials of living.'[392] The young apprentice suffered from violent cramps and was plagued by blisters and sores on his hands and knees. He was advised to remedy all this by urinating on his hands, and to 'rub tobacco juice in my cuts until I toughened up and grew hooves instead of blisters'.[393] He soon appreciated why unrestrained cursing and swearing was so commonplace.

Bullock could also empathise with the strong priority placed on loyalty and camaraderie. Of no lesser importance were unwritten but unwavering codes of honour and integrity. Thus, as David Rutherforth explained,

> On every tub you filled, you had a 'motty'. It might be number fourteen; a piece of shrug or tar-band. There'd be two holes in the tub and you'd slip your motty through before it went out of t' pit. Well, one or two got caught: they'd be waiting on the main road to change t' motty; and if you'd got no motties, you used to have to chalk it on t' tub and one or two got caught altering the chalk. Some got the sack and some got three months [suspension]. And nobody talked to them again, of course. (Interview, 1987)

Feelings of dread were aroused whenever the pit buzzer sounded to signify that the pit was 'flushed'. This indicated that an accident or explosion had occurred and that one or more miners had been injured in the process. All work was instantly suspended and, if necessary, part or, even, the whole of the pit was evacuated. Often, the next shift did not take place as scheduled. In worst case scenarios, a brutally unsentimental ritual was observed:

> If anybody died down t' pit, they just brought them home on a stretcher and put them wherever there was a space – as if to say, 'Right, that body's yours. You deal with it.' No compensation for that sort of thing. The pit flushed and all the men stopped at home. You had a shilling levy stopped off at the weekend to go towards the burial and help the wife out a bit. (Ex-Fryston woman, 1987)

Jim Bullock recalls that every worker he came across was a member of the Miners' Federation of Great Britain (MFGB). Bullock formed part of the minority of Fryston miners who attended local branch meetings, but never became a union official. Whenever he occasionally lay-preached in chapel, however, Bullock deliberately included some coded criticisms (subtly hidden within the appropriate scriptures) of any member of colliery management who happened to be seated amidst the congregation (interview, 1987).

Fryston's Black Friday
It was not long before Bullock and other Fryston miners and their families were embroiled in nationwide industrial action. The inevitable decline of the 'coal boom' which had accompanied the First World War was paralleled by the Government's decision to return its temporary control of the mines back into the hands of private coal owners. With great predictability, the owners announced 'drastic wage cuts', which they sought to impose by a lockout. The MFGB responded by invoking the support of their partners (the railway and transport workers) in the 'Triple Alliance' and sanctioning a strike, commencing on 15 April 1921.[394]

Troops were moved into the coalfields under the Emergency Powers Act, passed only five months earlier; and, in many cases, machine-guns were set up in readiness for potential 'trouble'. It was confidently assumed that the Triple Alliance would now spring decisively into action, but the prospect of a highly conflictual dispute was balked at by the establishment oriented MFGB General Secretary, Frank Hodges, and his equally 'moderate' counterpart, the railwaymen's leader, J.H. Thomas.

> Hodges was prepared to accept a wages freeze while negotiations to secure a national wages board went on. [...] Most miners, however, wanted to heed a fight to the finish and heeded the radical oratory of the rising star of the MFGB, the Yorkshireman, Herbert Smith. The miners' executive rejected Hodges's proposals by one vote. At this, Thomas and the transport workers pulled the rug out from under the miners by abandoning their own strike a few hours before it was due to begin. This was 'Black Friday' (15 April 1921) — the end of the Triple Alliance and a dark day for radical trade unionism.[395]

Not for the last time in a dispute of this magnitude, the mining communities were left to fight alone. Few of those interviewed in the 1980s had retained precise impressions of the 1921 strike. Two major exceptions were a man and a woman who were aware, even as children, of the selectiveness and restraint shown by strikers, even though they were clearly angered by the presence of the troops:

> You may have heard when the men came down to actually break into the pit when they were locked out. [...] The troops were billeted in the grounds at Fryston Hall. The men came down with clubs and everything. I always remember my father saying, 'You keep indoors. You keep out of this.' You get a vivid memory of an angry crowd and you being told to keep out of it. (Ex-Fryston man, 1986)

> My father was a charge deputy in 1921, so he was one of the last to come out of the pit and, this particular day, he was down the pit. Well, my mother and I set off walking to Castleford and, just as we'd set out, this great parade of men came walking through the field with great big hedge stakes and sticks with big knobs at the end, and they were going to 'kill everybody that was still at the pit'. My mother said, 'I'm not bothered about them!' and I followed her, half-scared to death! We passed all these men. Some of them knew her; they were from Wheldale and places like that. They knew her and they were going to 'kill' her husband, but they each said 'Good morning,' just as nicely as that. (Ex-Fryston woman, 1986)

The efforts of the miners and their families were all to no avail. After three months, the MFGB sanctioned a return to work on the terms offered by the owners, leaving a legacy of distrust towards the Government and — perhaps more importantly — key trade union partners, which would resurface later in the decade.[396]

Women's Work

Death, injury and the absence of financial compensation for such setbacks were not the only vicissitudes making the daily lives of Fryston women in the early 1920s equally, if not more, arduous than those of their menfolk. The lack of modern contraception gave rise to typically large families. A woman's personal esteem and reputation within the village was measured by her capacity to keep a clean and well-managed home, provide adequate and well-prepared food and clothing for her husband and their family, and make sure that her children were as polite and well-dressed as possible.

Jim Bullock famously referred in *Them and Us* to 'Aunt Jenny' (or 'Jinny', as she was known), a senior member of the Astbury family who had thirteen children of her own, but also once acted as 'wet nurse' to five babies belonging to other family members who chose to work in a wartime ammunition factory.[397] As one ex-Fryston woman explained,

> The women seemed to be forever having babies. Otherwise, it was just scrubbing, cooking and baking. I mean, I used to bake between four and four-and-a-half stones of bread a week. There were eight of us and, after mam died, I used to bake every day. I could bake three loaves of bread a night just for their 'snaps'. (Interview, 1986)

Cooking facilities were limited. Meals were cooked on the lip of a coal fire, inside a coal-fired oven, or in a free-standing 'set pot', conveniently described by one ex-Fryston woman as 'built-in copper constructions: brick-built columns with room for a fireplace underneath and a bowl for your water that you put a lid on top' (interview, 1986). These pots constituted the solitary means of hot water, making them fundamental to such routine household activities as cooking steam puddings and stews, or boiling work clothes clean. Once extracted from the set pot, such clothing would then be scrubbed with soap in a 'peggy' (wash) tub, with the help of a rubbing board. Water from the set pot would also be used to fill a big zinc or tin bath (usually located by the hearth or hanging on a nail on the outside wall) for miners to wash themselves clean following their latest shift.

Collective standards of cleanliness were reflected in a weekly ritual whereby each woman 'swilled down' her section of the street.

> The streets were beautiful. You couldn't say there was a dirty person in it. They all used to swill. We used to start from the top – we all had a concrete square in front of the house – and swill together in turn. (Ex-Fryston woman, 1986)

This was equally true of the water grates located outside every home. These were scrubbed until they shone, using a combination of black lead and 'elbow grease'. Should any woman fall ill or, perhaps, be expecting a child, her neighbours would rally round by doing her 'blacking' for her.

Just as every Fryston-born boy was destined to follow his father and older brothers down the mine, young women invariably conformed to a set 'career' pattern. 'From when you left school to the moment you got wed, it was either stay at home and help your mam; work in a factory like Burton's the tailors in Leeds; or, if you were really lucky, go into domestic service,' said one ex-Fryston woman (interview, 1986).

On the face of it, Fryston women were condemned to lives of drudgery and servitude; but the overwhelming majority derived great personal esteem from knowing that they were making such a highly significant — and, indeed, *essential* — contribution to the economic, social and physical well-being of their families and wider community.

Family Life
Family life in Fryston operated according to strict patriarchal principles, whereby the needs of the senior male (the 'head of the family' and 'breadwinner') were considered paramount:

> Our fathers were very Victorian. Strict? You never dared step out of line. He was your mother's Lord and Master. [...] It was his 'snap' on the table as soon as he walked in and you didn't dare breathe until he went up for a nap or went out for some beer. They were always in beer: £3 for your mam and the rest kept back for beer. They were hard days and there was always the thought that this drink might be his last. Besides which, the only time she got a minute's rest was when he was doing his supping. (Ex-Fryston woman, 1986)

It was customary for each miner to determine *unilaterally* how much his wife would receive from his weekly wage packet. 'No man ever tipped his money out in those days,' one ex-Fryston woman explained. 'Your mam never knew your dad's wage from first to last' (interview, 1986).

Strong privacy norms dictated that whatever went on within a particular family home was of no concern to anyone else. One ex-Fryston woman recalled how the couple next door used to 'fight like cat and dog' – to the extent of striking one another with pots and pans. 'All this would go on and, with the walls being so thin, you could hear every word, but dad used to sit there and read his paper and say to us kids, "Come on and mind your own business"' (interview, 1986).

Women considered it permissible to complain to relatives and very close female friends about their husbands' behaviour, but they would not confide in this way to anyone else. It was strictly taboo for men to talk in such fashion about their wives. Children were generally excluded from discussion, while gossiping about other villagers was severely frowned upon:

> He'd talk to my mother, but he'd never say anything in front of the children. Never. And he never liked anyone coming into the house if they'd come to tell tales: 'That's enough, missus, my wife's enough to do by looking after her own business.' There were scandals and skeletons in the cupboard, I'll bet, but we never, ever, got to know about 'em as kids. (Ex-Fryston woman, 1986)

From an early age, village children were required to perform helpful activities on behalf of immediate family and close neighbours, such as cleaning the outside windows of the house. Play, in those days, was largely improvised – and often risky by today's standards. This might range from mischievously knocking on outside toilet doors when the cubicle was occupied, to more dangerously adventurous exploits:

> There was a tow-path on our side of the river where the horses used to pull the barges. Occasionally, as kids, we'd walk alongside these horses or hitch a ride on a barge. But in those days, The Aire and Calder Navigation people used to have what they called these 'Tom Puddings'. The towing vessel was at the front with something like nineteen of these things fastened to one another by chains. They had a sort of bow in the middle of each one and, at the back, an indentation so they all slotted into each other. They used to carry up to 80 tons of coal in one of these and they had a loading basin at Wheldale and another one at Fryston. And we used to spend all our spare time at the Fryston

Basin – especially on a Saturday when we knew the men had gone – and we used to climb all over the place. How we weren't killed I don't know! (Ex-Fryston man, 1987)

Children typically acted according to their own devices. 'We used to go down the river as girls and shout to the "Boaty-ies", the people with the barges, "Throw us a rope, mister!" and they'd throw us a rope to go and play with' (ex-Fryston woman, 1987). More collective – and inclusive – play activities sometimes occurred on Sunday afternoons, when skipping ropes were stretched from one side of a village street to the other, providing an opportunity for local children, their mothers, and in some cases their fathers, to skip together by the dozen.

Although Christmas was celebrated in relatively modest fashion by today's standards, it was a time of profound pleasure and excitement. Each youngster would hang up his or her stocking on Christmas Eve and rise on the following morning to discover they had received the obligatory orange, apple, some nuts and a new penny. In those cases where the father's wage packet did not contain an actual new penny, he would take the time to polish up an old one, using ashes from the fire. 'Main presents' were gender demarcated – typically, a 'smokers' outfit' (consisting of a chocolate pipe or cigars) for boys, and a chocolate selection box for girls.[398]

A Flavour of Community

Interviews with residents emphasised the community-wide priority placed on mutual supportiveness. 'They'd lend each other bedding or anything like that, especially for childbirth or when anyone passed away,' one ex-Fryston woman maintained. 'And if anybody ever got married, there was coloured string on the knives and forks to remind us who they all belonged to' (interview, 1987). Likewise, if any local woman was poorly, she went on, 'two or three women on either side would come in and clean through the house and look after t' kiddies for 'em' (interview, 1987). This also applied whenever any woman had recently given birth.

Fundamental to village cohesion were the back-to-back terraces of the 'low buildings' of Oxford Street, Castle Street and Wellington Street.

They had to share a 'ginnel' full of toilets and you could see 'em every morning emptying 'slops'. And there was an 'ash pit', or 'midden', where you took everything from your ashes to your old shoes. Every week, a horse and cart came round and an old bloke called Lodge used to shovel the rubbish out. The stench was awful! Two families used to share a toilet between them. But the corner house of any terrace was always known as a good 'calling house' [pronounced kal-ling] where you could meet and have a natter. (Ex-Fryston woman, 1987)

This spirit of mutuality might temporarily break down in cases where family honour was a superseding issue:

Nearly all the village was related and, when they got half-drunk, they'd say something about some lass or the other and, straight away, one half of the pub was up in defence of the lass and the other in defence of the man. It was nothing fresh for the pub to have a wholesale brawl! (Ex-Fryston man, 1986)

The village was invigorated in this era by the presence of a thriving local economy. One ex-Fryston woman recalled, for example, how her mother would bake bread for the benefit of the aforementioned 'Boaty-ies'. This woman described how groups of these workers would regularly knock on the family's front door in School Street, to be handed a warm bundle of eight loaves in a pillow slip. Sometimes, the same mother would cook batches of Staffordshire oat cakes and have her daughter deliver them to the Boaty-ies for breakfast:

Listen, after she'd done for t' Boaty-ies, she baked for all t' village, did my mother. She came from North Staffordshire. I'd to deliver bread and buns to all t' village for her. And when I got to t' bottom where the Land Sale used to be, I'd bob round a corner and think – I couldn't read or write very much but I used to stop and study: 'Now, they'd had one and they've had it… I think I'll have a bun!' and I'd have summat out of the basket. (Interview, 1987)

Nothing succeeded in bringing the village together like such annual events as the visiting funfair or indigenous annual street carnival and chapel anniversary.

When I was a little lass, just after World War One [...] right up to the railway and the chapel was just a meadow. They called it 'Fryston Common'. The 'feast' [funfair] used to settle there every year. That was the highlight of the village in the 1920s: roundabouts, coconut shies, donkeys. Some lovely donkeys. (Ex-Fryston woman, 1987)

The anniversaries occurred on the two Sundays falling closest in proximity to Whitsuntide. Here was an occasion on which everyone in the village was decked out in new clothes. 'They'd all sing their hymns, present some poetry or give a recitation,' remembered one ex-Fryston man. 'It was quite an event in the village calendar' (interview, 1986).

Each year, Fryston's carnival organising committee selected a 'Carnival Queen' from all the girls of the village; but everyone dressed ostentatiously for the occasion, with some mimicking high-profile figures of the era, such as Nurse Edith Cavell or, later still, Mahatma Gandhi. All village streets were trimmed up accordingly, with an annual prize awarded to the most impressively decorated. 'It was nearly always Oxford Street,' one ex-Fryston woman explained. 'With them being back-to-back houses, they could fasten their trimmings across the street' (interview, 1986). Each street also decked out its own wagon and horses, in keeping with their specially chosen 'theme', for inclusion in the street parade:

Every street was sworn to secrecy — we did keep secrets in those days — and I remember when they had their very first wages for holiday with pay, our street, School Street, had that as their theme. You know? A flat cart with nothing on but a bit of sand and the kiddies playing in it. (Fryston woman, 1987)

Football Crazy

Jim Bullock recalls how, soon after joining Fryston, he not only began preaching occasionally in chapel, but also helped run 'physical culture' classes for young men and women, and assisted in boxing classes set up by the curate at St Peter's. 'My boxing ability stood me in good stead,' he said, 'and I think they respected me more for this than they would have done otherwise.'[399] Even at this stage, Bullock was aware of the paramount importance of association football, both as a means of leisure enjoyment per se, and source of village prestige within the wider Yorkshire coalfield.

The resumption of organised amateur league football in the 1918-19 season coincided with the emergence of an extremely talented and tough-tackling Fryston villager called Dick Foulkes. This young man had arrived in the village as a three-year-old in 1906, along with his parents and younger brother, Charlie, as part of the influx of Staffordshire people occurring at this time. Fryston were eager to shake off the trauma of 1915 by entering both senior and junior teams in the reformed Castleford and District league. The senior team performed without distinction and finished only in mid-table. It was left to the junior eleven, featuring sixteen-year-old Foulkes, to secure the village's only triumph — a 1-0 victory after extra time over Pontefract YMI in the twice-replayed final of the Castleford and District FA Junior Cup.[400]

Starting in the 1920-21 season, Fryston became a founder member of the new Yorkshire league, competing with such teams as Harrogate Town and the Bradford Park Avenue and Halifax Town reserve elevens. A new manager, Mr E. Purcell, sought to reinvigorate the colliery's footballing heritage by attracting a plethora of new players, including a pair of ex-professionals and the cream of local amateur clubs (e.g. Cyril Soar, the Fryston-born son of the retiring colliery manager, who had previously played for Selby Town). These incomers began playing alongside such established Fryston 'stars' as Dick Foulkes.[401]

Fryston struggled in the next three years to establish themselves in the new league. During this time, Foulkes briefly left Fryston (and the pit itself) to play for and work at Frickley Colliery, following a wage-related argument with a check-weighman. The argumentative but highly principled young man then returned to Fryston in 1922-23, having fallen out, this time, with the Frickley club committee. In most respects, Foulkes's first season back in the Fryston fold (1923-24) proved disappointing. A major exception occurred in the first qualifying round of the 1923-24 English Cup competition (the equivalent of today's FA Cup).

'The Colliers' were drawn against their Midlands League neighbours, Castleford Town, in a match played at the latter's home stadium of Wheldon Road (which now belongs to the Castleford Tigers rugby league club), less than two miles away from Fryston. Local interest was enhanced by the presence in the Castleford ranks of the ex-Fryston stalwart, Harry Millership, who had recently returned to Castleford following an illustrious career in professional football with Blackpool, Leeds City, Rotherham County and Wales.[402]

Buoyed up by the promise of a £1 win bonus, Fryston tore zealously into their more illustrious opponents. According to the *Pontefract and Castleford Express* (12 October 1923), 'Fryston were out to win, and they played very vigorously, and the methods of some of their players provoked the ire of the Castleford spectators.' Only Millership and the England amateur international left-half, Prentice, managed to keep their composure. The first half was scoreless; but shortly after half-time, Castleford were awarded a penalty, which Millership uncharacteristically sent ballooning out of the stadium.

The Midlands League team gradually asserted control and had twice gone close to scoring when the ball was desperately cleared up-field by a Fryston defender: 'Play then went to the other end, where Connor took the ball to the line. It came back to Foulkes, who headed into the net. It was an easy and unexpected goal.'[403] Fryston then resisted strong Castleford pressure to pull off a famous victory, but the ensuing euphoria was short-lived. The Town management successfully complained that Fryston had fielded an unregistered player and the result was overturned. In May 1924, Dick Foulkes and his brother, Charlie, were both signed on by Second Division Bradford City, thus opening a new chapter in the history of this rapidly emerging Fryston footballing dynasty.[404]

The Beloved Dr Sloan

In 1923, the people of Fryston welcomed a new doctor into their midst, a young man from Lurgan in Northern Ireland, whose unwavering kindness, good humour and selfless devotion to his patients over the next four decades would leave him fondly remembered, even to this day. 'I remember him coming,' one ex-Fryston man recalled:

> I think he started out on a push-bike. He lived at the bottom of Park Dale, then, in that little crescent. Then he acquired a Douglas 'square tank' motorbike and he used to come flying up

that road with his trilby front turned up in the air. He was a
proper doctor. He'd a proper bedside manner. (Interview, 1986)

George Sloan was born in 1898. His father, Francis, was the headmaster
of John's Street Primary School in Lurgan, whilst his mother, Georgina
Sarah Wake, was a home maker. Sloan was the eldest of six children.
He and three brothers all went on to study medicine at Queen's
University, Belfast, while Georgina took in needlework to help pay
their fees. Sloan's youngest brother died of a neurological complaint
before he had chance to qualify. A second brother, Sam, became a GP
in Wakefield. Sloan undertook maternity training in Dublin, earning
an additional degree (Bachelor of the Art of Obstetrics) in the process.

George spent two brief periods in Blackburn and Halifax. It was
not long before he was persuaded to go into partnership in Castleford
with Dr Gilfillan, a fellow student from Queen's. As Sloan's son,
Richard, subsequently explained,

> They worked together for a while, then had a sort of argument
> and they divided the town in two: they drew a line across a
> map. My father had Airedale and Dr Gilfillan had Castleford.
> Airedale had no houses at that time, so my father had a bad deal,
> but he did have Fryston. He lodged, at first, in Park Dale and
> I think he had a surgery in Fryston in the pit buildings. This
> house was built very soon after he arrived by Fryston Colliery.
> (Interview, 1987)

The five-bedroom dwelling was built by the colliery in 1923,
especially for the benefit of Sloan and his family, who had previously
been renting their much smaller house in Airedale. The property was
one of five originally built for senior people at Fryston: the colliery
manager, bookkeeper, the doctor and two undermanagers. The Sloans
decided to call their new abode 'Tieva Tara' – the Gaelic for 'House
on the Hill'. They initially rented the house, before buying it outright
two years later. At this time, George Sloan was married to his first
wife, Matilda (who was known as PiPi) and they had three children,
Geraldine, Dorothy and Frank.[405]

Sloan would eventually divorce, remarry, and become the father of
a second son (Richard), who was destined to follow him into general

practice. Richard Sloan remembers his father as someone who 'had a great sense of humour and was always telling jokes and laughing'.[406] He was a 'short fellow of around five-foot-eight' – a chain-smoking teetotaller who maintained fitness by playing his patients at table tennis. This capacity to engage, compassionately and without any obvious concession to status difference, was one of the secrets of his popularity:

> I know once, when my first daughter was born – they were born at home then – my wife had a bad time with her. He called three times a day to see her. One day, we were playing Ludo on t' bed and he comes in and says, 'Now then, what's this?' and we all says, 'Ludo. Don't you know it?' He says, 'No, how do you play?' 'Well,' I says, 'you shake a six, then you can move from here, right round and then home.' He says, 'Oh, aye, let's have a go.' Anyway, we were playing half-an-hour or more and I said, 'Hey, doctor, haven't you any more patients to attend to?' and he says, 'Aye, but they'll wait. Whose turn is it?' (Ex-Fryston man, 1987)

Another interviewee looked back fondly on the occasion when, as a seven-year-old with a neck boil, he was visited by Dr Sloan:

> The doctor said to me, 'That's a bad 'un. Let me squeeze it and I'll give you a penny.' So, he squeezed it, like. Then he says, 'Let me squeeze it again and I'll give you tuppence.' Finally, he says, 'One more squeeze and I'll give you a threepenny bit.' Anyway, he finally squeezed it till he got the core out and I walked away with a tanner [sixpenny piece] profit! A smashing bloke. Say you were cooking chips, he'd sit down and have a few with you. If some families hadn't enough to pay him for seeing their kids, he'd overlook it completely. (Fryston man, 1986)

Such was George Sloan's sensitivity to the economic plight of his registered patients that he would often waive his fees in this manner. Richard Sloan believes that the conditions of relative austerity endured by his father, his first wife and children may well have contributed to the breakdown of his marriage.

> To a non-Castleford person like my father's first wife, it was a sort of shock. It was really hard going for her. My father got a

lot of satisfaction from the job but, as a wife who was not born in Castleford, it was very different and I think it contributed to the divorce. (Interview, 1987)

Calling the Midwife

From the mid-1920s until well into the 1950s, Fryston also had its own midwife, Nurse Emma Box. 'She was someone special,' was how one Fryston woman described her. 'She was spotless. I'll bet she delivered every man or woman of a certain age ever to come out of Fryston – and I don't remember her ever losing one' (interview, 1988). Another ex-Fryston woman also recalled how:

> She was very, very strict; meticulous, but lovely with it! No matter who or where you were, she'd stop her bike and know your name. Always talk to you, whether you were nine or 90. She was smallish, thin. I should imagine she'd once been a very good-looking woman. She was always very smart. She lived on Fryston Road. (Interview, 1986)

Born in Ferrybridge in 1893, Nurse Box moved with her husband, a Fryston miner, into 33, North Street, but eventually had to vacate the house to make way for an undermanager. They and their four children (Jane, George, Eileen and Gordon) moved briefly into a house on Brook Street; but, once the Airedale estate had been built, they ended up at 301, Fryston Road. As the nurse's eldest child, George Box, explained,

> My father worked at Fryston Pit for a time, but he was a sick man: they diagnosed a tumour on his brain when he was just past 30. They gave him six months to live, but he lasted nine years. When he died, that's when my mother took up midwifery – to keep us in bread and butter. (Interview, 1986)

George recalls how his mother 'went away' for six months in order to qualify as a registered midwife. Having returned to Airedale and Fryston, she became one of the most ubiquitous and revered people in the area. 'She worked right round the clock,' said George. 'Many's been the time a husband would arrive to find a note in the window telling him where to find her' (interview, 1986). Like George Sloan, whom she often worked alongside, she projected a striking and unforgettable image and was immensely popular among village residents:

> She used to wear a kind of white headdress, just like a nun wears now, that used to flow out in the wind as she swept in on her bike with her black bag at the ready. She was small, wiry and extremely fit – she had to be fit to ride a bike around Fryston and Airedale. She was well-liked. She always did good. I've seen her empty one of our drawers to make a bed up for a baby. But people were good to her in turn. She'd often come back with an armful of tea cakes as 'payment in kind' or a measure of appreciation. (Interview, 1986)

Nurse Box would eventually remarry, to a local man called Fred Hopkins, with whom she had a fifth child, Margaret. George Box eventually became a well-known Castleford hairdresser. His brother's (Gordon's) wife, Edna, would follow in her mother-in-law's famous footsteps by also becoming a greatly revered local midwife.

Chapter Ten
Matters of Life and Death

Post-War Reconsolidation

The first post-war general election (of 14 December 1918) resulted in the continuation of a Coalition Government, consisting primarily of Conservatives and 'Coalition Liberals' under the leadership of David Lloyd George. Sensing, along with other senior members of his party, that it was imperative that they organise 'a proper Opposition' in both Houses of Parliament, Lord Crewe resumed his role as Leader of the Liberal Party in the House of Lords. 'Only now,' as Pope-Hennessy elaborated, 'his role was to criticise rather than to defend or explain the actions of His Majesty's Government.'[407] Crewe's wife, Peggy, continued in the meantime to chair the re-named Central Committee on Women's Training and Employment. The work of this committee now seemed more vital than ever, given that thousands of women were being displaced from wartime jobs by de-mobilised ex-servicemen.

The passing (on 23 December 1919) of legislation allowing women, not only the novel legal right to enter the law profession, but also to begin serving as Justices of the Peace (JPs), conferred further, much-welcomed, responsibilities on the Marchioness. Peggy was asked to chair a committee, assembled by the Lord Chancellor, charged with the task of compiling a list of potential female JPs. Perhaps not surprisingly, she was appointed one of the initial Justices for London (along with such distinguished fellow committee members as the labour historian and social reformer, Beatrice Webb; and the author, trade unionist and social worker, Gertrude Tuckwell). Peggy was also appointed President (in 1921) of the Mary Macarthur Holiday Home for Working Women, following the latter's untimely death, aged 40.[408]

These, then, were the immediate post-war preoccupations of Lord and Lady Crewe. In the remainder of this chapter, we transfer the focus of our attention onto a miscellany of important developments in the lives of other Crewe family members of significance to this volume. These brief updates specifically relate to: the second marriage of Lord Crewe's eldest daughter, Annabel — a formal liaison not universally approved of within the wider family; the entry into royal circles of her younger sibling, Cynthia; and, on a more depressing note, the deaths of Lord Crewe's sister, Florence Henniker, and — even more tragically — his son, 'Jack' Madeley.

'Lead, Kindly Light'

Eight years had now elapsed since Annabel Crewe-Milnes lost her first husband, Captain Arthur O'Neill, Unionist MP for Mid Antrim, who was killed in active service. Annabel was married for the second time of asking (on 9 February 1922) to James Hugh Hamilton Dodds. Decades later, Quentin Dodds (later, Quentin Crewe), one of the two sons that the couple would have together, referred in his autobiography to the obvious 'tensions' endemic to his parents' relationship. Quentin attributed these difficulties to the snobbish and disapproving attitudes exhibited by Annabel's own father, stepmother and in-laws from her previous marriage:

> My mother's first husband, Arthur O'Neill, had been killed in the First World War. They had had five children. My mother's father, the Marquess of Crewe, was a not very inspired statesman from an ancient Whig family, although he had the distinction of being the first Secretary of State for India to think it worthwhile going to that country. He and particularly my mother's stepmother together with her O'Neill in-laws, who claimed descent from the oldest recorded family in Europe, regarded my father, Hugh Dodds, who came from a line of Scottish Covenanters, sons of the manse, as irredeemably middle-class. They had done everything to dissuade her from marrying him. Her children too had discouraged her. But he was handsome, a brilliant horseman, the most elegant fencer in Britain, and she was in love. So, in 1922, when he was forty-two and she was one year younger, they married. At their wedding they chose for one of the hymns 'Lead Kindly Light Amid the Encircling Gloom', which her children affected to believe was a reference to them.[409]

Quentin spoke subsequently of the scarcely concealed snobbery that his mother also displayed towards her new relatives by marriage. This, according to Quentin, was a matter of 'family name'. His mother 'loved titles,' he explained, 'and could weave a gossamer-thin pattern of cousinship over half the peerage'.[410] It was the absence of corresponding lineage on her new husband's side of the family that she was evidently contemptuous of.

Woman of the Bedchamber

After World War I, Labour won the Shoreditch seat; and, in 1919, the Borough Council also became Labour-dominated for the first time ever. One of Lord Crewe's three daughters, Cynthia Colville, was co-opted onto its Maternity and Child Welfare Committee, which was committed to improving living conditions for the area's working-class residents. The committee soon demonstrated its effectiveness when intense lobbying on its part helped secure a new nursing home. Eager to ensure that the opening ceremony would be a truly special occasion, local councillors turned for assistance to Cynthia, and she, in turn, to her father:

> I was asked whether I could approach the Queen [Mary] to carry out this function – admittedly not impressive sounding to the outer world, but of acute significance to the entire East London Borough. I did not really know the Queen, and I felt that Her Majesty would have the haziest awareness of my existence. My father came to the rescue and composed a beautifully expressed and persuasive letter to the Queen's Private Secretary, Sir Harry Verney, emphasising the enormous pleasure that would be caused to Shoreditch if Her Majesty were to be so kind and gracious as to accede to the Borough Council's request. To the delight of everyone concerned the Queen consented to open the new Nurses' Homes, and on Saturday the 18th March 1922 the great event took place.[411]

Cynthia fondly recollected how, even in an area heavily blighted by widespread poverty and high unemployment, the Queen received a 'tremendous ovation'. The costermongers' barrows were decked out with flags; and, on Ware Street, where three-quarters of all residents were receiving outdoor relief, Mary was presented with a bunch of flowers, paid for by donations of a penny at a time.[412]

On the day of the royal visit, Cynthia received two letters at breakfast time: one inviting her to stand at the next general election as Liberal candidate for Shoreditch; the other from the Mistress of the Robes — the Duchess of Devonshire — inviting her to become the Queen's Woman of the Bedchamber for an initial period of six weeks per year. Cynthia conceded that her eventual decision to accept the Duchess's invitation, in preference to entering politics, was primarily driven by financial and practical considerations. For one thing, the £2,000 required to cover her election fee would have eaten catastrophically into the children's school fees. The palace job also came with the proviso that Cynthia would not be required to attend work during school holidays.[413]

While the title of Cynthia's new role might well suggest a position of servility, she was actually responsible for numerous high-level administrative tasks. The Queen's staff within the Royal Household was headed by the Mistress of the Robes (usually, as we have seen, a Duchess), who accompanied her on major state functions, such as Courts and Court Balls. At the next level of the hierarchy came four Ladies of the Bedchamber (peeresses, who attended the Queen on other impressive occasions). Then came a third group, made up of the four Women of the Bedchamber — usually children of marquesses or earls, who invariably 'lived in and did a good deal of ordinary secretarial work', e.g. issuing 'personal correspondence which demanded unofficial hand-written replies'.[414]

Cynthia maintained that it was here that her wartime training as a correspondence clerk in the Ministry of Pensions proved helpful: 'I found that being "commanded by the Queen" did not differ profoundly from being "directed by the Minister of Pensions."'[415] She quickly settled into a regular daily regime:

> Household breakfast would be at 9 a.m., and I must be ready by 9.30 for the summons by a bell from the Queen's sitting-room to take to Her Majesty, in my official basket, every letter addressed to the Lady-in-Waiting, duly opened and read. The Queen would first of all give me the letters addressed to herself that she desired me to answer, having already marked in pencil the appropriate sort of reply, such as: 'Sorry, impossible', 'Thank, but refuse', etc. I would then produce my correspondence and receive orders as to how it should be dealt with. I was unlikely to see the Queen again before luncheon, which would be in the Household dining-room, but tea would be for us all in the

Hall at Sandringham, and dinner too, with their Majesties in the large dining-room.[416]

The Queen was a person who, in Cynthia's estimation, possessed 'sturdy common-sense', allied to a 'subtle understanding of, and sympathy with, the anxious and varied problems of ordinary people'.[417] She was, according to Cynthia, a 'giver', driven by innate kindness and consideration to 'help the suffering and unfortunate'.[418] The monarch once confided to Cynthia that, but for an accident of birth, she would have been a Liberal. 'And,' as Cynthia explained, 'I believe this was a true estimate of her personality — a judicious mixture of reverence for tradition combined with enthusiasm for improvement and the capacity to move with the times.'[419]

Cynthia's working year was spent primarily at Buckingham Palace. It was an arduous existence, requiring her to be close at hand on evenings and at weekends, but not without its many compensations. Cynthia explained how each Woman of the Bedchamber enjoyed the comfort of 'a suite of rooms on the second floor, overlooking the forecourt, and a footman in constant attendance. She also had the use of a one-horse brougham to take her about London.'[420] During temporary stays at Windsor Castle, Cynthia had a ground floor sitting room and bedroom. She especially loved the quiet Easter gatherings of the royal family and revelled in travelling at the tail-end of the annual royal procession at Ascot racecourse.

It is evident, for all this, that Cynthia Colville's respect for her compatriots transcended class affiliation. This was exemplified by the especially close and enduring relationship she enjoyed with the people of Shoreditch. As Jock Colville once stated of this matter,

> She had worked there tirelessly since well before the First World War, running an Infant Welfare Centre, acting as Secretary to a School for Mothers and co-opted to the Public Health Committee of the unanimously Socialist Borough Council. She travelled eastwards two or three times a week by Underground, spent long hours visiting the poorer slum families and was familiar to many of the impoverished dwellers of a socially derelict square mile in the East End of London. She loved Shoreditch and felt as much at home in its squalid streets as she did at Buckingham Palace. To my mother all human beings were equally interesting

and she discoursed in the same genuine unaffected way with the King and Queen as with the citizens of Shoreditch. Thus, without seeking popularity, she was equally popular at both social extremes.[421]

'And Out from His Spirit Flew Death'

This was an era in which there was just as much to lament as celebrate. In an eleven-month period from March 1922 to April 1923, the deaths occurred of two of Lord Crewe's closest relatives, his son, Jack Madeley, followed by his sister, Florence Henniker. The demise of Mrs Henniker was not entirely unanticipated, and its impact therefore less traumatising than the premature death of her nephew.

The passing of the woman widely acknowledged as the muse for the character of Sue Bridehead in Thomas Hardy's *Jude the Obscure* occurred on 4 April 1923 when Mrs Henniker succumbed to the effects of heart failure. A fitting testimonial was volunteered by her brother, Lord Crewe, who reported that, although she had suffered 'a long and painful illness', she had nonetheless left behind 'a memory of undying youthfulness, of observant humour, of earnest faith and of unchanging affection'.[422] It is evident that Henniker's enduring relationship with Mr and Mrs Hardy remained a salient feature of her final years.

There is no doubt, either, that Henniker continued to serve as the great novelist's literary muse until the day she died. Tomalin[423] suggests that the poem, 'Without, Not Within Her', appearing in his *Late Lyrics and Earlier* anthology of 1922, referred to her directly:

> It was that strange freshness you carried
> Into a soul
> Whereon no thought of yours tarried
> Two moments at all.
>
> And out from his spirit flew death,
> And bale, and ban,
> Like the corn-chaff under the breath
> Of the winnowing-fan.[424]

Henniker and Hardy were certainly continuing to see each other often at this time. In a letter received by Hardy on the morning of 28 May 1922, Henniker informed him that she was planning on renting rooms at the King's Arms, Weymouth, from 26 June to 1 July, and therefore wondered whether he might provide her with a guided tour of *The Woodlanders* country.[425] This was a reference to the novel of that name, which focused on a woodland village in north-west Dorset. Hardy responded within the next 24 hours, enthusiastically agreeing to her request and informing her that he and Florence were excited by the prospect of her visit: 'We are both so glad,' he wrote, 'and will certainly show you the country of *The Woodlanders*, which is only about 12 miles from here.'[426]

Hardy and his wife were entirely true to their word. Both Henniker and her 'old faithful servant', Anna, were treated to a guided tour of the Dorset area in question. So entranced was the former by the sights of relevant places like Blackmore Vale and Sherborne that she seriously considered buying a house in the locality.[427]

The weather accompanying Henniker's visit was unseasonably wet. She explained in a letter sent one month later that, although she was not feeling well at the time of writing, this was unrelated to the rainy conditions she had encountered. She concluded by stating that she was already intent on visiting Dorchester again – while nonetheless recognising the need to remain 'careful for a good while after such a bad illness'.[428]

This was a portent of her gradual decline: 'In early January 1923, stricken by illness and by the death of her long-time maid and companion, Mrs Henniker telegraphed to ask if Florence could come and keep her company for a while.'[429] Mrs Hardy therefore arranged for her own sisters to come and stay with her husband in Dorset while she set off, as requested, to see Mrs Henniker, who had temporarily abandoned her London home for a 'damper and colder' property in Epsom. This was the beginning of the end: 'Already broken down in both health and spirits at the time of Florence's visit, Mrs Henniker died of heart failure in early April.'[430]

Henniker was subsequently buried alongside her husband, Arthur, in the churchyard at Thornham Magna in Suffolk. According to Millgate, Thomas and Florence Hardy each 'felt the loss severely, and the empty place she left in the ranks of Hardy's trusted friends and comfortable correspondents would never be filled'.[431] Though not immediately apparent, Henniker had already bequeathed to the Hardys a legacy which would have a peculiarly unsettling impact on the couple's relationship.

Five months before her eventual death, Henniker had written a letter, dated 9 November 1922, to her brother, Lord Crewe, stating that she wanted all the correspondence sent to her by Thomas Hardy to be given back to his wife.[432] A parcel-full of these letters eventually arrived at the Hardy home of Max Gate, where Florence Hardy immediately opened them up, in the misguided belief that the package was likely to contain 'an autograph album from some tiresome stranger'.[433] The actual contents proved extremely disconcerting: 'I think the most painful experience one can have,' she explained, 'is to receive a legacy from someone one has loved. I have put them away for the present, but later on shall carefully type them.'[434]

The friendship between the two Florences in Thomas Hardy's life had flourished even though his second wife was already aware of the enduring attraction he felt for Mrs Henniker. Now, though, this ancient correspondence made her husband's past relationship with Henniker more tangible and difficult to come to terms with, not least 'because they made the violence of his feelings clearer and showed his capacity for a near-obsessive sexual love'.[435] It is a testament to her selflessness that, following her husband's death, she chose to type up the letters for eventual publication before depositing them in the Dorset County Museum.[436]

This stash of 40 such items highlights a strongly compassionate side to Henniker's personality, reinforcing her preoccupations with anti-vivisection and the alleviation of animal and human suffering. Her wartime correspondence refers, for example, to the vast sum of money she raised during the World War, for the relief of wounded war horses, and to the scores of books she sent out to wounded British soldiers or prisoners of war in Egypt and Mesopotamia.[437]

The same letters also sometimes betray a strong underlying conservatism, reflected in Henniker's aversion, both to the rising phenomenon of motion pictures, and to contemporary female fashion trends – exemplified by 'transparent stockings and cardboard shoes with high heels'.[438] Generally speaking, 'The letters are not literary masterpieces, but they complement Hardy's to her, in a measure, and transmit something of the essence of a brave, intelligent, warm-hearted woman with a restrained, intuitive nature, streaked like his with irony and humour.'[439]

The feelings of grief accompanying Florence Henniker's passing were incomparable to the emotional devastation resulting from the sudden death of Lord and Lady Crewe's son, Jack Madeley. The ending of global conflict in 1918 had encouraged a new sense of optimism among Lord Crewe's generation. He had drawn solace from having been spared the suffering of so many of his close friends and relatives who had lost their children in the war: 'His child at least, Crewe might have thought, was safe to carry on into another generation the ideals and traditions, the interests and the tolerant beliefs that had inspired Crewe's own career.'[440]

Tragically and unexpectedly, however, Richard George Archibald John Lucian Hungerford Crewe-Milnes, Earl of Madeley passed away, aged eleven, on 31 March 1922, having suffered a severe mastoid infection.[441] A few days later, his funeral was described as follows by *The Times*:

> The funeral of Lord Madeley took place yesterday at Barthomley Church, a few miles from Crewe, where the ancestors of the Marquess of Crewe are buried. A large crowd of villagers, tenantry, and others of neighbouring places were present. The procession came by road from Betley Road Station, the coffin being placed on a wagon and bearing several beautiful floral tributes. [...] Workers on the estate acted as bearers.[442]

Some three years later, Lord Crewe would commission the Gothic Revival architects, Austin and Paley, to rebuild the chancel of Barthomley Church in memory of his son; but, in the meantime,

> The death of his son extinguished Crewe's hopes and projects for the future. For the time being, also, it dimmed his interest in current affairs, and although even amongst his friends he treated his loss with customary reticence, it seemed to them that, now in his middle-sixties, he neither wanted nor hoped for further public office.[443]

Chapter Eleven
The French Connection

Our Man in Paris

It was the Conservative Foreign Secretary, Lord Curzon, who, in 1922, invited Lord Crewe to cease leading the Liberal Opposition in the House of Lords and take charge of the British Embassy in Paris. Crewe had been earmarked as a possible Ambassador ever since 1917, when the incumbent, Sir Francis Bertie, had nominated him as someone whose 'noble yet democratic' views and natural sympathy for the French 'would render him irresistible to them'.[444] Crewe had hitherto been determined to stay in the House of Lords to keep a close eye on the Prime Minister, David Lloyd George, whom he distrusted immensely. This paved the way for the seventeenth Earl of Derby (1918-1920) and Lord Hardinge of Penshurst (1920-1922) to occupy the position in turn. The collapse of the Lloyd George regime in 1922, allied to the resignation of Lord Hardinge, created a belated opportunity for Crewe to become Ambassador.

In writing to the Marquess on 30 October 1922, Curzon explained that Lord Hardinge was resigning this post for personal reasons, and argued most persuasively that Crewe, ably assisted by his wife, Peggy, was the ideal person to replace him.

> My experience, which is now rather long, convinces me that Paris is the pivot upon which our Continental policy depends and that there, more than anywhere else, we want authority, influence, distinction, power. Ordinarily I might hope or expect to find these in the ranks of the Service. I cannot at present do so: and looking round for someone who will speak with the voice of England to [the French Prime Minister] Poincaré or his successors, and who will at the same time maintain the dignity and prestige of a very high office, I have come to the conclusion, in which Bonar Law concurs, that no one would satisfy that criterion so well as yourself if you are disposed to consider it. The presence of Lady Crewe would add a further element of popularity

and charm which would be of the highest value. I hope that you will both seriously consider the suggestion, even though it means an uprooting for a time of political and social ties at home.[445]

Crewe hesitated before responding. He and Peggy were still grieving over the loss of their son, Jack. A general election was also looming, and to accept an offer from the opposition party might undermine his political allies: 'They would regard it,' he wrote in reply to Curzon's letter, 'if not as a desertion, at least as a significant withdrawal from the field – presumably on the grounds that their cause is already hopeless.'[446]

Having contemplated long and hard before finally acquiescing, Crewe did everything to ensure that his Parisian lifestyle would be every bit as comfortable as the one he had become accustomed to in Britain:

> Free with money, and a perfectionist in comfortable living, Crewe determined to keep up the Embassy in what he felt to be an appropriate style. He sent to Paris a number of the famous Crewe family portraits, a quantity of his books, some of the specially fine French and English bindings from his father's collection and his own, together with all his gold and silver plate, his china and glass, and the Irish state liveries for his servants. At the Embassy, he found that Hardinge had left a staff comprising a French groom of the chambers, four men in livery and three men out of livery, a French chef with three assistants, four English housemaids, two chauffeurs and two odd men. This establishment Crewe supplemented by his own housekeeper from London, his butler and his valet, his chauffeur, a steward's room-boy and most important of all his English cook, the skilful and expert Mrs. James, who worked as *adjointe* to the chef.[447]

Pope-Hennessy maintains that Crewe's appointment was greeted positively by the French. The latter was a fluent speaker of their language; he was familiar with their literature; and (above all) he represented a great improvement on Lord Hardinge, who had displayed a 'formal point of view and manner, and altogether lacked Crewe's outstanding qualities of highly cultivated mind and quiet charm'.[448] Gladwyn adds that, once settled in Paris, the Crewes were unremittingly kind and considerate to their staff, all of whom were proud from the outset of the dignified, but 'brilliant' impression the Marquess created in contrast to the sheer dullness exhibited by his predecessor.[449] They also responded enthusiastically to Peggy's vivacious yet capable personality: 'Lacking any form of snobbishness and with an instinct for detecting pose, she was too genuine a person to be merely a figurehead.'[450]

A key part of the couple's overall responsibility was to entertain French or visiting dignitaries, whether this amounted to dinner parties for 60 guests at a time or a small reception for (say) the Prince of Wales. During his period in office, 'Crewe made many friends among the French, and would also go shooting with the President and with other French acquaintances.'[451] It was evident, however, that his appointment represented far more than a mere sinecure, and was in no sense 'largely ornamental', as one of his detractors cynically maintained.[452]

Crewe's initial briefing by Curzon included two important directives: firstly, 'he should endeavour to persuade the French that continuing to view Germany with hostility and suspicion was likely to have a self-defeating effect on European security negotiations'; and second, he was to do his utmost to strengthen the Anglo-French entente, in order to ensure that such negotiations might run as smoothly as possible.[453] On a wider note, 'The Foreign Office also hoped that his personal and intellectual gravitas would prove to the French that the British government accorded high importance to its relations with France.'[454]

Friends in High Places
Crewe initially found himself hampered by the complicated relationship he shared with the Foreign Secretary. The two individuals were life-long friends; but it was also indisputable that, 'Abnormally touchy, alert to any whisper of criticism, Curzon was also vindictive and long-memoried.'[455] Indeed, the minister had never really forgiven Crewe and his party for reversing the partition of Bengal, two decades earlier.[456] Mercifully, this negativity was counterbalanced during Crewe's six-year tenure as Ambassador by the mutually respectful, confiding and affectionate relationships he enjoyed with two important colleagues: his 'right-hand man', Eric Phipps, and Curzon's eventual replacement as Foreign Secretary, Sir Austen Chamberlain.

The Cambridge-educated Phipps had resumed working in Paris in November 1922 in the role of 'minister plenipotentiary', having returned from a two-year spell as *chargé d'affaires* at the British embassy in Brussels.[457] According to Johnson, Crewe was content to allow his 'more gregarious' junior colleague to engage in direct communication with relevant French ministry officials:

> It was the more outgoing Phipps who better understood and fitted in with how the French government preferred to conduct diplomacy, with its emphasis on personal contact and private influence. In general, the more reticent Crewe simply did not win the confidence of the politicians and officials with whom he came into contact in Paris to the same degree as Phipps.[458]

Johnson does emphasise, however, that Phipps held Crewe 'in the highest personal and professional regard', and therefore always operated 'in a way that never compromised or exceeded Crewe's authority'.[459]

The second significant relationship was not forged until 1924, the point at which the former Conservative Party leader, Sir Austen Chamberlain, took over as Foreign Secretary. Johnson forcefully maintains that 'many of Chamberlain's ideas about Anglo-French relations were shaped by the ideas and influence of Crewe'.[460] The Ambassador's wise counsel would invariably influence the content and tone of ongoing dialogue, policy and strategy formulation. Thus, as Johnson points out,

> Unlike Chamberlain, who frequently spoke and wrote with great passion about foreign affairs, Crewe's strength was that he displayed none of these traits. Instead, he presented an unruffled, reliable consistency of approach and argument that Chamberlain frequently, eventually came to accept.[461]

We shall see in what remains of this chapter how it was Crewe's stolid good sense and powers of influence that helped persuade Chamberlain to adopt the more concessionary attitude towards Germany that resulted in the Locarno Treaty — a multinational security pact involving the major European powers. It is evident that these qualities also permeated Crewe's involvement in two earlier crucial diplomatic episodes of the 1920s: the so-called Ruhr Crisis surrounding the terms of post-war reparation; and the Corfu Incident, involving an Italian invasion of the Grecian island of that name. His role in each of these three important historic examples is now examined in close detail.

Within three weeks of taking up the post of Ambassador, Crewe was confronted with his first major diplomatic headache. The so-called Ruhr Crisis came to a head in the autumn of 1922, when the French Government ran out of patience following Germany's repeated failure to meet the reparation demands placed on them under the 1919 *Treaty of Versailles*. A reduction in the financial amount involved had already been agreed by the Allies according to the *London Schedule of Payments* of May 1921. Further leniency was exercised in the summer of 1922, when the Allies accepted Germany's request to defer payment until 15 January 1923. It was only when Germany submitted an interim request to the Reparation Commission (on 14 November 1922) for a further respite that French tolerance finally expired.[462]

Allegedly 'incensed' by this situation, the French Prime Minister, Raymond Poincaré, decisively reacted. On 11 January 1923, French and Belgian troops marched, unopposed, into the German industrial heartland of the Ruhr valley. The German Government responded by calling a General Strike, whereupon the French reacted, in turn, by sending in troop reinforcements. Finding itself confronted, nine months later, by the possibilities of economic collapse and civil unrest, Germany called off this campaign of passive resistance.

> But this proved a hollow victory for France. France was also under severe economic and political pressure. In circumstances of chaos and confusion an agreement was reached in November 1923 to establish international committees of experts to report on the reparation issue. Meanwhile, France retained her presence in the Ruhr, but by January 1924 the economic strain proved too great. The franc collapsed and had to be salvaged by an Anglo-American rescue package. When the experts' reports were published, France had little alternative but to accept their proposals, especially those of the Dawes Committee, at the London Conference of July–August 1924.[463]

This so-called Dawes Plan required Germany to foot a much-reduced reparation bill, albeit based on a more modest and manageable schedule of instalments than had originally been stipulated. It was further agreed, however, that these payments would start to increase from the moment the German economy showed signs of strengthening.[464]

Lord Crewe played a low-key but important role in helping to ensure an eventual outcome was achieved in keeping with British objectives. This included a number of well-timed and deftly executed interventions in support of relevant colleagues. On 14 December 1923, for example, Crewe employed his intimate knowledge of French public and political opinion to inform the Foreign Office that an opportunity had arisen for the British to dictate the make-up of the subcommittee of experts held responsible for drafting a preliminary reparation agreement.[465]

The Ambassador began by observing how the French had been greatly perturbed by the result of the recent British general election where the Conservatives were unexpectedly ousted by the Labour Party under Ramsay MacDonald, which had taken advantage of a 'hung parliament' to form a minority government with the tacit support of the Liberals:

> A feeling prevails that the French government has allowed to slip an opportunity which may never recur of improving the chances of co-operation between the two countries. A natural result of this state of affairs has been a desire to avoid taking any step here which would be likely to complicate a delicate and somewhat uncertain situation. This may be said to some extent to have brought about an atmosphere of accommodation due to the realisation by the French government of the danger of doing anything at present directly contrary to the views of His Majesty's Government.[466]

Freshly realising, due to Crewe's prompting, that here was a helpful development that they must take full advantage of, Whitehall officials wasted no time in presenting the French with a battery of suggested protocols for nominating and appointing the relevant body of experts. Precisely as Crewe had anticipated, these procedures (so designed to facilitate a subcommittee membership in overall sympathy with British interests) were accepted, virtually without objection.

Crewe had another important intermediary role to play when, as the London Conference drew near, the French mass media almost scuppered British hopes of securing a reparation agreement based on the Dawes Plan. French journalists had aroused public concern that conference delegates were on the brink of ratifying protocols which inadequately addressed the possibility that Germany might default on future reparation payments. By now, Ramsay MacDonald had become established as British Prime Minister, and Édouard Herriot had succeeded Poincaré as MacDonald's counterpart. On hearing that the French premier was looking to MacDonald to help maintain the Dawes Plan's viability, Crewe wasted no time in helping to defuse this mini-crisis. More specifically,

> On 7 July Crewe telegraphed urgently that Herriot 'begs most earnestly that you will come to Paris if only for a few hours, believing that there is serious risk of defeat and consequent failure of conference plan unless French public opinion can be calmed'. MacDonald rushed to the aid of his fellow statesman. Discussions took place at the Quai d'Orsay on 8 and 9 July, resulting in the publication of a joint memorandum on the application of the Dawes Scheme.[467]

This message strove to reassure the French audience in particular that, in the event of any 'wilful default' by Germany, 'the Governments concerned will undertake to confer at once on how to put into operation such measures as they shall agree in order to protect themselves and the investors'.[468] This intervention succeeded, both in placating the concerned French media and ensuring that the outcome achieved was in keeping with British interests.

The 'Corfu Incident'

Lord Crewe's biographer observes how 'that talent for urbane and wise diplomacy which Crewe had signally shown throughout his political career [...] was exactly what was now required in the British Ambassador in Paris'.[469] He cites Crewe's handling of the 'Corfu Incident' of September 1923 as a major demonstration of these qualities.[470]

The political origins of this crisis lay in diplomatic attempts to determine the precise frontiers of the state of Albania, which had become internationally recognised in 1913. The demarcation of these boundaries had been deferred by the onset of World War I, but the task had now been regalvanised by a Conference of Ambassadors in Paris, which set up an Anglo-French-Italian commission under the chairmanship of the Italian general, Enrico Tellini.

In August 1923 the commission was engaged in a survey of the Greek-Albanian frontier roughly fifteen miles from the Greek town of Janina. Early in the morning of the 27th three cars left Janina for the border. In the first was an Albanian delegation, in the second [...] the Greek delegation, and in the third Tellini with three fellow Italians and an Albanian interpreter. There was an interval of 30 minutes between the departure of the Albanians and that of the Greeks; the Italians left Janina a few minutes after the Greeks. En route the Greek car developed engine trouble and was passed by the Italians. After making repairs the Greeks continued. Further on, while still unmistakably in Greek territory, they came upon the Italian car. It had run into an ambush formed by tree branches hastily thrown across the road, and its five occupants had been shot to death.[471]

Exactly who perpetrated these killings. and their motives for doing so, has since remained a matter of great contention. A subsequent investigation, authorised by the Conference of Ambassadors, maintained that the assassins arrived from Albania and immediately returned there once the deed had been done. It noted that, by now, the Greek Government had already lodged four complaints to the Albanians regarding the activities of armed bandits breaking across the Greek border. Thus, 'The implication could be drawn that the Janina crime was simple brigandage. Yet the perplexing fact that it was the second car that was attacked suggest that this was an attack made *with fine timing, planning, and possibly a political motive.*'[472]

This uncertainty was not sufficient to prevent the Italian Prime Minister, Benito Mussolini, from authorising a subsequent retaliatory invasion and occupation (on 31 August) of the strategically important Grecian port of Corfu. Greece appealed for this matter to be taken to the League of Nations, which happened to be in session at the time. The Italians succeeded, however, in diverting the controversy in the direction of yet another Ambassadors' Conference, which was also meeting in Paris. Mussolini, meanwhile, set a fine of 50 million liras as his price for withdrawing Italian troops from the island of Corfu.

It was generally accepted that the Greek government had a clear responsibility to ensure the safety of the representative of a foreign power on its territory, and was thus liable to make substantial apologies and reparation to Italy and probably also to the allied Conference of Ambassadors whose agent Tellini had been. But it was also felt that Mussolini's [...] bombardment and seizure of an undefended island was an outrage comparable with the behaviour of Austria-Hungary towards Serbia after Sarajevo in 1914.[473]

The Ambassadors' Conference immediately commissioned a three-person Commission of Inquiry into the assassinations. Without awaiting its outcome, the Greeks declared a readiness to compensate the Italians by fully meeting their financial demands – a move which undoubtedly influenced the nature and outcome of subsequent negotiations regarding the latter's withdrawal from Corfu.[474]

Given the level of prestige already attached to role of British Ambassador to France, and the reputation he already enjoyed on the strength of a distinguished political career, it was almost inevitable that Crewe would play a central part in these negotiations. However, once the responsibility for resolving the crisis had been passed onto the Conference of Ambassadors, Sir William Tyrrell (an influential senior British civil servant and diplomat) complained to Lord Curzon that Crewe was lacking the strength of character to stand up for himself in the context of testing negotiations, and that a sturdier substitute was required. Curzon kept faith in his Ambassador; and, as Barros puts it, 'Lord Crewe continued sitting in the meetings of the Conference where in the days to come his tenacity, good sense, and tact proved invaluable in what was to become a demanding and trying situation.'[475]

While the was no doubting Crewe's readiness to behave in concessionary manner whenever the situation dictated (e.g. by consenting to Italian demands to have a representative of their own on the above-mentioned Commission of Inquiry), he also displayed an early air of characteristic fortitude in demanding that the Italians immediately evacuate Corfu on production of the Commission's report. As the official American observer of the conference maintained in his report, Crewe was only partially successful in achieving this objective:

> Lord Crewe, he reported to Washington, had been unsuccessful in securing a 'categorical Italian assurance of [an] immediate evacuation' of Corfu upon Greece's acceptance of the Conference's note. Since it had been imperative to reach some

sort of a decision on this point that same day, Crewe, strongly supported by the French, contented himself with placing Italy 'under a very strong obligation' to evacuate Corfu. This obligation, according to Whitehouse, was 'evidenced partly by [the] unusually solemn statements spread on [the] record – which [...] will be most difficult for [the] Italian Government to evade'.[476]

Crewe nonetheless continued to demonstrate the type of resolute attitude that many detractors considered him incapable of. This was true of his reaction to an especially unhelpful cable delivered to the Conference by Mussolini on 8 September, in which the Italian Prime Minister insisted that his country would have no intention of evacuating Corfu even after the Greek's had deposited the 50 million liras they demanded. Mussolini stated that he was unwilling to authorise such an evacuation until those people responsible for the assassinations had been identified and duly executed. This proviso was reiterated once the Conference reconvened, two days later, by the Italian delegate, Roman Avezzana.[477]

Crewe immediately put his foot down, emphatically maintaining that the British Government would be 'greatly disappointed' by this stipulation, since they had always assumed that the evacuation would proceed once the deposit had been secured and the funeral of the politicians taken place. He added indignantly that: 'Avezzana's assertion that his government desired very much to leave Corfu, but that only Greece had the power to hasten this evacuation by swiftly arresting the culprits, placed him in an "absolutely new situation," which obligated him to consult again with London.'[478] Crewe issued a stern, thinly veiled threat to the Italians, emphasising that the position they were adopting would not go down well with his government or, indeed, the British public as a whole.

This coded warning immediately paid dividends. Avezzana cautioned Mussolini that the issue was in danger of becoming transformed into a patently undesirable Anglo-Italian dispute. In the early hours of 12 September, Mussolini informed Avezzana that he would be prepared to evacuate Corfu without the immediate arrest and punishment of the culprits, on condition that the 50 million liras be deposited on an interim basis by the Greek Government.[479]

A provisional deadline of 27 September was set for the Italian withdrawal. With typical doggedness, Crewe strove to have it formally documented that the Italians were under an official obligation to have *completed* their evacuation — and not merely got it underway — by this agreed date. Conference rejected this proposal, however. Afterwards, the official American observer referred to above was critical of Crewe's behaviour, complaining that his comments 'had put in doubt the good faith of the Italian Government,' while adding that, 'if Lord Crewe and the British desired to antagonise Rome, they certainly had succeeded.'[480]

Clearly impervious to such criticism, Crewe presided over discussions taking place on 25 September, when Conference reconvened to consider the Commission of Inquiry's report, which had been published only three days earlier. He was adamant from the outset that the report said nothing to justify the imposition of a 50 million liras fine.

> He was willing to admit it indicated that the Greek authorities had not arrived at any results, but it did not prove that the Greek Government had been guilty of negligence. It was possible that after further investigation the Commission of Inquiry would succeed in establishing in a more precise manner the responsibility of the Greek Government. At the moment, however, this responsibility was not clearly established. Crewe, therefore, thought that the Greek Government and public opinion had good grounds for believing that the amount of the penalty would not be immediately determined, but that the Conference would have to leave it to the Permanent Court of International Justice at The Hague for final settlement.[481]

Crewe's Italian counterpart, Avezzana, stridently objected that a financial basis of agreement had already been reached, which made no allowance for the procedural digression that Crewe was suddenly proposing. Moreover,

> The French delegate backed Italy's claim to the full indemnity, while the Japanese was evasive. Romano Avezzana, knowing Mussolini's temper, declared flatly that he could not reaffirm the promise of a Corfu evacuation on the 27th without the entire 50 million lira. The Paris embassy alerted the Ministry of Marine in Rome to the renewed danger of an Anglo-Italian conflict. But before matters reached the boiling point and before Mussolini

could use the situation to revise his flickering hopes of remaining in Corfu, the crisis passed. Overnight, Crewe received instructions from Curzon in London to yield, and in the morning session on the 26th he gave his sanction to the full indemnity.[482]

Curzon subsequently justified the sending of this directive on the grounds that the Foreign Ministry had been keen to avoid any accusation of having been 'responsible for a great European conflagration which really was on the verge of bursting out'.[483] Far from satisfied with this rationale, Crewe nonetheless wrote to Curzon on 26 September, conceding that things had turned out as well as could have been expected:

> [He] believed that under the circumstances it was the 'best conclusion that could have been reached,' and he certainly did his 'utmost to make it a better one.' The major achievement was to have 'secured a definite promise of the immediate evacuation of Corfu,' but since the occupation was 'an invasion of public right,' one could not 'regard the outcome as a triumph.' On the other hand since 'nobody was prepared to take stronger measures, there may have been no other way.'[484]

While clearly recognising the importance of the part he had played in the resolution of the crisis, Crewe followed up with a second letter, one day later, explaining that he was still struggling to come to terms with the outcome he had helped achieve. It represented, he regretted to say, a 'sorry instance of the low level which postwar morality had reached'.[485]

The Treaty of Locarno

Jacobsen paints a vivid impression of the collective euphoria accompanying the signing of the so-called Treaty of Locarno, which took place on 16 October 1925 at the Swiss lakeside town of that name. The normally aloof and reserved British Foreign Secretary, Sir Austen Chamberlain, is said by Jacobsen to have 'trembled and wept with joy', as did his French counterpart, Aristide Briand. In a rare display of pro-British affection, Benito Mussolini kissed Chamberlain's wife on the hand. Locally assembled crowds danced deliriously as brass bands played on. The following day's *New York Times* approvingly proclaimed: 'France and Germany Bar War Forever'.[486]

The underlying cause of this jubilation was the formal ratification of the Treaty's five constituent components. Four of these related to agreed arbitration protocols concerning Germany and four neighbouring states: France, Belgium, Poland and Czechoslovakia.

> The other, the Treaty of Mutual Guarantee, was a multilateral regional security agreement. It was, first of all, a reciprocal treaty of nonaggression by which the powers situated on the Rhine — Germany, France and Belgium — promised not to attack, invade, or resort to war against each other. Secondly, it was a treaty of mutual guarantee and assistance by which the nations of Western Europe — England, France, Germany, Belgium, and Italy — promised to observe the demilitarisation of the Rhineland, to defend the existing borders between Germany and France and Germany and Belgium, and to render military assistance to any signatory who was the victim of a violation of these two promises.[487]

Furthermore, as Johnson points out, the Treaty helped secure German membership of the League of Nations.[488] Taken as a whole, the historical significance of the Treaty was that it formally terminated the First World War, while its breakdown, eleven years later, represented the prelude to the second.[489]

Relevant negotiations had first begun in January 1925. The avowedly pro-French Chamberlain was initially in favour only of a tripartite military alliance in which Britain would come to the aid of France and Belgium in the event of any German aggression. This contrasted with the standpoint of the British Chancellor, Sir Winston Churchill, who argued that the exclusion of the Germans would encourage the French 'to continue antagonising Germany and ultimately lead Britain into a war which would destroy both nations'.[490]

A pivotal influence on Chamberlain's eventual change of strategic direction was exerted by Lord Crewe. Johnson points out that, although Chamberlain enjoyed a close rapport with his French opposite number, Aristide Briand, the most significant behind-the-scenes activity was undertaken by Crewe and *his* French counterpart:

> While it is true that he savoured the opportunity to talk to Briand at Geneva when they gathered for League Assembly and Council meetings, much of Chamberlain's communication with

the French government concerning the negotiation of the security pact was done by conventional diplomatic channels, through the Marquess of Crewe, the British ambassador at Paris, and through Crewe's opposite number, Aimé de Fleuriau. Indeed, the impact that Chamberlain's relationship with these two men had on Anglo-French relations in the mid-1920s is an important gap in our knowledge of Locarno diplomacy.[491]

Johnson attempts to close this 'gap' by outlining in close detail the process by which Chamberlain was brought round to his Ambassador's way of thinking. She begins by explaining that,

> Although Chamberlain later embraced the idea of a tripartite agreement with Germany, his preferred course of action was to conclude a treaty of mutual guarantee with France that would later be extended to include Germany. Crewe, on the other hand, believed that the British government should be willing to give greater acknowledgement to the fact that the most recent impetus for a multilateral security pact had come from Berlin, not from Paris. It was thus important that the British government focus on German suggestions and requirements and weave those of France into the process of negotiation only as and when they fitted the Anglo-German agenda.[492]

Crewe subscribed, in Johnson's estimation, to a 'much less sentimental' view than Chamberlain of the significance of the Entente Cordiale. The Ambassador reckoned that the French harboured misguided notions of why Britain had gone to war in 1914. The latter's involvement had not been driven primarily by any desire to 'defend Belgian neutrality' or, more pertinently, to 'rescue' France.

> Instead, Britain took up arms because 'if we had stood aside in 1914, and the Germans had become the undoubted masters of Europe, our turn would have come next, even to the point of our probably losing command of the sea'. Although [Crewe] agreed that European security and disarmament were of central importance to the British government, such matters should be primarily discussed to protect British interests against a potentially resurgent Germany. Bolstering the entente with France should not necessarily be the first priority. Furthermore, France's blossoming relationship with the successor states in Eastern

Europe, especially Hungary and Poland, should be encouraged by the British government and viewed as a way of moving away from 'our being represented as simply the saviours of France'.[493]

Chamberlain's thinking had hitherto been influenced by the views of Aimé de Fleuriau, Crewe's opposite number in London, who was resolutely averse to the idea of including Germany in initial negotiations. By contrast, Crewe was sympathetic to the position adopted by Lord D'Abernon, his counterpart in Berlin, who advocated an attitude of reconciliation with Germany. In striving to convert Chamberlain to this standpoint, Crewe wrote to the Foreign Secretary in March 1925, reminding him that: 'It must be borne in mind that France is now, and will be for the next few years at any rate, in a position, both on land and in the air, of overwhelming military preponderance over Germany.'[494] It was by such means of influence that Chamberlain eventually adopted a more inclusive and sympathetic attitude to the Germans.

The euphoria associated with the signing of the Treaty of Locarno subsequently evaporated, of course, with the onset of the Second World War. This is not to diminish the scale of Lord Crewe's accomplishments, both in relation to Locarno, and throughout his wider period in office:

> Although Crewe was undoubtedly a steadying influence on the way in which the British and French governments viewed each other during the mid-1920s, when his embassy began, relations between Britain and France were at their lowest ebb since the end of the First World War. When his embassy came to an end, the negotiation of the Locarno treaty had done much to repair that damage, but did not result in the entente between Britain and France emerging as the driving force behind further attempts to prevent a second European war.[495]

It would certainly be unfair to question the worthiness of his intentions. Writing in 1940 of his time spent in Paris, he said how he continued to take pride in his efforts because, as he put it, 'war smothers all the aspirations of Liberalism'.[496]

Chapter Twelve
Locked Out and Betrayed

Red Letter Days

The 1924-25 football season represented the pinnacle of a golden era in the history of the Fryston Colliery football team. The club attained its highest-ever position (fourth) in the Yorkshire League and ran their Midlands League opponents, Wombwell, close in the preliminary rounds of the English Cup, losing out 3-2 in a fiercely contested replay, having drawn the original tie, 2-2.[497]

Still desperate to bring home the coveted West Riding County Challenge Cup, Fryston had the satisfaction of overcoming their old nemesis, Goole Town (3-0), before eliminating another traditional rival, Rawdon of Bradford, 2-1, in a semi-final played on Leeds City's ground at Harehills. The team now squared up against Harrogate Town on a rain-swept Elland Road ground in their first county cup final since World War I. Despite a promising first half hour which Fryston easily dominated, the opposition gradually established superiority, eventually prevailing 3-0. For all this relative success, this major sporting prize continued to elude them.[498]

Meanwhile, inside the mining industry, major conflict was brewing. A point had now been reached whereby the revival of the coal trade in 1923-1924 had not been matched by a commensurate rise in pay. Thousands of miners were therefore developing a more militant mindset.[499] By the following year, a resurgence in the supply of foreign coal onto world markets (notably emanating from the rejuvenated German Ruhr), the loss of market share in the USA following the termination of the American miners' strike, and an elevation in the cost of British coal exports due to a return to the Gold Standard[500] severely disadvantaged the UK mining industry.[501]

The coal-owners reacted by insisting on drastic cost-cutting measures, including immediate wage reductions and the abolition of a guaranteed minimum wage. On discovering that the miners would be supported

174

in their opposition to these measures by the Trades Union Congress (TUC) General Council (which was prepared, if necessary, to sanction a General Strike), the Prime Minister, Stanley Baldwin, agreed to extend the coal subsidy until 1 May 1926. Baldwin further authorised a special Samuel Commission (named after its Chairman, the Liberal, Lord Samuel) to examine 'the economic position of the coal industry and the conditions affecting it'.[502]

The day on which the Prime Minister's concession was announced became known, thereafter, as 'Red Friday. Some saw it as a triumph of 'revolutionary socialism', which 'was supposed to have beaten the government to its knees'.[503] The Miners' Federation of Great Britain (MFGB) President, Herbert Smith, harboured no such illusions. 'We have no need to glorify about a victory,' he soberly cautioned his members. 'It is only an armistice, and it will depend largely how we stand between now and 1st May next year as an organization in respect of unity as to what will be the ultimate results.'[504] While the Samuel Commission was conducting its inquiry, the Government steeled itself for possible confrontation by setting up the supposedly neutral Organisation for the Maintenance of Supplies (OMS). Eager to avoid doing anything seen as 'provocative' the TUC mounted no such preparations.[505]

Prelude to Disaster

In the 1925-26 football season, Fryston appeared to have been dispirited by their ultimate failure of the previous campaign. The Colliers not only ended up in bottom position of the Yorkshire League, having won a mere four games out of 28, but were thrashed 7-0 by Mexborough in the preliminary round of the English Cup, and beaten 2-1 — this time by Rawdon — in the first round of the WRCC Cup.[506] It is possible that this dramatic loss of form was connected to parallel developments in the industrial relations sphere, where neither the miners nor coal-owners were unduly impressed by the recommendations of the Samuel Commission.

The long-term prosperity of the industry depended, in Samuel's view, not on the nationalisation of the mines, per se, but on the amalgamation of smaller pits into more efficient units. The short-term salvation of the industry was to be achieved, not by imposing longer hours and indefinite wage cuts, or by replacing the existing national wages agreement by district settlements (as the owners might prefer), but by implementing temporary wage reductions for all but the worst-paid men. The Commission also argued against further extensions of any government subsidy.[507]

Battle lines were immediately drawn once the subsidy expired, with the owners declaring a lockout of all miners, and the MFGB defiantly coining the slogan 'Not a penny off the pay; not a minute on the day'. Careful to insist that what followed was nothing more than a conventional (i.e. *non-revolutionary*) case of industrial action, the TUC's General Council called out four million members in sympathetic support of the miners. It was with increasing trepidation – based on fears that that the strike would be repressively put down as an insurrection – that the General Council strove desperately to broker an immediate settlement.

This sense of urgency became even more apparent when, on Sunday 2 May, printers working for the *Daily Mail* refused to prepare for publication an editorial condemning the General Strike as 'a revolutionary movement, intended to inflict suffering on the great mass of innocent persons in the community and thereby put forcible constraint on the Government'.[508] This was the Prime Minister's cue to break off negotiations with the Council and insist there would be no resumption of talks unless they formally called off the strike.

The General Council was in no doubt that 'this incident had deliberately been used as a means of terminating the negotiations'.[509] Egged on by Jimmy Thomas, the right-wing leader of the railway workers' union (and strident opponent of the strike), the General Council engaged covertly in talks with Lord Samuel, whom they deluded themselves into believing was acting as a mediator with Baldwin's knowledge and consent. Much to the miners' consternation and chagrin, a Council delegation went round to Downing Street to inform him of their decision to terminate the strike. Their 'surrender' was unconditional.[510]

The miners were now left to fight alone. Their efforts in this regard were greatly inspired, at least in part, by the spellbinding, almost evangelistic, oratory of their charismatic General Secretary, A.J. Cook, a man fiercely denounced by Conservative politicians and newspaper editorials in the seven months that followed. Less widely acknowledged is the arguably more significant role of Herbert Smith, who, according to Brendon, led his men 'with the skill of a Great War general'.[511] Here, on a national stage, his manner was consistent with that displayed in the 1902-04 Wheldale-Fryston strike.[512]

Undeferential and unintimidated to the last, Smith once paused during discussion with Baldwin to take out his dentures and wipe them clean with his handkerchief. As one historian observed:

> Herbert Smith, in his sixties, was almost the stereotypical Yorkshireman whose utterances became legendary in the 1920s. Deriding the timidity of the TUC and its reluctance to back the miners to the hilt, Smith exhorted them thus: 'Get on t' field. That's t' place.' His response of 'nowt' when asked what concessions the MFGB was prepared to make likewise placed him as an almost Old Testament figure in his righteousness and inflexibility. 'Nowt. Nowt doin'. We've nowt to offer,' became almost a mantra from Smith's lips. [...] The received opinion early in 1926 was that Smith was the old-fashioned unionist, perhaps slightly out of his depth. But by the end of the year most observers had seen the truth. The alleged demon, Cook, turned out to be moderate and accommodating, but Smith was a rock that the elements could not shake.[513]

Contrary to popular characterisations, it was the firebrand Cook, rather than his more stolid presidential colleague, who engaged in secret negotiations – starting as early as July 1926 – with individuals close to the Government and/or owners, such as the industrialist, Seebohm Rowntree, the editor of *The Economist*, W.T. Layton, and Rowntree's Private Secretary, F.D. Stuart.[514] Such revelations chime, as we shall see, with the commonly levelled allegation that it was Smith's legendary 'stubbornness' and 'intransigence' that stood in the way of a negotiated settlement and led to the unnecessarily prolonged hardship of mining communities like Fryston.

The eventual termination of the strike was precipitated by the organised return to work and formation of a breakaway union in Nottinghamshire, instigated by the Nottinghamshire Miners Association's (NMA's) General Secretary, George Spencer, MP. Things came to a head at an MFGB conference at Kingsway Hall, London, on 8 October 1926, where a bitter confrontation took place between Smith, and Spencer, after the former had read out a newspaper report from the previous day which claimed that Spencer had facilitated a return to work of men at two Nottinghamshire collieries.[515]

Spencer was duly expelled from the conference and an NWA Inquiry into his activities authorised; but this did not prevent inevitable damage from being done, especially as 'This intervention by the NWA's best-known leader lent legitimacy to the return to work and extended it.'[516] Building on the momentum he had now created, Spencer led an organised return to work in the Notts coalfield on 7 November. Three weeks later, the MFGB Executive resigned themselves to defeat by calling off their action in a bid to halt any further spread of 'Spencerism'.[517]

Henceforward, agreements were forged, not nationally but at district level:

> The terms of the return to work varied but usually included an eight-hour day and the wage conditions as at 1921 rather than 1924. The owners scored a total victory. The miners had to work longer hours for lower wages (in 1927 an average of 7d loss per shift).[518]

As forecast by Samuel and the miners, unemployment in the coalfields rose in consequence of longer hours, reaching 200,000 by January 1927, and over 300,000 by July 1928. The human cost of such joblessness – in terms of chronic malnutrition, the out-migration of young men in search of jobs, and closure of local shops due to lack of trade – was every bit as tangible.[519]

We now examine the lived experience of striking Fryston villagers and their families (including one man who famously returned to work), starting from the perspective of Jim Bullock and his wife. In an important supplementary section, we focus on the recollections of a Durham-based priest, who would subsequently play a crucially transformative role in terms of Fryston and its neighbouring localities, and on the emergence in the immediate post-strike period of a young Frystoner who was to become a celebrated professional footballer.

Making a Song and Dance About It
In the months immediately preceding the General Strike, Jim Bullock had been courting his eventual first wife, a Skipton girl called Anne, who was a friend of one of his older sisters. Anne came from a

well-known family of pacifists, her father being a quietly spoken and deeply philosophical founding member of the Labour Party. It was during the earliest of Bullock's visits to see Anne in Skipton that he was introduced to such eminent figures in the Labour movement as Philip Snowden, Sir Stafford Cripps and Herbert Morrison, and became even more politicised in the process:

> Under her [Anne's] father's influence and guidance I began to take a really keen interest in Labour party politics, my conversion was different to that of my brother. He was converted to religion many times. I was converted to Socialism once.[520]

Undeterred by the onset of the General Strike, Bullock and Anne were married at Skipton Baptist Church on 22 May. The couple had already begun paying rent on a terraced house on the newly-created Airedale estate which they were due to start occupying 28 weeks later. The newlyweds therefore stayed for the duration of the strike with Anne's parents in Skipton, where Bullock became part of a fund-raising 'Miners' Concert Party and Dance Band':

> We worked to a programme, well planned. We arranged with the local Labour Party to book the biggest hall in their locality. The miners then gave a concert and I made a speech to let the audience know what the Strike was about. We then took a collection and appealed for hospitality for the miners. The remainder of the evening was spent with our orchestra playing for dancing.[521]

During one such engagement in Silsden, Bullock appalled his pacifist father-in-law, who was told by a fellow Labour Party member all about the methods the young man had employed in dealing with a group of youthful Conservatives ('Young Imps') who were boisterously disrupting the dance and physically harassing the band's drummer. When Bullock delivered the ultimatum that the hecklers either leave quietly or opt to stay and fight, the Imps chose the latter course of action.[522] Bullock's father-in-law looked more approvingly on the occasion when the former and his colleagues accompanied Philip Snowden to a lecture at Sedburgh public school, which raised the impressive sum of £7,500.[523]

While Jim and Anne Bullock were able to continue a style of life largely protected from the financial and emotional consequences of the strike and subsequent lockout, the same, alas, could not be said of his fellow workers and their families back in Fryston. Local people struggled in various ways to offset the extreme financial hardship resulting from the dispute. Jack Hulme and Jack Caulkin set off on push bikes, harmonicas in hand, to go street busking in places as far afield as Staffordshire. No less enterprising were those families who resorted to 'scratting' coal from surrounding tips and selling it on to diverse commercial entities:

> Some sold theirs to John Smith's Brewery; but Salts of Saltaire, the woollen weavers, sometimes took ours. You used to store it all in sacks in your yard. If you got a right good hole on the tip, you used to leave somebody there overnight to guard it! (Ex-Fryston man, 1987)

Reflecting a staunch collective ethos, striking families engaged in a variety of innovative fund-raising activities. Thanks in large part to the extraordinary talent of Jabez ('Jabie') Foulkes, the latest member of the Fryston footballing dynasty, the local schoolboys' team was proving all-conquering in the Castleford area. One Fryston woman gleefully reported how she had borrowed Jabie's boots to score the winning goal in a specially arranged fixture against Pontefract liquorice workers:

> There were a few of us formed a team to go to 'Ponte' to raise some money to feed all t' kids. I'm not kidding, they were as big as horses, some of their team! (Ex-Fryston woman, 1986)

Complementing all this was the kindness and paternalism displayed by the local chapels, the village schoolteachers (Mr and Mrs Rickaby), and the village shopkeepers, Albert Firth and Cuddy Bateson. The Rickabys helped sustain the village by dispensing gallons of home-made soup:

> Day after day, the kids used to take their bowls and have 'em filled, and Mrs Rickaby used to go to [the top of the street] where all the men were stood and give 'em fistfuls of 'cigs' and

'bacca'. Mr and Mrs Firth used to have the shop and they were very good. They used to let everybody have 'tick'. They say he lost a goldmine through people never paying him back. (Ex-Fryston woman, 1987)

An equally vital, if more surprising, part was played by the notoriously cantankerous village butcher:

Cuddy Bateson was marvellous during that strike. Every bit of meat he could scrape together used to go in t' set pot for soup for the adults and kids. Sometimes, we'd come back from butcher Bateson's and bob the soup straight through a colander to get rid of lumps of fat that were floating on the top. (Ex-Fryston man, 1986)

In the absence of any state provision for striking workers and their families, local residents were dependent on means-tested handouts from the Board of Guardians. One woman recalled how her father received a weekly voucher of ten shillings and sixpence to feed a family of eight, but that this had only amounted to a loan — scheduled to be repaid in the form of weekly deductions of sixpence per week from his pay packet. In some instances, parents were forced by poverty into temporarily re-housing their children with strike sympathisers elsewhere in the county:

I was sent away to a place called Silsden in Keighley where the people were working and better off. They sent a few of us away to be fed. I've never been back since. Nor do I want to. The people were absolute gold but, as hard up as we were, I was despondent. I remember sitting on the bank of the river where they had their little allotment and hens — absolutely beautiful — but I couldn't see it for tears. The food they were offering me, I was so ill through worry, I couldn't eat. (Ex-Fryston woman, 1987)

Although local miners stayed generally resolute, the conduct and experience of separate individuals was often complicated by matters of personal pride and ideological conviction. One ex-Fryston woman recollected that her father was privately opposed to the strike on the grounds that 'they never gained anything from it' (interview, 1987).

This man would play no part in deterring the handful of strike-breakers who dared to enter the mine. His pride also discouraged him from receiving various forms of charity: 'We used to say, "They're giving boots away at school, Dad. Can we go? Can Mam go with us?"' the woman recollected. 'He'd say, "No, if there's any for you, they'll give you them." He never borrowed or asked for anything.'

'Judas Iscariot Lives Here'

One former male resident of Fryston, who was eight years old at the time, reflected that the colliery entrance was patrolled by police dog-handlers, intent on escorting potential strike-breakers ('blacklegs' or 'scabs') into the mine. Although a 'couple of scuffles' occurred, there were few other instances of violence. 'People were more together in them days,' he maintained. 'They were against the "Establishment" and there was only a small percentage of "scabs"' (ex-Fryston man, 1986). Sometimes the consequences of strike-breaking were unexpectedly indirect:

> They used to make this soup at chapel and, whenever you went, you got a big jug of soup and what they called 'a bag of buns'. Well, when my dad got to hear that the chap who organised it all was a 'blackleg', he wouldn't let me go again. Anyway, one day I went back and my dad got to hear about it, and he gave me a belting with the big buckle end. I'd all weals across my back for going against him. He nearly killed me for it. (Ex-Fryston woman, 1986)

It is almost certain that the 'blackleg' alluded to above was a local man called Albert Saunders. This Staffordshire-born individual had begun living in Fryston during the Wheldale-Fryston strike of 1902-04. By the time the General Strike occurred, Mr Saunders had left the village and taken up residence with his wife, Hannah, on nearby Fryston Road, Airedale. He was now working at Glasshoughton Colliery, rather than Fryston. Broadly built and five-feet-eleven-inches tall, Saunders was a self-educated man 'of firm religious beliefs' whose commitment to non-conformity 'extended beyond the bounds of the church which he served for nearly 50 years as a Methodist Lay Preacher'.[524] In keeping with his beliefs, Saunders stridently denounced the strike, erecting 20 posters outside his home which mostly condemned the role played by the MFGB's 'communist faction'. Local strikers responded by painting the words 'Judas Iscariot lives here' across the adjoining pavement.[525]

Totally unfazed, Saunders placed an advertisement in the local press, informing everyone that he would be reporting to work as usual at 6am on the following Monday. Jim Bullock surmised in *Them and Us* that this may have been the first instance of strikebreaking in Yorkshire.[526] Bullock magnanimously acknowledged that 'it took a courageous man to blackleg in mining', and that Saunders was 'a strong man', a local preacher who 'nobody could class as a weakling'.[527] His colleagues at Glasshoughton drew a less charitable conclusion:

> When he came out of the pit at the end of the day the colliery band was waiting to welcome him and they marched in front of him all the way to his house playing a funeral march. He had to follow the band and keep to their pace because all the miners and their families were stood on each side of the roads, bareheaded, with their heads bowed as if it was a funeral procession.[528]

Following Holy Orders

Eight days after Jim Bullock's marriage to Anne (on 30 May 1926), a much grander religious ceremony took place, involving the ordination of Father John Charles Sydney Daly at Durham Cathedral. The Surrey-born Daly had hitherto enjoyed a comfortable middle-class existence as the son of a successful stockbroker and his wife, a trained nurse. The Cambridge-educated 23-year-old had previously looked upon his undergraduate career as a stepping-stone into the City, where he might eventually emulate his father. More recently, he had experienced a growing desire to enter the Anglican priesthood and was encouraged by his college dean to seek Holy Orders. Daly therefore spent a year at Cuddesdon Theological College (Oxford), before agreeing to become a curate at St Mary's in the slum parish of Tyne Dock.[529]

Daly has since recalled how the onset of the General Strike had enabled some of his Cambridge peers to fulfil their childhood ambitions to drive a train – albeit in the controversial capacity of replacement labour for striking railway workers. The Surrey man had been resigned to cycling all the way to his ordination, due to the rail workers' involvement in the strike. Following its termination, it still took him fourteen hours to travel north, due to the continuing disorganisation of the railway network. This marathon journey enabled the ordination to proceed as scheduled, before Daly then moved into a clergy house at St Mary's, where he began overseeing a generally impoverished parish of 18,000 people.[530]

As in Fryston, the Geordie miners and their families invariably lived in overcrowded houses characterised by poor or no sanitation, the presence of outside 'earth' (non-flushable) toilets and a single wash house shared by multiple residents. Tuberculosis was also rife in the area, particularly among children. Compounding all of this was what Daly described as the crushing impact of the ongoing lockout:

> There was no welfare state in those days, the Union funds were soon used up and the Parish Council had to supply food to the women and children. The widow of the first man whom I was sent to bury told me that her husband had been a coal miner on strike, but refused to sit down with the family to eat. 'Nay lass,' he would say, 'there's nowt for me: that food is for you and the bairns.' He would go out into the street, as did tens of thousands of other miners, walking in all weathers to pass the time. He had caught pneumonia and, having no strength, he had died.[531]

Daly was referring to this man in stating that: 'The first person I buried was a coal miner. He died of starvation at the end of 1926. It was the General Strike' (interview, 1986).

The Final Reckoning

Jim Bullock maintained that, amidst the many forces stacked against the striking miners and their families, 'The only thing on our side was the glorious weather. It was a marvellous summer. Nobody wanted coal and we could practically live outside.'[532] Bullock explained how, as the drift-back to work of the Nottinghamshire and Derbyshire miners gathered pace, Fryston miners 'were bitter enough to insist then that the ponies were fetched out, that the safety men were brought out, that the pumps stood. That's how bitter it got — we got to such a state that we didn't even care if we sacrificed the pit itself.'[533]

As mentioned earlier, subsequent lay and academic analysis generally attributed the miners' eventual defeat to the intransigence of Herbert Smith. By contrast, the equally prominent figure of A.J. Cook is customarily exempted from accusations of culpability. Typical of this tendency are the claims of Cook's biographer, who maintains that the Welshman grew progressively disconcerted by his president's harmful displays of obduracy and poor judgement.[534] By the final stages of the lockout, Cook had already 'embraced a conciliatory, face-saving position'; but the fact that he regarded Smith's position as 'unchallengeable' and saw any public criticism of the MFGB president as potentially detrimental to the miners' cause, encouraged him to adopt a more covert modus operandi, involving secret backstage manoeuvring.[535]

A predictably kinder, countervailing view is represented by Herbert Smith's biographer, Jack Lawson, who posits that his subject's determination to resist the coal-owners' and government's demands for a decrease in wages and increase in working hours was driven by a special form of insight and empathy not shared by his detractors:

> Herbert Smith knew the secret hidden places and what goes on in them. He had seen so much that he lived there in mind, even when he was in the council room where great decisions were made. Only those who could project themselves into such places, conditions, and experiences, can judge whether he made mistakes and how: those in the coalfields did not so judge him.[536]

No criticism was directed at Smith or, for that matter, Cook, by those Fryston residents old enough to have witnessed the strike first-hand. Jim Bullock recalled, for example, how he had seen Herbert Smith addressing a miners' rally in Castleford. 'He was as blunt as he was indomitable,' was Bullock's abiding impression. 'Even when the end was seeming probable, Herbert stoked our determination to continue with an honesty and rectitude that would have made us follow him to hell — and, by God, we almost did' (interview, 1987).

Another Fryston stalwart, Frances Payne, was also in her twenties when the lockout took place. She had never set eyes on A.J. Cook before, but such was the MFGB president's mythical reputation that she still felt compelled to stop off and pay tribute to him, four decades later, while travelling to meet a friend in continental Europe:

> When I went to London to set off to Germany, I went to find A.J. Cook's grave. I didn't know where the hell I was in London. Father had put me on t' train. [...] I was supposed to be meeting a woman, but she was delayed because of a rail strike. So, while I was waiting on my own in this hotel, I decided to find it. I saw this bus that had 'Golders Green' on it and I thought, 'That's it!' and I caught the bus to the cemetery where he's buried and searched out his grave. Aye, A.J. Cook: the greatest union man that ever was. (Interview, 1987)

Emerging From the Ruins

For two of the individuals already mentioned in this chapter, the collapse of the great lockout heralded momentous changes concerning their personal and career development.

The following football season (1926-27) was one in which Fryston, having dropped out of the Yorkshire League into the less prestigious Castleford and District League, suffered the ignominy of a 10-0 hammering against Denaby United in a preliminary round of the English Cup. Dick Foulkes was among the tens of thousands of miners now languishing on the dole. Making matters worse, his two-year professional footballing career had been permanently curtailed by a knee injury; but he was able to draw some consolation from the fact that his younger brother was about to embark on an even more illustrious footballing career.[537]

The meteoric rise of the 14-year-old Jabie Foulkes was manifested in a series of trophy-winning exploits he produced as centre-forward and captain of the unstoppable Fryston school football team of 1926-27. 'I broke all records that year,' Foulkes later recalled:

> I scored seven goals in each of two semi-finals. A teacher called Baxter took us, but old Rickaby was as keen as mustard. We won the Jackson Shield, League Championship and Sanders Cup. They were all good lads that year. I thought they'd all turn pro but, in the finish, there was only Freddie Astbury, who played for a Cheshire League team, other than me. (Interview, 1986)

On leaving school, Foulkes began playing open-age football, not as anticipated with Fryston, but with Whitwood Mere of the Leeds and District League. He had already followed his brother Dick's recent advice by switching from centre-forward onto the right wing. The young man had also recently begun working on Fryston pit top. He had played only three matches for Whitwood when he was invited to join First Division Huddersfield Town:

> After four matches with them, they put me in their second team and asked me to join their ground staff. My father went with me to sign on. I'd only been earning 12s 6d [63 pence] on Fryston pit top so, when [Huddersfield's manager] Clem Stephenson said, 'Will £4 10s [four pounds and fifty pence] be enough?' I felt like a millionaire! (Interview, 1986)

This was the start of a fantastic footballing adventure in which Foulkes would eventually rub shoulders with such greats of the game as Stanley Matthews and Len Shackleton, before returning to Fryston in the 1940s and helping to transform the colliery team into one of the greatest in the county.

The three years that John Daly had spent, in the meantime, as a curate on Tyneside were, as he acknowledged, among the happiest of his life. 'Working on the Tyneside, I loved the people, the Geordies,' he maintained.

> The old ladies would say, 'Where are you going next, hinny?' And I'd answer, 'Well, I'll go anywhere the church wants me to go. If they want me to go to Timbuktu, I'm ready to go to Timbuktu; but I do hope they don't send me to Yorkshire!' I thought they were too tough − I shouldn't know how to stand up to them! (Interview, 1986)

This statement was to prove unwittingly prophetic. Three years after arriving on Tyneside, Daly was summoned by his old College Principal, Jimmy Seaton, who was by now the Bishop of Wakefield. Seaton explained how he wanted Daly to apply his recent experience by setting up a new parish and building a new church in and around Airedale, deep within the Yorkshire coalfield. 'It was one of those queer things,' Daly recollected. 'The Lord just took over. I don't want it to sound a silly, sentimental sort of reason, but that's how it seemed, looking back. I'd certainly got no bright ideas of my own' (interview, 1986).

Daly had already signed a form on leaving college, promising the Missionary Committee that he would be willing, after serving as a curate, to go wherever the Church might subsequently decide to send him. The young cleric therefore approached the Bishop of Durham in search of permission to leave the diocese. The latter's response was profoundly inspirational:

> On the eve of his ordination in the Oxford diocese, he told me, he had made a vow, kneeling before the High Altar in Cuddesdon Parish Church, that he would never seek preferment. 'The result has been,' he said, 'whenever I have been asked to move to another sphere of work, I have not had to calculate where this falls in with my plans for the future, for my ambitions, but simply whether there was any good reason why I should not accept. Then if there is no good reason, I should take it to be a call from the Lord.' I went to Yorkshire in 1929.[538]

Chapter Thirteen
Homecoming

Freed of the Burdens of Statesmanship

It was sometime in 1927 that Lord Crewe reasoned that, since his seventieth birthday was now looming, he would like to spend the remainder of his lifetime back in Britain, in the comfort of his own homes, and in the company of his own friends and relatives.[539] He was persuaded by the Foreign Secretary, Austen Chamberlain, to stay on as Ambassador until the summer of 1928, at which point he received 'the usual formal despatch' from the Foreign Office, in appreciation of his six-year term of office. A more affectionate tribute was sent by the Foreign Secretary himself, who was unstinting in his praise:

> I cannot be content without saying to you in a more personal form how much we owe to you. You have enhanced the dignity of a great post. You and Lady Crewe have won the hearts of the Parisians, but you have done more than this: in the early days of your Mission, relations with France were difficult and sometimes came very near to breaking-point. I believe it to be largely owing to your judgement and courage that even then our differences were kept within bounds, whilst since those relations have improved you have at every turn contributed to the restoration of confidence and to the close co-operation which it was essential for us to secure. For all this I am grateful, not only as Secretary of State and as such the mouthpiece of His Majesty's Government, but because I could have had no more able and willing helper in the post which you have filled. Nothing could have been more delightful than my relations with you, both public and personal.[540]

Freed of the burdens of statesmanship, Crewe applied himself assiduously to the difficult but highly rewarding task of writing a two-volume biography of his late father-in-law, Lord Rosebery. Crewe would later reveal in the introduction to the first volume that he had been asked by Rosebery's family to undertake this project. Although he had known the former Prime Minister for 50 years – first as a longstanding family friend then as Rosebery's son-in-law – he did not underestimate the complexity of the task. 'There was a great mass of material, of which some important elements were separately sorted, while others were indiscriminately dotted about at his different homes,' he revealed. 'He seldom destroyed even a trivial letter, so the work of selection was arduous. And the multiplicity of his interests made it imperative to include some illustration of each.'[541] The overall undertaking was greatly simplified by Crewe's decision to avoid focusing in too much detail on Rosebery's political career – even of the brief period he served as Prime Minister.[542]

In the remainder of this chapter, we dwell, not only on the content and significance of Crewe's biography of his distinguished relative by marriage, but also on the latest phase of the career development of Crewe's daughter, Cynthia Colville, who became established in this era as trail-blazing female member of the justice system. We begin by focusing, however, on the formative years of Cynthia's nephew, Quentin Dodds. This latter discussion is chiefly drawn from Quentin's memoirs.[543] It provides an illuminating insight into the way in which the personal outlook of this future cultural icon of the 'swinging sixties' of British society was shaped by early childhood experience – not least, his problematic relationship with his mother, Annabel, the daughter of Lord Crewe.

Falling Down

Quentin Dodds was two years old when his grandfather returned from Paris to London. Though perfectly healthy during infancy, Quentin would spend most of his life (from the age of six onwards) as a victim of muscular dystrophy. As we shall see in later chapters, this did not prove an obstacle to the remarkable success he achieved in later life. In the words of one contemporary observer, Quentin 'fell down so much as a child and bounced back with such good cheer that he grew up to challenge prevailing stereotypes as an iconoclastic journalist, an innovative restaurant critic, a high-spirited social lion, a high-minded gossip columnist, a globe-trotting adventurer, a prolific author and an even more prolific lover'.[544] Quentin's own daughter reports that, even as a toddler, 'with his cherubic face and blond curls', he was regularly summoned from his bedroom to delight his parents' guests with tall stories and 'merry recitations'.[545]

Quentin moved, during the first year of his life, from London (the city of his birth) to Tripoli, and then on to Sicily, where his father, Hugh Dodds, was ostensibly British Consul, but spent long hours lounging on the beach or playing rounds of golf. His mother (Annabel), meanwhile, spent much of her time 'writing letters' – but only after spending the first hour of morning on such mundane matters as discussing the daily menu with the chef. The family enjoyed a very privileged lifestyle, often spent in the company of the Sicilian aristocracy. Quentin and his older brother, Colin, who was four years his senior, were both taught by a governess. According to the former, 'Colin had a cleft palate and a scarred lip. He spoke indistinctly. My mother was ashamed, so he was kept in the schoolroom.'[546]

Although the Dodds family was based, primarily, in Sicily, they spent entire summer seasons with relatives in England and Northern Ireland. Such occasions allowed Quentin to draw unfavourable comparisons between the relatively cold disposition of his mother and the more engaging characteristics of his aunts (Celia and Cynthia), each of whom 'used to recount stories, in special, would-be authentic voices, of the curse on this or that family; of the monster at Glamis Castle; of Lord Halifax's stepping back out of a lift when he remembered the liftman's face from a dream. The lift fell to the basement, killing all.'[547] Though 'undemonstrative' as a mother, and driven by an innate but well-concealed snobbery, Annabel was, in Quentin's estimation, 'an entertaining and informative companion'.[548]

Following one such visit to England, Quentin decided to stay on for a while longer at his half-sister's idyllic home in Epping Forest. It was Quentin's brother-in-law who noticed something wrong with the young man's ability to walk in normal fashion. The latter was also showing an increasingly disconcerting tendency to fall over unexpectedly. Annabel therefore took Quentin to see a distinguished Harley Street neurologist, who not only diagnosed muscular dystrophy, but also made the alarming prediction that he would not live beyond the age of sixteen. Annabel's reaction was simply to avoid mentioning Quentin's illness for the next twelve years. The latter had his own ideas as to why she adopted this coping strategy:

It may have been that she thought it pointless to fuss about something when there is nothing one can do to change it. [...] Alternatively, it may have been a shrinking from responsibility. When, so much later, we did speak of it, my mother blamed my father. It was suggested to her that muscular dystrophy came, like haemophilia, through the female line to boy children. This was unacceptable. Without troubling to look it up, my mother could name her mother's mother's mother back through five generations to Mrs Sheridan, wife of the playwright. There was no history of any kind in her family. She had had five perfect children with her first husband. It was plain that Colin's cleft palate and my dystrophy must come from our father.[549]

While attending preparatory boarding school, Quentin endured persistent teasing about his illness, but his teachers remained unflinchingly indifferent to his plight, insisting that he face up to it like a man. Both inside and outside of his family, Quentin was being 'trained to be tough', and not question the stability and rectitude of the current World Order:

My mother once told me that, when she was a girl in the 1890s, she and her sisters would wander listless by the lake at Crewe Hall and wish that something would happen in the world. In their sheltered youth, no hint of revolution ruffled their confidence in the eternal nature of the British Empire.[550]

Among other memorable features of Quentin's early childhood were his occasional visits to see his half-siblings, the O'Neill's, at their ancestral seat of Shane's Castle in Northern Ireland, which was located on the shore of Lough Neagh. 'Shane's', as the castle was known, consisted of three parts: an old castle ruin, from which eight cannons still protruded from battlements, and two more recently constructed mansions. The 'Shane's' estate resembled a small village, characterised by the incessant activity of all manner of gamekeepers, grooms, dairymaids, laundrymaids and electricians. The park consisted of 2,000 acres of fertile land, surrounded by a protective wall. It required a five-mile drive to get from one side of it to the other.

A prevailing system of primogeniture dictated that the O'Neill estate belonged to the family's eldest son, Shane, who was also set to inherit the even larger Crewe estates. According to Quentin, Shane displayed no more than an 'uninterested friendliness' towards him and his brother, Colin. Shane was, in Quentin's opinion, 'a sad man lacking overt joie de vivre and warmth – qualities which were ever thinly spread in the O'Neills'.[551] His seemingly unhappy life was destined – as we shall see in a later chapter – to be tragically curtailed.

A Crowded Life

In contrast to the sedentary lifestyle led by Quentin's mother, Annabel, the boy's aunt Cynthia (Colville) was ceaselessly engaged in charitable, professional and committee work of palpable humanitarian significance.

During the relevant era of the late 1920s, the infant death rate in Britain had fallen from 154 per thousand just after the war, to a more encouraging 69; but the still-birth rate and death rate during the first month of life had not improved commensurately. Additionally, some 3,000 mothers per annum were dying while in the act of giving birth. It was against this background that Cynthia was invited, in May 1929, to serve on an eighteen-person Ministry of Health Departmental Committee, set up by Neville Chamberlain to consider the problem of maternal mortality. She and her colleagues interviewed scores of mothers, their doctors and midwives, in the process of compiling a greatly enlightening and influential pamphlet, *Motherhood,* which had an initial run of 20,000 copies.[552]

It was also around this time that Cynthia became vice-president of the Women Public Health Officers' Association (the trade union for health visitors) and its president one year later. She was also appointed a Justice of the Peace for the Hanover Square Division of London, where she dealt primarily with education summonses and issues relating to licensed premises. Cynthia then began working at the East London Juvenile Court, and soon graduated into the role of Juvenile Court Chairman [sic]. These activities were carried out in conjunction with the three months per annum she also spent in the service of Queen Mary.[553]

Cynthia's professional approach was undoubtedly shaped by the knowledge and experience she had gained in Shoreditch and the insight she had also derived into the problems of local families. Thus,

Rather than going to families' homes to meet with the parents, Colville and colleagues had children and their families summonsed to them. In many ways, the juvenile court was family case work *par excellence*, as detailed investigations of children were frequently presented to the court. For the more troubled children and young people, such investigations also sought to explore their inner lives and emotions. [...] Colville and her colleagues at the Inner London Juvenile Court [...] were outspoken on matters concerning juvenile justice, particularly where they felt there was a universality to the cases in question.[554]

She and her co-workers were strong advocates of continuing support and after-care for the young people they were dealing with, especially those who had been sent down for their misdemeanours.[555] This philosophy underpinned her day-to-day conduct as one of only two female magistrates appointed on a Home Office committee charged with establishing the set of rules governing the conduct of juvenile courts under the Children and Young Persons Act 1933.[556]

In Praise of the Lord

Cynthia's father was, meanwhile, utilising his new-found sense of 'freedom' to complete his two-part biography of Lord Rosebery. Among the impressive range of source material he employed were: the former Prime Minister's vast collection of personal journals and diaries; a trove of correspondence between Rosebery and all manner of individuals, including such eminent figures as Queen Victoria and Lord Gladstone; and the richly-detailed diaries diligently kept by Lady Rosebery. Crewe also drew on his own correspondence with Rosebery, and insights based on their innumerable conversations.

In one such instance, described in Volume 1, the author refers to a letter he received from Rosebery, dated 29 December 1916, which contained a heart-warming tribute to Crewe's father, Richard Monckton Milnes:

> My dear R. As a very young fellow I made some speech in the House of Lords (I forget anything else about it), which seemed to me a dead failure, and I was greatly depressed. But next morning I received a note from your father congratulating me upon it in cordial terms. This warmed me once more, and

raised me from the ground. It might have been the frigid dignity of the House of Lords which had made me unduly dejected. My conviction, however, still remains that the speech was a failure, and that your father, realising this, and the mortification of a young friend, took the trouble on returning home to write a letter to cheer him from the pure tact of kindness.

That was the sort of thing that he did I fancy pretty often, and that is why his memory is so sweet to scores of others as well.[557]

Both volumes of Crewe's biography are imbued with strong feelings of affection for his subject and are heavily concentrated on the loving relationship that Rosebery enjoyed with all sections of his family. Crewe maintains, for example, that Rosebery 'was all that a father-in-law could be to the wives and husbands of his sons and daughters,' adding that 'His affectionate regard for them was amply returned.'[558]

The author further explains how, not surprisingly, it was the death of Rosebery's grandson, Jack Madeley, which caused the former Prime Minister's greatest sorrow in life. Crewe quotes relatedly from a letter which Rosebery sent to one of his closest friends, thanking him for his expression of sympathy. 'The blow is indeed a heavy one,' he wrote, 'heaviest of course for my daughter and son-in-law, but scarcely less heavy for me, who adored the child.'[559]

Critical reaction to Crewe's two volumes was variable. Pole, for one, complimented him for having displayed 'amazing' frankness in producing such a 'graceful and painstaking' biography.[560] Phelps Hall decreed along similar lines that Crewe had made 'an excellent contribution to scholarship', his book possessing 'dignity, charm and sympathy — no mean accomplishment in view of the enigmatic character of Mr. Gladstone's successor as leader of the Liberal party'.[561]

It was left to Marriott, however, to most effectively encapsulate the general feelings of ambivalence shared by so many reviewers. 'There is probably no one but Lord Crewe who could have painted it half so well,' he asserted. 'But it is not entirely illuminating.'[562] Marriott, like Pole, considered that, whilst Crewe's biography undoubtedly provided an excellent insight into Rosebery's character, and into his relationships with friends, relatives and fellow politicians, this was at the relative expense of any sustained discussion of his fundamental political beliefs or spellbinding parliamentary oratory.

Quietly Integrating

In the early 1930s, Lord and Lady Crewe decided to look for a country home capable of providing them with the opportunity to occasionally retreat from their London residence of Crewe House. As one observer explained, 'Lord Crewe had always had extravagant tastes but, by the 1930s, it was time for retrenchment.'[563] He and Peggy had already been selling off their assets, such as a prized Romney painting, which had helped pay for the expensive lifestyle they had enjoyed in Paris. Now was the time for strategic downsizing:

> After looking for many weeks at many houses, most of them too big and none of them sufficiently appealing, they chanced upon West Horsley Place, a low, sixteenth-century house built of small red bricks, which lies at the end of a sloping avenue, and with walled gardens and orchards behind it, near Leatherhead in Surrey. Although larger than they had intended their new house to be, West Horsley, with its singular quiet charm, airy well-proportioned rooms and fine staircases won their hearts. They bought it, and settled there in 1932, filling the house with pictures, furniture and objects from Fryston Hall, and installing in a long, dim book room hung with curtains of red brocade the great library collected by Lord Houghton and amplified by Lord Crewe. So large is this collection of books that it overflows into several other rooms and lobbies of the house. In keeping with the Whig traditions of Crewe Hall, two bedrooms at Horsley were re-christened the Buff Room and the Blue Room and furnished in these colours.[564]

Since returning to Britain from France, Peggy Crewe had become chairwoman of the Liberal Social Council and played a key part in establishing townswoman's guilds. Being a keen gardener, she also took charge of the landscaping of the grounds: 'She had a clear idea of the effect she wished to create. [...] There were borders of perennials and annuals, winding along the serpentine wall, stocks in the walled garden, a phlox border and an antirrhinum garden, as well as an informal corner of cape hyacinths.'[565] Henceforward, she and the Marquess would become quietly integrated into local village life, worshipping at St Mary's Parish

Church, walking through the village and countryside, and (in Peggy's case) declaring the annual village fete 'open'.[566]

It was not long before Crewe began selling off parts of his ancestral estates: 'His father's lands in Yorkshire had gone and, in 1933, he sold the bulk of his 20,000 acres in Cheshire, including Crewe Hall, to the Duchy of Lancaster, typically for far less than it was worth, on the grounds that the Crown would look after the tenants better.'[567] Socially, the Crewes settled into the lavish style of life they had grown accustomed to in Paris:

> The entertaining resumed on the same generous scale as before. Their daughter Mary was growing up and her friends remember that visits to the house were, for young people, awesome experiences at which they were banished to the furthest end of the dining room. Mary had her coming-out dance at the house in 1933. Lord Crewe's granddaughter, Mary O'Neill, and Mr Derick Gascoigne (the parents later of Bamber Gascoigne) had their wedding reception there in April 1934.[568]

Bouncing Back

In the mid-1930s, Quentin Dodds's parents relocated from Sicily to the French Riviera, where his father was entering a new ambassadorial role. It had become increasingly untenable for his father to stay in Italy, on account of an extremely controversial relationship he had recently cultivated:

> Even before Mussolini actually invaded Abyssinia in 1935, it was impossible for my father to stay in Sicily. Haile Selassie had become a friend during the thirteen years Father spent in Abyssinia. He had, improperly perhaps for a diplomat, encouraged Ras Tafari, as he then was, in his revolution against his libertine, syphilitic cousin, Lij Yassu, the regent. Colin had been born in Abyssinia and the Emperor was his godfather.[569]

Quentin maintains that it would have been difficult to find two people more socially ill-equipped than his conservatively minded parents to integrate into this chic and fashionable section of French society.

Quentin's father had previously abandoned an unfulfilling career as a merchant banker in Hong Kong and Shanghai to fight in the Boer

War. He had then chosen to stay in Africa, initially within the South African police force, then as a District Commissioner in British Somaliland, and finally in the Abyssinian consulate. This was, as Quentin explained, a form of existence 'lived mostly out of doors, on horseback or on foot, in wild country'.[570]

Annabel Dodds had experienced in the meantime 'the quiet upbringing of a landowner's daughter'. Quentin clearly attributed her emotionally withdrawn adult demeanour to the way that she had been brought up by her own father (Lord Crewe), following the untimely death of her mother when Annabel was only five:

> She [Annabel] might have expected, as his eldest daughter, to have become my grandfather's hostess, but at her 'coming-out' dance he announced his engagement to someone only a year older than she was. He was a man of few feelings, certainly as far as children were concerned, having, for example, gone abroad on a long journey when he knew that his only son, aged eight and motherless, was dying. It may have been this complete lack of outward affection that inhibited maternal feeling in my mother.[571]

This prior experience of both parents helped to explain why, in Quentin's estimation, neither of them was inclined to mix within the 'smart society' so closely associated with pre-war Rivieran culture — or, indeed, to form friendships with French people, per se.[572] Theirs was a conservative style of life that their second son would consciously and ostentatiously rebel against in subsequent decades.

Chapter Fourteen
Cleanliness is Next to Godliness

Divine and Secular Inspiration

Fryston's history of the early 1930s is dominated by two major developments: the opening of the pithead baths in 1932, and the creation of the Holy Cross Church, one year later, when volunteer labourers – the majority of them Frystoners – used materials extracted from Fryston Hall to help construct this local place of worship. We shall now see how contributions made by two prominent individuals, Jim Bullock and the Reverend John Daly, proved highly inspirational in these developments. The chapter begins by highlighting the rise to prominence of this pair during the late 1920s, and outlining the crucial influence they both had on Fryston's dramatic evolution of the following decade.

Searching for 'A Bit of Heaven'

Once the 1926 lockout was over and the miners returned to work, Jim Bullock and his wife finally moved into their first home on Fryston Road. The house initially contained nothing more than a solitary armchair, a second-hand bed, a table, knives and forks, bedding linen and towels.[573] Bullock resumed working with the Kelsy brothers; but, following 28 weeks of inactivity, he developed a huge carbuncle in the middle of his palm and managed to throw his knee out of joint when slipping at the coalface. Eager to clear debts accruing in the strike, Bullock was forced to carry on working, and resorted to filling coal tubs while leaning against a pit prop. The Kelsys never complained or criticised him for slowing down their progress. In fact, they touchingly 'carried' him until he was injury-free.[574]

Bullock continued to study copiously and soon obtained a colliery deputy's certificate, authorising him to perform such vital tasks as detecting the presence of gases and measuring the quantity of air flow. At Oscar Fisher's invitation, he became a deputy at the tender age of 25:

The manager then gave me a lot of useful advice telling me that I now belonged to them and that I had to have the interests of the company at heart at all times. I had to treat men fairly but firmly. He then gave me a note entitling me to carry a deputy's safety lamp and to carry a deputy's yardstick. This yardstick is used to measure distances and is also used to sound the roof to see whether it is safe. It is also used for inserting powder into shot holes and ramming in the stemming before you fire a shot.[575]

The new appointee ran home to tell his wife that he was now 'on the first rung of the ladder'; but this was only the start of Bullock's meteoric rise: he privately swore he would never go back to being an 'ordinary' miner.[576]

Young Jim and his wife each threw themselves into a variety of village activities. They helped form 'a very amateur dramatic society', for example, with Bullock taking on the role of Ebenezer Scrooge in his own adaptation of *A Christmas Carol*. During this period, Bullock also pressed on with further studies. A mere three years after passing his deputy exams, he became suitably qualified for the role of Fisher's undermanager — the first man from Bowers Row ever to attain this position.[577]

There seemed no limit to Bullock's ambition. He had become increasingly aware of the massive discrepancy between the quality of life he had initially been consigned to and that enjoyed by 'the boss class', as he called them. As he conceded with typical candour,

I was envious. I wanted a bit of heaven down here. I was not content, as my father was, to wait for my eternal reward in heaven. I wanted security of tenure. I wanted a carriage and pair. I wanted holidays with pay, a pension, education for my children and more than anything I wanted the 'house on the hill'.[578]

Ruthless and Domineering

Bullock considered himself fortunate to have originally been mentored by Oscar Fisher. 'He took me under his wing,' the younger man acknowledged, 'and he gave me the full benefit of his many years of mining experience.' However, Fisher also gradually introduced Bullock 'to the other side of those techniques that I had always hated'.[579] Bullock was especially disapproving of Fisher's disdainful and exploitative attitude towards the men: 'He [Fisher] was a good pitman, he was a hard taskmaster, he was loyal to his owners and always maintained that that was where his only loyalty lay.'[580]

As other interviewees confirmed, Fisher projected an intimidating presence:

> He was a huge man: domineering, both physically and mentally. Ruthless with it. In those days, a pit manager was a hard man – he had to be – and that's what Oscar Fisher was. (Ex-Fryston man, 1986)

Such was the personal power he commanded that Fisher could sack or suspend any worker at a stroke, assign him to a harder task, reduce his wages, or even evict the man and his family from their home. With organised trade unionism still reeling from the 1926 lockout, it took a man of exceptional courage to display overt defiance. As Nancy Oxtoby explained in a 1987 interview, her father, Joe Spedding, was one such individual:

> How my dad came to be on the union, I do know because he did talk to me about it. The manager was called Mr Fisher and they used to have to do a job called 'drawing timber off' and my father refused to do it. So, Mr Fisher called him into his office and said, 'Now, Spedding, if you don't draw that timber you can clear off and I'll not set you on till I want to set you on.' But my dad said, 'It's not my job and I'm not supposed to do it,' and off he went. He was out of work through that for nine months.

Apart from the 20 or 30 colleagues who initially laid down their tools in solidarity with Spedding, the wider workforce had no appetite for a strike. Consequently, Spedding turned up to work every day for nine months to be greeted in predictable manner:

> They used to say, 'You can clear off! There's no job for you, Spedding!' But he went in one day and Fisher said, 'Well, I think you've had enough. I'm letting you come back.' But that was the turning point for him – why he became the official. (Nancy Oxtoby, 1987)

Conditions of social and economic austerity, combined with the waning of trade union power, encouraged a particular style of management that Jim Bullock found detestable: 'Kidding, lying, giving wrong impressions, deliberately deceiving men, cheating men, all done by professing Christians was something I just could not understand.' Why was it so difficult, he asked himself, for men and management to be straight with one another and mean exactly what they said?[581]

Old Rugged Cross

It was not long after the Reverend John Daly had been licensed as Priest in Charge of Airedale with Fryston that he first became acquainted with his new parish. As he subsequently recollected:

> Airedale was a red brick housing estate built shortly after the war by the Pontefract Council. It had been well planned along the shoulder of a hill with a square in the centre with shops, a large pub and a fine site which the brewery had given for a Church. Nearby was an Army Hut, one end of which was the cosy little Holy Cross Church and the other end was the Church Hall. There were more shops and another pub, and a cinema further up Fryston Road. There was a fine modern school building. About five thousand lived in Airedale and another five hundred in Townville where the houses were privately owned. It made a good, consolidated parish, easy to visit on a bicycle or on foot with my Scottish sheep dog Rover.[582]

Daly's first strategic move was to enlist the services of his sister, Barbara, who selflessly resigned from her job as a London secretary to join him as his 'housekeeper, secretary and unpaid curate' in his Airedale council house.[583]

The new priest was greeted on his arrival by the intimidating presence of 'a large roughly hewn wooden cross', marking the designated location for a permanent church building to replace the existing temporary construction. Five years had elapsed since the ecclesiastic district had been approved, during which time local people had succeeded in raising £300 towards the building of the new church. The Bishop of Wakefield became more and more insistent that the project must be completed without further delay. As Daly recollects, 'The Bishop left us a free hand, except that we must employ the architect of his choice.

In those days an ecclesiastic district could not become a parish until it had a church large enough for a congregation of 500.'[584]

No-one was more impressed by the newly arriving cleric than Jim Bullock. 'What a wonderful character,' he said of him in *Them and Us*. 'Forceful, upright, a real man's man. Tall, good looking. A man who commanded respect throughout the whole of the village.'[585] As Bullock also emphasised, Daly was a personal friend – and ex-colleague while he worked in London – of the Reverend Philip ('Tubby') Clayton, who was the founder of Toc H, an institution dedicated to applying the skills and expertise of male volunteers to the needs of their neighbourhood and community.

Daly took the decision, shortly after arriving, to form an Airedale branch of Toc H. He subsequently reflected that 'it was in this way that I became adopted into the mining community'.[586] Jim Bullock was among the dozens of local colliery workers who immediately enlisted:

> I joined and I was given the post of 'Job Master'. This was not an easy position to fulfil for everybody had to work for nothing. We did all sorts of jobs. We ran classes for young people in various subjects. We worked for the hospitals. We took old people out on trips. We did gardening and interior decorating for the old people. All this was organized by the Job Master and done by the miners after a full shift down the pit.[587]

Soft Soaping the Workforce

Jim Bullock was not altogether averse to using the type of deceitfulness he purportedly deplored in others to push through potentially unpopular or unpalatable decisions. He candidly admitted that, sometimes, the colliery manager 'uses method that are not strictly according to the book of rules,' adding that, 'if his object is right – and is proved in practice to be right – then the means are proved worthy by the results'.[588] This is the philosophy he employed in his first real task as undermanager – that of overcoming workforce opposition to the introduction of pithead baths at Fryston.

Under the terms of the Mining Industry Act 1926 a one-shilling levy (known as 'The Royalties Welfare Levy') was taken from each ton of coal sold, with the objective of providing pithead baths for each colliery in Britain.[589] A decision was made at national level by the

Miners' Welfare Committee that, to offset any accusations of favouritism, each colliery would be offered (according to alphabetical order) the total funding required to construct pithead baths. As Bullock explained, not all employees were keen to see baths installed as this was contrary to mining tradition. A ballot was therefore undertaken at each colliery. Wherever there was a majority vote in opposition to the proposed scheme, the relevant colliery was automatically relegated to the bottom of the list of possible beneficiaries.[590]

The Fryston management and union committee were united in their determination to see pithead baths installed. The problem was:

> The men did not want them. There was an old faith – not superstition – that bathing every day weakened your back and softened your limbs; that you were more likely to catch cold, these fears were very real. I knew all about these fears. I knew the inconvenience of washing at home, particularly to the miners' wives and families.[591]

Bullock sought to counter this opposition by bringing in medical experts to convince the men that bathing would not weaken their backs, and to persuade them of the merits of leaving any coal dust at the pit 'where it belonged'.[592] This failed to have the desired effect. On the day of the ballot, the union representatives were gathered in Bullock's office, where they had been invited for a drink.

> When the union officials knew how the ballot was going, they were as disappointed as I was. I filled up their glasses, then went into the next room where the count was taking place and told my secretary and his assistants to keep on counting but to count the 'Nays' as 'Yays'. If I didn't tell them as plainly as this I let them know what I wanted to happen. I went back and joined the union committee and later my secretary came into my office proudly bearing the result – two-thirds majority vote in favour – to an inebriated but now jubilant management committee.[593]

On the following day, Fryston miners read Bullock's notice of the outcome with incredulity. Each accused the others of having lied about their intention to vote against. As Bullock subsequently recollected,

They spent all day trying to find out who had voted for it, but I said, 'You're not accusing me of twisting a ballot, are you?' I said, 'Your union committee was there!' Of course, within a fortnight, the ventilation plant broke down and the baths broke down, so the men went home. They said they weren't going to work without a bath! (Interview, 1987)

Pithead Baths for Fryston

A ceremony took place on 16 January 1932 to commemorate the opening of the baths. The *Pontefract and Castleford Express* for 22 January 1932 eulogistically hailed them as 'Practically the finest in Europe.' Its reporter noted that, 'While adding a beautiful architectural feature to the village, they will add immensely to the comfort of the miners who are employed there by the Airedale Collieries, Ltd.'

This novel structure comprised two storeys, each housing a first-aid and ambulance room. The building also incorporated a time office and lamp room. Linking the baths to the colliery's No. 2 shaft was a covered, steam-heated gantry.[594] The new powerhouse, which had been cleared to accommodate the many guests, was packed full of dignitaries, such as the Bishop of Wakefield and the local MPs for Normanton and North Leeds, who sat alongside such familiar figures as the Reverend John Daly, Percy Greaves, Herbert Smith, Jim Bullock, Oscar Fisher and Dr George Sloan.[595]

The opening address was delivered by Hugh F. Smithson, the General Manager of Airedale Collieries, who began by apologising on behalf of Lord Crewe, who had been scheduled to formally open the baths, but was prevented from doing so by illness. Smithson had seen a letter from Crewe to the Chair of Directors 'in which he expressed very sincere regret at not being able to be with them, the reason being that he was laid up with a severe chill, and his doctors would not allow him to go out of the house. It was regrettable having regard to his long association with that particular colliery.'[596]

The privilege of opening the baths was therefore extended to the next speaker, Colonel Lane Fox, who was a former Minister of the Mines. Lane Fox informed his audience that he had already been given a guided tour of the new complex. Having viewed a variety of similar schemes quite recently, he felt justified in declaring that he had never come across anything so complete and impressive as the Fryston installation. The new baths would not only produce 'greater comfort' for those using them directly, but also bring considerable relief to housewives no longer having to scrub pit clothes clean and leave them hanging to dry for hours. In concluding,

> He congratulated the management of the colliery on the part they had been able to take in getting that installation put in, also the local Welfare Committee for the details they had gone into since, and his old friend Mr. Herbert Smith, of the Central Committee, for the large part he was sure he had taken in the matter [...] In declaring the baths open, he hoped they would prove a constant source of encouragement to welfare work, and an example to neighbouring areas to the men who knew their job and were prepared to carry it out.[597]

Votes of thanks were delivered, in turn, by George East, President of the Fryston MFGB branch, and Oscar Fisher. East made a point of thanking the colliery management for the 'tremendous amount of work' they had devoted to implementing a scheme which looked, according to him, like something out of a Jules Verne novel. Fisher reciprocated by thanking local union officials for having helped secure the men's approval of the scheme. Seemingly unaware of Jim Bullock's illicit intervention, Fisher proudly emphasised that, 'When a ballot of the men was taken there was a majority of 3 to 1 in favour, and he believed that was one of the best ballots taken on the matter, showing that their men were strongly in favour of the provision.'[598]

The ceremony was closed by the old MFGB warhorse, Herbert Smith. His speech included the little-known revelation that he had started his career with a brief spell at Fryston Colliery:

> Mr Herbert Smith, replying, said he had been trying to look back to 1874, when he started to work at that colliery. He had seen the colliery pass through many stages, but he had never seen it brighter than it was that day (applause). The baths were more up-to-date than any he had seen. They wanted baths in homes as well as at the pits. They were anxious to go on with this work, and they were not keeping the money locked up unnecessarily, but spending it. The Welfare Committee undertook many different kinds of work and one he was strongly

in favour of was research work to avoid accidents and save life, and everyone would agree that more money still should be spent in this direction.[599]

Rolling Away the Stone

John Daly had, meanwhile, been shrewd enough to realise that the sum raised by local people of £300 was insufficient to finance the building of a church. In casting around for a cheap source of stone, he came across a disused church on the corner of the 'Shambles' in York's city centre, but the Archbishop denied him permission to use it. Then fate appeared to take a hand. One day when he was being given a tour of Fryston Woods by a local Rover Scout, they came across 'a large, derelict manor house', comprising the remains of Fryston Hall.

> I was immediately interested because the stone looked good and we'd obviously got to get some stone if we wanted to build a church. So, I reported it to the Bishop and, a few weeks later, he said, 'You can have it for £300,' which was exactly the amount of money we had managed to raise. Having blown the whole of our £300, we still needed someone to pull the building down. (John Daly, 1986)

Once the purchase had been approved by the Bishop's nominated architect (Sir Charles Nicholson), Daly set about dismantling the building in such a way as to preserve the magnificent pillars (porticos) forming the entrance to the hall.[600] On Easter Monday, 1931, local worshippers conducted a short service in the old Ballroom at Fryston Hall, seeking Divine Blessing for the stone, and those responsible for its deconstruction and removal.[601] Jim Bullock maintains that Daly turned to him to see that the job got done: 'He came down to see me and I took a team of men with blasting material from the pit and blew the whole place up, but we protected the pillars.'[602]

The manager of nearby Glasshoughton Colliery (a Mr Elliott) agreed to provide an old T-Ford Truck, capable of carrying the stone up the hill to Airedale. He also paid for the petrol and driver's wages. When it became necessary for the latter to resume working down the mine, John Daly personally took over the driving:

They were big, big pieces of stone, but we tried to move them without chipping them. Some of them were approaching two tons and we only had a one-ton truck. On one occasion, we were going along with certainly more than one ton on the back and the front wheels came off the ground and our load slid onto the floor! These types of thing tended to happen, but we were generally ok because we took our time. We used over 600 tons of stone, but we also needed to put in 400 tons of reinforced concrete because, as they explained, the church needed to be built on a 'raft' as the coal had been taken away underneath. For this we needed broken brick. Again, Mr Elliott sent me a chit saying they were going to lower a 100ft chimney and we could take what we wanted as long as we looked sharp about it. (John Daly, 1986)

Once again, Jim Bullock volunteered his services and those of other colleagues. It was Bullock who also provided a brick-crushing machine. Each morning, after mass, but before breakfast, Daly would drive off to collect a ton of bricks from Glasshoughton, before depositing them at Fryston to be broken up for the foundations.[603] There were no limits, Jim Bullock maintained, to Father Daly's resourcefulness:

The vicar went round all the pits and building yards begging old girders, borrowing cement mixers and lorries. I understand he even sacrificed six months of his own salary in advance to pay for materials we needed – a truly wonderful character – he really did know how to get the best out of people.[604]

'The Church's One Foundation'
Bullock also recollected how John Daly had turned up at a Toc H meeting and requested that local miners engage in the digging out of the foundations for the new project.[605] The first sod was dug out by Oscar Fisher in February 1932, after which local women and children all pitched in with commendable enthusiasm.[606] Bullock duly arranged for teams of Fryston miners to work on successive shifts. One such group (of cement mixers) consisted of six of the 'roughest' and 'strongest' men in the pit. Fortunately, as Bullock explained, 'John Daly didn't mind my miners swearing, what he wanted was to get some work out of them – and he did.'[607] Once the foundations had been laid, an invitation was despatched to Lord

Crewe, asking if he would do local people the honour of laying the altar stone.

'Stone By Stone, A Hall Becomes A Church' was the headline accompanying the report by the *Pontefract and Castleford Express* (24 March 1933) on the events of the previous Saturday, when Lord Crewe obligingly laid the altar stone, as requested. This Holy Cross Church was being built, of course, from materials emanating from his former ancestral home. It was, as the *Express* put it, 'a day of reminiscences', adding that many of those in the audience could 'remember the old days at Fryston Hall, the Christmas parties and the Bible classes held there'.[608]

The laying of the stone was preceded by a short service. Aside from Lord Crewe, the ceremony was attended by: the Bishops of Wakefield and Pontefract; officials of Airedale Collieries; the Mayor and Mayoress of Pontefract; and companies of Girl Guides and Boy Scouts. Following the singing of the hymn, 'The Church's One Foundation' (set to music provided by the St John's Ambulance Brigade) and the offering of prayers, the altar stone was blessed by the Bishop of Wakefield. The Bishop marvelled that the stone, which had been extracted from Fryston Colliery's Beeston Seam, was in the region of 500 million years old.[609]

Lord Crewe was presented with a mallet, which he then used to lay the stone, 'in the faith of Jesus Christ our Lord [...] that here true worship may for ever be offered, and true faith, with brotherly love, may for ever flourish and abound'.[610] He commenced his speech by casting his mind back, some 60 years ago, when his parents lived at Fryston Hall and he had the pleasure of cutting the first sod for the new Fryston Colliery. In turning to the present day, he glowingly observed that:

> Nothing was more striking or admirable than the way in which the people of Airedale had interested themselves in the scheme for the new church and had worked very hard for its erection. The church, when complete, would be an enduring monument of what could be done by the efforts of the many. The times had gone when churches could be built through the generosity of individuals, but the Airedale Church would be no less worthy and no less holy because it represented numbers rather than individuals. Times had changed from the days when the valley

of the Aire was one long stretch of smiling country, and salmon could be caught in the river. Those days seemed almost as remote as the days of Oliver Cromwell and the Battle of Marston Moor. One thing had not changed, however, and that was the spiritual need of mankind. It was to satisfy those needs that the church was to be built, and he hoped to fulfil its purposes.[611]

In thanking his lordship, the Bishop of Wakefield declared that this was a singularly happy occasion. 'Nothing could be more fitting,' he confidently stated, 'than that stones so rich in English literature should be preserved and sanctified, and become the spiritual home of the people.'[612] The Bishop applauded the ordinary people of Fryston and Airedale for all the hard work and financial generosity they had committed to this project, and heartily complimented the Reverend Daly for the 'inspiring leadership' he had exhibited. The Bishop thought it 'fitting' that the altar stone should have been excavated from Fryston Colliery: 'It was perhaps millions of years old, and would remind them of the One Eternal Father. The name "Holy Cross" spoke of sacrifice, and the building was being erected by the sacrifice of working people in very hard times.'[613] Then, once the ceremony was over,

> Lord Crewe was surrounded by residents, and appeared to enjoy his chats with the old people. He also joined the company who took tea in the Airedale Council School, and again chatted freely of former days. He left to the accompaniment of hearty cheers.[614]

Mission Accomplished

The completion of the project proved even more arduous than anticipated. It had first been necessary to strengthen the foundations by employing countless yards of steel rods to offset the risk of subsidence posed by underlying worked-out coal seams.[615] Daly had set on an unemployed former bricklayer, George Westerman, to perform and oversee the actual building of the church. Since October 1932, four further workers (a combination of stone masons and site labourers) had been signed up to hasten the completion of the foundations and assist in the stone and brick work. One day, as Daly explained,

> George told me that the wall was getting too high for them to lift the stone and proposed that I should ask my sister to donate

the front wheel of her bicycle; it was with that, as a pulley wheel, that the whole church was built. Many minor miracles accompanied the building: we were never overdrawn at the bank; a firm saved us hundreds of pounds by lending us tubular scaffolding on the understanding that we could return it to their warehouse within two weeks of their recall; they recalled it two years later, ten days before we had completed the work. When all was done, we found that there was just enough stone left to build a surrounding wall. No one was hurt and we never had a strike![616]

The Holy Cross Church was finally consecrated on 14 July 1934. With the project now completed, Daly received a call, one year later, from the Bishop of Rhodesia (now Zimbabwe), inviting him to become one of his mission priests. Excited by the prospect of a new challenge, Daly wrote to the Bishop of Wakefield, seeking his permission to leave Airedale.

He surprised me by replying that he did not think that I should, but that I must go to see him in a fortnight's time. Meanwhile coming home one very cold morning from the Daily Eucharist in our new church I saw a pile of letters on the breakfast table. My sister remarked, 'There is an envelope there marked Lambeth Palace, I expect the Archbishop wants to make you a Bishop!' and we both laughed. The letter had been written by the Archbishop's Senior Chaplain, who had been my theological college chaplain. It started 'Dear John, I'm afraid that I am going to put a bomb under your chair.' He continued that I was summoned to London to see the Archbishop who was considering me as the first bishop of a new diocese in West Africa. And so it was that in 1935 I was consecrated and sent to the Gambia with my first Mitre.[617]

Daly's consecration as Bishop of Gambia and the Rio Pongos, at the age of 32, made him the youngest person in the Anglican Communion ever to achieve that status. He subsequently became Bishop of Accra in 1951 and of Korea in 1955, and the first-ever Bishop of Taejon in 1965.[618] A heart-warming acknowledgement of the fabulous legacy bequeathed by Daly to the residents of Fryston, Townville and Airedale was subsequently proffered by his old friend, Jim Bullock, who wrote:

John Daly has gone to a much bigger job – he is now a bishop – but as long as ever Holy Cross church in Airedale stands it will be a testimony to John Daly, for without his vision and his drive it would never have been built. It is also a testimony to hundreds of miners, to some colliery managers and to many other people who did what they could to help him in this wonderful project. Wherever John Daly is I am sure he will never forget the days he spent at Airedale or the friends he made while he was there.[619]

Chapter Fifteen

Pre-War Village Heyday

Stalwarts, Past and Present

The 1930s was a decade in which the curtain finally came down on a period of intense industrial conflict, exemplified by the General Strike and Lockout of 1926. As if to mark the closure of this era, the deaths occurred of two heroic stalwarts of the strike – one known nationally, the other locally. The first section of this chapter dwells on the passing of these two historically significant figures.

The same decade was equally noteworthy for seminal local developments which would help shape the experience of Fryston people, both in the armed services and on the 'home front', during the coming global conflict of 1939-45. We focus, by way of illustration, on the adolescent and early adult lives of two romantically entwined Fryston individuals whose singular wartime exploits in the armed services are described in Chapter 18.

The current chapter also continues to trace the progress of two Fryston men (Jabie Foulkes and Jim Bullock) already featuring prominently in this volume. The exploits of these individuals – one in pre-war professional football, the other in realising his lifelong ambition to become colliery manager – would also prove pivotal to significant developments in wartime Fryston and in the aftermath of military conflict.

'Lest the Humble Perish'

The tragic death in 1936 of the seemingly ever-present village butcher, George ('Cuddy') Bateson, was due to an act of suicide, in which he cut his own throat with a knife normally used for severing and trimming meat. Cuddy was discovered at approximately 11am on the day in question, along a small, tree-lined valley, beside the River Aire. Fryston-born David Rotherforth was one of two local youths who first came across the butcher's corpse, which was sat, propped up against a willow tree. Rotherforth and his close friend, Tommy Bailey, had been making their way to the river, when their shocking discovery unfolded:

> We were just about to go through this gully down to t' riverside. Tommy were about ten yards in front of me and he gets through t' bushes and says, 'Oh, bloody hell, Dave! Look here!' He said, 'Old Cuddy's nearly cut his bloody head off!' I said, 'I don't want to see it! I'm off!' Well, Tommy went and reported it to t' police. Course, he hadn't far to go. First house on Brook Street were t' bobby's house. (Interview, 1987)

Some claimed, with the benefit of hindsight, to have witnessed Bateson steadfastly preparing to kill himself. One Fryston man had been in the butcher's shop with his mother, earlier that morning, when they saw Cuddy assiduously sharpening his knives. Bateson's wife subsequently disclosed how, a few hours beforehand, her husband had been dismayed to discover that a delivery of meat was badly infected by tuberculosis:

> His wife told me that she was cutting some stew-meat up for their dinner and she said to her niece, 'Annie, where's that sharp knife?' She said, 'I don't know.' Well, somebody came in then and said, 'I've just seen Cuddy going over to Brook Street.' But she thought no more about it; she just thought he'd gone collecting money off people who'd been 'ticking' with him. Anyway, half-an-hour later, a knock came at the door and Mrs Pilkington said her son-in-law had found him and she'd gone and thrown a pinnie [apron] over his body. They said it was over this beast — with it being so full of TB. (Fryston woman, 1986)

Complementary accounts emphasise that Bateson was already suffering from clinical depression at the time — perhaps related to the presence of crippling arthritis in his wrists and elbows (which he tried to relieve by drinking rum or whisky), or on account of his daughter's severe learning disability. Local folklore dictates that 'Cuddy stayed in character to the end. They say he even had the dignity to fold his knives away in the cloth after he'd cut his throat' (ex-Fryston woman, 1986). Few would have put it past him.

Two years later, on 16 June 1938, the venerable ex-president of the MFGB, Herbert Smith, died unexpectedly, confounding recent assumptions that he was in robust health. Smith's personal fortunes had oscillated throughout the 1930s. He stood, albeit unsuccessfully, for the MFGB presidency in 1931 and 1932. The esteem and affection in which he was held by fellow miners was nonetheless reaffirmed in 1931 when the 'Herbert Smith Testimonial' fund paid for the unveiling of a bust within the Miners' Hall at Barnsley, with surplus money being donated to a housing project for aged miners, to be named in his honour.[620]

Smith's biographer reflected that, of all his subject's many virtues, it was his constant readiness to become personally involved whenever mining disaster and tragedy occurred that set him apart from others.[621] Most recently, Smith and the future Yorkshire Miners' Association President, Joe Hall, both attended the Wharncliffe Woodmoor explosion of 1936 in which 56 lives were lost. Smith was participating in a Miners' International Congress in faraway Prague on the day in question. He received a wire that same afternoon, informing him of the tragedy.

> At six o'clock the next morning he and [Joe Hall] landed by plane in Yorkshire. At nine o'clock that morning they were down the mine. When one remembers that Herbert Smith was, at this time, seventy-four years of age, his vitality and energy seem amazing. This tireless driving power was characteristic of him to the last hour of his life.[622]

Smith had spoken prophetically of his death in a speech delivered in Pontefract, on 15 June 1938, to celebrate the creation of a new miners' banner. Shortly after breakfast on the following day, he set off to cast his vote in favour of the local Labour Party candidate in the general election. 'That done,' Lawson explained, 'he returned to his office, sat down in his chair – and died. When he was found his diary lay open before him, with a list of engagements for the day.'[623] Lawson writes touchingly and elegiacally of the way in which 'The Man in the Cap' was honoured by the society he served:

> His body was carried to Castleford – as he desired – where he had worked in earlier years. It was the day of the Yorkshire Miners' Demonstration, but instead of carrying banners to a great meeting, they carried them behind their great leader. All along the 20-mile route from Barnsley to Castleford, miners at collieries joined the procession. Schoolchildren lined the roads.

Crowds were massed behind them. All the industries and professions were represented. All ranks of society followed Herbert Smith when he went back to his old colliery for his first and final rest. For he was one of the most valiant of a valiant generation of workers' champions. He was the unique product of an age that has passed, but of that character which must live lest the humble perish.[624]

There was no such official commemoration for Cuddy Bateson, except for a well-attended and dignified funeral service and burial. A local myth endures that, at the foot of the willow tree which the butcher chose as his final resting place, springtime flowers perennially adorn the patch of earth where Cuddy's blood was spilled – nature's way, perhaps, of thanking him on behalf of 'the humble' he once famously refused to let perish.

Village Sweethearts

The 1930s represented a heyday in the history of Fryston village. A vivid taste of daily life in this close-knit, socially vibrant and self-sufficient village is contained in the adolescent and early adult experience of two members of established Fryston families, Bill Spedding and Frances Griffiths, who developed a strong romantic attachment during this economically challenging era.

Spedding was born in the back-to-back dwelling of 18 Oxford Street, where he, his parents and siblings lodged with a family called Moseley. He was one of three brothers and four sisters whose father had travelled widely before eventually settling in Fryston. 'I'm a bit vague about when my dad first came to Fryston,' Spedding conceded.

> I do know that he used to keep a chest upstairs that he and his brothers had when they were in Canada. I understand they worked on a horse farm. Then they came back to Workington where he was born. That was a depressed area and he came here looking for work. There was a short period where our Mary and myself went back to Cumbria to go to school there, but we came back to Fryston a few months later. (Interview, 1987)

Frances Griffiths's father was a Welshman, who initially lodged in Fryston with his oldest sister, Mrs Morgan. *His* father (Frances's grandfather) was among those killed in the Gresford pit disaster of 22 September 1934. Frances's mother came from a relatively well-established Fryston family which originally arrived from Lancashire. Frances was the eldest of nine children (four brothers and five sisters). She, too, lived in one of the back-to-back terraces comprising the 'low buildings' – in her case, Castle Street.

Spedding left school when he was fourteen years old. His employment options were limited and career trajectory virtually preordained. 'Scholarships were rare,' he shrugged.

> You were lucky to be considered. That wasn't the criterion, anyway. When you were like us, you didn't look to the future: you had to be finding a job and I started at Fryston Pit. School broke up and they let me start a couple of weeks before I was fourteen. The day I started was the day before they opened the baths in 1932. That big lamp in the 'Bullring' [to commemorate the opening of the pit-head baths] is a constant reminder for me! I felt so proud of starting, I walked round the village in my pit muck! (Interview, 1987)

Frances Griffiths's school career was regularly interrupted each time her mother gave birth to one of her eight younger siblings. 'Every time that Nurse Box came into the village,' she chuckled ironically, 'I used to say, "I hope you're not coming to our flaming house!"' (interview, 1987). Her after-school chores were even more arduous.

> I used to have to take a note to school. When it became dusk at four o'clock, with my dad working I had to get up and feed t' pigs: two buckets of potato peelings strapped to my shoulders. Can you imagine that, with the size of me? Potato peelings and what they called 'sharps' – a kind of bran. I used to have to carry this, and it was quite a walk to where t' allotments were, down towards Water Fryston. And I used to have to stop at t' tap and run water into it and mix it with my hands. Mind you, I used to love doing that! And my three younger sisters wouldn't believe me, and my three younger brothers weren't old enough to do owt like that. I just happened to be t' eldest in t' family. They used to let me out of school early to go and feed my father's pigs. Mrs Rickaby used to have a down on me because of that! (Interview, 1987)

Leisure relations were similarly gender demarcated. Having emerged from the pit baths, Spedding and his male colleagues would stand talking at the top of the street. 'And after you'd had your supper,' he recalled, 'you might do the same again. Either that or you might go for a walk, half-a-dozen of you' (interview, 1987). Griffiths would likewise spend her leisure time in the company of other women. For example,

> There was a place in Fryston, women and children used to go to it on Monday nights. They called it 'Sunshine Corner' and it was where they'd have their little gatherings. There was a song: 'Sunshine Corner, oh it's jolly fine/It's for children under 99/All are welcome/Seats are given free/Fryston Sunshine Corner is the place for me.' (Interview, 1987)

The self-sufficient character of Fryston village was exemplified in the 1930s by the presence during this and subsequent decades of a thriving local economy. In addition to the home-made toffee apples, sweets, cakes, scones, vinegar and 'pop' (home-made fruit cordials) peddled by other village residents, Frances Griffiths's own auntie sold delicious, home-made meat pies that villagers used to queue up for every Saturday, and baked traditional oat-cakes which people ate with bacon and eggs for breakfast. Griffiths recalled how this economy was enriched by a regular influx of outside entrepreneurs:

> All t' street traders used to come round on their horses and carts, each with their own character. It was an event when they came round, especially for t' kids. Roundabouts or 'joy rides', fish, fruit and vegetables; all the lot. There used to be a chap come round selling 'finney' haddock and that, called Mr Fairey. Old Joe Crowther used to bring vegetables from out of Wheldon Lane. Then the highlight of the lot for t' kids were Bill Grundy's hot pies from Airedale. They used to bring 'em in a big barrow with like a tub in the middle. There was one bloke used to sell paraffin, which he brought from Sagar Street in Castleford. You could get a can of paraffin for tuppence. (Interview, 1987)

The romance between Bill Spedding and Frances Griffiths had begun when they were childhood sweethearts. Their relationship was soon taken for granted by most of their immediate relatives. As Frances recalled, 'Bill's mother used to say to me, "Will you look after our Billy's supper for me while I go up to our Ada's?" That was her sister's. We used to stand talking long before then' (interview, 1987). Not everyone in the family was approving of their courtship. 'I've had many a good hiding off my dad for it,' said Frances. '"Home!" he'd say. "He'll do you no good." That was from just leaving school and yet I was 25 and he was 27 when we got married.' This called for a slightly furtive approach which left Bill vulnerable to a rival for Frances's affection:

> I'd spend some hours at what we called 'top of t' street' where the Bullring is in Fryston, opposite t' pit baths, when Bill was on afternoons. I'd stand up there and I could see him pass this window where he'd be coming down the steps. He always had a cloth cap on and – I can see it now – that checked scarf he used to wear, just thrown around his neck! And I used to get serenaded while I was waiting for Bill: a lad called Georgie Dean – 'Dixie Dean' we used to call him – from Brotherton. He was a lovely singer, and he knew that I adored Bing Crosby. If he came out of the baths before Bill, Dixie used to come over talking to me and start singing in that nice voice of his. I used to tease my Bill, I did: 'Oh, I've been serenaded while I've been waiting!' (Interview, 1987)

It was during the early stages of their relationship that Frances first became aware of her suitor's talent for sketching portraits. 'I'll tell you when I first noticed Bill's drawing,' she recollected.

> I was only thirteen or fourteen and he'd drawn a portrait of Alice Faye, who was his favourite film star at that time. I used to go up to their house every night and, when I saw this drawing, I started daubing her hair with this bit of yellow paint. Bill wrote underneath it – he'd already signed his own name – 'Painted by Miss Frances Griffiths.' He didn't want people to think he'd done it and he was mad as hell because she was his favourite star! (Interview, 1987)

Spedding remained steadfastly self-effacing about this talent, insisting that he could not be considered 'an artist'. 'I just seemed to have a good eye for picking a photograph out,' he modestly insisted. 'Probably, there's a bit of artistic ability comes in there because I can look at a dozen photographs and maybe pick out only three that I want to draw.' He maintained that his skills were more in keeping with those of a draughtsman. 'I have a really good eye for perspective and proportion,' he maintained, 'and putting that photo on that piece of paper' (interview, 1987). Little did he and Frances imagine that, as the 1940s beckoned, Bill's talent for drawing would help sustain him when the pair subsequently become separated by war.

Which One Was Matthews?

Important wartime and post-war developments in Fryston's history were signposted by events occurring in the unfolding professional career of the village-born Jabie Foulkes. It had not taken Foulkes too long, on leaving the village, to discover that Huddersfield Town already had a surfeit of top-quality outside-rights (some of them established internationals) when he first joined them. With his career prospects therefore restricted, he was given a free transfer to Stockport County of Division Three (North) in the summer of 1932. It was at this point that he linked up with the club's greatest ever goal scorer, Alf Lythgoe.[625]

Both players made their debuts in the 1932-33 season, in which Foulkes scored seven goals in 36 appearances, and the more prolific Lythgoe nineteen in 20. The two goals they each scored in Stockport's amazing 8-5 home win against Chester marked the high point of a season in which 'County' achieved a highly respectable third place in their division. The club then attained the equivalent position in 1933-34, a season in which the ever-present Foulkes scored thirteen goals, and Lythgoe a phenomenal 46. Their most notable occasion occurred when Foulkes scored once, but laid on four other goals, in Stockport's record-breaking 13-0 home win against Halifax Town on 6 January 1934.[626]

Alf Lythgoe's transfer to Huddersfield Town early in the 1934-35 season predated a predictable dip in County's form. The club slipped to seventh in the league, but Foulkes had good reason to remember one game in particular – in January 1935: 'The most important goal I ever scored was against West Ham in an FA Cup tie when they were in t' First Division and we were in t' third. It was an equaliser three minutes from time at Upton Park. And we beat 'em one-nowt in the replay' (interview, 1986).

Stockport finished a healthy fifth position in Foulkes's final season with the club. His personal contribution of four goals in 30 league appearances was curtailed by a chronic shoulder injury. Had it not been for this physical setback, Foulkes would have signed for Second Division Manchester United in November 1936. The ex-Frystoner was taken on, instead, by Second Division Bradford Park Avenue, although the appearances he made for them during his two-season stay were heavily restricted by his shoulder impediment.[627]

This injury did not prevent him playing a starring role in Park Avenue's historic 2-1 FA Cup Fourth Round victory over Stoke City in the 1937-38 season — a game played in front of 31,000 people. By common consensus, Foulkes completely overshadowed the opposition right-winger, none other than the legendary Stanley Matthews. 'Next day,' Foulkes recalled, 'the *Daily Herald* said, "Which one was Matthews?" Mind you, I did play a blinder that day.' It was an all-too-brief encounter: 'I never met him to talk to; just to shake hands on the pitch,' Foulkes continued. 'Then we went off to Roker [Park] where Sunderland beat us one-nowt' (interview, 1986).

During his brief spell at Bradford, Foulkes had sufficient time to acquaint himself with another all-time great, the mercurially entertaining Len Shackleton. 'Shack was only a kid then,' he remembered:

> He used to come and train with us at Bradford. He would have been at Bradford Grammar School, I think. He went to Arsenal first off; then, according to form, he got homesick and returned home to Bradford. He had it, then — that touch of class — even when he was a kid. (Interview, 1986)

Foulkes spent an injury-ridden season (1938-39) with nearby Halifax Town, and played three matches for Crewe Alexandra the season after, before his professional career was terminated by war. This distinguished career coincided with a correspondingly undistinguished era in the history of Fryston Colliery FC. The club fared only moderately during the 1930s, failing to lift a single trophy (with the exception of a league title in 1929-30), though playing in the modest environments of the Castleford and District League, followed by the newly formed Pontefract

League. Between 1937 and 1942, Fryston failed to enter any of the local football leagues.[628]

As we shall soon see, the wartime and post-war resurrection of Fryston Colliery FC would become closely associated with a renewal of the club's relationship with Jabie Foulkes and his brother, Dick, and with its strengthening ties with Bradford Park Avenue. The nurturing and enthusiastic attitude of the newly installed Fryston Colliery Manager, Jim Bullock, would also prove fundamental to this process.

The Key to the Door

It was in the pre-war year of 1938 that Bullock finally achieved his twin-objectives of becoming manager of Fryston Colliery and obtaining the key to the door to the much-coveted 'house on the hill'. This was a considerable accomplishment on his part. Bullock had been told informally a few months earlier that, were he to obtain his First-Class [Managerial] Certificate, there was a good chance that he would be invited to take over as manager from Oscar Fisher. Spurred on by this incentive, Bullock spent four nights per week at night school. He also received the crucial advice and support of his Colliery Overman and Bachelor of Science, Ernest Mason, who gave him private tuition at weekends.

Bullock had only one year in which to complete a three-year course. As the final examinations grew near, his wife was on hand to provide post-midnight cups of coffee and occasionally apply cold towels to his head. It was a brutally taxing regime:

> Remember that all this time, I was up at four-thirty in the morning, looking after a big pit, and was doing all the studying in addition to this work and by the time I sat for the examination I was practically a nervous wreck. But, my goodness, I knew my stuff and I can say that I literally blinded the First Class Certificate and within six months of having got it I'd become the manager of Fryston Colliery.[629]

The young man was understandably delighted by this stunning achievement. 'In every truth,' he maintained, 'I'd landed "the house on the hill". I'd got, and become, everything I had set out to be.'[630] But this promotion did come at a cost: Bullock soon discovered that the job of colliery manager was one of the most difficult and exhausting in British industry. 'I know of no job,' he wrote, 'so arduous, carrying such responsibility, with such dire penalties if things go wrong, with such little reward – materially – when things go right.'[631] This was especially true in the case of explosions or disasters where, according to Bullock, the pit manager inevitably 'stands in the dock, like a criminal, a lonely figure, with his critics gathering like vultures to destroy him'.[632]

Bullock also discovered that, on becoming colliery manager, he had not only widened the social distance between himself and ordinary mining families, but also been left floundering on the margins of the social class he had ostensibly just joined.

> There was a distinct dividing line, particularly for the boss's children. If you sent them to an ordinary school, they had it a bit rough because everybody knew they were the boss's kids. The miners didn't sort of fancy going out with the boss's daughter and the owners were a bit too good for her, so she weren't quoted as a prospective marriage partner; she was in a sort of marriage no-man's-land. I mean, they doffed their caps. I always remember that, when I was first made undermanager, my name immediately changed without me asking to 'Mr Bullock' and, when you got to manager, 'Sir' was added to it. (Interview, 1987)

We have already seen that Bullock's desire to occupy the house on the hill was driven, not solely by the prospect of sharing the 'coach and horses' lifestyle associated with the bosses. He also felt that he 'could do more for my own people as a colliery manager'.[633] He explained in one television documentary how, in the process of rising from pony lad to colliery manager, he had been forced to cultivate an 'elasticity of conscience', in such a way as to persuade himself, let alone others, 'that I could do far more good staying in this village, and far more good for t' Labour Party as a manager speaking on a socialist platform than I could as a trade union leader speaking on socialism'.[634]

The new pit manager felt sure that his longstanding relationship with local miners would work to his advantage:

> You see, I'd seen my grandfather when he was very old. I'd seen my father when he was very old. I'd had a brother killed down the pit; I saw the distress it brought into our house. I was

a different type of manager because I'd come from the ranks. I'd known what it was like to work in this hot pit 'bollock naked' like they were. I'd worked with them, I'd worked among them; I'd 'deputied' over them, been undermanager, assistant manager, manager. They knew this. (Interview, 1987)

He thus strove to maintain a close and consistent rapport with his followers, and consciously employed such devices as his inherent sociability, knowledge of all sports, and ability to reel off gripping and humorous anecdotes, to win over his workers' co-operation. Sometimes, though (as in the case of the pithead baths ballot, referred to earlier), his methods contradicted the principles he espoused. Responding to the charge that he occasionally adopted an autocratic style, he unashamedly declared:

Well, when I first went there, it needed it. We were given six weeks to either alter the ventilation or shut the pit. And I found out early on that one man could do more by himself in ten minutes than a committee could do in a fortnight. So, I used to do it and consult them afterwards. (Interview, 1987)

Local sentiments towards Jim Bullock were cautiously ambiguous. 'He was a pretty straight fellow, was Jim,' is how one ex-Fryston miner described him. 'He called a spade a spade, but you knew where you stood with him. Not all sections liked him because of it' (interview, 1986). Another ex-miner expanded on the complex nature of Bullock's relationship with the men:

Bullock was this kind of man: if you showed you were with him, he'd stick with you through thick or thin. If you were against him, then he was definitely against you — in a cool, rather than nasty, sort of way. Unfortunately, you could get yourself a bad name with people who weren't with Bullock: you were a 'boss's man'. In fact, to be a boss's man you were called upon to make far more sacrifices than any of the name-callers. But I'll say this: you don't see that sort of loyalty from a manager now. Bullock would go down the pit and know every man by name. He'd talk to them about their families — if there was a baby born yesterday, he'd know all about it. There was never any *love* for him, but there was no shortage of loyalty and respect. (Interview, 1986)

Needless to add, Jim Bullock was destined to play a central role in the most notable developments occurring in Fryston, both in the context of the forthcoming war, and in the peacetime era that followed.

Chapter Sixteen

Storm Clouds Gathering

Looming Global Conflict

During the remaining years of the 1930s, two lavish ceremonials (in the form of a Crewe family wedding and the coronation of a new king) gave way to looming global conflict as fascism threatened to disrupt the existing world order. In the first two sections of this chapter, we review events surrounding the marriage of Lord and Lady Crewe's daughter, Mary, and the crowning, after much national controversy, of George VI. Subsequent sections then examine the experience of two of Lord Crewe's grandsons as they encountered the rise of fascism while each studying abroad. A final section follows the experience of a Jewish German medical student who was forced to take refuge in Great Britain, where she was to embark on a new domestic and professional life in a now-familiar West Yorkshire mining village.

The 'Society Wedding of the Year'

On 24 October 1935, the 'society wedding of the year' took place when 20-year-old Mary Crewe-Milnes was married in Westminster Abbey to 22-year-old George Innes-Ker, the 9th Duke of Roxburghe. The couple had become engaged the previous June when the young Duke had presented his wife-to-be with an opulent ring from Cartier, incorporating two pear-shaped diamonds.[635] Mary was, of course, the 'beautiful and glamorous' daughter of the Crewes, while 'Bobo', as he was known by his friends, was the Scottish landowner of an 80,000-acre estate.[636] Having recently graduated from Sandhurst into the Royal Horse Guards, the Duke was reputed to be 'perhaps the best shot in the kingdom'.[637]

A post-wedding ball was held at Crewe House. The service itself and subsequent reception were deemed of such national significance to warrant being screened in cinemas across the country. The *British*

Movietone broadcast of 28 October 1935 ('Ducal Wedding at the Abbey', by Beryl De Querton) summarised the occasion thus:

> One of the most brilliant events of the season, the wedding at Westminster Abbey by special permission of the King of Lady Mary Crewe-Milnes to the Duke of Roxburghe! The bride arrives with her father, the Marquess of Crewe, and there's a huge crowd, mostly women, waiting to see the happy pair leave the Abbey. The bridegroom is 22 and a second Lieutenant in the Royal Horse Guards. His bride of 20 is now the youngest duchess in the land, and both are godchildren of the King and Queen. They drive away to the reception at Crewe House, which was attended by Her Majesty. A feature of the wedding was the bridal retinue – one of the biggest ever seen at the Abbey, for there were fourteen bridesmaids.

Subsequently, Crewe House was used to a much lesser extent as a venue for such lavish entertainment. Lord Crewe agreed to a request by the National Art Collections Fund in 1936 to allow public viewings of family portraits and other works adorning the walls of the building. One year later, the Crewe family moved into Argyll House on the King's Road, Chelsea, and sold off Crewe House to Thomas Tilling Ltd, a well-established bus company which had recently branched out into construction work.[638]

High Constable of England

A constitutional crisis had meanwhile been raging, relating to the fact that the reigning British monarch, King Edward VIII, had refused to yield to political, religious and legal pressure by insisting on marrying the American divorcée, Wallis Simpson. By now, Lord Crewe was leading 'the dignified life of a trusted elder statesman, an old man universally respected and consulted frequently'.[639] It therefore came as no surprise when, during the early stages of the crisis, the Prime Minister, Stanley Baldwin, wrote to him, saying, 'I should be very grateful if I might consult you as an old servant of the King on a very private matter in which your counsel would be of great value.'[640]

Crewe responded proactively. Baldwin was subsequently told by Lord Salisbury of a plan to send a delegation of 'elder statesmen no longer involved in everyday politics' to inform the King that they would resign their membership of the Privy Council unless he agreed to choose between the Throne and Mrs Simpson. Baldwin saw the five men involved (Lords Crewe, Derby, Fitzalan and Salisbury himself, along with Sir Austen Chamberlain) for an hour-long meeting on 17 November 1936, when they told him of their 'great perturbation at the information which had reached them concerning the King's intentions'.[641]

It is impossible to say how far the political pressure exerted by Crewe and his like-minded colleagues helped steer the eventual course of history. All we can say with certainty is that the crisis was finally resolved when, in December 1936, Edward chose to abdicate, rather than terminate his romance. He was replaced as monarch by his younger brother, who succeeded him to the throne as King George VI on 11 December 1936, three days before his 41st birthday.[642]

Three days after succeeding to the throne, the new King delivered a hand-written message to the House of Lords, which was read out by the Earl of Cromer, The King acknowledged therein that the circumstances in which he was succeeding his brother were unprecedented and that he was doing so at a time of great personal distress. He confessed to finding great solace in the good will and sympathy of all his subjects; and promised that he would endeavour, with God's help and the support of the Queen Consort, 'to uphold the honour of the Realm and to promote the happiness of My peoples'.[643]

The King's written message followed the time-honoured custom of communicating to Parliament in this way. It was equally customary for Parliament to respond without delay, confirming all Members' devotion to the new King and Queen. In keeping with this convention, the Lord Privy Seal, Viscount Halifax, replied that it was 'good augury' that George VI was succeeding to the throne as a 'second son', just like his father before him. As with his father, 'the King's first service was as a sailor, in which capacity he shared the fortunes of the Grand Fleet at Jutland, and like his father, most especially, he has been privileged to know the happiness of an ideal marriage and the background of a perfect home life'.[644]

Next to speak was Lord Crewe (re-elected in 1936 as Leader of the Liberal Opposition in the House), who wholeheartedly supported the Motion on behalf of the Liberal peers while endorsing Halifax's optimism:

I agree altogether with what fell from the noble Viscount opposite that it can be no disadvantage to His Majesty that he attained his present age as a younger son of the Royal House. It was certainly no disadvantage to his illustrious father, though his experience of it was somewhat shorter. We must all feel, I think, that it will stand the King in good stead that he has been able, in a simple and informal way, to see much of the condition of some of those of his subjects who do not belong to the prosperous classes; and we feel, with the noble Viscount opposite, that he will be assisted in his work by the presence of his Queen, who has already earned such esteem and regard, even outside her own native land of Scotland. Also, we know that both Sovereigns will find the example and the help of Her Majesty Queen Mary of perpetual assistance in the arduous task to which they have been called. I join with the noble Viscount opposite in hoping – and I am sure Parliament and the whole nation hope – that his Majesty King George will have before him many birthdays, in health and happiness and in a peaceful world.[645]

The Coronation of King George VI and Queen Elizabeth took place at Westminster Abbey on 12 May 1937. The Duchess of Roxburghe's 'striking deportment' and dark good looks' were in evidence once more, when she was one of four duchesses (alongside those of Buccleuch, Norfolk and Rutland), chosen to carry the Queen's train.[646] Also present was Cynthia Colville, who enjoyed 'the added personal excitement' of watching her father (Lord Crewe) occupy the role of Lord High Constable of England (with his grandson, Colin, acting as his page). Cynthia was clearly aware of the immense constitutional significance of her father's role in the proceedings:

This office carries, I believe, supreme authority and command over all the forces of the realm, so that it is thought too dangerous to be held for longer than a few hours by any individual and is therefore only conferred for the actual day of the Coronation. Queen Mary was present in full State, with her Mistress of the Robes, Lord Chamberlain and all her Household in attendance on her.[647]

Winds of Change

The optimism evoked by these ceremonial events was soon tempered by sobering developments arising elsewhere in Europe, related to the growing threat to world peace posed by the rise of fascism in Adolf Hitler's Nazi Germany. Such developments were witnessed, first-hand, by two of Lord Crewe's grandsons, Jock Colville and Terence O'Neill, while they were each studying abroad.

On leaving school in the spring of 1933, Colville had gone to Germany for three months with a view to improving his spoken usage of the language before entering Cambridge. Colville stayed at Marxzell, in the Black Forest, with a professor who taught German to young Jock and half a dozen other pupils. Three months prior to Colville's arrival, President Hindenburg had appointed Adolf Hitler as Chancellor of the German Reich. Colville initially saw nothing too perturbing in this development:

> To those owning no crystal ball this was not particularly alarming, though Dr Cyril Norwood, the Headmaster of Harrow, told me he thought it a disaster for Europe, and my mother said that everything she read about Hitler and his National Socialist Party filled her with revulsion. After I had been in the Black Forest for a week or two, I concluded that these prejudiced views showed a total misunderstanding of the youthful and infectious spirit sweeping across Germany. Much as I respected Dr Norwood, and deeply though I loved my energetic, fearless and liberal-minded mother, I now perceived that the older generation at home were, and doubtless always had been, hopelessly biased and out of touch with the modern world.[648]

Colville was able to perceive from this close vantage point a 'visible determination to put the country soundly on its feet again'.[649] Every weekend, boys and girls dressed in brown, and armed with picks and shovels, happily engaged in voluntary work. They were evidently undeterred by the presence of 'fat middle-aged Storm-Troopers, dressed like boy-scouts', persistently shaking collection boxes for donations 'earmarked to build an air-force which the vicious, punitive and inequitable Treaty of Versailles forbade Germany to possess'.[650] Equally undeterred, Colville admitted to becoming 'infected' by the universally held enthusiasm spreading all around him.[651]

Further evidence suggests that Colville may also have been 'infected' by the explicitly anti-Semitic sentiments expressed by the group of German students he mingled with during a weekend spent at Tübingen

University. These students referred, for example, to the Hebrew-originating names of two British Government Ministers (Sir John Simon and Sir Samuel Hoare) to substantiate their conspiratorial belief that Britain was being 'governed by the Jews'.[652] It seems that Colville not only internalised such views, but also promulgated them in the presence of family friends and relatives. Following a visit by young Jock to the home of the Jewish Mr Lionel de Rothschild, his host complained to Cynthia Colville that: 'Your son comes to stay in my house, shoots my pheasants, drinks my champagne, smokes my cigars and then tells me that there is a lot to be said for Hitler.'[653]

During the next four years Colville's enthusiasm for Herr Hitler progressively wore thin. Having spent time more recently in Italy (where 'patriotic fervour' extended to using bombs and mustard gas against Abyssinians) and then Russia (in which 'old Bolsheviks were being liquidated and the Kulaks deported to prison camps in Siberia'),[654] Colville began preparing for a set of exacting Foreign Office entrance exams. As part of his preparation, he returned in 1937 to Marxzell with a view to brushing up on his German. Among the first things he discovered was that, following the death of President Hindenburg, Adolf Hitler had now become both Head of the German Government and Head of the State, and was attracting unbridled devotion in his exalted position of 'Führer of the German Reich'.[655]

One of Colville's primary means of improving his spoken German was to engage in conversation with 'an ebullient' 19-year-old, non-English speaker called Max. Such regular dialogue provided Colville with an alarming insight into the contemporary German way of thinking:

> The only thing that made a man of one, [Max] said, was war. Germany having first rooted out all the poison in her own system — Jews, Gypsies and other lesser breeds — would soon dominate the world; for the Germans were real men, not decadent, pleasure-loving lounge-lizards like the Latins or money-grabbing Jewish financiers like the Americans. There was, he thought, some hope for England, if she accepted the hand of friendship which the Führer offered and put her own corrupted house in order. 'Strength through Joy' was no longer much in evidence, but Max was sure that the current slogan, endorsed by the Führer, reflected the future. It was '*Heute gehört*

uns Deutschland, morgen die ganze Welt' – 'Today, Germany is ours; tomorrow the whole world.'[656]

Events arising in the following few weeks confirmed Colville's gravest fears. Prevailing social attitudes were suddenly transformed: an immediate ban was placed on the music of Felix Mendelssohn, while authorship of *Die Lorelei* was now attributed to 'Anonymous', rather than its actual creator, the Jewish poet, Heine (whose work had won the devotion of Richard Monckton Milnes). Worse still was the evidence Colville was now witnessing first hand:

> In Karlsruhe and in Munich I saw shops and broken windows and in Stuttgart I walked behind a frightened, cringing man wearing the Star of David. I was warned again and again by the Professor not to air my views in restaurants or indeed anywhere in public. I heard, for the first time, of a place called Dachau and another called Buchenwald to which people who spoke out of turn might be sent for reformatory purposes. In Baden-Baden I stood beside a large bonfire into which the citizens were hurling books. I picked up a singed one; it was a calf-bound edition of Buddenbrooks by Thomas Mann. 'Throw it back into the fire', said a stern Storm Trooper who strode towards me when he saw me pick it up. This was no occasion for argument: I did as I was told.[657]

By 1936, Colville's two older brothers had taken up positions as a banker and stockbroker in the City of London. Colville's interest in politics and current affairs prompted him to apply for a career in the Foreign Office. Having succeeded in passing his exams at the first attempt, he entered Whitehall in 1937. Colville, who was living with his parents at 66 Eccleston Square, was assigned to affairs in Turkey and Persia.

'Wheels Turning' and 'Hammers Falling'

In contrast to his cousin, Jock, Terence O'Neill had already formulated a robust anti-fascist (and anti-appeasement) philosophy prior to studying abroad. It was during his teenage years that O'Neill first adopted the anti-fascist stance already subscribed to by his mother, Annabel:

> From the late-twenties to the mid-thirties my stepfather was the British Consul in Sicily and she knew what fascism was at

first hand. She was not sorry when my stepfather became Consul General at Nice. Nevertheless, during the latter part of the thirties appeasement was the official policy of the National Government and those who did not support that policy were unpopular in many quarters.[658]

This sentiment was also shared by O'Neill's brother-in-law (husband of his older sister), Edward Buxton. O'Neill spent many enjoyable vacations with the Buxton family at their home in Epping Forest. On one such occasion in 1935, O'Neill attended a local pony club meeting with his niece, which was addressed by the Member of Parliament for Epping, and future British Prime Minister, Winston Churchill, who stepped forward while puffing characteristically on a long cigar:

> He clambered on to a farm wagon and after a few remarks about the importance of these 'equestrian events' — I had never heard this slurred enunciation before — he plunged into his speech. I seem to recall a sentence which went like this: 'For as I am speaking to you the wheels are turning and the hammers are falling in Nazi Germany.' It was one of his long series of warning speeches which were unfortunately ignored by most of the British population. His audience consisted of about thirty children, their ponies and their parents. I remember thinking at the time what a waste it was that this oratory was being poured out in a forest glade to this small, uninterested audience. [...] I was sorry that more people were not here to listen to his well-reasoned arguments.[659]

It was shortly after leaving school that O'Neill chose, like his cousin, Jock, to move abroad with a view to improving his command of foreign languages. He initially stayed in France before moving on to Austria with a view to learning German. The Austrian family he boarded with (in Salzburg, in the spring and summer of 1936) was 'violently anti-Nazi'. One of the family's boys had been a member of the *Österreicher Front*, in opposition to Austria's eventual annexation (the *Anschluss*).[660]

According to Mulholland, 'This experience turned him [O'Neill] into a convinced opponent of appeasement back in Britain, a position which disturbed Lord Crewe and his family who were partisans of Neville Chamberlain.'[661] In fact, O'Neill became an active

233

anti-appeasement campaigner, firing off a stream of letters to *The Times*, though none of them was actually published.[662]

On returning home from Europe, O'Neill briefly entered the Stock Exchange. It was not long before his aunt, and surrogate mother, Sylvia O'Neill, arranged in 1939 for him to become civilian aide-de-camp to the Governor of South Australia in Adelaide. Mulholland maintains that this ploy was strategically designed to curtail O'Neill's growing political ambitions.[663] O'Neill considered this a 'memorable and happy occasion', during which time he developed a lasting fondness for Australians; but his brief stay would be cut short when war eventually broke out and he was compelled to return to Britain.[664]

The Road From Berlin to Fryston

While Colville and O'Neill may have been exposed in contrasting manner to the theoretical and practical manifestations of fascism and anti-Semitism, neither had become an actual victim of these scourges. In many cases, of course, the threat posed by the pre-war expansionist and racist ambitions of the Third Reich was experienced first-hand – as in the case of Gerda Laura Clara Alice Friedmann, who had the 'misfortune' to have been born (on 24 March 1912) into a wealthy Jewish family in the German city of Berlin.

Gerda Friedmann's father was an eminent Berlin lawyer, 'the German equivalent of Lord Arnold Goodman, who was a Jewish lawyer and political advisor in London'.[665] It was indicative of the family's relative affluence that Gerda and her two brothers were taught by a live-in English governess. Not surprisingly, from a young age they were able to speak English almost as adeptly as their native German. As Gerda's son, Richard Sloan, subsequently explained,

> Their house in Berlin was huge and furnished with antiques and with significant works of art. They often holidayed in Monte Carlo, where my grandfather could play roulette and poker. He owned racehorses, and my mother was an accomplished rider. At one time he also owned a film starring Richard Tauber, the tenor, with whom he was a friend. The film was a flop. My grandfather had someone visit the house to shave him each morning. They had lavish dinner parties and I possess the table plans and menus from some of these. At one point he owned

a telephone factory and installed the telephones in the Vatican. A Pope died soon after the phones were up and running. There is a family joke that the Pope, when he felt terribly ill, could not reach the phone on his bedside table and that this resulted in his death.[666]

This was by no means the Friedmann family's only distinguishing feature. Gerda's cousin was married to an internationally renowned bacteriologist. Her paternal uncle was an equally famous biochemist who eventually became a professor of biochemistry at Cambridge University. One of *his* mother's aunts by marriage was the granddaughter of the scientist who discovered both the bacterium responsible for causing gonorrhoea, and the causative agent of leprosy. Finally, a cousin of Gerda's mother was married to the grandson of the famous composer, Felix Mendelssohn, alluded to above.

Blessed with so many advantages, Gerda opted to pursue a career as a doctor. In 1933, her parents emigrated to Great Britain, where they initially settled in London's Maida Vale and became naturalised British citizens. Gerda stayed on in Germany to study medicine at the University of Berlin; but, following Hitler's rise to power, she and some of her fellow students were forced into wearing yellow armbands, signifying that they were Jewish. It was ironic that she, along with the rest of her family, were part of a Lutheran Church congregation, and that she had never seen the inside of a synagogue.[667]

Gerda qualified as a doctor in 1938 and left Germany for Great Britain just in time to save her life. She was not accorded any favours by the British Government, who announced that foreign doctors were required to retake their final examination as a prerequisite for working in this country. Gerda duly sat and passed her conjoint finals – 'Member of the Royal College of Surgeons' (MRCS), and 'Licentiate of the Royal College of Physicians' (LRCP) – in Edinburgh in 1939. She was now well positioned to start applying for a post in general practice; but, as Richard Sloan explains, 'She applied for about three hundred jobs and got nowhere'.[668] The sole exception was the invitation she received to attend an interview in the small, West Yorkshire mining village of Fryston.

Chapter Seventeen
Posh Folks' War

Those Who Served

Prior to the Second World War, Jock Colville had been ensconced in a relatively routine Foreign Office job. His political responsibilities were irrevocably transformed when the German Chancellor, Adolf Hitler, reneged on the terms of a 'Munich Agreement' he had reached in 1938 with the British Prime Minister, Neville Chamberlain. This agreement provided for the permanent German possession of an area of land recently seized from Czechoslovakia on condition that it would refrain from any further territorial expansion of its borders. Hitler's lack of true commitment to this undertaking was laid bare by his further invasion of Czechoslovakia in March 1939, and of Poland some six months afterwards. Following the latter incursion, and Hitler's flouting of a directive to instantly withdraw his troops, Britain declared war on Germany on 3 September 1939. Colville had been about to set sail for New York on the first leg of a month's holiday in Wyoming. With war now declared, all such leave was cancelled.[669]

At the outset of the conflict, Chamberlain immediately applied to the Foreign Office for an Assistant Private Secretary. Sir Alexander Cadogan, the Permanent Under-Secretary, decreed that Colville would be ideally suited to the post. Thus, at the age of 24, Colville found himself 'seeing the Cabinet minutes every day and familiar with all the secrets of State and of the war'.[670]

From 10 September 1939 to July 1954, Colville kept a diary of his diplomatic and military experience.[671] The present chapter draws primarily on this diary, but also on memoirs, and biographical and autobiographical accounts of the wartime experience of Colville himself and, to a lesser extent, his mother, Cynthia, and cousin, Terence O'Neill.[672]

As we shall see below, Colville served two separate spells in the RAF. These took the form of secondments from his more enduring role of Assistant Permanent Secretary – firstly, to Neville Chamberlain, and then to his successor as Prime Minister, Winston Churchill. The following discussion will focus on the nature of Colville's relationships with these two immensely significant wartime individuals and outline his personal assessments of their respective conduct and personalities.

The chapter also focuses on the important wartime position occupied by Colville's mother (and Lord Crewe's daughter), Cynthia, who was continuing in the role as Woman of the Bedchamber to Queen Mary. She would have the unenviable responsibility thrust upon her of having to break tragic news of great personal significance to her monarch. Finally, the chapter includes overviews, not only Jock Colville's military experience of the war, but also of the brief spell of armed service undertaken by his cousin, Terence O'Neill.

Early Wartime

Jock Colville's first encounter with his new employer, Neville Chamberlain, took place in October 1939. On this occasion, the Prime Minister proved endearingly shy and welcoming; but it soon became obvious to Colville that Chamberlain was an aloof individual who steadfastly subscribed to a rigid pattern of work and showed an unwillingness to be disturbed at weekends or after his evening meal. He was certainly not one to socialise or even exchange pleasantries. Yet, as Colville states in his diary, 'this austere man had such integrity, such devotion to duty and such high ideals and standards, that if it was at first difficult to feel affection for him it was impossible not to feel esteem'.[673]

From working within such close reach of Chamberlain, Colville was able to detect in the Prime Minister 'an element of damaged vanity', resulting from the notorious act of deception perpetrated by the German Chancellor:

> At Munich, in September 1938, he had trusted Hitler in the face of strong remonstrances from the Foreign Office, but with encouragement from our gullible Ambassador in Berlin, Sir Neville Henderson. Hitler had betrayed that trust and made a dupe of Chamberlain. One evening when I was returning with him from the House of Commons, he spoke angrily of some Opposition member who had been attacking government policy. 'I believe,' said I, 'that he is sincere in his views.' 'What of that?'

replied the Prime Minister sharply. 'I am sure Hitler was sincere at Munich, but he changed his mind a few days later.' I thought that remark explained quite a lot about Chamberlain's ingenuous faith in the Munich agreement – and perhaps something about Chamberlain himself.[674]

Colville still found time alongside his wartime duties to occasionally meet up with close relatives, such as his mother, his grandparents, and his mother's half-sister, Mary Roxburghe, who was a devout critic of the Government's apathetic approach to the conflict. When Jock visited Mary on 28 September 1939, both she and Colville expressed concern about the Government's apparent lack of conviction:

> We agreed that it would probably be a good thing if Chamberlain resigned soon and left the conduct of the war to some younger and forceful successor. Unfortunately, I can see no Lloyd George on the horizon at present: Winston is a national figure, but is rather too old; and the younger politicians do not seem to include any outstanding personality. Halifax would be respected, but he has not the drive necessary to keep the country united and enthusiastic.[675]

The Duchess courted controversy in the spring of 1940 by travelling with a party of 'illicit wives' to the Middle East, where they were temporarily reunited with their Army husbands. Speaking in April 1940, Peter Coats, the garden designer and aide de camp to General Wavell, complained that: 'Palestine is more like Ladies' Day at Ascot than ever. Actually, I disapprove of them being here, just because they can pull strings and have the fare. But as they are all friends, I can't work against them.'[676] It was Coats who had to intervene several weeks later by rescuing the Duchess when she found herself hemmed in by a herd of goats in the city of Jerusalem.[677]

In the early stages of the war, Jock often escorted his mother, Cynthia, to dinner with Lord and Lady Crewe. On one such occasion (on 12 October 1939), it occurred to Jock that his grandfather was now looking 'rather old', but that his mental alertness remained unaffected:

> When mother and Peggy had left the dining-room, I sat a long time with him, sipping old brandy, and hearing him talk of his

active political days. He told me that when at the India Office and Colonial Office he had known every member of the staff and had always considered it important that a Secretary of State should be able to judge the individual capacities of those beneath him.[678]

Crewe considered it imperative that Churchill – who was War Lord at the time – must not be elevated to the position of Prime Minister. In his view, Chamberlain must continue in office, since he possessed 'both the necessary drive and the confidence of the public'.[679]

Jock Colville was equally averse to the prospect of Churchill succeeding the appeasement-oriented Chamberlain, a man who, nonetheless, continued to command his professional loyalty. 'Provided the P.M. and Halifax remain in the War Cabinet there will at least be some restraint on our new War Lord,' he comfortingly told himself.

> He [Churchill] may, of course, be the man of drive and energy the country believes him to be and he may be able to speed up our creaking military and industrial machinery; but it is a terrible risk, it involves the danger of rash and spectacular exploits, and I cannot help fearing that this country may be manoeuvred into the most dangerous position it has ever been in. […] Everybody here is in despair at the prospect. Personally, I shall be sorry too, because I feel a greater loyalty towards the P.M. than I had supposed.[680]

The hopes of Colville and many others were dashed when Chamberlain resigned as Prime Minister and was succeeded by Winston Churchill. Seasoned Tory grandees, like Rab Butler, would have chosen the steadying hand of someone like Lord Halifax in preference to 'the greatest adventurer in modern political history'. Colville was equally in little doubt that:

> The King, although he gave Winston all the support in his power once the choice was made, certainly disliked the change and would have preferred Lord Halifax; and the feeling in Conservative, or at any rate old-fashioned, circles, was represented by a letter which Queen Mary wrote to my mother saying how much she hoped I would remain with Mr Chamberlain and not go on with the new Prime Minister.[681]

Queen Mary's hopes were dashed when Colville was reassigned from Chamberlain to the incoming Prime Minister. Against all expectation it was not long before his opinion of his new political master became radically transformed. Colville soon saw in Churchill a unique and fascinating outlook on life. The latter, he maintained, possessed 'some strange intuitive power' which often induced him to adopt positions that flew in the face of conventional ways of thinking.[682] While open to persuasion by anyone courageous enough to contradict him, Churchill 'always retained unswerving independence of thought', and exhibited in numerous contexts 'a quite inexplicable facility for reaching the right decision on faulty logic and against all the best advice'.[683]

Colville acknowledged that the Prime Minister was often guilty of 'terrifying' displays of anger. He could be 'violently offensive' or 'bitingly sarcastic' to his staff; and, 'though he would never say he was sorry, he would equally never let the sun go down without in some way making amends or showing that he had not meant to be unkind'.[684] Churchill was also resolutely loyal and affectionate towards longstanding friends and acquaintances, or those who had served him well. He was not inclined to hold grudges and detested all forms of vindictiveness.[685]

That said, the Prime Minister was, in Colville's opinion, someone 'not easy to work for'. He was totally lacking in patience and made unreasonable demands of his staff. Thus, for example,

> As soon as he had ordered something to be done, he expected that it had been completed. Many was the time when he told me to do something and before I had time to get back to my telephone he had rung the bell to enquire the result. [...] His own rapidity of thought and expression was partly responsible for this, together with the fact that having been in a position to give orders all his life, and seldom obliged to execute them, he had no conception of the practical difficulties of communication and of administrative arrangements.[686]

Colville discovered to his surprise that Churchill's political credo was 'as strange a mixture of radical and traditionalist as could anywhere be found'.[687] He soon learned that the Prime Minister was not politically conservative by nature; neither was he a committed supporter of the

'One Road In, One Road Out'. A bus trundles off towards Castleford town centre, having crossed the railway bridge linking Fryston to the outside world.

Two views of the village during the post-war period: one panoramic, the other taken from the vantage point of the pit entrance.

Lord Crewe (see inset photograph) enjoyed a long and distinguished political and diplomatic career. He is seated on the extreme left of the main picture, talking to Queen Mary on board HMS *Medina*. As Secretary of State for India, he accompanied the Queen and King George V on a royal visit there in 1911.

Crewe served with great distinction as British Ambassador in Paris from 1922 to 1928. He worked in close conjunction with the Foreign Secretary, Sir Joseph Austen Chamberlain (front centre), who is seen talking with some amusement to his French counterpart, Aristide Briand (front left). Crewe is listening in from the favourable vantage point of the second row.

Crewe's son-in-law, Captain Arthur O'Neill, was elected Member of Parliament for Mid-Antrim in January 1910. He is the shorter of the two men in lighter suits, pictured during his election campaign (top left). O'Neill was shot dead while serving in the 2nd Life Guards during World War 1 (top right), thus becoming the first MP to perish in the conflict.

Captain Reginald Rhys Soar of the Royal Navy Air Service (RNAS) is pictured (second from left) with his first wife (extreme left) and close friends while briefly stationed in Pembrokeshire in 1917. The son of the Fryston Colliery Manager, Soar was an ace fighter pilot in the First World War, often taking to the air in his trusty Sopwith aircraft, *Hilda*.

The indomitable 'Man in the Cap', Herbert Smith (front row, fifth from the left), attending a union-management meeting at Fryston in the 1930s. Smith was President of the Miners' Federation of Great Britain (MFGB) during the General Strike and Lockout of 1926. Jim Bullock (back row, third from the right) was an active campaigner and fundraiser in the Lockout but had since joined the colliery management.

The village headmaster, J.S. Rickaby (seen here with the all-conquering school soccer team of 1926-27 and in the inset photograph), was one of several teachers and retailers whose generosity helped local families survive the hardship of the Lockout. Holding the ball is the team's star player and captain, Jabie Foulkes, who subsequently played professionally for Stockport County, Bradford Park Avenue and Halifax Town.

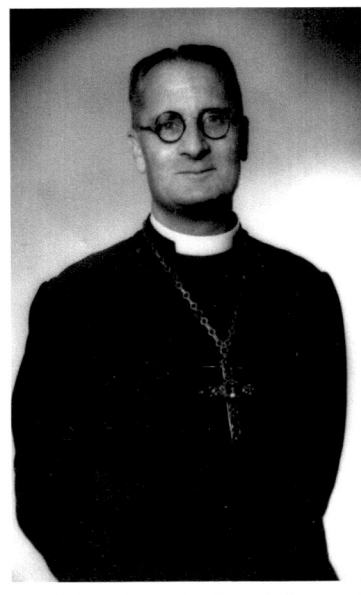

Top left: Father John Daly had spent the Lockout as curate in an impoverished coalmining area on Tyneside, before transferring to the newly emerging parish incorporating Airedale, Fryston and Townville in 1929. Daly is pictured (top right) in the company of George Westerman, the only man he employed full-time to work on the construction of the Holy Cross Church, Airedale.

Most of the relevant spadework was undertaken by local volunteers, including the wives and children of Fryston and Airedale miners. The foundation stone of the new church was formally laid by Lord Crewe on 18 March 1933.

The completed building incorporated the entrance porticos and other stone materials once belonging to Fryston Hall.

Several of Lord Crewe's relatives shared his connections with the royal family. His wife, 'Peggy', is centrally seated at the races in 1928, with the Queen and King George V's only daughter, the Princess Royal and Countess of Harewood, reading avidly on her right.

King George V and Queen Mary (both central, holding walking sticks) attend a social gathering in Buckinghamshire, in January 1934. The Queen's close confidant and Woman of the Bedchamber — Crewe's daughter, Cynthia Colville — is standing next but one on her left.

Queen Mary's goddaughter (and Crewe's youngest child), Lady Mary Evelyn Hungerford Crewe-Milnes, was married to George Innes-Ker, 9th Duke of Roxburghe, at Westminster Abbey on 24 October 1935. The marriage ended in an acrimonious and highly publicised divorce.

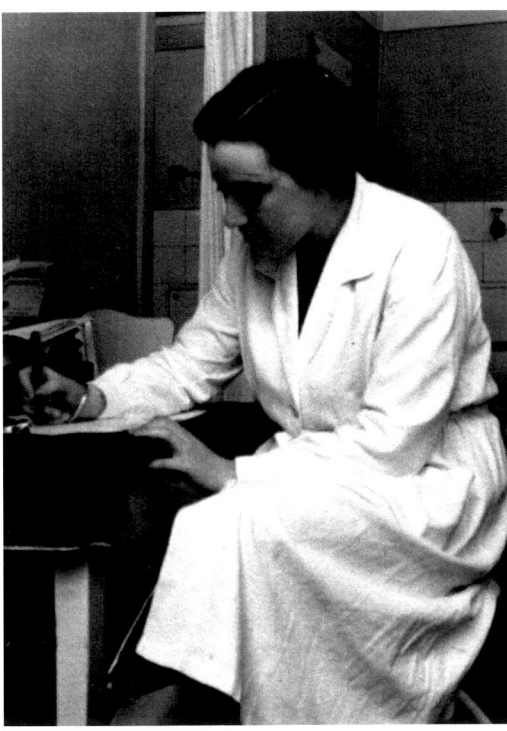

The Second World War gave rise to many daunting and memorable experiences. Shortly before hostilities broke out, the Jewish medical student, Gerda Friedmann, fled from Berlin to Edinburgh, to complete her studies before arriving improbably in Fryston.

Frances Griffiths and Bill Spedding were two Fryston sweethearts who spent five years apart when she served in the Women's Auxiliary Air Force on the south coast of England while he was imprisoned in a concentration camp a stone's throw from Auschwitz.

Having served with great distinction in the First World War, the former Fryston miner, John Whetton, set up a special survey unit which helped identify the precise locations of enemy personnel, weaponry and armoured vehicles.

Among the 'Bevin Boys' working at Fryston during the war and in its immediate aftermath were star professional footballers of the calibre of the great Len Shackleton (left) and Jimmy Stephen (right). These and other professionals helped organise and took part in a series of charity matches in which local amateur footballers were also present.

On one such occasion, a star-studded Bradford Park Avenue team took on a Fryston eleven at Castleford's Wheldon Road rugby stadium. Included in the Park Avenue line-up was Ron Greenwood (middle row, extreme right), the future West Ham United and England manager.

These and other fundraising initiatives enabled Fryston to pioneer the provision of powered invalid carriages and other facilities for permanently disabled miners.

Once settled in Fryston, Gerda Friedmann worked alongside (and eventually married) the beloved village doctor, George Sloan, who had arrived from Northern Ireland in 1923. The couple were ultimately succeeded in local general practice by their only child, Richard (also pictured here).

An equally beloved contemporary of Dr Sloan's was the local midwife, Nurse Emma Box. For three decades or more, she was responsible for the delivery of virtually all new-born babies in Fryston and nearby Airedale.

In 1951, Fryston miners constructed their own welfare hall, all in the space of thirteen days.

Local men then set about building their own athletics stadium one year later with the aim of creating a 'White City of the North'.

The Fryston pit deputy, Lister Addy, is seen chatting with a grateful haulage hand, Jim Winterbottom, whose life he saved on 3 May 1952 by conducting a daring underground rescue.

The charismatic Fryston Colliery Manager, Jim Bullock, bade farewell to his workforce in 1954 to take on the presidency of the nascent British Association of Colliery Management (BACM), a position he occupied until retiring in 1969 (see inset photograph).

Bullock formed a warm and mutually respectful relationship with the controversial Chairman of the National Coal Board, Alfred (later, Lord) Robens (right). On the left of the picture is Geoff Lofthouse, a one-time administrative officer within the NCB, who became personnel manager at Fryston in the early 1970s, prior to his election as MP for Pontefract and Castleford in 1978.

Three of Lord Crewe's grandsons each rose to fame. John ('Jock') Colville had two spells as private secretary to the Prime Minister, Winston Churchill, and spent a two-year secondment as private secretary to Princess Elizabeth (soon to become Queen Elizabeth II).

The journalist, author, restaurant critic, traveller and bon viveur, Quentin Crewe (seen on the right), was already in the advanced stages of muscular dystrophy when his close friend, Princess Margaret's husband, Lord Snowdon (seated opposite), helped customise a special 'Chairmobile' on his behalf.

The election of Terence Marne O'Neill as Prime Minister of Northern Ireland in 1963 heralded a major resurgence of sectarian violence. O'Neill is seen here with his Westminster counterpart, Harold Wilson.

The Fryston pit banner is proudly held aloft amidst a demonstration by members of the National Union of Mineworkers (NUM) and their supporters during the 1984–85 miners' strike.

Fryston's NUM delegate, Brian Dakin (left), about to address a strike rally also attended by the NUM National President, Arthur Scargill (seated on the right of the picture).

The strikebreaking Fryston miner, Michael Fletcher, is visited in hospital by the Chairman of the NCB, Ian MacGregor, after the former was allegedly attacked and beaten in his own home by local strike activists.

A mere nine months after the strike Fryston Colliery ceased production. Its head gear was demolished less than two years later.

In the wake of pit closure, the Fryston-born octogenarian, Jack Hulme (seen here with the freelance journalist and fellow photographer, Stephen McClarence), belatedly rose to fame when the Yorkshire Art Circus stumbled across the massive collection of images of village life he had amassed during previous decades. Two such photographs are featured on this page.

The Yorkshire Art Circus also helped launch the artistic career of the former Fryston miner, Harry Malkin (pictured right), whose charcoal drawings and paintings evocatively recall the experience of working underground (centre). Malkin created a specially commissioned three-dimensional clay 'wall sculpture' for Fryston (bottom picture), partly modelled on the Jack Hulme photograph appearing on the facing page.

As part of an early 21st century millennium regeneration initiative, Fryston was provided with a new village green and play area, all designed by the renowned American landscape architect, Martha Schwartz. The symbolic significance of a conspicuously protruding cairn statue (locally derided as 'Martha's finger') was lost on most observers.

Bamber Gascoigne, presenter of the *University Challenge* TV quiz show, and his wife, Christina, are shown standing in front of the West Horsley mansion he inherited in 2014 from his great aunt, Mary, Duchess of Roxburghe. This bequest included many priceless family heirlooms and cultural artefacts once belonging to Lord Crewe and Richard Monckton Milnes. The vast contents of the West Horsley library, including scores of books once residing at Fryston Hall, were bequeathed to Cambridge University, in keeping with Mary's wishes.

Conservative Party, per se. He nonetheless harboured a profound and unshifting regard for the British monarchy; and, while religiously agnostic, he wholeheartedly recognised 'the divine right of Kings'.[688] As Colville points out, 'as the years went by, and I think more particularly as a result of the Battle of Britain, [Churchill] slowly began to conceive that there was some overriding power which had a conscious influence on our destinies'.[689]

Diary entries referring to this iconic airborne 'battle' provide a vivid insight into the impulsive, enthusiastic and ultimately warm nature of Churchill's essential character. In one such entry (for Thursday, 15 August 1940), Colville begins: 'Today there took place the greatest and most successful air battle of all.' With German planes reportedly falling like flies, Churchill ('consumed with excitement') sped off to Fighter Command at Stanmore.

> When he came back, he told me the total was well over a hundred and asked me to ring up the Lord President, who is in the country recovering from an operation. I did so and found Mr Chamberlain somewhat cold at being disturbed in the middle of dinner. However, he was overcome with joy when he heard the news and very touched at Winston thinking of him. It is typical of W. to do a small thing like this which could give such great pleasure.[690]

What impressed Colville most of all was the inspirational nature of Churchill's leadership style and of his unflagging faith that Germany would eventually be overcome. Colville accepted that Churchill 'was no Jeremiah':

> Indeed, he was at his energetic, pugnacious and unconquerable best when the clouds were darkening for an approaching storm, and though he was wise enough to offer blood, sweat and tears rather than manna from heaven, he never lost faith in his conviction that all would be well in the end.' Like Isaiah, he prophesised salvation.[691]

The Human Cost of War

No level of British society was exempt from the human cost of war. This reality was underlined by the deaths during active service of two sons of Annabel Dodds (formerly, O'Neill), and the son of her sister, Celia Coates. These fatalities are discussed in more depth in Chapter 19. Here we focus on a similar tragedy befalling an individual of the greatest importance in British society: the reigning monarch, Queen Mary.

Jock Colville reports in his diary that his mother spent most of her early wartime days waiting on the Queen at Badminton, where the monarch was persistently unsettled by the sound of air-raid sirens. Whenever Cynthia returned briefly to London, she invariably brought back small presents for Jock from Her Majesty: 'The old lady is extraordinarily thoughtful and methodical,' he wrote, 'and is always fond of doing small things which give pleasure. She still continues to send me large packets of monograms, the envelopes addressed by herself – a practice she began when I was ten.'[692]

Mary's regal status did not render her immune to tragedy. In August 1942, Cynthia Colville was called upon to break the news to the Queen of the death of her son, the Duke of Kent. Cynthia was, at this time, part of the Queen's entourage visiting Badminton as guests of the Duke and Duchess of Beaufort. The Duke of Kent had also been present early in the proceedings. Being a high-ranking RAF officer, he eventually set off to join up with his squadron in Iceland.

It was only a few days after his departure that Cynthia was asked to break off from reading a book out loud to the Queen and receive a telephone call in her own room from the King's Private Secretary, Sir Eric Miéville. Once there, she was told the terrible news that the Duke of Kent had died in an air crash when his plane failed to clear a range of hills, shortly after setting off for Iceland. Cynthia then steeled herself in readiness to inform Her Majesty.

The Queen had already concluded that some form of bad news was in the reckoning, otherwise the phone call could have waited until the morning. Cynthia recalled that, 'As I came into her sitting-room, the Queen said, "What is it? Is it the King?" I said: "No, Ma'am, I am afraid it is the Duke of Kent," and then proceeded to relate all that I had been told.'[693] Cynthia wrote in admiration of the way in which the Queen's attention immediately re-focussed unselfishly onto the emotional needs of her daughter-in-law:

'I must go to Marina tomorrow,' she said. Shattered as she herself was by the horror of this dreadful accident, her immediate reaction was to help and comfort one who would be even more heartbroken than herself. So the car was ordered for 10 a.m. next day and we started off on the drive to Iver, where the sorrowful mother and widow could share their overwhelming grief.[694]

Active Servants

Cynthia Colville was narrowly spared from experiencing similar personal anguish. All three of her sons enlisted at various stages of the war in the British armed services. First to join up was her unmarried middle boy, Philip, who was a stockbroker at the time. He had acted on the advice of a cousin (who was already enlisted in the Army) in becoming a Grenadier Guard. Following four months of training at Sandhurst, Philip served in the 4th Battalion for the duration of the war, eventually rising to the rank of Major.[695]

Cynthia and Geordie Colville had reason to feel alarmed when nothing was heard of this son for several weeks after the Dunkirk landing. Such anxiety reached a peak when, in dining with the Queen one evening at Badminton, Cynthia was suddenly called upon to take a message.

> So, with a sinking heart I went off to the telephone and was greeted by Lord Burlington in these words: 'I thought you would like to know that Philip has crossed the Seine!' This seemed too good to be true and my thankfulness knew no bounds. He still had a long way to go, through the forests of Normandy, hampered constantly by German attacks of one kind and another, but ultimately his platoon (the last Brigade of Guards Platoon to leave France) reached Cherbourg, and my son actually returned home on 18th June, 1940.[696]

Philip was then assigned to a long period of training on Salisbury Plain, before finally returning to France with the 6th Guards Tank Brigade in the summer of 1944, where he assisted them in their 'triumphant progress from Arromanches to beyond the Rhine'.[697]

The eldest of Cynthia's three sons, David, joined the Navy. As he was an excellent linguist, he was appointed liaison officer to a Free

French minesweeper and saw active service in the Atlantic. He was eventually redeployed into an onshore position on the River Clyde, thus providing his parents with reason to feel more settled.[698]

Cynthia Colville maintained that her third son, Jock, was 'mortified' to be working all this time in a 'safe civilian job' and yearned to follow his brothers' example by enlisting.[699] Far from seeking to deter him, Winston Churchill actively encouraged Jock to pursue this noble ambition: 'At your age I would have fought with the cavalry,' the Prime Minister confessed. 'The R.A.F. are the cavalry of modern war, and if you want to join them you may.'[700] Despite opposition from the Foreign Office, which was fearful of creating a precedent, Jock successfully applied to undergo training as a pilot.

Following confirmation of his formal acceptance by the RAF (in August 1941), Jock Colville received a moving letter from his mother, stating that she was 'very proud to hear of my new Air force son', and fervently hoped that 'the *ardua* won't be too tedious or exacting and that the *astra* will fulfil all your hopes concerning them'.[701] Colville was presented with a commemorative Cartier silver cigarette case by Winston and Clementine Churchill, each of whom attended a farewell party (along with Cynthia Colville and 'the whole of Whitehall') in late September. Jock Colville took his leave a few days later, pausing only to bid farewell to Churchill, who had just made an impassioned speech in Parliament:

> I went into the Cabinet Room to say goodbye to him. He said it must only be 'au revoir' as he hoped I should often come back and see him. He ought not to be letting me go, and Eden had been 'very sour' about it and about recalling a trained officer from the army to take my place; but I had so much wanted to go and he thought I was doing a very gallant thing. He said, 'I have the greatest affection for you; we all have, Clemmy and I especially. Goodbye and God bless you.' I went out of the room with a lump in my throat such as I have not had for many years.[702]

The British RAF training facilities were universally at risk of German bombing, so Colville received his training in the South African Transvaal. This proved a long and laborious process – primarily because aircraft spare parts were in such short supply. It was not until 28 January 1943 that Colville returned to England ('adorned with my pilot wings') with the aim of flying Mustangs in cross-channel missions.[703]

Above the Clouds

Colville had scarcely settled into his new aerial role when, in December 1943, he was unexpectedly recalled to Downing Street by the Prime Minister, who had impatiently insisted: 'It is time that you came back here.'[704] Not long afterwards, however, Colville received 'inside information', that an invasion of northern France by the British and Americans had been scheduled for the coming spring. Churchill fully empathised with the younger man's desire to take part in this operation and therefore permitted him a second period of leave.

The Secretary of State for Air appealed to Churchill to rescind this decision — on the grounds that it was 'unsafe and unwise to allow a man who knew the invasion plans to fly over enemy territory'.[705] Whitehall colleagues complained in parallel of the potential difficulties involved in finding an adequate replacement for Colville while he was serving in the RAF. A compromise was achieved, decreeing that Colville would not be allowed to cross the English coastline into France until D-Day itself. The further understanding was reached that Colville would return to Downing Street by no later than the following August. Thus, on 20 May 1944, Colville arrived at the RAF Station at Odiham, 'from which No. 168 Squadron was flying its P.51 Mustangs, taking low level photographs of target areas, firing cannon shells at trains in occupied France and sweeping the enemy coast in search of shipping'.[706]

The day chosen for the D-Day operation 'was unseasonably vile'.[707] Following an early morning briefing, Colville and his RAF colleagues flew over Hampshire, prior to entering France:

> The Channel was teeming with ships: convoys of landing craft, large and small; big troop-ships; destroyers and cruisers; thousands of ships with their white bow-waves and thousands of barrage balloons. In the sky we mingled with an equally vast array of Spitfires and Typhoons of the RAF and Lightnings and Thunderbolts of the US Army Air Force. We were in the van of the greatest Crusade of all times, elated to the extent of spiritual intoxication, and so instilled with a sense of unity with

those thousands of others who were setting forth on the same venture that the hazards ahead were of no consequence, and fear was a forgotten emotion. War in these conditions is, for a short span, magnificent.[708]

This was the first of several such missions, which eventually resulted in the Allies establishing a Normandy beachhead. Fighting had been fierce: Colville's squadron alone lost a quarter of its aircraft in the week after D-Day. At no time was Colville directly involved in dogfights, although he was once forced into escaping from no fewer than nine chasing German planes.[709]

That said, he also survived three near-death experiences. On 13 June 1944, an enemy shell pierced his port wing, 'missing both the vital aileron cable and the flap by a hair's breadth', otherwise his aircraft would have spun uncontrollably to earth.[710] Then, sometime in mid-July, his petrol tank was penetrated by a shell, leaving him to 'limp back home', grateful for the fact that his plane did not explode.[711] The third close shave occurred as Colville occupied one of four planes returning over American lines from a low-flying reconnaissance mission:

> Failing to distinguish Mustangs from Messerschmitts, the Americans greeted us with a storm of machine-gun bullets. One passed through my tail-plane, two through a wing, but fortunately none through the cockpit. One of my companions whose aircraft was alongside me, had bullets through both his feet but contrived to hold on long enough to make a landing. When our Group Captain telephoned to remonstrate, the American commanding officer said that he really must get round to having the gun-crews brush up on their aircraft recognition.[712]

Colville conceded that he was one of the few members of his squadron *not* to have experienced direct aerial combat in the war; but, he maintained, 'I had at least flown on more than forty operations and could tell myself that my training as a pilot had not been wasted.'[713]

Cousins in Arms

It was on an unspecified date sometime in 1944 that Jock Colville met up in France with his cousin, Terence O'Neill, who was serving as a captain in the Irish Guards. O'Neill had borrowed his Brigadier's jeep for the occasion, thereby enabling the two relatives to engage in a spot of wartime sight-seeing. They were accompanied on their journey by one of O'Neill's friends, an Australian fellow officer.

Part-way into their voyage, the three men pulled over to a cornfield, where they enjoyed a brief lunch together. They then progressed on foot towards the nearby Carpiquet airfield but were suddenly forced to take sanctuary in a Canadian trench when heavy shelling broke out. This was only the start of a decidedly hair-raising adventure:

> After being unceremoniously ejected when we ventured into Caen, of which our troops only held half, we crossed the Orne at Bénouville, were shelled again and were within a mile of the factory at Colombelles, still held by the enemy, when we all but stumbled into a minefield. We were saved in the nick of time from driving straight into the enemy lines by a soldier with a blackened face who leaped out in front of our jeep. Terence O'Neill, totally unperturbed, went into reverse and drove backwards to the Orne bridge singing, in his excellent tenor voice, '*Tout va très bien, Madame la Marquise*.'[714]

Following this 'foolish escapade', the two cousins and their Australian companion returned to Terence's headquarters, whereupon he treated them to a luxurious banquet. The meal was in stark contrast to the 'dull and repetitive' food typically served up in the RAF. With hindsight, Colville ought not to have been surprised by O'Neill's culinary extravagance:

> In addition to [O'Neill's] other duties, he was a catering officer with a flair and had imported, as a useful addition to more war-like equipment, a poultry farm. It had crossed the Channel in the recesses of a L.S.T. (landing craft for tanks). The Brigade of Guards, as magnificent fighters as any in the world, saw no virtue in austerity on active service.[715]

While awaiting the invasion of Europe, O'Neill married Jean Whitaker in February 1944. He then served, during the Allies' advance, as Intelligence Officer for the second battalion. According to Mulholland, O'Neill enjoyed 'a particularly patrician war-experience'.[716] There was only one notable exception to this rule:

By 10 September 1944 the Guards had fought their way to the Dutch frontier. They stayed for a week, and here O'Neill was injured, hit on the sciatic nerve by shrapnel when brigade headquarters came under artillery fire. As they were temporarily cut off, O'Neill was tended in a local house by the Ten Horn family in Holland. [...] Captain O'Neill was evacuated back to England and the war came to a close before he could return to active service.[717]

The termination of conflict had not come soon enough for O'Neill's brother, Shane, who was killed in action in October 1944, adding to the earlier death of Terence's brother, Brian, in May 1940. Details of these fatalities (and the impact they had on close relatives) are discussed in greater detail in Chapter 19, where we examine the wartime experience of those members of the Crewe dynasty not bound by such prominent political, military, or regal obligations.

Chapter Eighteen
Pit-Folks' War

A 'Singularly Vibrant Village'

From September 1939 to September 1945, the people of Fryston experienced similar sensations of fear and uncertainty to those gripping the nation as a whole; but, leaving aside the conditions of austerity and occasional danger associated with this conflict, this remained throughout a 'singularly vibrant village', and 'by no means the sober or depressing place one might have anticipated'.[718]

Jim Bullock, for one, was 'busier than ever', organising such nightly, morale-boosting activities as dances, whist drives, discussion sessions and amateur dramatics.[719] As a result, Fryston was 'alive, teeming with activities every night'.[720] Bullock also set up a co-operative pig-breeding venture, providing pork to the pit canteen. 'Everybody was short of food,' he wrote, 'but we in the mining industry had extra food rations and we served meals in the canteen.' Generally speaking, 'The war was a bad time but probably better for miners than for some.'[721]

It was the enduring threat posed by German air raids which local people found most perturbing. Bullock explains how, during the first such raids, the colliery placed 'firewatchers' on top of the pit-head baths. On one occasion, a 'bomb' was thought to have dropped directly into the pit yard. It turned out to have been the empty casing of an incendiary bomb, jettisoned by a German aircraft.[722]

As one ex-Fryston woman relatedly explained:

> They used to drop incendiary bombs somewhere over Fairburn and, when the buzzer went, my mam and my brother and sisters used to wait for my dad to tell 'em when to go to t' shelter. But because I was little more than a baby, he'd take me upstairs and lie in bed with me. Either that or he'd sit with me and talk to the ARP [Air Raid Precautions] wardens. Being so little, I had a Mickey Mouse gas mask. I was petrified of it. I couldn't get my breath when I had it on. (Interview, 1986)

A second Fryston woman was old enough to recall the vivid sights and sounds of the ongoing conflict, and to remember the active part she played in it:

> When the Germans bombed Leeds, they dropped what they called 'chandeliers', which lit up the sky and made it seem like daylight. They dropped hundreds and hundreds of incendiary bombs round here: down the 'old lane' and up the fields. Well, my dad was the ARP man and he said, 'I want some volunteers to help put the incendiary bombs out,' and we all volunteered. You could tell who the aeroplanes belonged to by the sound of their engines. Whereas ours were Rolls Royce that went 'Purr! Purr!' there's somehow went 'Der-um! Der-um!' (Interview, 1986)

In the remainder of this chapter, we turn our attention onto the well-documented and highly notable wartime activities of prominent individuals already referred to in earlier chapters. Discussion will therefore focus on Jim Bullock's experience as captain of the Fryston 'Home Guard' and of his attempts to harness the sporting talents of an influx of 'Bevin Boys' into Fryston for the benefit of the colliery football team. A further section will explore the singular experience of the German-born Gerda Friedmann who, having recently been taken on as an assistant by Dr George Sloan, was subjected to a strict wartime curfew. Three final sections then consider the 'remarkable' nature of the spells of active service undertaken by John Whetton, who used civilian surveying techniques to help pinpoint and disable enemy artillery, and by the romantically involved Bill and Frances Spedding. Theirs was a marriage which, as we shall now discover, was interrupted by a six-year separation during which Frances served in the Women's Auxiliary Air Force (WAAF) while Bill was held captive by the enemy.

Fryston's 'Dad's Army'

Jim Bullock's role as colliery manager made it almost inevitable that he would be made Captain of one of Castleford's platoons of the Home Guard. With such a huge workforce of miners at his disposal, he was predictably able to recruit and organise the numerically strongest platoon in the district. One major drawback, here, was that Bullock did not share the Army's fondness for discipline, ritual and regulation: 'To me the protocol and red tape seemed ridiculous,' he wrote. 'Too much time was spent showing people how to salute, slope arms. My idea was, we should train to fight in the way that Hitler was proving successful.'[723]

Bullock scornfully describes in *Them and Us* how, in preparing for a possible enemy attack, all Home Guard platoons underwent a mock training scenario, requiring them to mount a unified attack on Castleford, which was to be defended by troops from the Regular Army. As leader of the largest platoon in Castleford, Bullock was given overall command of the operation, his somewhat nebulous directive requiring him to organise the attack in whatever manner he saw fit. Matchboxes were to be used as 'hand-grenades'. Each time one of these was dropped into a Regular Army 'machine-gun post', the infantrymen concerned were considered 'wiped out'. This task proved ridiculously easy to execute:

> Before the attack started, we got all of our platoons over at Allerton Bywater, which is about two miles away from Castleford, and I sent two of my men down to the Drill Hall in Castleford, where the Regular Army were parading. There they heard the officers and sergeants telling them just which points they had to defend. My men immediately got on the telephone to me at Allerton Bywater and told me exactly where the Regular Army was stationed. So, when the time came for me to attack at ten o'clock, we walked straight into Castleford and wiped out every machine-gun post by about half past ten![724]

A de-briefing session was staged in which an Army General asked the 'commanding officer' (Jim Bullock) to step forward and explain how victory had been achieved. The General was appalled to discover that it had succeeded according to a policy of 'infiltration'. 'Damn it man,' snapped the General, 'you can't do that, it's not playing the game.'[725] During the heated exchange that followed, Bullock argued that Hitler had conquered Holland, France and Belgium by smuggling men behind their lines and engaging in acts of sabotage. Tiring of Bullock's attitude, the General stridently complained: 'I don't admire your methods, and I don't want any more questions from you at all.'[726]

Bullock angrily retorted that it was no wonder that Hitler was winning. It was the *Regular Army*, he maintained, whose methods were not fit for purpose. 'If he can play the game as he thinks fit and you insist on playing the game as it ought to be played, you'll lose,' Bullock argued back. 'So surely it's time to change your tactics.'[727]

The wartime experience of the Fryston Home Guard was largely uneventful, in fact – the one major exception being the occasion on which a barrage balloon came adrift in Sheffield and its anchoring rope fell off in Fryston Wood. The alarm was raised that German parachute troops were dropping into the trees. The Home Guard quickly surrounded the area – armed only with picks, hammers and pitchforks – but it proved to be a false alarm.[728]

Bullock's Bevin Boys

Jim Bullock freely admitted to having employed his natural enthusiasm for sport as a means of forging a closer and mutually respectful relationship with his workforce. This was especially true of his relationship with his talented football team.[729] Midway through the war, Bullock sought to improve the team's quality by re-employing Dick Foulkes as a miner and appointing him first team coach. He also tempted Dick's brother, Jabie, into returning to the mine and signing on as the team's star right-winger. Most advantageous of all was the incorporation of fifteen 'Bevin Boys' (men who chose to work in 'reserved occupations' like mining rather than enlisting in the armed services) into the workforce, all of whom were professional footballers at the time. It was these men who, according to Bullock, 'coached my boys into one of the finest junior sides in the country'.[730]

The fact that five of these players were drawn from Second Division Bradford Park Avenue helped create an important and enduring relationship between the club and Fryston Colliery. Three established Park Avenue stars, the full-backs Arthur Farrell and Jimmy Stephen, and the inside forward, Len Shackleton, joined the workforce just after the war. Their two relatively junior colleagues, the Bradford-born left-winger, Geoff Walker, and the Scottish inside forward Johnny Downie, came to Fryston in the early 1940s, while both were still in their teens. It was this pair (but Downie in particular) who engaged most earnestly in mining work, and who successfully slotted into village life.[731]

Downie had only recently been playing for the Park Avenue 'nursery' team, East Bierley, who played in the West Riding Amateur League. Although he had set his sights on joining the RAF, Downie was persuaded by the Park Avenue manager to enter the mines and continue playing football at weekends. His fellow Bevin Boy, Geoff Walker, had previously been working as the accountant for his parents' greengrocery business.

These two underwent their basic training at the nearby Prince of Wales Colliery, before moving on to Fryston, where they began working underground on the 'trolleys'. At first, Downie and Walker commuted daily from Bradford into Castleford.

> They looked after us quite well there and allowed us to come home to Bradford. Each day I got the bus to Leeds, Leeds to Pontefract, Pontefract to the colliery; and it was very good. I wouldn't like to do it again, though: I wasn't happy down below. Up on top was all right, but we were a long way down below, most of us. I was at the loading end of the operation. When they got the coal out, we put it into trolleys. That was all the skill we had, really, for mining. To be fair, they couldn't allow us to be in a position where we could jeopardise others. So there was no working at the coalface, or anything like that.[732]

Walker had a harder time of it than Downie, injuring his leg so badly on one occasion that he was forced to miss five Park Avenue fixtures. Although Walker continued to commute for the duration of his stay, Downie eventually entered lodgings at the bottom of Fryston Road, Airedale, and only returned to Bradford to train and play in matches. This made him especially popular within the village.[733]

With all these resources to draw upon, Fryston were all-conquering in the 1943-44 season, winning the Pontefract League championship and four local knock-out cup competitions. They enjoyed similar superiority in the following season, winning three more trophies, despite encountering stiffer opposition in the more competitive West Yorkshire League. Fryston were on course to win the coveted WRCC Cup, having beaten Leeds United Reserves in the semi-final. By uncanny coincidence, their opponents in the final were the reigning cup holders, Johnny Downie's former club, the formidable East Bierley.

Fryston was deserted on match day, with the final taking place at Elland Road, Leeds, before a crowd of 5,000 people. The colliery team was no match for an opposition side containing seven men currently registered with Bradford Park Avenue. Fryston had been well on top in the early stages, when Foulkes deservedly opened the scoring with a 25-yard screamer; and it was well against the run of play that East Bierley equalised just before half time. Once the game resumed, 'Roberts, in heading a ball, was injured in the face and although he carried on, the effect was felt in the Fryston defence.'[734] An unfortunate defensive lapse allowed Bierley in for a goal, which was arguably offside. It was only in the final minutes that a third Bierley goal secured a deserved win.[735]

In the first week of May 1945, Fryston played the first of an unforgettable series of charity matches which sought to take full advantage of their developing relationship with Bradford Park Avenue. Fryston miners had already donated generously to a huge collection on behalf of merchant seamen, and it was anticipated that a charity match setting the Fryston first team against a Park Avenue XI at Wheldon Road would further enhance their contribution. The Bradford team included such existing and future Fryston Bevin Boys as Stephen, Farrell, Walker, Downie (who came on as substitute) and the rapidly emerging, crowd pleaser Len Shackleton, who had just returned to Bradford after an unhappy spell as an apprentice at Arsenal FC.

Soon to achieve legendary status as a star of Sunderland, Newcastle United and England, the immensely talented and free-scoring Shackleton had already forged a reputation as an irreverent 'showman', whose bag of tricks included teasing opponents by sitting on the ball, or 'under-cutting' the ball with his foot in such a way as to make it roll tantalisingly close to an opponent before wickedly spinning backwards.[736] Not surprisingly, Shackleton was the star attraction as Park Avenue ran out 4-0 winners at Wheldon Road – although Jimmy Stephen was also mentioned in despatches. 'Shackleton soon became a favourite with the crowd, and gave a faultless exhibition of forward play,' said the *Pontefract and Castleford Express* (11 May 1945). 'On one occasion he dribbled his way from near the half-way line to score a fine goal. Fryston made one or two promising raids, but Stephen was up to his football International form.'

An equally popular, though locally based, individual also played an active part on the 'home front'. Dr George Sloan had been too young to enlist for the First World War, and too old to serve in World War II. Nevertheless,

> In the Second World War, he was in charge of a single-decker bus equipped to deal with medical emergencies if there was an air raid. Bombs were only dropped once or twice on Castleford when it was mistaken for Leeds. An incendiary bomb landed in the garden during one of these raids and he kept its remnants in his consulting room desk drawer. He was a nervous man and for a while after that he had a hosepipe set up in the house in case of fire.[737]

Dr Sloan was in the middle of a 'very difficult divorce' from his first wife and was also advertising at the time for a medical assistant to work alongside him at Tieve Tara. Fortunately for him, his surgery was one of the three hundred or more being applied to by the recently qualified Gerda Friedmann. Sloan is said to have told a friend, 'I only hope she is not good looking,'[738] but the application was the prelude to a marital, as well as professional relationship. They would eventually have a son, Richard, who regarded it as indicative of his father's 'individuality' that, of the countless candidates who applied for the vacancy in question, he opted to take on *a German*:

> What always amazed me was how the people of Airedale and Castleford took to my mother, a German, in the middle of the Second World War. She, at the same time, took to the people of Airedale and was always grateful for their giving her such a warm welcome. This was because she was a refugee but also because she was so kind and caring to her patients. She was so thankful that Great Britain took her in and let her do the job of her dreams.[739]

It was a time in which the need for vigilance was considered paramount. Gerda's brother, Herbert, and sister-in-law, Sania, were both interred on the Isle of Wight for the duration of the war. Gerda, herself, was subjected to a curfew, requiring her not to venture out at night. This naturally interfered with her ability to fulfil her responsibilities towards her patients. The curfew involved regular checks by a visiting police constable, who came round every night to share a pot of tea.

Gerda was undeterred by these obstacles. According to Richard Sloan, his mother was a 'cultured', modern thinking person ('the first woman in Castleford to wear trousers').[740] She had a pronounced German accent, but her English diction was impeccable. She and Richard's father laughed a lot together and quickly fell in love. The two were married on 30 November 1944; and, on 26 November 1945, Richard was born in a Leeds nursing home. 'My father was so happy after the birth,' he humorously declared, 'that he put a roll of five-pound notes in an empty Elastoplast tin and gave it to the consultant obstetrician.'[741]

It is indisputable that this wartime experience left lasting mental scars on Gerda Sloan (Friedmann). 'I saw how the war affected my mother for the rest of her life,' wrote Richard.

> She had problems sleeping and, like she did in the war, listened to the news half the night on the BBC World Service. She knew that if Hitler had won that she was on a death list. She had a serious guilt complex that she had survived and not died in a concentration camp. There is a known condition called survivor guilt. Her mother's cousin Peter Speyer died in Auschwitz in 1943. I think I know to an extent what it must feel like to leave one's country and become a refugee.[742]

It is nonetheless undeniable that Gerda's wartime introduction to Fryston heralded the start of a warm and memorable relationship between the German-born doctor and the people of the village.

From Coalfield to Killing Fields

Away from home, courage and devotion to the war effort was displayed by Fryston men and women located elsewhere in Britain, or in the European and Middle Eastern theatres of war. In John Whetton's case, this involved a resumption of the military service he had undergone in World War I.

Having graduated, with a Masters degree from the University of Leeds, Whetton rose to the position of research assistant at Armstrong

College in Newcastle-upon-Tyne. He soon became a lecturer in mining, surveying, and applied geophysics, and was eventually made a Reader. Whetton's academic career was then interrupted by the growing likelihood of war following the rise of Adolf Hitler.[743]

In 1936, at the age of 42, Whetton was asked to establish a specialist volunteer unit – known as the 4th Durham Survey Regiment Royal Artillery – within the Territorial Army. Whetton was initially reluctant to take on the 'formidable task' of attracting recruits 'with sound technical training, particularly in mining, surveying, civil and mechanical engineering and man management and, indeed, men with knowledge of pure science, especially in physics, and others of professional standing'.[744] An overriding sense of duty nonetheless prevailed. On 1 January 1937, a temporary headquarters was set up in Gateshead. The preliminary training of recruits was completed later that July.[745]

Here was an innovative approach to using wartime intelligence. As Whetton and Ogden point out, 'Artillery survey can be described as the practical application of the techniques of co-ordinate geometry to the use of artillery in war, with the objective of increasing its effectiveness.'[746] It involved the implementation of such civilian survey methods as 'flash spotting' or 'sound ranging' to coordinate British artillery fire power, thus guaranteeing its greatest possible accuracy in relation to enemy targets. Survey Units of this nature were previously unheard of.

The '4th' embarked on their first mission – to Egypt in 1940 – where they discovered on arriving that they were the only Survey Regiment in the entire Middle East.[747] Finding itself 'constantly in demand',[748] the Unit served with distinction in Eritrea, Greece, Palestine, Syria, Tunisia, and Libya. They also participated in the Battle of El Alamein in 1942 and the invasion of Sicily in 1943. In recognition of the part he played in these exploits, Whetton was decorated with an Africa Star, the Italy Star and the Distinguished Service Order. Finally, the regiment took part in the D-Day Landings at Normandy in June 1944, followed by 'Operation Market Garden' in Belgium and Holland.

Writing decades later, the celebrated military commander, Lieutenant-General Sir B.G. Horrocks, said he doubted whether any other Army unit had done more to secure a British victory:

Although I am an infantryman, and proud of it, in my opinion, the Royal Regiment of Artillery did more to win the last War than any other arm of the Service, and the core of the R.A. was the fantastic accuracy of their Survey Units. This enabled me, as a Corps Commander, to switch the fire of several hundred guns in a matter of minutes, and thus bring down a devastating concentration on some vital sector of my Corps front. Neither the Germans, the Russians, our U.S. allies nor the French (supposedly masters in the art of handling artillery) ever came up to the high standard set by the British.[749]

It was a freak accident that put paid to the continuation of Whetton's military career. A visiting Army officer, Lieutenant Colonel Clegg, C.O., of the 7 Survey Regiment, was about to sit down with Whetton for lunch. However,

Whilst Colonel Clegg was taking off his webbing, his revolver fell out of its holster, hit the ground and went off, the bullet hitting Colonel Whetton in the leg and breaking his fibula. Although unlucky to be hit in such a way, he was also lucky that the random shot did not do more damage. The result was that he had to be evacuated and was later invalided out of the Army.[750]

Following his evacuation back to England, Whetton had many honours bestowed on him, including the Order of the British Empire, the Croix de Guerre and the Belgian Order of the Crown. On 6 September 1946, the 4th Survey Regiment's return to Gateshead was commemorated by a welcome-home banquet. A plaque was subsequently unveiled in Durham Cathedral in honour of the Regiment's dead and wounded.

By now, Whetton had resumed his academic career, having been promoted in 1945 to a Chair of Mining at the University of Leeds. He eventually rose to the position of Vice-Chancellor, which he occupied from 1955-1957. Following his retirement in 1960, he was elected president of the Midland Institute of Mining. In 1978, Whetton co-wrote the book, *Z Location or Survey in War – The story of the 4th Durham Survey Regiment Royal Artillery,* with his co-commanding officer, Lieutenant Colonel Robert Ogden. This was published shortly before he died, aged 84, on 23 September 1978, with a second edition following in 2004.

It was not only the menfolk of mining villages who were actively engaged in war. Many Fryston women worked slavishly for long hours in munitions factories. Others, like Frances Griffiths, worked in military support units, such as (in her case) the WAAF. Though prohibited from engaging in direct conflict, such women provided essential back-up support. Frances had planned to marry her childhood sweetheart, Bill Spedding, but this ambition was thwarted by the outbreak of war. In this and the section that follows, we retell the remarkable story of how the couple navigated their way through their six-year separation.

Bill Spedding was called up to serve in the Royal Engineers, as part of the First Militia in July 1939. He and another young Frystoner, his close friend, Henry Eddy, were initially stationed in Catterick, near York. They had previously been told that, because miners were classed as a reserve occupation, they could opt out of serving in the Army, but both rejected this possibility. Each man relished the opportunity for adventure and the respite offered from life spent chiefly underground. It was clearly advantageous that they were such inseparable friends.

Having passed through a series of other preparatory camps, Spedding and Eddy travelled to France as part of the intended 'big breakthrough of the Allies'. The two friends were separated when their unit was forced into a temporary retreat. Being Royal Engineers, it was their responsibility to hang back and stall the advancing enemy by blowing up bridges and felling trees across roads and railway lines. Eddy still managed to make his escape and successfully returned to England. Spedding progressed to a beach just outside of Calais, only to find that the boats transporting servicemen out of danger had recently departed.

Worse still, Spedding was shot in his side; but, being only lightly wounded, he volunteered to stay put and help tend to other injured colleagues.

> We had to leave the really bad ones, but we got back inland
> and ended up in Belgium. That's where I got captured. We'd
> just pinched a couple of geese or hens off a farm. It was pitch
> dark and we were sneaking through an orchard when we came
> across four tanks! Somebody spotted us, there was a shout and
> that was it. No real point in resisting. As any soldier will tell

you, eight out of ten Germans speak English, so there was no communication problem. It was a case of a brief chat and quickly on our way. The real soldiers weren't the bad people that many would have you believe. I mean, when I was wounded, I was dressed by a German doctor who couldn't have been a nicer bloke. (Bill Spedding, 1987)

Spedding and most of his British colleagues were originally imprisoned in one camp, Stalag VIII B in Lamsdorf, and then forced to march a total of 500 miles across France, Belgium and Holland into Germany. From there, Spedding passed through four further camps and finally ended up in Poland, along with 250 other prisoners. These men were consigned to a life of hard labour, which they strove to make the best of:

The neighbouring village was a pit village, funnily enough. It didn't take us long to realise that, if you worked at this pit, even on the pit top, you got more food and the chance of a bath every day. We didn't do it for long, though, because we caused 'em that much trouble and upset that they kicked us out and, like most other prisoners, we ended up doing forestry work. (Interview, 1987)

Similar attempts were made to make life as bearable as possible. Prisoners sought to employ their diverse talents to the benefit of everyone. Concert parties were staged, for example, in which men with a penchant for acting, singing or playing music performed in costumes made out of Red Cross string and other makeshift material.

Spedding was part of a group of intrinsically artistic and literary individuals who published a regular camp newspaper called *Reverberations*.

I was sub-editor and I used to do the drawings for it. I also sketched quite a lot of photographs for our soldiers. The Germans once asked me to draw Hitler, but I drew a line at that! I applied to the Red Cross for drawing materials, but the Germans wouldn't entertain it for some reason. Eventually, they relented and allowed me to draw. I had a lot of drawings confiscated because they used to do periodical searches and go through all your stuff. (Interview, 1987)

A sinister presence cast its shadow, however, insofar as the camp was located within a mile-and-a-half of Auschwitz, the 'death camp' in which 'impure' minority groups, such as Jews, gypsies, communists, trade unionists and the disabled, were systematically exterminated in gas chambers. 'You could see the big smoke-stacks over the hill, but you could smell it just as easily,' said Spedding. 'We once went up there for a big de-lousing machine. German logic being what it was, they were gassing twenty thousand a day and, though we were being kept alive, we were having to borrow their de-lousing machine!' (interview, 1987).

It was not until four years later – on the bitterly cold morning of 19 January 1945 – that Spedding could reclaim his freedom. For the previous three days, the locality had resounded with the booming of big guns and zooming of aircraft overhead. Suddenly, the German camp guards came running in with the repeated shouts of 'Raus! Raus! Raus!' ('Out! Out! Out!'). They were followed in by the British commanding officer, who informed the prisoners that they had only one hour in which to pack their things together as there had been a breakthrough by the Allies.

> There must have been four-foot of snow on the floor when we set off to march to where they were collecting the British prisoners. We saw some atrocities along the way. The first fifteen miles were littered with them. It appeared that they'd been trying to move the inmates from Auschwitz. All the non-British – the Jews especially – were dressed in this kind of pink and white pyjama suit with the 'Star of David' on and there were quite a few lying around who'd been shot in the back of the head. It didn't do a lot for you, other than to make you walk much quicker. We ended up marching 873 miles – I've since worked it out! – to Bavaria, where we were released by the American Third Army under General Patton. (Interview, 1987)

Spedding eventually reached a repatriation camp in Brussels, where he was medically examined. 'I was lucky,' he joked. 'I didn't even get a blister on that march' (interview, 1987). Spedding was five-feet-eight but weighed only eight stones at the time. Having been pronounced 'A1 but emaciated', he was quickly de-loused and demobilised forthwith.

Most of the above events took place while Frances Griffiths was serving in the WAAF. She explained in interview how she had been called up as part of the 'Twenty-ones': the passing of the National Service Act in December 1941 had provided for the conscription of all unmarried women and childless widows aged between 20 and 30. It was shortly after this legal enactment that Frances received her notice. She found herself stationed for the next four years at the RAF Titchfield base, located between Southampton and Portsmouth. This was the home base of the No. 12 Balloon Squadron, which consisted of approximately 600 service personnel, charged with making hydrogen-filled barrage balloons, and deploying them over the Hampshire coastline. Frances worked chiefly in the stores, dispensing equipment and materials requested by RAF personnel (interview, 1987).

The young Ms Griffiths was still serving at Titchfield when she heard of Bill Spedding's release. Being unmarried, she was not permitted immediate leave of absence. Spedding had already been back home for two weeks before she was allowed to travel back to Fryston.

> He came home with a Scottish lad [called Walter] who'd lost all his family while he was a prisoner. His mam said they laid on this party, but Bill was nowhere to be found. Eventually, they found him on some muck-stacks at the back of Brook Street. He was giving some kids a ride on a bike. Sooner do that than mix back in. (Interview, 1987)

The couple had not seen each other for such a long time. On the day they were due to be reunited, Frances 'felt poorly wondering what he'd be like and what he might think of me' (interview, 1987). She boarded the train for Leeds at London's Kings Cross and entered a compartment already occupied by four cheery sailors. It was clear from the outset that Griffiths was ill at ease. One of the sailors sympathetically asked her whether she was feeling alright. She responded by pouring her heart out.

The sailor kindly set about reassuring her. He told her not to worry.

> 'When you get to Leeds, you walk through that barrier and you meet your Bill. Everything will turn out fine.' I'd got all my

gear – respirator and all sorts – on my shoulder, but he said, 'We'll see to that.' He said, 'I'll tell you what, I wish I was your Bill!' He really cheered me up. (Interview, 1987)

Griffiths duly made her way through the ticket barrier – albeit 'in a trance' – where she was greeted by Spedding, his brother, Jack, and Walter. Within seconds, Bill Spedding had thrown his arms around her – though not with the desired effect.

My first thoughts when I looked at him when he first grabbed hold of me were, 'Oh, God! I'll never marry him!' He was right thin and covered in spots and he'd this Tam o' Shanter thing on. I glanced up and thought, 'I'll never marry him!' (Interview, 1987)

The train ride on to Castleford was even more excruciating. Griffiths recalled how Walter started handing round cigarettes in a bid to settle everybody down. He never offered her one, but she was a non-smoker, anyway. She suddenly remembered, however, that she had a stash of tobacco in her bag:

When I came home every six months, I used to bring a case full of cigarettes for my dad because t' Canadians and t' Yanks used to come through our camp and throw packs to us in t' stores: I used to help out in t' men's end sometimes; and if I fixed 'em up with clothes, they'd throw me a pack, although I never smoked 'em. I used to save them up for my dad, though. But that day, I was so on edge that I went to take one out and Bill said, 'Do you smoke?' And you'd have thought I'd committed a crime! And as I went to smoke one, he saw that I'd got some very thin, pink nail varnish on – another thing I seldom used to do – and he said, 'Nail varnish as well!' *Right put out!* (Interview, 1987).

The situation thankfully improved. By the following day, Spedding had jettisoned his cap and looked decidedly more appealing while relaxing in his shirt sleeves. It was not long before the couple resurrected the idea of getting married. Griffiths was given a one-month period of leave in which to tie the knot. The couple eventually moved from Fryston to settle in nearby Glasshoughton. As Bill Spedding explained in interview, 'The supreme irony of it all was that, while she was in t' WAAFs, she had to have a serious operation, and we've never been able to have any kids' (interview, 1987). The couple fostered a succession of local children, before eventually adopting a son of their own.

Chapter Nineteen
Passing On

Port in a Storm

Of all the branches of the Milnes-Crewe dynasty, the outbreak of war initially impacted least of all on the lives of Lord Crewe's daughter, Annabel Dodds, her husband and their two sons. Over in the South of France, the lights continued to shine brightly while England was, meanwhile, 'shrouded in the blackout';[751] but, in April 1940 (two months before the German conquest of France), Colin and Quentin Dodds returned to England, to be followed one month later by their mother. The boys' father stayed on in France, where he was entrusted with the task of driving the Duke of Windsor all the way to Lisbon to ensure he could not be captured by the Germans. He returned, not to his former base of Nice, but to the more westerly coastal city of Marseille, where he was assimilated into the American Consulate.[752]

Having arrived back in England, Colin enlisted in the Army. Quentin stayed with his mother at Aunt Celia's house in Yorkshire, before spending the next two years at Eton. This constituted a very 'confusing' experience, whereby 'Nearly everything about the school seemed absurd and unnatural.' House discipline was enforced by 'an autonomous clique of senior boys', who randomly meted out corporal punishment for which there was no right of appeal.[753] Quentin recalls that: 'Intelligence was not admired, unless accompanied by athletic talent, but coupled with poverty or social inferiority it was unforgivable,' adding that 'To be Jewish was even worse.'[754]

Quentin's father returned to England in late 1941. Acutely aware of his son's disillusionment with Eton, he made him sign a written pledge to continue doing the best he could, otherwise his parents would transfer him to some unspecified local school. Quentin was becoming increasingly conscious, however, of his physical difference from other boys, and contemptuous of the school's seemingly ridiculous attitudes and conventions. He ultimately 'rebelled' by truanting off to

London. He then jumped at the subsequent suggestion that he leave Eton altogether and went off to be taught by 'an impoverished vicar' from Henley, before settling with his family in their new home in Madeley, Staffordshire.[755]

By this time, Madeley Manor had become an important hub in the wartime experience of Lord Crewe and his extended family. The safekeeping of the property had, as Quentin explained, just been entrusted to his parents:

> The house had stood empty for twenty years or more. The original Madeley Manor had been left to fall down in the seventeenth century, when the owner married the Crewe heiress and moved to Crewe Hall. This new one, some nine miles from Crewe, just over the Staffordshire border, was built in 1805, for a great-aunt of my mother's, or rather a white stucco wing was added on an Elizabethan timber-framed farmhouse. The farmhouse collapsed at the turn of the century and a plain, practical block replaced it.
>
> My mother's father [Lord Crewe], who was both extravagant and poorly advised, money and business being unmentionable topics, had sold Crewe Hall as well as his house in Yorkshire. Madeley and some four thousand acres, and two thousand or so in Wiltshire, was all that was left of the thirty thousand he had inherited. He lived in a house in Surrey. Madeley was to belong to my mother.[756]

The Manor thus became a temporary place of refuge for members of the Crewe dynasty – not least of all, Lord and Lady Crewe, who sought to escape the bomb-ridden locations of Surrey and London. It also served as a repository for many, often valuable and extravagant artefacts previously belonging to the family's ancestral homes at Fryston and Crewe. Details of this era are scattered throughout the memoirs of Quentin Dodds and in Jock Colville's diary.

By drawing on these accounts, this chapter provides an insight into the problematic contemporary relationship between Quentin and his parents, and the historical relationship between his mother, Annabel, and her father, Lord Crewe. The chapter also reveals the ways in which the Crewe family both learned of, and was affected by, the deaths of close relatives perishing in action, and of the demise through illness of

Cynthia Colville's husband and, more latterly, her father. It concludes by examining seminal developments in the early careers of three of Lord Crewe's grandsons, who would each go on to play significant parts in major cultural, political and ceremonial events in later decades of the twentieth century.

A Moving Experience?

Quentin Dodds saw the move to Madeley as an opportunity to belatedly draw closer – both geographically *and* emotionally – to his parents, although he also realised that there were many obstacles to the possible formation of a warmer relationship with his mother, who was notoriously unemotional.

It is possible that at least part of Annabel Dodds's outwardly 'cold' demeanour was attributable to the fact that she had already lost one of her sons in battle by the time she moved into the Manor. Jock Colville records in his diary that, on Thursday, 16 May 1940, he was informed by the War Office that his cousin (and Annabel's son), Captain Brian O'Neill of the 1st Battalion of the Irish Guards, had been killed two days earlier while sailing aboard the troopship, *Chobry*, which was sunk while close to the Norwegian coast. 'This is the first casualty of this horrible war that has really brought the full meaning of it home to me,' Colville observed. 'He had great charm and was, I believe, a most efficient soldier,' he said of his cousin. 'He also had considerable brain-power of which he might one day have been able to make real use.'[757]

Quentin Dodds surmised that other, more intrinsic factors were more responsible for his mother's emotional inertness. He ventured that the death of Annabel's own mother when she was only a child, allied to the presence of a 'distant father' had prevented her from getting close to her own children.[758] She also lacked the experience necessary to prepare her both for the relative social isolation involved with the move to Madeley and the extra responsibility entailed in running a house, even though she was able to depend on the support of a cook, an 'occasional butler', and local girls who did all the cleaning.[759]

At Madeley, Annabel endured a 'life of exile', spent reading the daily news, writing letters, occasionally entering Newcastle-under-Lyme to pick up the rations, and cleaning out the chickens. Aside from that,

She was absorbed by other people's lives, and her only real enjoyment at Madeley was in the hours she spent visiting families in the village. When I went back to live in Madeley thirty years later, my wife was irritated by the number of old people who would say to her, almost, she felt, accusingly: 'Everybody loved Lady Annabel, she was a real lady, always had time for everyone.'[760]

Annabel was also universally popular with Quentin's cousins, such as David, Philip and Jock Colville, all of whom considered her 'wonderful'. Quentin regarded this as a failure on their part to see through an illusion: 'Their mothers, her sisters, had their oddities, but they were loving – it never occurred to their children that my mother was not the same.'[761]

By contrast, the move to Madeley provided a context in which Quentin and his father were able to do some 'bonding' while sorting through and cataloguing the vast quantities of furniture, china crockery, paintings and books now occupying the house and stables, having been deposited there from Crewe Hall or sent up from Surrey and London to protect them from possible bombing. Quentin joked that whilst there were no 'rude prints' for the pair to get excited about,

> I had high hopes of the Monckton Milnes books, because he was known in the nineteenth century to have the largest and best library of pornography in Britain, if not in Europe. It was a spur that prevented me from groaning when Father said: 'We'll do six packing cases of books this afternoon.'[762]

Much to Quentin's dismay, he and his father came across only two 'rude' books of this nature – one an illustrated catalogue of prostitutes, the other an original edition of Rochester's *Poems*.

> Both, oddly enough, came from the Crewe library. My grandfather, with Victorian prudery, had somehow managed to get rid of the whole of Monckton Milnes's pornographic collection. It would have been illegal to sell it and he would never have committed a crime. Against that, I find it hard to believe that he could ever have brought himself to destroy a book.[763]

In addition to such treasures, a number of infinitely more precious *human* objects entered Madeley Manor in order to safeguard their security. Two of Lord Crewe's daughters, Lady Celia Coates and the Duchess of Roxburghe, lived in the relatively safe rural isolation of Helperby (North Yorkshire) and Floors Castle (Kelso), respectively. Further south, repeated air raids were becoming increasingly disconcerting. Lord Crewe and Peggy yielded to medical advice by moving up to Madeley from Surrey.[764] Furthermore, when Cynthia's 75-year-old husband, Geordie, fell ill, and could not sleep for the sound of the bombing, he, too, was transferred to the relative tranquillity of the Staffordshire border.[765]

These moves were not to everyone's satisfaction. According to Jock Colville's diary entry for 7 October 1940, 'Mother is much disgruntled at leaving London – she is afraid of nothing – but Father is desperately anxious to go. He will also be able to affect great economies by living at Madeley and that becomes increasingly necessary.'[766] It was a ramshackle but cosy existence. As Quentin explained, 'Carpets were flung down, beds put up, odd pictures hung, some books stuffed in shelves.'[767]

The presence of these new residents inevitably attracted a steady flow of visitors. On Friday, 7 February 1941, for example, Jock and Philip Colville took the train together from Euston Station to Crewe, where they then caught a taxi to Madeley. As Jock stated in his diary,

> The first impression of Madeley is pleasing, in spite of the overcrowding with furniture and pictures from Crewe, Crewe House, Horsley and Eccleston Square. The rooms are well proportioned and spacious and large fires burn in every grate.[768]

One day later, the two men accompanied their mother on a pleasant stroll through the nearby park and village. Afterwards, Jock wrote in complimentary manner about the local landscape, which he described as 'undulating and pretty, quite unspoilt by the sight of an occasional colliery and the nearness of the Potteries and the Five Towns'. He was decidedly less impressed by the external appearance of Madeley Manor itself, which struck him as 'much less attractive than within, in fact distinctly disappointing as it was built in a good period (c.1800)'.[769]

Following an 'agreeable' meeting with Peggy, who was keen to elicit 'top secret' information from her grandson, Jock engaged in long discussion with her husband, who was not enjoying the best of health:

> After tea I went to see Grandfather in his room upstairs. He has had a touch of pleurisy, which at eighty-three is serious. However, he looks astonishingly well and youthful, his cheeks have sunk a little, but his eye and brain are clear and he expresses himself well if sometimes haltingly. His memory is remarkable, both for what he has seen and what he has read. We talked of politics. He said the Prime Minister had greatly mellowed of recent years and had, he thought, lost the sudden fits of unreasonable temper to which he had once been subject. He agreed that Baldwin would receive the roughest treatment at the hands of posterity, rougher than Chamberlain, but he did not believe this would be entirely justified although Baldwin's understanding of foreign affairs had been very slight. In other circumstances he might well have been a great Prime Minister. He had the capacity as his handling of the Abdication had shown.[770]

In fact, Lord and Lady Crewe proved incapable of tolerating a long stay in Staffordshire. Life proved too dull for Peggy in particular. As Quentin pointed out, 'My step-grandmother, an easy victim of ennui, soon removed my grandfather back to London. She would rather be bombed than bored.'[771]

One Tragedy After Another

Madeley Manor nonetheless continued to represent the epicentre of family life. It was during a week's leave spent there in August 1944 that Jock Colville was informed of the death in action of his 24-year-old cousin, Lieutenant Anthony Coates of the Coldstream Guards. Colville's Aunt Celia had heard of the news by letter from Jock's brother, Philip.

> We were all plunged in gloom and mine was still further thickened by confirmation of a previous report [...] that Sidney Cuthbert too had been killed. Both Sidney and Anthony had

admirable qualities and no ordinary charm. So had a long list of my air force friends who have died in the last year. It is indeed uncanny how the best go. It is as if they had reached the standard set for us in this world, and need undergo no further trials, while the more imperfect live on, requiring more time and further chances. In no other way can I explain the constant decimation of the best.[772]

On a later visit to the Manor, Jock learned of the death of Lieutenant Colonel Shane O'Neill, of the North Irish Horse, the eldest son of Quentin's mother, Annabel. Jock had gone there with his mother on 27 October in order to collect some winter clothes. Soon after arriving, he had to retire upstairs with chicken pox. He spent the next ten days reading classic novels. It was during this time that he learned that Shane had been the victim of enemy shelling while serving in Italy. It was, as he stated in his diary, 'a tragedy which Aunt Nancy [Annabel] took with her usual philosophy'.[773]

Cynthia Colville spoke in similar vein of her sister's stoical reaction: 'I have always thought that Annabel inherited my father's wonderful spirit of fortitude; she faced every disaster in turn with unshaken courage, and never clamoured egotistically for sympathy.'[774] Annabel's son, Quentin, adopted a less charitable perspective. He found his mother's 'stillness' perplexing: 'Was it that emotions should never show, or did she have none, or were they different from other people's? Her unquestionable gift of prescience possibly detracted from feelings, certainly from surprise.'[775]

This final sentence alludes to Annabel's allegedly uncanny gift of foresight, as well as her ability to avoid outward displays of grief. These characteristics had been strikingly evident regarding the earlier death of her son, Brian. The first inkling of this tragedy had occurred when her father's butler had telephoned her on the morning in question to inform her that a telegraph had been received on her behalf. Knowing, somehow instinctively, that the message had been sent to inform her of the death of her son, Annabel delayed collecting it until later that afternoon, choosing to get on instead with other scheduled activities.

Annabel was mercifully spared a third such tragedy. 'There was one terrible moment when her elder Dodds son was missing for some time and it appeared only too likely that he had been killed and his body not found,' her sister, Cynthia recalled.[776] The telegram confirming that he was missing at Anzio had the word 'Priority' ominously stamped on the envelope. 'However,' Cynthia continued, 'it turned out, mercifully, that the Germans had made him a prisoner and before very long this news reached my poor sister and put an end to her agonising suspense.'[777] Quentin's father had already concluded that his older boy was still alive – because Annabel had not experienced a relevant premonition: "'Your mother didn't know. He must be all right,'" said my father. Nine days later we heard that Colin was safe, a prisoner of war.'[778]

Lord Crewe's Demise

During the war period, the Milnes-Crewe dynasty was further depleted by deaths occurring due to natural causes. Cynthia Colville had not endured the sense of tragedy suffered by her sisters in losing sons in battle. She was nonetheless affected by other forms of personal loss:

> My husband had been very poorly for some time and during the war his health began to deteriorate rapidly. Alas, in September 1943, he died on the same day of the month that my mother had departed this life. He was buried at Cowes in the island that he loved so dearly and which to him was essentially 'home'.[779]

It was not very long afterwards that Cynthia also experienced the passing of her father.

On an earlier unspecified date, 'late in the war', Lord and Lady Crewe had learned that their daughter, Mary, had been involved in a serious car accident up in Scotland. Only 24 hours earlier, Lord Crewe had informed his wife that he had practically lost his sight, after a period of progressive deterioration. He nonetheless insisted that Mary's plight be prioritised:

> The raids were frequent, but he supported me in my wish to go to our daughter at once, and I left a few hours later for Edinburgh. We all knew the fearful raids, but not many of us, I hope, had to lie there at that time in perpetual darkness, and helpless. I found my daughter with multiple injuries and concussion, but after about a fortnight I heard from my husband asking that if she were out of danger, I would return, and as

that was the case and she was surrounded by friends, I did so. He told me there had been several bad raids, and I realised all the implications.[780]

Shortly afterwards, Peggy hosted a dinner party of eight people at Argyll House. Lord Crewe was meanwhile confined to bed, and enemy planes flew overhead while flares 'like scarlet maple leaves' rained down profusely onto their garden. 'The forces of evil were abroad that night,' Lady Crewe maintained:

> The bombs kept dropping and the noise was terrific. Suddenly, there was a lull – and then an earthquake. The target had indeed been found, and farther down the King's Road several hundred people had been plunged into eternity. Argyll House shook, and I raced upstairs to my husband, thinking the house would fall and we should have to carry him out. I passed my maid, Sparks, who seemed to have the same idea, as she was standing there in outdoor clothes, needless to say perfectly calm, with her cat in a basket on one arm and my fur coat on the other. I hurried on into my husband's room – the light had gone out and the nurse was quietly lighting candles – and then I heard a low clear voice saying: 'Why are you here? Go down and look after your guests.'[781]

On Thursday, 18 January 1944, Jock and Cynthia Colville paid a brief visit to Argyll House. Jock brought with him a batch of lemons and oranges (both rare wartime luxuries), which he had obtained while serving abroad. Mother and son spent a good half-hour with Lord Crewe, who was 'in bed but looking well and cheerful in spite of having now gone all but stone blind', before turning their attention to Peggy, who had just returned from a dinner date at the Spanish Embassy.[782]

The decision was taken, only a few weeks later, to relieve Crewe of the stress being caused by the continuing air raids by arranging for him to be transferred to Peggy's family seat of Mentmore. A vivid description of their living environment is provided by Jock Colville, who visited the pair on Tuesday, 16 May 1944, during a period of leave:

> Went for the night to Mentmore where Grandfather and Peggy are living in the gaunt and almost deserted house, crammed with evacuated treasures from museums and galleries. Grandfather,

racked with sciatica, was lying dressed in a chair. Though physically worn, he is still very much alert mentally and was full of political conversation.[783]

This proved the first in a series of occasional visits by Colville to see his grandparents. On the week commencing Saturday 10 March 1945, for example, he travelled down to Mentmore to enjoy a few more days with them. He spent the first morning in prolonged conversation with Crewe. 'Talked to Grandfather before dinner,' he reported:

> Though very old, blind and in constant pain, he keeps up a gay demeanour and talks with grasp, wisdom and concentration of the present as of the past. He says he thinks the continuation of a coalition Government after this war will prove to be essential in some form. He told me Lord Randolph Churchill had more charm than Winston but, if that were possible, worse manners.[784]

On the following day, Colville enjoyed another long conversation with his grandfather. He spent the remainder of his time reading a batch of Lord Rosebery's original essays and being introduced by Peggy to some of the treasures being stored at Mentmore (including refugee items from Westminster Abbey). An otherwise enjoyable and relaxing stay was spoiled when, on Thursday 15 March, Colville received a phone call from his aunt, Lady Adelaide Colville, informing him that his godfather and first cousin, Alick, Viscount Colville of Culross, had died when his plane crashed while taking off in the Azores.

The war in Europe was ended when the Allies accepted Germany's surrender on 8 May 1945. Just over one month later, on 20 June 1945, Lord Crewe died at his home at West Horsley, 'in a room overlooking the flower-garden and lined with books'.[785] The funeral service was held at the 'lovely red sandstone church' at Barthomley.[786]

'A Perpetual Fountain of Good Sense'
Political tributes to Crewe were led in the Lords Sitting of 22 August 1945 by Viscount Addison, the Secretary of State for Dominion Affairs. Crewe had died, Addison began, 'full of years and full of honour'. He had bequeathed an example, the Viscount explained, 'of a long life of

public service which will be difficult to emulate, but of which we are justly proud'. In reviewing the many highlights of a distinguished 60-year political career, Addison pointed out that Crewe had held the unique distinction of having served under five successive British Sovereigns. He further maintained that Crewe had employed his social advantages, not selfishly, but in the interests of the wider society. To that extent, 'he was in all his life a devoted public servant, and he was a splendid example of a great English gentleman'.[787]

This moving tribute was underscored by Viscount Cranborne, who ventured that there had not been anyone in the House 'more universally respected, indeed beloved, than Lord Crewe'. He was, said Cranborne, the member of a dying breed: 'Gifted, charming and kindly', he was an elder statesman on a par with 'those wise men described in Ecclesiasticus', who used their wisdom and understanding to inform, guide and direct the people. Cranborne revealed that he had visited Crewe only a few weeks before he died:

> I had gone down to the country where he was then living, and I was taken up to his room. He was lying on a sofa close to the window. He was an old man, his sight had almost gone, and I believe he was in constant pain. One might have expected that even his great spirit would have showed signs of weakening. But he was entirely serene. He talked with the greatest interest of the affairs of the day, of the latest developments of the war and of the last debates in your Lordships' House. His mind was as fresh and receptive as that of a young man. I thought I had never seen so magnificent an example of the triumph of the spirit over the infirmities of the flesh. My Lords, what is the supreme test of greatness? It is not that it should be said of a man that he did this or that, but that one should say, 'I should like to have been that man.'[788]

A final tribute was delivered by Crewe's old friend and fellow Liberal, Lord Samuel, who reminded the House of the well-known story that, when Asquith was Prime Minister, and 'faced by some problem of special difficulty', he would always turn in the first instance for Crewe's advice, in preference to that of any other minister. Moreover, declared Samuel,

So did the other members of that and other Governments, and many more as well, and seldom indeed it happened that Lord Crewe's opinion was not justified by the event. It might be said of him, as was said of a great Englishman in an earlier century: 'He was a perpetual fountain of good sense.'[789]

Moving On

Jock Colville had gone straight from attending his grandfather's funeral to boarding Winston Churchill's train at Leeds, where the Prime Minister and his entourage were seeking to generate Conservative support for a general election called in the wake of the Allied victory. This decision to capitalise on prevailing post-war euphoria unexpectedly backfired on the Tories. Contrary to all expectations, Labour was elected on 26 July 1945 with a landslide majority.[790]

In keeping with civil service tradition, Colville automatically transferred his professional allegiance by becoming an Assistant Private Secretary to the newly elected Labour Prime Minister, Clement Attlee. Colville served only a few brief months in this role before returning, as per prior agreement, to the Foreign Office. 'I left No. 10,' he wrote, 'glad to have served, for however short a period, a man whom I could not perhaps love, admire, laugh with and be uplifted by to the extent that I could feel and do all those things with Churchill, but one for whose integrity and competence I have an imperishable respect.'[791]

It soon became apparent that Jock Colville now entertained ambitions of entering Parliament. In October 1945, the Chelsea seat became available when the local MP succeeded his uncle into the House of Lords. Colville's bid to secure the Tory Party nomination was endorsed by Winston Churchill. He was dismayed to discover, though, that by the time the Conservative Association received his application, they had already chosen an alternative candidate. Colville briefly rued his luck before settling back into life at the Foreign Office, following a six-year leave of absence.

Similar political ambition was harboured by a second of Lord Crewe's grandsons. In late 1945, Terence O'Neill returned to his Irish roots by settling with his family in a converted Regency rectory near Ahogill, Northern Ireland. O'Neill had not previously spent any longer than the occasional holiday season in the country.[792] He had already tried

— albeit unsuccessfully — to persuade his uncle, Lord Rathcavan, to secure him a nomination for a safe Westminster seat. He was now setting his sights on winning a Northern Irish constituency according to his own devices.[793]

Lord Crewe's death in 1945 had elicited a change in his daughter Annabel's family name from Dodds to Crewe. This was to enable her to assume her inheritance of designated parts of her father's estate. It was therefore in the name of *Quentin Crewe* that the third of Lord Crewe's grandsons entered Cambridge in 1944 to study for a degree in Law. Quentin found his chosen subject so 'dreary' that he switched, after less than a year, to reading Economics. His new discipline proved equally tiresome.[794]

The 'two academically hopeless years' he spent at Cambridge were not entirely wasted, though. Aside from helping him to mature as an individual, Quentin's Cambridge experience equipped him with an enhanced appreciation of the theatre, broadened his knowledge of literature, and fostered a greater political awareness.[795] Early in his Cambridge career, he was advised by a fellow muscular dystrophy victim to prepare for the deterioration of his condition by pre-emptively using a walking stick. He left Cambridge prematurely, and physically more unsteadily than he had entered, but now re-set his sights on pursuing a career in the arts.[796]

In Chapter 21, we trace the continuing career trajectories of Quentin, his half-brother, Terence, and cousin, Jock. Their progress is thus examined with a view to emphasising the profound impact they would each eventually create, whether in the nation's political or diplomatic circles, or as part of its wider cultural character.

Chapter Twenty
New World Order

'Owned and Managed on Behalf of the People'
Already basking, like countless other Britons, in the post-war afterglow of a victory over fascism and the landslide election of the Labour Government, Jim Bullock oversaw the replacement of the colliery's eight original (though now antiquated) Lancashire boilers by seven high-pressure state-of-the-art alternatives. Informed opinion now estimated that Fryston possessed another 150 years of coal reserves.[797] The manager also re-embarked with renewed vigour and confidence on his mission to improve local social and welfare facilities.

> When I was a Fryston man at first, the only thing they got was a ton of coal per month. There were no canteens or anything like that. So, we built a canteen and we started selling miners their clothes. The Committee paid cash to the dealer in Castleford and the men and women could get their clothes and suits off us without the usual charge for deferred payments. From the money that we made at the canteen, we started selling radios and, later, televisions and washing machines. And we were able, for the first time in history, to take old people away for a week's holiday and I used to take them to the pantomime at Leeds. It enabled me to act as a sort of Robin Hood with other people's money because it was the miners' money; they'd made it. The Committee, under my leadership, spent it all on improving facilities in the village, particularly for the old people. (Jim Bullock, 1987)

Bullock's lifelong commitment to using his managerial status to secure better living and working conditions for those under his authority was epitomised by charitable activities designed to obtain invalid carriages for local miners with serious spinal injuries incurred underground. The first section of this chapter examines the broad nature of these charitable endeavours, while a second section focuses more specifically on yet more fund-raising football matches involving Fryston's post-war Bevin Boys — most notably, the legendary 'Clown Prince of Football', Len Shackleton.

Pit men and socialists like Bullock were understandably buoyed up by the advent of a majority Labour government, pledged to creating a thriving welfare state, full employment, a public health service and, most significantly for our purposes, the nationalisation of the mines. Fishman makes the point that this new state ownership of the mines saw the incorporation of 800 privately owned collieries into a single, centralised entity, 'owned and managed on behalf of the people'.[798]

Fishman also asserts, however, that ideological commitment was not the sole driver of governmental policy. Rather, nationalisation was regarded as the surest and most expedient way of addressing the severe and intensifying coal shortages continuing since the war. The euphoria that greeted nationalisation was short-lived. Eager to vindicate the government's decision to nationalise, the coal unions collaborated in a programme of work intensification: 'The pursuit of increased output by both management and union men was unremitting. If anything, the union campaign for more production was intensified after Vesting Day.'[799]

This chapter will go on to explain how these changes had the net effect of wresting the responsibility for planning and negotiation out of the reach of colliery managers like Jim Bullock, and placing the emphasis on centrally determined production and performance targets. The centralisation of such procedures imbued, not only senior NCB officials, but also trade union leaders — like the Yorkshire Area NUM President, Joe Hall — with immense personal power and prestige. This undoubtedly lay at the root of an unsavoury confrontation between Bullock and Hall (soon to be described, below) and helped fuel the former's determination to help found a trade union for the benefit of mine managers like himself.

Nationalisation was not, of course, the only significant socio-political development of the post-war period. The inception of the National Health Service (NHS) in 1948 represented the second monumental achievement of the new Labour Government. In the final section of the chapter, we examine the way that the transition from private to *publicly funded* general practice was met with disapproval by most

General Practitioners in Castleford. Conspicuously supportive of this more egalitarian system were George and Gerda Sloan, whose patient numbers expanded significantly while they personified a compassionate approach to medical intervention, in keeping with the intended ethos of the freshly minted NHS.

A 'Thing of Right, Not of Charity'

Jim Bullock recalls in *Them and Us* how his colliery was able to boast a relatively low accident rate in the immediate post-war years, but that this was still no cause for complacency: in one twelve-month period, Fryston incurred four serious accidents, all involving spinal fractures. Bullock had been aware since childhood that such hapless victims were invariably 'doomed' to spend their remaining days (an average of two more years), lying on a water bed in misery and pain caused by bed sores and bowel infections. His 'heart ached' to witness the plight of young men cut down in their prime, and to see the despair felt by their dependents. Bullock therefore resolved to do everything he could to improve the fortunes of such victims and their families.[800]

The Fryston manager drew inspiration from work undertaken at Pinderfields Hospital, Wakefield, where a local surgeon was exploring ways of improving the mobility of disabled miners. Bullock set about raising sufficient funds to provide motorised invalid carriages for disabled miners and additional amenities for their loved ones. His preferred approach was to establish 'concert parties', comprising local musicians and other entertainers, who performed at local pubs within a ten-mile radius of Fryston.[801]

Bullock could recall that one particular concert party member – a 'very talented London lad' called Les Aplin, who had married the Fryston-born Annie Holmes during the war – was capable of playing seven instruments to a professional standard. It was Aplin who helped crystallise the overall objective of the concerts by writing songs about injured miners and members of the colliery rescue team.[802] The popular, Bromley-born Aplin joined fellow Fryston musicians (such as Joe Smith, Herbert Brace and Harry Gilliver), and other entertainers, such as the local amateur comedian and 'drag queen', Asher Astbury, in putting on a string of well-received performances:

The first one we gave was at Knottingley. Hudswell-Clarks, the big pit suppliers at Leeds, contributed to it and, in fact, they paid for the hall for us. I wrote a monologue called 'The Broken-backed Miner'. I can't recall it now, but I know it finished up on the line, 'There but for the grace of God go I.' And in the little hush before the clapping started, the director of Hudswell-Clarks said, 'Hear, hear!' and I felt so proud that someone of his stature – 'cos I didn't know too many great men in those days – should appreciate what I'd done. (Les Aplin, 1986)

This was the first of many triumphs. One member of the party was the close friend of an ex-checkweighman from Fryston Colliery who played bass in the orchestra pit at the Theatre Royal in Castleford. It was owing to his influence that they were allowed to play this venue.

The show was on a Sunday night and Albert Modley, the very famous Yorkshire comedian, who was at the absolute height of his fame, volunteered his services for free. The concert was a great success. I finished it by singing 'Frankie and Johnny', which was very popular at the time. (Les Aplin, 1986)

An equally memorable concert was staged in Normanton High Street, where the Doncaster-born European Heavyweight (boxing) Champion, Bruce Woodcock, was guest of honour, and took his seat amidst a huge entourage.

Within twelve months, Bullock and his concert party had amassed enough money to buy motor-propelled carriages for every disabled Fryston miner. Then, as concert bookings continued to proliferate, the Fryston welfare committee was able to purchase such immensely helpful items as a washing machine and television set for each miner and his family, and to pay for them to spend a fortnight by the sea. This soon became, in Bullock's words, 'a thing of right and not of charity' (interview, 1987).

Fryston's example was imitated nationwide. An appropriate administrative infrastructure was soon established: the Yorkshire NUM President, Alwyn Machin, agreed to chair the first County Paraplegic Committee in Yorkshire, that also included Jim Bullock, Miss Pearson (the surgeon from Pinderfields) and Bullock's future second wife, Jay

Barstow, who was the coalfield's medical social worker at the time. Following the nationalisation of the mines (see below), a National Paraplegic Committee was formed, on which Bullock served as a founder member. The Fryston boss was therefore justified in maintaining:

> The things we had done and started at Fryston as an exception now became the rule throughout the whole of the mining industry. This was a development that has been rich in its rewards. The way the disabled are looked after now in the mining industry, compared to how they were previously neglected, is one of the most satisfying things in my whole career.[803]

Return of 'The Clown Prince'

The colliery's once formidable football team lost its momentum in the first post-war season of 1945-46, with only the Embleton Cup to show for their efforts. Fryston had been eliminated 4-2 in the second round of the WRCC Cup by a strong Selby Town Yorkshire League eleven.[804] Some consolation came in the form of their final fixture – a second, well-publicised charity match which pitted a Fryston XI against a Bradford Park Avenue first team, containing, not only Johnny Downie (who was a 'regular' by now), but also the future West Ham and England manager, Ron Greenwood.

The game, which was played, according to recent custom, on Castleford RLFC's Wheldon Road ground before a packed crowd, was predictably one-sided, with Downie playing a starring role in a 6-2 win for the visitors. A post-match 'smoking concert' was held at the Grosvenor Café, Castleford, in honour of both teams. Jim Bullock half-jokingly thanked Ernest Bevin for inventing the scheme which allowed so many talented sportsmen to work at Fryston. He derived great pleasure from knowing that the handsome gate receipts would enable the colliery to turn out a team for at least another season.[805]

In the following season, Jim Bullock's fund-raising activities were given a further boost by the arrival of two more Bevin Boys, the Bradford Park Avenue stars, Len Shackleton, and his colleague, the future Scottish international full-back, Jimmy Stephen. Faced with the post-war alternatives of engaging in some form of 'essential' factory work, undertaking National Service, or entering the mines as Bevin

Boys, Stephen and Shackleton each regarded the third option as least detrimental to their footballing careers.

Shackleton's decision was influenced by the fact that the firm he had recently been working for, the General Electric Company (GEC), was about to relocate from Bradford to Coventry: 'Deciding that, in the pit, I would at least be fairly near home – and Park Avenue football ground – I said I would have a crack at it.'[806] The future England international left readers of his autobiography, *Len Shackleton, Clown Prince of Soccer*, under no illusions that he lacked any appetite for pit work. 'My papers to report as a Bevin Boy duly arrived,' he recalled, 'even though I had warned the postman not to worry if he accidentally mislaid an OHMS envelope addressed to Len Shackleton.'[807] Psychologically unprepared for the task at hand, Shackleton began setting out on the 60-mile daily return trip from Bradford to Fryston and back in the company of his Avenue team-mate.

Jimmy Stephen spoke with similar distaste of the 'horrendous' six-hour round trip he and Shackleton daily embarked on. 'We had to get a bus from home to the centre of Bradford,' he later complained.

> Then we got a bus to Leeds, a bus from Leeds to Castleford and, finally, a bus from Castleford to Fryston. We used to have to leave our homes at six o'clock in the morning to start work at nine; and it was the same coming back, of course. It was a dreadful way of life, really.'[808]

For Shackleton, the 'shock' of having to leave Bradford so early each morning was one thing, but this was nothing compared to the experience of descending in the pit cage (or 'torture box', as he described it):

> Going down in a pit cage is a terrifying experience: it is like being suspended on a piece of elastic. One minute you are rushing into the bowels of the earth, imagining Brisbane to be the next stop; the next minute you stop suddenly and [...] just dangle. One day at Fryston was sufficient to convince me I had made a real blunder by volunteering for mining, and I soon started investigating ways and means of 'dodging the column' without being reprimanded for absenteeism. To be perfectly frank, I did not overwork myself.[809]

Shackleton's attitude to working underground was in stark contrast to that of the more committed Johnny Downie. Jim Bullock had not only assigned Shackleton and Stephen to significantly less arduous jobs, but also allowed them to work custom designed 'nine-to-five' shifts to compensate them for the additional travelling they endured. Downie spent life underground, loading the freshly won coal onto trolleys. Asked by Shackleton's biographer what the Clown Prince was doing in the meantime, Downie replied, 'Oh, I don't know. Wasting his time, I would think. He didn't go very often; he didn't go as often as us.'[810]

Bullock's lenient attitude was handsomely rewarded when Shackleton and Stephen heeded his request to help select and prepare a 'Fryston' team to play Frickley Colliery of the Midlands League in yet another charity match, staged with the objective of funding a further fleet of invalid carriages. By this time, Shackleton had recently been signed by Newcastle United, and transferred from Fryston to the north-eastern Gosforth Colliery, where he now worked in the company of the famous 'Magpies' and England centre-forward, Jackie Milburn. This recent development in Shackleton's career had considerably enhanced the appeal of the Fryston-Frickley contest.

In the run-up to this fixture, Shackleton had played only a handful of matches for Newcastle, following his British record-breaking £13,000 transfer from Park Avenue. His efforts had proven typically newsworthy: having scored six goals on his debut (on 5 October 1946) in a 13-0 win over Newport County, Shackleton suffered the ignominy of having a penalty saved, three games later, during Newcastle's Fourth Round FA Cup defeat by his former club.

Jimmy Stephen, for his part, had recently made his international debut as captain of Scotland in a 3-1 defeat against Wales. Perhaps not surprisingly, the Fryston team to play Frickley contained a sizeable Park Avenue contingent of Maddison (in goal), Farrell, Downie, Walker, Dix, Mordue, Stephen and Smith, supplemented by Shackleton (Newcastle United), Roberts (Fryston) and Gledhill (York City). During the actual game, a succession of more indigenous Fryston players came on as substitutes.

Though the occasion was badly affected by heavy rain, the players all contributed to an entertaining and highly competitive match, which was predictably won by Fryston:

In the early stages both Shackleton and Walker netted with first-time drives, and Walker got a third goal before the change round. In the second half a grand movement from one end of the field to the other saw Shackleton thread his way through the opposition for a fourth goal. Just on time Lunn succeeded with a lovely goal to make the result a win for Fryston by 4 goals to 1. In spite of the clinging mud and greasy ball some skilful work was put in by both teams, and the match was thoroughly enjoyed. The Fryston team were provided with kit, except boots, by the Bradford Park Avenue club.[811]

It was not long before Fryston said farewell to its remaining Bevin Boys. Shackleton's decision to join Newcastle, and his accompanying transfer to Gosforth, also put paid to Jimmy Stephen's Fryston career: 'When Len left, that was the end of our friendship – going to work and that,' the Scot explained, 'and I was so sick of it, I became what you'd call an "absentee".'[812] Stephen was therefore forced to complete his National Service in the RAF. He was eventually transferred from Park Avenue to Portsmouth in 1949. Of the other Fryston Bevin Boys, Arthur Farrell moved from Bradford to Barnsley in 1951; Geoff Walker spent eight more seasons with Middlesbrough before joining Doncaster Rovers in 1954; and Johnny Downie was transferred to Manchester United, for the then British record fee of £18,000 in 1948.

'Shack' played only two seasons for Newcastle before teaming up with their bitter north-eastern rivals, Sunderland, in 1948. Looking back on his experiences at Fryston and Gosforth, the Clown Prince reflected that, while he was clearly 'not cut out to be a miner', he had nonetheless developed 'a lot of admiration' for those he had been privileged enough to work alongside: 'They work hard, are never lavishly paid,' he commented, adding that they are 'among the most likeable and genuine people one could wish to meet.'[813]

No Longer the 'King of the Village'
'Vesting Day' of 1 January 1947 heralded the historic moment when the nationalisation of the mines at last became a reality. The occasion would always be remembered by Jim Bullock for the 'great celebrations' that accompanied it.

We had the village band out; the vicar was there and blessed the new N.C.B. flag and the pit; speeches were made from management and trade union leaders, pledging utmost cooperation and goodwill. Then the miners gave three cheers for the Labour Government and we set about our new task: To get more coal out; to make Nationalization really work. We all agreed ours – Fryston – was the pit to show how it could work. A Socialist Manager had already been there over twenty years, knew everybody by name in the pit, coupled with Trade Union leaders, respected and trusted by the men and the manager. What could stop us now?[814]

Bullock had been one of the most ardent, vociferous and optimistic proponents of Nationalisation; but his initial enthusiasm quickly turned into disillusionment once he became aware of the typical backgrounds of men who were appointed to the newly created levels (Pit Consultative, Area Consultative, Divisional Consultative and National Consultative) of the recently conceived National Coal Board. 'We'd got generals and admirals, and aristocrats and discarded food ministers – a real motley selection,' Bullock ruefully recalled. 'I mean, the chief qualification, well one of 'em, was they had to run a pit. I should think half of them had never seen one!'[815]

At a stroke, the authority of managers like Bullock was severely undermined: they were, in his words, 'no longer the king of our village'. Negotiations and discussions over wages, conditions and forward planning were now undertaken by trade union leaders and senior NCB officials. The priority for each Pit Consultative Committee was to establish 'tonnage targets' for each separate colliery. All mines achieving such targets were entitled to fly the NCB flag from their pit head for a period of five days. As Jim Bullock soberly recalled,

The first week our output was eight hundred tons more than we had ever had before but it was a few hundred tons below the target we had set. Result – a letter from the Divisional Board wanting to know the reason why we had not got our target, it wasn't a nice letter either.[816]

This had been a miscalculation on Bullock's part. Neighbouring collieries had all set their targets far more conservatively and received congratulatory letters by the hatful. Having learned this lesson the hard way, Bullock's committee simply dropped their targets to more achievable levels, with the result that 'We quickly wore our flag threadbare.'[817] Progress was discernible: in its first year as part of the 'NCB North Eastern Division No. 8 Castleford Area Sub Area "A"', Fryston's 1,478 employees produced 406,000 tons of coal. This had risen to a total of 446,663 tons, achieved from the same Beeston and Flockton 'Thick' seams by 1,754 personnel by 1954.[818]

Jim Bullock Versus Joseph Hall

Not long after Nationalisation had first arrived, Jim Bullock experienced an important epiphany when an unsavoury encounter with a miners' union leader convinced him of the urgent need to form a management trade union.[819] The first big union–management meeting to occur at Fryston since Vesting Day took place in Bullock's office. Management was represented by Bullock and his Area General Manager. The union delegation was led by the Yorkshire Area NUM President, Joseph Hall, a forceful and pugnacious character who was physically and intellectually well-qualified for even the most embittered confrontation with management or politicians.

This Barnsley-born Methodist lay preacher could boast an impressive trade union pedigree. Having risen through the ranks as branch secretary and checkweighman at Cortonwood Colliery, then Miners' Safety Inspector, financial secretary for the YMA and executive member of the MFGB, he succeeded his great friend, Herbert Smith, as YMA President in 1938.[820] Though consistently ebullient and unyielding, Hall undoubtedly possessed a softer and more cultured side: since starting work, he had been a committed autodidact, spending his early wages on classic novels, poetry books and the works of Shakespeare.[821] All told, as Jim Bullock acknowledged,

> Joe was already a veteran, a real fighter, either with his knuckles or with words. He made quite a reputation at inquiries held into various explosions when he represented the miners. Even before Nationalization he was an opponent to be feared. He would break forth into torrents of abuse against bosses in general and managers in particular. When addressing big miners' meetings, he had been known to descend from the platform and personally attack a heckler in the crowd.[822]

According to Bullock, Hall was apt to impose his authority over colliery managers by deliberately arriving hours late for meetings, and then quoting long sequences of poetry, Shakespeare and the scriptures to emphasise his intellectual superiority.[823] Such was the case in question: 'On the day he arrived in Fryston village (two hours late) he met a Fryston miner – a real idle fellow – who asked him to go into his coal cellar with him and see the sort of "home coal" that Bullock was sending him.'[824] Bullock explained how Hall had duly escorted this old miner down the cellar stairs.

> And everybody gets a bit of muck in their coal at times, you know, and they get it for nowt – it isn't as if we're frightened of losing their custom, either. So, therefore, probably this coal that he saw in this cellar had been the accumulation, well, not of centuries, but many, many years. And he had a big heap of muck.[825]

Hall preferred to accept the word of the Fryston miner, who alleged that this dirt had accompanied a single delivery of coal. The Yorkshire Area President not only fumed at this discovery, but also promised the miner that he would *insist* that Jim Bullock come over within the next half hour and personally shovel every speck of 'muck' into the back of a lorry.[826]

Within minutes, a still-furious Joe Hall burst, without knocking, into Bullock's office, where he declared himself 'astounded' by what he had just witnessed in the cellar. He then repeated the promise he had just made to the miner – followed by an astonishing ultimatum: 'I'm giving you five minutes to pick up that telephone, order a lorry to come round here and then you, Jim Bullock, will go and you [will] shovel that muck out yourself, put it in the lorry and see it is carried away.'[827]

Bullock remained defiantly uncompromising, even when Hall threatened to throw him out of the window and 'down the bloody stairs'. A brief, 'deadly' silence ensued before Bullock 'dropped his bombshell' by threatening Hall in turn that, whilst he 'might have got away with this in any other office in Yorkshire', he was not going to get away with it in Fryston. Bullock then turned the tables on Hall by insisting that, if the *union leader himself* didn't go and shovel the dirt out, *he* would be the one flying down the stairs.[828]

The tension had now become unbearable. The Area Director appealed to Bullock to accompany him over to the old miner's house, where they could attempt to sort things out. Bullock remained unrepentant:

> So I says, 'There's no compromise wi' me,' I says, 'If thy's frightened of him, I'm not.' So I started taking my coat off and hanging it up on this peg, and I began to wonder how we were getting out of this because I knew I wasn't going down for that coal, and I knew Joe, and I knew that he didn't like being shown up. But he suddenly showed what a great man he is in other ways: he turned round and he says to t' union committee, 'There you go,' he says. 'Do you think you're gonna have me falling out with the best colliery manager we've got?' He says, 'T' only bloody socialist we've got as a colliery manager! Falling out?' he says. 'I've only done this to let you know he's got some bloody guts. So look after this lad! Learn to help this lad!' And before long, we were shaking hands, and it was absolutely marvellous.[829]

Bullock recalled how the incident was over in a flash. Afterwards, though, he shuddered to think what might have happened in the offices of managerial colleagues too afraid, unlike him, to stand up to the likes of Hall. He therefore committed himself to helping create the British Association of Colliery Management, the institution he would one day become National President of.[830]

Always Prescribing the Best

The second monumental development of the immediate post-war period was the foundation of the NHS in 1948. According to Richard Sloan, his parents were among only a small minority of consultants and General Practitioners in their district who readily welcomed and embraced this new development. George and Gerda's historically benevolent attitude to local people immediately paid dividends: 'Because of [my father's] kindness for many years during the depression and my mother's compassionate approach, patients were queuing hundreds of yards on the approach road to the surgery to register with them as NHS patients in 1948.'[831]

This constituency of patients eventually peaked at around ten thousand, encouraging the Sloans to take on a partner, the Scottish-born

Dr Smith, an entertaining man who raced greyhounds and, one New Year's Eve, fell drunkenly through the door of Tieve Tara, much to the disapproval of the teetotal George Sloan.[832]

More recent generations might understandably feel envious of the system of medical general practice prevailing in the early days of the NHS. As Richard Sloan recalls,

> My parents would spend part of the evening updating a large ledger in which was kept lists of patients who required revisiting the next day. The phone would start ringing at about 8 a.m., and there would be scores of new visit requests to be undertaken as well as the revisits. There were two people living in different parts of the housing estate who also took messages and visit requests. This was because a large number of patients did not have telephones and the telephone boxes were often vandalised. The GP could park his or her car at the address of one visit and do a further six without driving. Visits were undertaken in all weathers and at all times.[833]

It was customary at this time for Richard to escort his mother round Fryston and Airedale as Christmas approached, delivering mince pies to poorer families in the area. 'We arrived at one house, and I thought there was no-one in because there were no lights on,' Richard disclosed. 'My mother explained that this was Mr and Mrs Stevens and they were both blind.'[834]

In fact, Fred and Christine Stevens had come together in heart-warming fashion shortly after the war. Their relationship followed a period of correspondence in which Fryston-born Fred wrote loving letters in braille and Christine did likewise from her distant home of Sri Lanka. Eventually, the two met up in person, fell in love and married. Christine Stevens had particular reason to feel indebted to 'Dr Gerda' when Fred was admitted to hospital with a severe bout of pleurisy and pneumonia:

> Dr Gerda was very good. I mean, she was a real good friend to me. She tried to keep him at home with me being new to the village and only his parents there, but he was really, really ill and I was expecting our first baby. So, eventually she said, 'I'm very sorry, but I shall have to let them take him to hospital.' And they carried him out on a stretcher and, he was that ill,

nobody thought he'd come back in again. That was 34 years ago, so he managed to survive! Then, once we got a house outside Fryston, we started to do well. His parents didn't want us to get a house. They said we'd never manage. Then again, Dr Gerda stepped in and said, 'Please give them a chance. If you don't give them a chance, they'll never manage at all.' So, she helped to get us a 'prefab'. Things worked out just fine and she was very pleased for us. (Interview, 1986)

George and Gerda continued to operate in the relaxed, person-oriented style which had been the hallmark of their pre-NHS patient care. According to Richard Sloan,

My father rarely wrote in the patient's records and the practice consistently spent too much money on prescription drugs. Men from London were sent up to assess the situation and he was threatened with fines. He told them that he would always prescribe the best for his patients. My mother had the same approach.[835]

This is not to pretend that obvious class differences were not apparent. As Richard readily concedes, 'Being the only son of parents both of whom were GPs meant that I had a thoroughly middle-class and privileged upbringing.'[836] He was forbidden from going into Fryston village as his parents regarded it as too rough a place for him. In contrast to other families, his parents employed a housekeeper, gardener, chauffeur and someone to wash their car.[837]

Richard also had a live-in nanny and acknowledges that his mother 'doted' on him and spoilt him until the day she died. Having initially attended Airedale infants and primary school, Richard was enrolled at the age of six at the more prestigious Queen Elizabeth Grammar School in Wakefield. His birthday parties were held in the Tieve Tara waiting room. On one such occasion in 1951, Gerda Sloan hired the famous children's television personality, Harry Corbett, who came, along with his famous glove puppet, 'Sooty' the bear, to entertain Richard and his guests.[838] As a rule,

We went on great holidays, and when I reached the age of about seven, the holidays alternated between Lake Tegernsee in Bavaria and a cruise. On the German holiday, we met with her brother, Herbert, and his Russian wife, Sania. They lived in Munich. My mother made sure my father and I were introduced to the theatre and the arts. She took my father to hear Richard Tauber (the German tenor) sing at the Grand Theatre, Leeds. After the performance, to my father's delight, they went backstage and she introduced him to Tauber. Richard Tauber had been a friend of my grandfather in Berlin.[839]

It was not, however, a life entirely devoid of tragedy. Gerda Sloan's parents had returned to London at the end of World War II. Her father died suddenly in 1952 and her mother, Lily, killed herself by slashing her wrists soon afterwards. What Richard refers to as this 'selfish act'[840] magnified the blame cast on Gerda by her brother for failing to come quickly enough to Lily's assistance following her husband's death. This had a lasting impact on his mother's mental health: the trauma added, in his opinion, to Gerda's 'already significant guilt complex as a survivor of the war', causing her to drink too much, especially in the evenings.[841]

Sloan is careful to insist that this did not affect his mother's medical work, although it would eventually take its toll on her physical well-being. Gerda's 'excessive' drinking became the subject of rows between mother and son;[842] but as we shall see later, they nonetheless maintained a personal and professional relationship of inestimable benefit to the people of Fryston.

Chapter Twenty-One
Ceremony, Secrecy and Discord

Peace In Our Time

The termination of global conflict enabled some members of the 'Milnes-Crewe dynasty' to re-enter their peacetime roles. Lord Crewe's daughter, Cynthia Colville, continued to occupy the position of Woman of the Bedchamber to Queen Mary, while her younger half-sister, Mary, resettled into the privileged Scottish lifestyle commensurate with her ducal status.

Two of Crewe's grandsons, Jock Colville and Terence O'Neill, returned home from active service to resume civil service and political careers, respectively. O'Neill began fulfilling a political ambition which would eventually see him elected as Prime Minister of Northern Ireland. Terence's cousin, Jock, briefly returned to the Foreign Office before strengthening his family connection with British royalty by becoming Private Secretary to the young Princess Elizabeth, and then switching roles again to become peacetime Joint Principal Private Secretary to Prime Minister, Winston Churchill.

Another grandson, Quentin Crewe, had abandoned life at Cambridge University and was languishing in relatively menial jobs. This did not prevent him from forming an ill-fated relationship with the daughter of the future British Prime Minister, Harold Macmillan, and his wife, Dorothy.

This chapter comprehensively outlines these developments, many of which would significantly help shape the course of British history in the decades that followed.

Born to Rule

Having set his sights on entering the British Parliament as a Northern Irish MP, Terence O'Neill quickly seized an early opportunity to do so when, in October 1946, a by-election arose in the Stormont constituency of Bannside. O'Neill leaned heavily on 'the prestige of his family name', both to secure the Unionist nomination and be elected unopposed in November 1946. It was regarded as irrelevant that he 'had neither previous reputation nor experience' with the party.[843]

In addition to the ancestral advantage he enjoyed, O'Neill was fortunate to have served as an army captain:

> A military tradition carried an important kudos in Unionist politics. [...] It marked him out as one of a long line of aristocratic warriors who had served queen and country with savoir-faire and an upbeat combination of duty and adventure.[844]

Mulholland adds that, in common with most 'unionist liberals', O'Neill's personal life had been 'almost hermetically sealed off' from any contact with the Catholic population.[845] Somewhat disconcertingly,

> There was little sign in O'Neill's personal life of any particular sympathy with the Catholic minority. Notoriously, in the 1950s he placed an advertisement in a Belfast newspaper seeking a protestant housemaid. This, he explained unapologetically in 1972, was because on previous occasions there had been 'some trouble' over Catholic staff, so they had 'advertised for a person of the Protestant religion to stop Catholics turning up'. His daughter, Anne, born 1947, reminiscing in 1969 of her Ahoghill childhood, recalled that she was warned to steer clear of Catholics as dangerous rowdies. The image of an aloof ascendancy family is inescapable.[846]

By his own later admission, O'Neill's English upbringing had not prepared him for the 'intricacies of Ulster politics'. Thus, 'The impression gained is that of a British constitutionalist to whom the passions of Irish nationalisms were quite alien.'[847]

O'Neill's first political role of any distinction was secured in 1948, when he was appointed Parliamentary Secretary to William Grant, Minister of Health with special responsibility for housing. The time spent in this ministry provided O'Neill with a crash course in Unionist political sensibilities: lacking any real apprenticeship in the ranks of the party or the Protestant Orange Order, O'Neill's association with Grant, a minister with rare working-class credentials, was perhaps the closest he ever came to working with Unionism's plebeian core.[848]

In October 1945, Jock Colville returned from his secondment and re-entered the Foreign Office, where the country allocated to him was Yugoslavia; but, in the spring of 1947, he was unexpectedly offered the role of Private Secretary to the 21-year-old Princess Elizabeth.

> There was no interviewing, no overt headhunting for jobs like these. Colville was a member of the magic circle of courtiers and aristocrats, known at court almost since his birth as the son of Lady Cynthia Colville and the grandson of the Marquess of Crewe. His training had been in the Foreign Office, traditionally regarded as a seed bed for royal officials. Colville knew enough about court life not to want to become a permanent part of it.[849]

Colville certainly had no desire to abandon his blossoming civil service career; but whatever hesitation he may have felt was ameliorated by a guarantee that this secondment would be limited to two years. His decision was also influenced by the words of Winston Churchill, who insisted that it was his duty to accept. Colville later reflected that 'It was in the event a greater pleasure than a duty, for I served a young lady as wise as she was attractive.'[850]

A mere four months into his appointment, Colville played an important, but little-known, role in Princess Elizabeth's marriage to Lieutenant Philip Mountbatten, which took place at Westminster Abbey on Thursday, 20 November 1947. Colville was meant to ride, decked out in Air Force uniform, amidst the Queen's procession to Westminster Abbey, but things did not proceed strictly according to plan:

> Half an hour before the Queen's procession was due to leave, I received an urgent summons to go to Princess Elizabeth's sitting room. She stood there, radiant and entrancing in her wedding dress. One thing and one only had gone wrong. The superb pearl necklace which the King had given her had been left with the other presents at St James's Palace, where they were to be on display to the public, and she particularly wanted to wear her father's present at her wedding. Could I, somehow, make my way to St James's Palace and retrieve the necklace?[851]

Colville galloped immediately down the palace staircase into the main quadrangle, where he jumped into a conveniently parked Royal Daimler. Finding himself confronted by a fifteen-deep crowd across Marlborough Gate, he was forced to abandon the vehicle and cover the remaining distance on foot:

> I ran as fast as I could to Friary Court, St James's Palace. All was still and there was not a living soul to be seen. I rang the doorbell and nothing happened. I rang again and after a minute or two a suspicious face appeared as the door opened a few inches. I was asked what my business might be. My story sounded improbable and the ancient janitor evidently thought it so. He was clearly undecided, so that I began to wonder whether to push him aside and force an entry. Finally he let me in with a warning that upstairs, guarding the wedding presents, I should find representatives of the CID.[852]

Colville was duly met by burly-looking officers who were immensely suspicious of his request. It was only when his name was identified on the Wedding Programme that Colville was finally allowed to retrieve the necklace and deliver it to the Princess in time.

Among those also playing important supporting roles was one of the Princess's Ladies-in-Waiting, Lady Margaret ('Meg') Egerton. The fifth daughter of the fourth Earl of Ellesmere, Egerton had spent World War II in the Kelso Auxiliary Territorial Services, when she found herself posted to Edinburgh Castle as a clerk at Scottish Command (HQ of the Scottish Army). She was accorded the distinction of leading the ATS in the victory parade along Princes Street.[853] According to Bradford, Egerton had been 'recruited in the same, apparently informal way after the shy Princess had stayed with her family in March 1946 for a race meeting'.[854]

Subsequently, this Lady-in-Waiting had not only enchanted her royal employer by singing, in beautiful voice 'in the heather of Balmoral', the metrical psalm, 'The Lord's My Shepherd', but had also taught Elizabeth and her younger sister, Margaret, a little-known descant.

> Princess Elizabeth decided to have this at her wedding, but nobody could find the score of the descant. Lady Margaret,

tunefully accompanied by the two princesses, therefore sang it to the Organist and Precentor of Westminster Abbey who took down the notes in musical shorthand and taught it to the Abbey Choir.[855]

By February 1948, Jock Colville had, by his own admission, 'fallen head over heels in love' with Egerton. She was, as he put it, 'strikingly good-looking, and no less strikingly vivacious'.[856] The fact that Colville's office at Buckingham Palace was located next door to the Lady-in-Waiting's suite of rooms gave him an 'unfair advantage' over rival suitors.[857] The couple were engaged in July 1948 and married at St Margaret's, Westminster, on 20 October 1948, 'causing a traffic jam in Parliament Square of major inconvenience to the public'.[858] Princess Margaret was one of the bridesmaids. Among other attendees was Sir Winston Churchill.

> He came to my own wedding and fell for the bride. Her vivacity and strikingly good features captivated him: they laughed together, they gossiped together and whenever he possibly could, he put her next to him at dinner, sometimes to the displeasure of ladies who thought they had a higher claim to precedence than the private secretary's wife. Churchill never failed to be attracted by the young of either sex. He encouraged the boys and he flirted, very mildly, with the girls, provided they were both good-looking and forthcoming.[859]

'Pledged to Stay Together'

Having left Cambridge in 1946, Quentin Crewe had moved to London, where he briefly helped run a bookshop. He then occupied equally short-lived roles as an organiser of art exhibitions, a clerical worker in a film-processing factory, and a receptionist for a travel agency. Quentin lived briefly with the Bonham-Carter family in Gloucester Square, before moving, in 1948, into a flat in Sloane Street with his brother, Colin. The two men attended twice-weekly debutante dances, sometimes attended by Princesses Elizabeth and Margaret. He had started to fall over regularly by now, and begun trying various forms of unconventional medicine, including acupuncture, in a bid to offset his illness.[860]

That year was also marked by the death of his mother, Annabel, whose funeral was held at Barthomley. It was attended by a host of family mourners, including her stepmother, the Marchioness of Crewe, and two sisters, Lady Cynthia Colville and Lady Celia Milnes Coates. The service was led by the Archdeacon of Macclesfield, with six tenant farmers acting as pall bearers. Quentin characteristically maintained that his mother's death had 'meant little' to him personally.[861]

In fact, he responded by embarking on a tour of Britain in the company of a Cambridge peer, Willy Mostyn-Owen. The two friends stayed at the homes of the latter's mother in Shropshire and Perthshire. During one such stay, Quentin met Sarah Macmillan, the youngest of four children belonging to the future Conservative Prime Minister, Harold Macmillan, and his wife, Lady Dorothy Cavendish.

> Sarah came, one weekend, to stay with Willy. She was not especially pretty. Her eyes were too small and her lips thin, but when she smiled her eyes crinkled in a way that was for years to make my heart turn over. She had a beautiful figure, which she spoiled much of the time by moving, when she was nervous, with a diffident crouch. There was a vulnerability about her that I found touching, but also, even at the very beginning, there was a waywardness that was challenging and an enigmatic quality that gave me no peace. By the end of the weekend we were lovers, pledged to stay together for a long time.[862]

The couple's future happiness was threatened by the fact that, as a teenager, Sarah had been cruelly informed by a male friend of Princess Margaret's that Harold Macmillan was not really her father, and that she was actually the daughter of his close friend and political ally, Robert (Bob) Boothby, MP for Aberdeen and Kincardine East.

Macmillan and Wife

Sarah's mother, Lady Dorothy, was the third daughter of the 9th Duke of Devonshire. Dorothy had met Harold Macmillan in 1919, while the latter was acting as aide-de-camp to *her* father, who was then Governor-General of Canada. Macmillan also worked at this time for his family's huge publishing corporation. In spite of their obvious dissimilarities (she being high-spirited, warm and outgoing, while he was sober and dreary, both in appearance and disposition), they were engaged after three months and married in 1920.

The couple had produced three children between 1921 and 1926, during which time Macmillan became a Member of Parliament (in 1924). By the late 1920s, a rift had developed in their relationship. Dorothy's parents had always wondered why their daughter had ever become attracted to this plain-looking and scruffily clad individual – undoubtedly the 'most stupendously boring man' they had ever clapped eyes on:

> By 1929 she was wondering why also. She had problems with her fierce American mother-in-law at Birch Grove, the family Edwardian mansion and estate in Sussex, and a husband whom she now regarded as unsatisfactory in most respects. She was bored. She was also exceptionally selfish and emotional, and craved excitement and drama. Macmillan, through no fault of his own, could supply few of her requirements.[863]

An unexpected twist occurred when the Macmillans were invited by Bob Boothby to form part of a shooting party at his parents' stately home at Beechwood, shortly after Macmillan had lost his seat at the 1929 election. As Parris points out, the glamorous and telegenic Boothby was everything Harold was not:

> He was a handsome, dashing, assured fellow who drove a two-seater Bentley. His oratory was commanding, as was his sureness of touch, whether with dukes or dustmen, complete. He was as at home in grand country houses as in a fisherman's cottage in his Scottish constituency.[864]

On the second day of the shoot, Boothby was astonished to find his hand being squeezed affectionately by Dorothy Macmillan. 'That was when it all began,' according to Rhodes-James. 'Dorothy was not beautiful, but she was highly sexed, seeking adventure and eager,' he added. 'However, what began as a casual affair initiated by her, and not by Boothby, very rapidly developed into something very serious on both sides.'[865]

The 'serious' nature of this relationship was re-emphasised on 26 August 1930, when Dorothy Macmillan gave birth to her fourth child – and third daughter – Sarah. Due to complications emerging during labour, Dorothy was confined to her bed for several months. Soon afterwards, she disclosed to Harold that Boothby was the father of her child and that she wanted the freedom to marry him. Macmillan rejected his wife's request for a divorce, but this did not deter Dorothy and Boothby from living together between 1929 and 1935. Meanwhile,

> Macmillan said he had done nothing wrong and refused to accuse his wife of adultery. Politically, it would have been damaging. Macmillan had won back his Stockton seat in 1931 and any suggestion of his wife's adultery would have unsettled his constituents.[866]

The affair nonetheless took its toll on Harold Macmillan. There was talk of an attempted suicide, and Parris suspects that, when Macmillan collapsed and briefly entered a Munich-based sanatorium in 1931, it was due to the strain induced by the Boothby affair.[867] Boothby, himself, tried repeatedly to extricate himself from the affair. Acting in desperation, he rashly proposed marriage to Dorothy's cousin, Diane Cavendish, in 1935; but the marriage soon failed, and he started seeing Dorothy again.[868]

Falling Down 'More and More'

Quentin Crewe believes that Boothby's relationship with Sarah was driven, not by genuine parental affection, but 'by a perverse pride in the scandal', which continued to swell alongside Macmillan's growing political celebrity.

> At the same time, he [Boothby] was generous and good company. He had a flamboyance so far removed from the modesty of my upbringing that I was dazzled. He used to take Sarah and myself to the opera, generally Wagner. He always had a box, so that when we got to those longueurs which bored him we could go out to have a glass of champagne and come back in time for the splendours.[869]

Such activities formed part of a wider, enviable style of life whereby Quentin accompanied Sarah and her mother to point-to-point meetings, local dances or shooting parties, or otherwise simply lounged around, 'happy to spend our weekends in indolent content'.[870] This idyllic form of existence was dramatically short-circuited when (in 1950) Quentin and Sarah impulsively announced their intention to marry. Lady Dorothy appealed to Quentin in writing to reconsider this course of action. She referred tactfully and sympathetically to the burden that his disability might place on her daughter, and to the fact that she was too young to be tied down so early in life.[871]

Quentin's relationship with Sarah would eventually break down, due to the latter's infidelity. The former attributed this outcome to two fatal 'strands' intrinsic to Sarah's 'complex character'. The first of these originated from 'a desperate need to be liked, to be reassured that her illegitimacy, as she thought of it, did not matter', while the second comprised 'a compulsive infidelity', marked by 'an emotional nomadism, seeking fresh pastures'.[872]

Sarah's proclivity for behaving in unfaithful and deceitful manner was ironically disclosed to Quentin in a letter sent to him in December 1950 by Bob Boothby, which implored him not to trust any of Sarah's statements or intentions. Boothby informed Quentin how, the previous evening, Sarah had secretly gone to a restaurant with another admirer and asked her date to ring Quentin with a bogus excuse for her lateness in arriving home. 'Now you do not do this sort of thing to someone you love,' wrote Boothby. 'The truth of the matter is that at present she is in love only with herself,' he continued. 'And if you persist in the delusion that she loves you, you are going to get badly hurt.'[873]

For the next few weeks, Quentin 'lived in a state of frenzy – crying to Lady Dorothy, abusing my friends in ways that I cannot really remember'.[874] Then Sarah announced that she was pregnant by another man. Quentin remained adamant that the child could just as easily have been his. He nonetheless acknowledged the mother's right to nominate the father, after which Bob Boothby wrote a second letter, reassuring him that he would soon feel better for finally having had his eyes 'cleared of illusion'.[875]

Calculations of political necessity and expediency by Lady Dorothy were the main drivers of subsequent events. The summer of 1951 represented a crucial political juncture.

> The country was facing one of its perennial economic disasters. It seemed certain that Labour would have to call an election, and more than probable that they would lose it. If the

Conservatives won, Harold would surely be offered an important job. Lady Dorothy decided that nothing must be allowed to damage his prospects. She thought that Sarah's having a baby would be a threat; she must have an abortion.[876]

The operation was legitimised by two psychiatrists, who vouched for the fact that having the baby might pose a grave risk to Sarah's health. Hard though Sarah protested, her mother's insistent attitude gradually wore her down. Lady Dorothy took Harold off for the summer break, leaving him none the wiser of relevant developments. Ironically, the abortion brought Dorothy and Quentin into a 'closer and more confiding' relationship and the latter spent a great deal of time at the Macmillan home.[877]

Up until now, Sarah had been living with the presumed father of her child, but the latter contracted tuberculosis and was admitted to a sanatorium, forcing Sarah to return home to her parents. Quentin discovered that he was still in love with her, but these feelings were not reciprocated: 'In different ways, we needed each other and comforted each other,' he observed. 'But, in the end, it was for me too painful.'[878] Quentin's inability to walk had worsened to such an extent by now that Harold Macmillan insisted on him seeing his doctor:

> I fell down more and more and the knees of my trousers now looked like tea cosies and my ankles wept copiously. The doctor thought that my struggling on buses to work and the uphill walk each evening up the Haymarket was bad for me. I seized happily on this opinion and left my tedious job on the French line.[879]

Just Say 'No'
When Jock Colville's royal secondment expired in September 1949, he moved to Lisbon, where he was appointed Head of Chancery in the Embassy. He returned to Britain on leave in October 1951. Eighteen months earlier, Clement Attlee's Labour Party had won the general election by five seats, but had since decided to try and increase their majority, only to lose out to Sir Winston Churchill's Conservatives. The Colvilles were heading for a holiday in Scotland, but stopped off en route to stay at Jock's mother-in-law's, near

Newmarket, where they all attended the Cesarewitch race meeting. Colville was approached in the Jockey Club Stand by an 'agitated official' who hastily informed him that the Prime Minister (Churchill) wanted an urgent word. '"Whatever he asks you to do," advised [his] innately cautious wife, "Say no."'[880]

Colville failed to heed his wife's advice. Later in the afternoon, he travelled by train to London, where he accepted Churchill's invitation to become his Principal Private Secretary. Colville had initially been hesitant in accepting, since he considered himself 'ten years too young for such an appointment', and also felt that he lacked sufficient knowledge of political issues arising outside of the Foreign Office.[881] Above all, it was only one month earlier that Churchill's predecessor (Attlee) had appointed to the role of PPS the extremely competent and highly regarded Treasury official, David Pitblado.

Jock had already taken the view that, 'If Pitblado were now required to make way for me, it would smack of favouritism and those who mattered in Whitehall would resent the imposition of a largely unqualified incumbent to replace a highly qualified one.'[882] The eventual solution to this dilemma was to have Colville and Pitblado act as Joint Principal Private Secretaries, with the former acting primarily as conduit between Churchill and his Cabinet, and the latter expediting the day-to-day running of the Treasury, the Civil Service, and economic affairs.

Many of Churchill's closest friends and relatives considered it unwise of the Prime Minister to return to office as his 77th birthday approached. Churchill initially informed Colville that he intended to stay on for only one year, before handing the reins to Anthony Eden: 'He just wanted, he said, to have time to re-establish the intimate relationship with the United States, which had been a keynote of his policy in the war, and to restore at home the liberties which had been eroded by war-time restrictions and post-war socialist measures.'[883]

Colville maintains that, during the three-and-a-half years of Churchill's second administration, he succeeded in returning the country from conditions of post-war economic malaise and rationing to a 'shedding of austerity, a return to comparative prosperity and a temporary restoration of peace on earth'.[884] It was indisputable, though, that the effort involved had taken its toll on Churchill's health.

Throughout this period, Churchill had shown an increasing proneness to tiredness, and the responsibility for writing his speeches was increasingly devolved to Colville.[885] The death of King George VI on 6 February 1952 reduced the Premier to tears; and, one week after the state funeral of 22 February, Churchill's physician, Lord Moran, informed Colville that the Prime Minister had experienced a small arterial spasm, which might prove the precursor of a stroke. A brief economic downturn unfolded, during which Churchill's popularity and that of his government was badly undermined.[886]

God Rest the King

The death of George VI had placed Cynthia Colville once more in the unenviable position of having to convey tragic news to Queen Mary. Cynthia was in the process of eating breakfast with two colleagues at Marlborough House when an emissary unexpectedly arrived at their table, bearing 'the horrifying news' that the King had 'expired quietly during the night without anybody at the time being any the wiser'.[887] Cynthia initially responded in disbelief. The King had seemed in such good health the night before. She also reflected to herself how 'energetic and cheerful' he had seemed at Sandringham over Christmas.

> I could recall how His Majesty had remarked to me one evening at dinner how foolish it was to confuse illness and operations. He pointed out how he had had an operation the previous autumn (for the removal of a lung) and now he was perfectly well again.[888]

Cynthia felt desperately sorry for her queen, who had now lost three of her six children and recently witnessed the abdication of her son, King Edward VIII. However, even in the grip of such tragedy, the Queen remained conscious of the need to comfort and console her widowed daughter-in-law. Equally, 'with her keen and dispassionate sense of the inherent vocation that alone justified the age-long tradition of the monarchy', Mary regarded it imperative that she be the first person to curtsy before, and kiss the hand of, the new Sovereign.[889]

Somewhat propitiously, Queen Elizabeth II had just arrived back in London, after visiting Kenya with Prince Philip, where they had both been told of her father's passing. Elizabeth had only returned to

Clarence House a matter of 30 minutes earlier when Queen Mary arrived to meet her. Mary had travelled over by Daimler, waiving all the while to the crowds gathering sympathetically on the street. She arrived at 4:30pm to find Elizabeth and her husband already waiting to welcome her.

> Queen Mary walked to her. Queen Elizabeth extended her hand, and her grandmother and subject took it and kissed it lightly. 'God save the Queen,' she said in a strong voice that had the ring of a declaration.[890]

Dancing Queen

A period of reconsolidation lay ahead. On 3 December 1952, Meg Colville gave birth to her and Jock's first child, a daughter who was originally called Harriet Jane. The infant was subsequently re-registered, however, as Elizabeth Harriet, in honour of the new Queen, who offered to be her godparent. A similar offer was extended by Winston Churchill, who also attended the christening.[891]

The Coronation of Queen Elizabeth II took place on 2 June 1953, but not before Queen Mary had passed away some two months earlier. On 31 May, Jock and Meg Colville had attended the grand Household Brigade's Ball at Hampton Court. Male guests all wore tailcoats and some of them knee-breeches, while most women wore tiaras and dresses 'worthy of the occasion'.[892] The Palace was bathed in floodlight, its fountains surrounded by floral banks. In one memorable instance, 'The Queen, dancing with the Duke of Edinburgh and looking as beautiful as the people imagine her to be, stopped to ask us how her goddaughter did and whether she was yet out of control,' said Jock.[893]

On Coronation Day, Jock and Meg left home for Westminster Abbey at 7:15am. The weather was cold and it was threatening to rain, but the anticipated downpour held off until well after the service commenced. The Queen had favoured Jock, Meg and Cynthia with seats in her box, immediately above the Queen Mother and princesses: 'Though we saw little of the procession entering the Abbey,' said Colville, 'we saw every movement of the Queen, including the anointing, better than 95 per cent of the people in the Abbey, and looked straight at the massed peeresses whose robes and jewels sparkled with unique magnificence and whose movement as, with white gloved hands, they put their coronets on was aptly compared to the corps de ballet in *Lac des Cygnes*.'[894]

Once the ceremony was over, Jock and Meg Colville sat down to lunch in Westminster Hall. Afterwards, they joined the Prime Minister in watching a magnificent firework display on the Thames from the vantage point of the Ministry of Materials. Cynthia Colville rushed back home from the service to change into more casual clothing before taking the Underground train to Shoreditch with the intention of sharing celebrations with her old friends in the borough:

> It was a Shoreditch far less poor than I had originally known it, and changed in many other ways too, but one thing it had certainly not lost — its loyalty. The gorgeously attired congregation of the Abbey that day, with coronets, ermine and sparkling diamonds, was no more united in its affection and allegiance to its new and beautiful young Queen than were the people of the erstwhile slums of Hoxton and Haggerston.[895]

The events of this day were a testament to Cynthia Colville's dual affiliation to two extremely disparate sections of society. The profound appreciation extended to her by members of both social strata was reflected in the fact that a housing complex in Shoreditch was renamed the 'Colville Estate' in her honour; while, in 1953, she was made a Dame Commander of the Order of the British Empire. These and her other accomplishments are modestly described in her autobiographical *Crowded Life*, published five years before she died, aged 84, on 15 June 1968.

A Stroke of Deception

By now, Winston Churchill's health was progressively deteriorating. Jock Colville had noted in his diary entries of June 1952 that the Prime Minister was often feeling depressed and claiming to have lost his political vigour.[896] A *physical* decline was equally palpable. On Sunday, 9 November 1952, Colville had observed in his diary that: 'He (W.) is getting tired and visibly ageing. He finds it hard work to compose a speech and ideas no longer flow.'[897]

An almost inevitable crisis arose on 23 June 1953, when Jock and Meg Colville were among Churchill's guests at a lavish dinner at 10,

Downing Street, held in honour of the Italian Prime Minister. As Colville put it in his diary,

> At the end of the dinner, W. made a little speech in his best and most sparkling form, mainly about the Roman Conquest of Britain! After dinner he had a stroke, which occurred while he was in the pillared room among the guests. After the guests had left, he leant heavily on my arm but managed to walk to his bedroom.[898]

No-one appeared to have noticed that Churchill had not risen from his seat to bid goodbye to all his guests. On the following day, the Premier presided over a Cabinet meeting. Colleagues noticed a slurring of his speech and slight drooping of his mouth but attributed this to nothing more sinister than tiredness.[899]

The immediate decision was taken to postpone a scheduled conference in Bermuda, involving Churchill, the United States President and the French Prime Minister. This heralded an unprecedented spell of political intrigue. According to Colville,

> Two days after his stroke, when I drove down to Chartwell alone with the Prime Minister (Lady Churchill having gone on ahead to prepare the household), he gave me strict orders not to let it be known that he was temporarily incapacitated and to ensure that the administration continued to function as if he were in full control. We realised that however well we knew his policy and the way his thoughts were likely to move, we had to be careful not to allow our own judgement to be given Prime Ministerial effect. To have done so, as we could without too great difficulty, would have been a constitutional outrage. It was an extraordinary, indeed perhaps an unprecedented, situation.[900]

Colville calculated that, if he failed to undertake immediate pre-emptive action, news of Churchill's stroke would quickly leak out to the press. He therefore contacted three prominent press barons, Lord Beaverbrook, Brendan Bracken and Lord Camrose – all close friends of Churchill – and invited them to Chartwell, where he briefed them of the situation. Colville describes how, having 'paced the lawn in earnest conversation', his three guests decided to circulate a health bulletin, explaining why Churchill would not be travelling to Bermuda.[901]

A preliminary memo was drafted by Lord Moran and another medical specialist, only for it to be rejected on the grounds that inclusion of the phrase 'disturbance in the cerebral circulation' might suggest the occurrence of a stroke and generate calls for Churchill's resignation. This phrase was therefore supplanted by the more innocuous assertion that Churchill was 'in need of complete rest'.[902] By such means

> They achieved the all but incredible, and in peace-time possibly unique, success of gagging Fleet Street, something they would have done for nobody but Churchill. Not a word of the Prime Minister's stroke was published until he himself casually mentioned it in a speech in the House of Commons a year later.[903]

This did not resolve the problem of how to fulfil the role of government in the absence of its leader. Colville was, fortunately, able to depend on the 'wisdom and coolness' of the Secretary of the Cabinet, Sir Norman Brook, whom he took into his confidence from the outset.[904] Acting in concert with another senior government minister, Rab Butler, and the Prime Minister's son-in-law (and Member of Parliament for Bedford), Christopher Soames, Colville was therefore thrust into running the show 'while the ring master was unavailable'.[905] In practical terms,

> My colleagues and I had to handle requests from Ministers and Government departments entirely ignorant of the Prime Minister's incapacity. Discussion of how best to handle such inquiries, whether by postponement, by consultation with the Minister or Under Secretary responsible or, in some cases, by direct reply on the Prime Minister's behalf were the subject of daily discussions.[906]

Protocol was ignored to the extent that Soames was granted access to all manner of Cabinet papers and other classified documents that he would normally have been forbidden from seeing.[907]

In the early stages of Churchill's illness, Colville was told by Lord Moran that the Prime Minister would not live beyond that weekend; but this was to underestimate the Premier's powers of recuperation. Less than one week later, Churchill was reading the novels of Anthony

Trollope; and, before July was out, he was 'sufficiently restored to take an intelligent interest in affairs of state and express his own decisive views', thereby enabling Colville and Soames to return 'to the fringes of power, having for a time been drawn perilously close to the centre'.[908]

Following Winston Churchill's subsequent resignation as Prime Minister in 1955, Jock Colville stepped out of political and diplomatic life and entered merchant banking. He would use his newfound contacts in the City to liaise with Cambridge University in setting up a College and archive, both named in Churchill's honour, and publish a series of high-profile books, based largely on diary records of his diplomatic and wartime experience.

The Siege of Floors Castle

In 1953, the eighteen-year marriage between George Victor Robert John Innes-Ker, the 9th Earl of Roxburghe and Mary, Duchess of Roxburghe (formerly, Lady Mary Evelyn Hungerford Crewe-Milnes) was terminated in a resoundingly controversial and acrimonious way. This highly infamous conclusion of their relationship occurred when Mary 'showed courage and tenacity'[909] in resisting a sustained attempt by her husband to evict her from Floors Castle, his 100-room ducal seat near Kelso:

> She famously endured a six-week siege [...] after he served her divorce papers on a silver breakfast tray; she barricaded herself in a wing of the house, and he cut off heat, electricity, telephone, and gas in an effort to oust her. He tried also to turn off the water, but a canny and sympathetic neighbour, the future Prime Minister, Sir Alec Douglas-Home, who eventually helped broker a resolution, advised her to alert the insurance company to the fire threat.[910]

The 9th Duke undertook this 'astonishing and controversial' course of action in accordance with Scottish common law, which decreed that a wife was entitled to live in her husband's house 'by license' only.[911] He gave no explicit reason for wanting to evict the Duchess quite so summarily.[912] Local aristocratic sentiment was geared largely in the Duchess's favour. Aside from the support provided by Douglas-Home, the second Earl Haig at Bemersyde also smuggled in supplies of food, candles, matches and paraffin lamps.[913]

The dispute was eventually settled out of court, and Mary was granted a divorce in December 1953, on the grounds of the Duke's adultery.[914] Mary spent the remainder of her life in a finely furnished apartment overlooking London's Hyde Park and (as we shall see in Chapter 30), at a sixteen-century mansion set in four hundred acres at West Horsley Place, Surrey, which she eventually inherited from her mother. Unlike her ex-husband, Mary did not subsequently remarry.[915]

Chapter Twenty-Two
With These Hands

Man of the People, Salt of the Earth

In the early 1950s, Jim Bullock's enterprising but community-centred approach to colliery management inspired numerous exciting innovations — both above and below ground. Bullock's charismatic personality and pioneering attitude to colliery life were regularly highlighted in local newspaper and magazine articles which generated considerable publicity for Fryston, both in Castleford itself and outside the town boundaries.

One such article appearing in the *Pontefract and Castleford Express* (6 October 1950) was typical. 'The petrol engine has its sparking plug,' it began. 'The cartridge has its percussion cap. Fryston has Mr James Allen Bullock, the Agent and Manager of Fryston Colliery, who went to the pit 27 years ago — as a pony driver.'

This feature article characterised Bullock as a non-stop human dynamo whose supreme imagination and enthusiasm was constantly inspiring and energising all manner of schemes, ranging from the securing of invalid carriages for miners to concert parties and sporting events:

> His working hours are always passed under pressure and, no sooner has he left the pit, than he is off to something else — perhaps a meeting of one of the many Coal Board committees of which he is a member, to discuss welfare or other mining matters. But with all the crowding that comes of a responsible career, he makes time always to tie up happily the ends of social and community life. He never neglects that. For this native of Bowers Row, who came from a family of 12 — and of mining stock — is a man of the people and takes his pleasures with them.

A similar article, 'Salt of the Earth', included two years later in the *Yorkshire Illustrated* magazine, also talked of Bullock's upbringing as the youngest member of a large mining family. It rightly speculated that the death of Jim's oldest brother had instilled in him a great desire to make mining a safer occupation. Underground developments during Bullock's tenure as manager were both a testament to this commitment and a vindication of Oscar Fisher's assertion, fourteen years earlier, that Bullock would rise 'to great heights' within the mining industry:

> For amazing things have happened at the colliery since. What were narrow airways have now become high and wide steel-lined roads. Great gusts of pure air are blown round pit-workings in which men and horses have almost suffocated in the past. Men, who once worked in semi-nudity, can now work fully clothed. And much has been accomplished. Small diesel engines installed by Mr Fisher were supplemented by larger, more powerful engines. The few pit ponies that remain, including the one Jim drove in his early days, are now given a well-deserved break. Men whose lives have been spent underground have been given a new conception of mining. Instead of the foul blackness and oppressive heat, they have been given bright electric lamps and the cool atmosphere that makes an appreciable difference to the production figures of deep-mined coal.
>
> Main haulage roads, cut after the fashion of London Tubes, are now fitted with specially constructed fluorescent tubes. The pit bottom is brightly illuminated and, nowadays, there are few – if any – parts of this Yorkshire coal mine where any real discomfort is felt.[916]

The remainder of the article focused on Bullock's corresponding commitment to social and welfare developments. It emphasised, for example, that he had recently been appointed as Director of the Coal Industry Social Welfare Organisation (CISWO). This role would be undertaken in addition to his existing responsibilities as Vice-Chairman, to the Divisional Paraplegic Miners' Committee, and patron of the Boys' Holiday Camps scheme he was also involved in.

In this chapter, we concentrate on a series of newsworthy developments occurring during this peak period of Bullock's career as manager of Fryston Colliery. The first two sections highlight a pair of innovative and unique projects – the building of a welfare hall, and the creation of a sports arena – both voluntarily undertaken by Fryston miners under Bullock's supervision. A third section then traces the steps in a daring rescue in which a Fryston pit deputy risked his life in going to the aid of a colleague who was trapped and stranded halfway down the mineshaft. In the final two sections we analyse Bullock's pioneering role in establishing a trade union for colliery managers, and describe his departure from Fryston, following his resignation as pit boss, to a new palatial home in Swillington, near Leeds.

A Different Kind of Fryston Hall

We have already seen how, during World War II and in its immediate aftermath, Fryston reaped the benefit of a thriving pit canteen, which evolved from selling food and beverages to retailing pit boots, work clothing, and even hand-made suits, which the men paid for by instalment from their wages. This practice was then applied to the retailing of radios, radiograms and television sets. Money accumulated in this way was re-invested in such worthwhile ventures as the installation of sunray and massage rooms.[917]

Jim Bullock discovered, by virtue of the position he occupied as an NCB National Director of Welfare, that the corporation was about to assume control of all pit canteens and any revenue they might generate. He therefore campaigned quickly and pre-emptively to ensure that Fryston retained autonomy over the running of this resource. This guaranteed Bullock and his local welfare committee the freedom to continue re-investing funds into village facilities and amenities.

Attention became focused on realising a longstanding local ambition to construct a welfare hall and community hub for Fryston miners and their families. 'I was now determined to do something about the dream,' Bullock wrote in *Them and Us*. He knew that, whilst it would be one thing to provide the requisite materials and labour, such a project also required 'vision, ingenuity, organization, planning and bold leadership and this I knew inside me was my job'.[918]

Bullock took the prerequisite step of cheekily asking NCB Area officials if they would be willing to lease to the people of Fryston 'an old, deserted, worked-out desolate quarry that was an eyesore adjoining the village' — all for a nominal rent of one shilling for every hundred years. The NCB unexpectedly agreed to these terms.[919] Bullock then used all his powers of persuasion to borrow bulldozers and cement mixers from surrounding collieries in the area. Thereafter,

Incredible things happened at incredible speed. When the big machines arrived the quarry was a mass of old lime kilns, tangled undergrowth, years and years of accumulated rubbish. But by nightfall on the first day, there was a beautiful level piece of ground fifty yards long and ten feet wide.[920]

Rubble, sand and cement was then delivered by a convoy of borrowed vehicles and all this material levelled off, in 36 hours, into a smooth, solid foundation by a squad of 80 volunteer miners who had just completed their shifts.

With only £7,000 to play with, the committee possessed neither the time nor money to enable them to construct a building out of brick or stone, so they settled instead for a pair of ex-Army Nissen huts. One of these was one hundred feet long, and the other 80. They were locked together in an L-shaped formation, with the bottom part functioning as an old folks' room. Volunteer miners applied skills ordinarily used underground to assemble the new welfare hall within one day of the huts having been delivered.[921]

Bullock was careful throughout not to mention – except to certain NUM committee members – all the red tape (such as government building regulations, permits, licenses, land covenants and delivery contracts) which should have been addressed but was systematically circumvented.

My theory was that, if I ignored the lot and then pleaded ignorance, I could create a delay in any official decision. Also, I felt that if I could get the Welfare Hall built – and opened – it would need a hell of a council – who were miners and elected by miners – to give orders to knock it all down.[922]

Once the shell had been erected, a custom-built bar was installed by a local brewery. The walls and backdrop to the concert stage were decorated in the form of murals painted by a wartime refugee, a highly talented Czechoslovakian artist and puppeteer called Francis Drilek. The brewery also loaned the committee enough money to furnish the hall and agreed to defer payment on the first intake of beer. Within one week of the project starting, invitations for the opening ceremony were already being printed off. A notice over the new hall proclaimed: 'This hall was built in twelve days by miners, out of monies raised by miners, for themselves and their families, for culture and entertainment.'[923]

The official opening took place on Saturday, 20 October 1951. Nine months later, the *Pontefract and Castleford Express* (18 July 1952) reported how the Fryston Welfare Club and Institute had been 'highly commended by the newly created Coal Industry Social Welfare Organisation, when they visited it on Friday to sign their names in concrete in one of the outside walls'. Among those present at Jim Bullock's invitation were: the Yorkshire Area NUM President, Joe Hall; the union's General Secretary (and Joint Secretary of CISWO), Arthur Horner; and Abe Moffatt, Chairman of the Scottish Area NUM.

The hall quickly became the hub of village life. Miners and their wives were royally entertained from the stage by specially invited performers. Sports nights were held involving guest appearances by well-known male and female athletes. Speaking over a decade later, Jim Bullock recollected how:

> It was a beautiful place. […] And at that side, we'd an old people's room where people could come and play cards and dominoes and watch television in it, and they could come up whether they drunk or not, which is not so in pubs. I mean, if you go in pubs, you're expected to buy drinks, but, I mean, here you could come and talk to each other and it was really a home from home for them. Well, I made it really beautiful. I mean, we'd got carpets – thick carpets – on the floor, and we'd strip-lighting, red, yellow and white, you know. It had a beautiful atmosphere. I went in really expecting a burst of gratitude, you know: 'What a wonderful place you've built.' And the first remark one old miner made was, 'Where the bloody hell do we spit?' And we had to finish up putting spittoons on the floor for 'em. But they looked after it, and they really enjoyed this place.[924]

Bullock praised the work of Francis Drilek in particular. 'That's a marvellous mural,' he enthused in referring to one decoration adorning the rear of the stage.[925] Bullock had first utilised the talents of Drilek and his wife, Vlasta (who had fled with him from Nazi-occupied Czechoslovakia in 1938) to put on puppet shows demonstrating health and safety principles to Fryston miners. A newspaper article of one such demonstration, attended by Joe Hall, included a photograph of a pair of dancing pigs.[926]

These pigs had initially been created by Francis at the suggestion of his wife, due to the fact that such animals were symbols of good luck in their country of origin. The couple initially practiced their puppetry within Fryston village itself before eventually branching out into a part-time, and then full-time, career as the husband-and-wife team of 'Jan and Vlasta Dalibor'.[927] The puppet pigs, popularly known by now as 'Pinky' and 'Perky' (originally 'Porky'), soon made appearances in summer seasons at the seaside, before being invited to perform in a BBC talent show. Shortly thereafter (in 1958), they began the first of a nine-year series of programmes for the Corporation, in the course of which Pinky and Perky became two of television's best-loved and most iconic characters.[928]

The 'White City of the North'

The late edition of the *Yorkshire Evening Post* for 6 September 1952 led with the seemingly incredible headline: 'Fryston Miners Build Super Sports Stadium: Ambitious spare-time project will cater for 20,000.' The *Post* explained how this open-air arena would eventually incorporate 6,000 seats and be able to accommodate boxing, tennis and football matches, as well as cycling, athletics and bowls competitions. Describing the project as 'the brain-child of colliery agent and manager, Mr J. Bullock', the article disclosed that work on the stadium had only been in progress for the last six weeks, but that the project was due to be fully up and running in the New Year.

As Bullock subsequently explained, his initial idea had been to blast out sufficient space in a nearby disused lime quarry to develop stone terracing and a banked-up cycle track. 'I wanted it to be the White City of the North,' he maintained. 'There isn't a stadium anywhere in the north of England except Bradford, but this was going to be a cycling track, a running track, a football field, and accommodation cut out of these cliffs for thousands of spectators.'[929]

'The boss' was capably assisted in his attempt to realise this ambition by some 70 local miners, working all day each Sunday. 'I am proud of them and their staunch effort,' Bullock said in the above-mentioned

Post article, adding that 'I am sure the venture will go far and resound for generations to the credit of the Fryston miners.' He insisted that, along with the welfare hall, the stadium was intended, not only for the benefit of Fryston people, but for everyone living in the wider locality.

Bullock confessed in *Them and Us* that he had resorted to various dubious ploys to sustain the enthusiasm and morale of his volunteer labourers. Initially, he put on a barrel of beer for them and arranged for the colliery band to provide music while they worked. He then used his contacts in the local and national news media to ensure that the men's progress was constantly being reported, especially by the BBC, whose Tony Van den Bergh provided regular updates. Before the project was completed, attendance started to dwindle.

> So one week-end I put notices out to say that the BBC were going to make a film on the Saturday and Sunday. I got my surveyors to take up their positions on the top of the quarry with their tripods. It looked like the real thing. Everybody worked like mad. Afterwards, the miners kept asking: 'When are we going to see the film?' But when I told them that – it was just a lie – they realized that the deception had got the required results and they forgave me.[930]

This 'White City of the North' was soon to be employed as a venue for charitable events, such as wrestling and boxing matches. Bullock made the point that, the colliery workforce included at this time a handful of former professional boxers, such as Jimmy Lumb, George Hinchcliffe and Chick Duggan. The younger pair of Hinchcliffe and Duggan gladly participated in Bullock's fund-raising schemes. 'Chick Duggan had over three hundred contests,' Bullock recalled:

> He was a tearaway fighter, cast in the same mould as the famous 'Yiddle' Kid Berg and Ted Kid Lewis. He fought fifteen rounds for me many times for nothing. Him and all the other boxers fought any opponent I picked for them, never asking for reward if they knew the proceeds were for our Injured Miners' Fund.[931]

The enterprising Bullock founded a colliery boxing team on the back of this new venture, and arranged fixtures with representatives of other Yorkshire pits, and organisations like the police. Following the precedent set by the footballing Bevin Boys, the ex-professionals referred to above helped cultivate the local boxing talent. As one Fryston-born man, Tommy Templeman, explained, 'We used to go up to t' old welfare and train up here. Jimmy Lumb used to help 'em. Him and Bullock used to run it hand in hand at that time' (interview, 1986). Lumb soon turned his hand to promoting professional contests and brought over numerous Tongan and West African fighters, a handful of whom (such as the famous Ghanaian boxer, Peter Cobblah) temporarily resided in the village.

The Lister Addy Rescue

Another memorable occasion on which Fryston attracted headlines in the regional and national press occurred in the period between the construction of the welfare hall and crafting of the sports stadium. 'Deputy's great courage in Yorkshire pit rescue: Lowered 450 ft. to miner trapped in cage', was the headline of an article appearing in the 6 May 1952 edition of the *Yorkshire Post*. The article described how residents of this 'little West Riding mining village' had been marveling, the night before, at the heroism of 39-year-old Lister Addy, who had risked his own life in rescuing a 25-year-old haulage hand, Jim Winterbottom.

In recognition of this outstanding act of courage, Addy and his wife were invited to Buckingham Palace, where Queen Elizabeth II awarded him the George Medal — the civilian equivalent of the Victoria Cross. The citation for this award appeared in the *Supplement to the London Gazette* (29 July 1952). Here, we relive the often frightening and death-defying experience of the main protagonists, Addy and Winterbottom, and other relevant actors, including the ubiquitous Jim Bullock.

The rescue attempt was activated from the instance that Bullock was woken up, at around 6:30am, on the first Saturday of May 1952 by a telephone call from Lister Addy, who hurriedly explained that Jim Winterbottom was stuck in a cage, which was lodged in the wall of the winding shaft, some 70 yards from the pit bottom and 80 yards from the top. Bullock rushed immediately to the mine, where Addy was already awaiting further instructions.

According to Bullock,

> He [Addy] was a strong, thick-set man with a face that looked
> as if it had been hewn out of rock. He was a good fighter, an
> old-type pit man who believed in authority. His methods of
> maintaining discipline were somewhat hard but very effective.[932]

One of no fewer than sixteen children, Addy had already lost two
brothers in fatalities down the mine, one of them having perished in
the Fryston underground fire of 1915, described in Chapter 7.

The younger Winterbottom was a quiet, softly-spoken individual.
Born in the 'low buildings' of Oxford Street, he was one of a family
of eight children. His grandfather, 'Yorkie' Winterbottom, had spent
all his life at Fryston Pit, and occupied the position of 'watchman' (or
'yard bobby') at the time of the rescue.[933] Winterbottom's uncle was,
like Addy, a Fryston pit deputy, although it was under the latter's
supervision that Jim occupied the role of haulage hand.

Winterbottom had gone into work on the Saturday in question,
only to discover that a senior colleague had reported ill, making it
necessary for Winterbottom to take over the task of pulling off and
loading coal tubs onto the cage. As Jim Bullock further explained,

> Jim Winterbottom was a very willing worker and when they
> were loading this tram containing rails one of the rails got fast
> on the side of the cage and Jimmy went into the cage to try and
> liberate the rail. While he was inside — we never did find the
> real reason — the cage suddenly set off at its usual speed. As the
> cage went higher the rail which was hanging out of the side of
> the cage embedded itself in the side of the pit shaft seventy-five
> yards up from the pit bottom. Now the cage was tightly jammed
> and young Winterbottom was trapped.[934]

The situation was complicated by the fact that the tub had dropped
on top of Winterbottom and was wedged across his chest. 'I shouted
to Jack Fox to drop the cage down just a little bit because I thought
it'd release the tub,' said Winterbottom, 'but this was a mistake; it
fetched it onto me even more, so I shouted them to stop' (interview,
1987). Although he was conscious of 'all the shouting and commotion'
going on below, Winterbottom could do nothing but lie there and
hope for the best. It was a physically — and mentally — uncomfortable
experience, he maintained: 'I was suspended there for two to three

hours before I got rescued and, I don't know if tha's ever been in a pit shaft, but it soon gets bloody cold!' (interview, 1987).

Jim Bullock explained how no fewer than four Fryston deputies, including Lister Addy, tried to reach Winterbottom by climbing up the tram cable, or via conductor ropes or pipes, but that all such efforts proved futile. Eventually, they decided that the only viable option was to lower someone by rope from an inset located above the cage, with a view to releasing it from the shaft wall and returning Winterbottom to safety. Lister Addy was not only captain of the colliery rescue team but also the person primarily responsible for Winterbottom's safety. It was he who therefore volunteered to be lowered.[935]

Bullock and the other deputies tied three lengths of rope together to provide Addy with sufficient means of reaching the cage. Addy was kitted out with a safety harness, goggles, and two pairs of gloves.[936] It would be easy to underestimate the profound trepidation he was forced to overcome.

> I could see the fear in his eyes. He looked so imploringly at me as if to say: 'Isn't there any other way?' But he knew, and I knew, there wasn't any other way. To his credit he never voiced his fear but to the other people present he hid it under an air of bravado.[937]

The rescue crew of Addy, Bullock and the deputies had originally counted on gaining access at the old Silkstone level, only to discover that the road had been blocked by a rockfall. They therefore ascended to the Flockton level, some 450 feet above the cage itself. It was here that Addy started his descent. It proved an almost insurmountable task.[938] The temperature of the shaft was below freezing point and Addy's goggles and cap lamp were both heavily smeared with grease from the winding rope. His original pair of gloves quickly wore out due to attrition, and he accidentally dropped the spare pair in trying to replace the originals. As Addy also observed,

> I went down holding one of the conductor wires which steady the cage, but I had only gone about 60ft. when I began to spiral round the wire. When I let go I was swinging in space and banging against the sides of the shaft.[939]

It seemed like the final straw when Addy discovered that the rope had run out of length, forcing him to use the shaft cable as his sole means of sliding onto the cage roof. It was a terrifying prospect. Not surprisingly, as Addy admitted afterwards,

> I hesitated a moment longer but I knew I had to get to young Jimmy Winterbottom, so I cut, the rope parted, now indeed I was on my own. I slid down the rest of the cable and landed on the roof of the dangerously tilted cage. I took off my harness, rested a moment and had a look around. The first thing I saw was the new pair of gloves I had dropped, they had landed smack on top of the tilted cage and had not fallen off, my first real bit of luck I thought.[940]

The pit cage had four compartments, each capable of carrying two trams. Addy found, by climbing through two trapdoors, that Winterbottom was in the second from the top. Winterbottom's feet were protruding from under the tram. Having established that the younger man was not too badly injured, Addy quickly got to work:

> Then he bent down, did Lister, and he was a strong-ish bloke and he lifted the tub off me, but he had to put it down because I said to him, 'Open thi legs because I can't get out.' So, he strode across me and opened his legs and lifted it again so I could wriggle out underneath him. We sat there and had a word, like, about the best way to get down. (Jim Winterbottom, 1987)

With Addy's encouragement and physical assistance, Winterbottom was able to slide from the compartment he initially occupied into the relative safety of the one directly underneath. Once this had been achieved, Addy set about shaking and swaying the tram in a sustained attempt to release it. 'I did this many times,' he later recalled, 'and this jerking eased the rail away from the shaft side and then, to my joy and relief, I felt the cage straighten.'[941] Addy then re-joined Winterbottom and called as hard as he could to get the winding man to lower the cage as slowly as possible. Unfortunately, the cage became stuck again, fifteen feet from the pit bottom, so Addy had to call for some rope to be thrown up, which he then tied round Winterbottom's waist before finally lowering him to safety.

Winterbottom was able to walk, unassisted, into the pit offices, where he was given a drink of sweet tea to counteract possible shock. Having been checked over by the colliery first-aid man, Winterbottom stood up with the intention of leaving for home, only to fall backwards and eventually be carried out of the pit.

> They took me to the hospital where they x-rayed me, said there was nothing wrong with me and sent me home. But I started vomiting blood, sent for the doctor, then another doctor came. They rushed me off to hospital where they discovered I'd got a collapsed lung. That was about it, though. I soon mended nicely and was glad to be alive. (Interview, 1987)

Details of Addy's heroism continued to resound – in one way or another – for decades thereafter. The story of the rescue was recounted, for example, in a radio drama, *Caged in Darkness*, written by Tony Van Den Bergh with Russell Napier and Ronald Baddiley, for BBC Home Service Radio. It was broadcast on 7 November 1961. The parts of Lister and his wife, Jim Winterbottom, Jim Bullock and the other deputies involved (Freddie Astbury, Ernie Bagnall and George Sharp) were played by professional actors. Five years later, the exploits of Mr Addy were vividly described in the informative children's magazine, *Look and Learn*.[942]

Jim Bullock's Farewell

We saw in the previous chapter how, in Jim Bullock's opinion, Nationalisation had created an ethos in which 'Threats to managers and sheer bullying were now commonplace.'[943] It had also quickly dawned on managers like him that, because they lacked a representative body of their own, they were being excluded from relevant conciliation or consultation procedures. There already existed a National Association of Colliery Managers, but its function was limited to promoting 'technical advance and knowledge'. Pit managers therefore 'realized that for the first time in history they had to unite and form a management trade union for their own protection'.[944]

A new management union, the British Association of Colliery Management (BACM), duly emerged, its structure (consisting of Area Committees, Divisional Committees and a National Executive Committee) corresponding to the existing organisational tiers of the

NCB. Successful attempts were made to incorporate other, closely related bodies, such as the Institute of Mining Surveyors, and the Association of Electrical and Mechanical Engineers (Mining). A large proportion of BACM's founding members were sympathetic to the Conservative Party and recoiled at the prospect of being called a trade union, or, worse still, becoming affiliated to the TUC. In keeping with its ethos, BACM's first president was a coal-owner, called Major Walton Brown, whose offices were based at the Association's headquarters at Neville Hall, Newcastle.[945]

Jim Bullock played an active part in the birth of this novel union and was initially appointed delegate for his own area on the BACM Divisional Executive. He knew from the outset that the union was regarded with scepticism both inside and outside its own membership: 'The miners scorned the idea and their leaders poured ridicule on it,' he wrote. 'Chairmen of the Divisional Boards, who were ex-generals, admirals, aristocrats and ex-cabinet ministers, thought it was ridiculous for management to form a union.'[946]

By 1954, Bullock had become conscious that he was spreading himself too thinly. He was particularly aware that he was spending so much time away from Fryston that he was no longer doing justice to the job of colliery manager. He made a simple calculation: 'I was convinced that I could make a greater contribution in national and international affairs than I could ever make locally.'[947] He therefore asked the NCB to formally relieve him of the roles of agent and manager of Fryston Colliery.

At a formal gathering, marking Bullock's departure from Fryston, the colliery undermanager, Edrich Sharpe, said: 'I want to pay tribute to Mr Bullock who has done more in the past hundred years to change conditions for everybody who worked at Fryston colliery, for everybody who lives in Fryston village so quickly and so efficiently.'[948] Twelve months after leaving Fryston, Bullock was invited back to an Old People's Dinner. His successor as colliery manager, Edgar Williams, extended him a warm welcome by generously stating that: 'I hope the day will come when the people of Fryston will show me the same affection and respect that tonight they have shown to Mr. Bullock.'[949]

Bullock replied, somewhat competitively, by recalling the tale of the rich American who set out to buy the best available turf in Great Britain. The American's first destination was Lord's cricket ground, where his offer of two million dollars was rejected. Now realising that the prospect of such a straightforward transaction was out of the question, the American therefore asked how he should go about growing his own vegetation. 'They sent for the groundsman,' Bullock continued, 'explained what the American wanted and the groundsman said, "Get some land, level it, weed it, make sure it is really good soil, cultivate it, get the finest lawn seed you can buy, sow it, roll it, feed it, cut it, roll it, feed it, and cut it for two hundred years and you'll have turf exactly like this."' At this point, Bullock turned round, looked Edgar Williams directly in the eye, and insisted: 'There's a moral in the story.'[950]

From 'Them' Back to 'Us'

When Bullock resigned as colliery manager, he was naturally forced to vacate 'the house on the hill' he had long cherished and eventually occupied. He and his wife soon settled in a pleasant, detached cottage in Swillington, the neighbouring village to his native Bowers Row. 'The Mount', as the new home was called, formerly belonged to a colliery engineer, whose widow cheerfully made the sale conditional on the Bullocks promising that they would do nothing to 'hinder the activities of the spirit' who reputedly haunted the property, or choose to kill three ancient-looking hens who had made it their permanent residence. 'We got it very cheap,' Bullock later recalled. 'Very few people wanted to buy a ghost with a house, so she went out and we moved in. It was surrounded by owls and inhabited by bats.'[951]

Jim and Jay Bullock remained in the cottage for five years, during which time they erected a garage, installed fireplaces and extended the kitchen – all without obtaining the requisite planning permission. Jay gave birth during this period to their daughter, Josephine Alwyn Bullock, who was named in honour of her father's great friend, the miners' leader, Joseph Alwyn Machin. Without realising it, the couple were already gravitating towards their next place of residence. 'We were both fond of riding and stabled our horse in the old ruined stables at Swillington House,' he later recollected.[952]

Bullock and Jay started to notice that, although the stables had no roof covering, windows, water supply, sanitation or natural light, they had nonetheless retained the original solid walls, constructed out of sturdy York stone. The pair wasted no time in purchasing the stables and surrounding lands. A deal was struck with the NCB (who had long since acquired the property), following an inspection and evaluation of the property by the Chairman of its Yorkshire Division.

Plans for reconstruction of the stables were drawn up by the same architect friend of Jim Bullock who had drafted plans for Fryston Welfare Hall. Once they had sold the Mount, the Bullocks moved into their ramshackle new dwelling – during the hot summer of 1959, the year in which their son, James Allen was also born.

The Herculean task of rescuing the stables from utter deterioration was simplified by the fact that surrounding mansions in the area, at places like Methley and Temple Newsam, were in the process of being demolished. The Bullocks were able to purchase huge fireplaces, cupboards, tables and other items from these former residencies – all at (literally) knock-down prices, due to the fact that modern houses were far too small to accommodate them. The renovation work itself was carried out by volunteers. 'We have received so much help from such a variety of people,' said Bullock:

> One of my nephews – Dick Milner – was a first-class builder and craftsman. He spent every minute of his spare time here. Another nephew – Freddy Bullock – a forester, helped us with the planting of Christmas trees and laying out the grounds. Miners from Fryston came at week-ends and worked as if they were on contract. My old friend Freddy Astbury, and his two sons, never missed a weekend for two or three years and worked as hard as if the place belonged to them.[953]

In the meantime, the Bullocks used every spare penny at their disposal to purchase the nearby lake, swamps and other surrounding land. Jim Bullock was therefore entitled to speak with justifiable pride of what they managed to accomplish:

> We have worked very hard indeed but it has been very rewarding work. We have something tangible to show for our efforts. We have recovered valuable land from swamp. We have set out plantations on scrubland. We have made ruined stables into a beautiful home. We have been able to entertain many visitors from all walks of life and many of my old friends from Fryston come down to see me.[954]

Chapter Twenty-Three
Back from the Brink

Under New Management

Just like his predecessor at Fryston (Jim Bullock), Edgar Williams had risen through the ranks, progressing from face-worker to colliery manager. He was once dismissed from a Castleford colliery for allegedly including too much 'dirt' among his coal. The thinly disguised animosity between Bullock and Williams, alluded to in the previous chapter, was exacerbated when the former continued to draw on Fryston miners to help restore his newly acquired Swillington property:

> No, I didn't get on with Mr Bullock at all. There was an occasion early on when he asked permission for two men to work for him. I thought, 'Well, as a gesture of goodwill, I'll allow him the men for two days.' But he encouraged them people to stay with him for a week and I stopped their wages. They told me that he said he'd made arrangements with me when he had not. I paid them their money. I told them that in no way must they leave this colliery without my permission for anyone. Of course, he thought I'd loaned them for the week, etc. I told him, 'Jimmy, I happen to be manager here. Anything you want I might give you but, after what's happened, I don't think you'll be getting any labour from this colliery again.' And he never did. No. I never got on with him, I kept him at arm's length. Course, he still went on and made progress. He became President of BACM for the whole of the country – that was in the days of Robens – but that didn't worry me. I had a pit to run. (Edgar Williams, 1986)

In this chapter, we trace notable developments during Edgar Williams's tenure as manager. We explore the nature and repercussions of the new manager's attempts to transform working practices and introduce greater mechanisation as ways of securing the colliery's future. We then outline corresponding transformations in village housing and welfare provision. Finally, the chapter dwells on parallel developments at the macro level of coalfield affairs – most notably: the progress achieved by Jim Bullock in establishing a trade union for colliery management; on Bullock's relationship with Alfred (later Lord) Robens as Chair of the NCB; and of the implications of Robens's policies for the future of collieries like Fryston.

Appointment With Fear

A few days after his appointment as manager, Edgar Williams discovered that both his immediate line manager in the NCB and his undermanager at Fryston had also been newly recruited to their roles. Williams was informed by his Group Manager that such changes had been undertaken in order to 'alter the life and ethos of the pit because it was badly in the red and we'd to do something about it' (interview, 1986). This problematic 'ethos' was a legacy, so Williams was told, of the laissez faire style of management practiced by his predecessor. Williams saw from the outset that discipline was lax: 'Men were coming out of the pit before time and working in various departments that seemed to have no bearing on the production of coal' (interview, 1986). Most prominent of all were groups of local sportsmen ('Bullock's Blue-Eyed Boys') who were allegedly assigned to lighter 'surface' tasks, even though they were qualified 'face-workers'. 'It wasn't long,' Williams declared, 'before I got them down the mine doing a useful job instead' (interview, 1986).

This had proved an uphill task. Strikes were commonplace. The first of these occurred when Williams unceremoniously removed a placard in the pit yard, proclaiming: 'This colliery is worked by the People for the People,' which had been a proud legacy of Vesting Day. Tonnage levels fell correspondingly, compared to those achieved under Bullock's supervision.

> This called for an inquiry by the Area General Manager, who came along and told me he'd expected better results. I told him he ought to have known the state of the colliery before he employed me and that I didn't care a damn whether he sacked me or not, but I was doing my best and results would come. He said, 'How long?' and I said, 'Four years.' (Interview, 1986)

The new manager quickly succeeded in reducing annual losses from £200,000 to £50,000, but this was still deemed insufficient to guarantee Fryston's future viability. The manager was therefore summoned to the NCB offices in London, where he was told that, unless he succeeded in securing the co-operation of the local NUM, the colliery would be closed. Informally, however, he was given some ground for optimism. 'As I was leaving the place,' he revealed, 'one of the seniors called me back for a word and told me that they'd noted that things were improving, and if I continued like this, the Board would alter the whole surface structure, electrify the mine and bring in modern conditions of pulling coal' (interview, 1986).

Williams maintained that further progress was made by using a combination of persuasion and deliberate persecution on his part. The ethos was gradually changing for the better, owing to a fairer allocation of work tasks. There were no longer any blue-eyed boys:

> They had a proper job to do, and when I sent them down the mine, it pleased the men considerably. It was these things that altered the workman's mind and attitude towards the colliery, and this is one reason why we made a steady improvement. (Interview, 1986)

A less benign tactic involved the direct persecution of individuals proving recalcitrant to managerial direction:

> The men were opposed to us and, naturally, they'd every right to be because we made many changes and, sometimes, we persecuted the wrong men; but you've got to take drastic action in these circumstances. One fellow who'd been at the colliery many years and was now overman knew practically every man. We had his support and he helped us to kind of sort the wheat from the chaff. Finally, the tonnage got better and we broke clean for the first time. It took about four years. (Interview, 1986)

Jim Bullock and Alf Robens

We have previously seen how, in the immediate post-war period, Jim Bullock became a founding member of the British Association of Colliery Management. BACM's President and Secretary during those formative years (Major Stanley Walton-Brown and Major Robert Anderson, respectively) had each been stakeholder-managers under private ownership, neither having 'risen from the ranks'. Like the majority of their Executive members, they were hostile to Nationalisation, and rarely oppositional towards NCB policy or sensitive to its negative implications for British mining communities.[955]

Bullock's advent as President – a position he held from 1956 to 1969 – and of George Tyler as his Secretary (1959-1973) saw the old guard replaced by a 'different breed' of BACM leaders. Both men came from mining communities and had actually worked down the pit; they were Labour Party members, and staunch advocates of Nationalisation. Together, they developed 'a stridently independent stance as a managerial trade union'.[956] According to one ex-BACM member,

> Bullock was the best leader that BACM have ever had, and, yes, there was a change in the attitude of the management union. [...] He came up, as you'll know, from the pit. [...] Brother, father, Uncle Tom Cobley and all were miners. He was from a mining village and he was a hands-on man.[957]

This 'watershed' period, marking a transition from BACM's preoccupation with the defence of management's working rights and conditions to a far greater concern with aspects of Coal Board and governmental policy, coincided with the appointment of Alfred Robens as NCB Chair in the autumn of 1960.[958]

The first NCB Chairman Jim Bullock had dealt with as BACM President was Sir Hubert Houldsworth, QC – 'a kind, honest man if ever there was one', in Bullock's estimation – but certainly no-one's fool. Houldsworth was succeeded by his Deputy Chair, Jim Bowman, an ex-Vice President of the NUM. Here, too, Bullock enjoyed a satisfying working relationship, largely because Bowman, 'spoke pit language of all types as good and fluently as any of us'.[959] When the demand for coal plummeted and oil imports rose correspondingly, Bowman preferred to stockpile output in the pit yards rather than close mines down prematurely.[960] Bowman retired in 1960, seemingly no longer capable of preventing closures from becoming more commonplace. As Jim Bullock put it, 'redundancy was *no longer an ugly spectre lurking in the background, it was here, it was a grim* reality'.[961]

The appointment of Alfred ('Alf', later Lord) Robens as Bowman's successor generated great controversy. It is indisputable that Robens did possess relevant experience, having served as Parliamentary Secretary to the Ministry of Fuel and Power from 1947 to 1951, and Minister of Labour in 1951. Now, though, he was a senior member of the Labour shadow cabinet. The fact that he was offered the job by the *Conservative* Prime Minister, Harold Macmillan, aroused suspicion that he was being used to 'put a human face' on the dismantling of the coal industry. Such consternation was exacerbated by the fact that news of Robens's appointment was leaked (in an article by John Cole, Labour Correspondent of *The Guardian*, on 13 June 1960), prior to Hugh Gaitskell, the Labour Party leader, having first been notified.[962]

Jim Bullock wasted no time in objecting to this appointment. He expressed his indignation directly to the Minister of Power and in the following letter to *The Times*:

> Management's criticism of the appointment is the appalling idea that in this industry there is no person capable of handling the business of this great, complex and complicated industry; but that someone from outside the industry with nowhere near the experience can do it better than those with a lifetime's experience.
>
> My union represents men of the highest skills and experience in the industry, men of high integrity and calibre, and this appointment comes as a distinct shock to all of them and makes nonsense of my union's efforts to establish an appointments procedure in the industry which would conform to the high principles for which in the past this country has so rightfully won great respect.
>
> It is in this context that the appointment of Mr Robens appears to us to be wrong.[963]

Robens disregarded this objection. He calculated that the chief problem confronting him on his arrival as Chair in October 1960 was the fact that markets for coal were rapidly diminishing due to the fierce competition posed by cheap oil, and that coal itself was being massively over-produced.[964] This was all occurring at great financial loss. Thus, in his parlance,

> The nettle had to be seized – if we didn't mechanise quickly, even more pits would have to be closed. There was only one course to pursue – mechanise as hard as possible and keep a

strict control over recruitment so as to enable natural wastage to take the load.[965]

Alongside this, it would be necessary to mount the 'biggest campaign to market coal that had ever been launched'.[966]

Robens therefore embarked on a sustained sales drive, not only consolidating coal supplies to power stations, but also persuading local authorities to rely on coal for heating new housing and office spaces. He also lobbied hard to discourage the use of imported foreign coal in the steel industry, and force government to consider the net financial costs involved in building expensive nuclear plants to the detriment of coal.[967] Robens chose to concentrate mechanisation in the most productive coalfields and introduced novel ways of distributing coal more efficiently – e.g. by using an innovative 'merry-go-round system', which enabled trains to unload coal at power station terminals without needing to come to a halt.[968]

Hall points out that, 'Above all, Robens gave the industry personality. He was a natural publicist, and at first spent a lot of time rebuilding the morale of the industry.'[969] His signature approach was 'highly personalised': advertisements invariably pictured him talking to miners at their workplace, attesting to the fact that the 'gaffer was prepared to get stuck in'.[970] He made the most of his working-class credentials and reputation within the Labour Party by travelling from pit to pit, staring down detractors as destructive 'Jeremiahs' and 'preaching his doctrine of vigorous competition' directly to the rank-and-file.[971]

No-one had become more impressed by this campaign than Jim Bullock. 'Within twelve months,' Bullock conceded, 'I had realized that in Alf Robens we had an outstanding man. He stood tall among tall men. He was no push-over. He was nobody's man but his own.'[972] Bullock therefore wrote a second letter to *The Times*, admitting that 'although my sentiments were right in my first letter my conclusions were wrong'.[973] It was not merely that output was soaring, or that the coal industry was starting to be viewed more positively by the public:

> We had now a chairman who was able and willing to oppose the reduction of output of the industry at all levels. He defied authority above him and he fought against decisions he felt were

wrong, but no matter how much he disagreed he supported these decisions once they became law.[974]

This revision of attitude was the first step towards a lasting friendship between Jim Bullock and Alf Robens. Feelings of mutual respect and co-operation soon emerged within an industrial context in which larger pits employing 2,000 men soon became the norm. These technologically advanced units required a more modern approach to management. 'Jim Bullock knew and understood all this,' said Robens:

> He was a practical person himself and his pragmatic approach to these new Management problems made him a tower of strength to both his union membership and the industry. These were the hard testing times for men with responsibility and he showed his sterling worth and quality of character, by refusing to seek refuge, as he might well have done, by saying that these were the Board's problems to solve and that his sole responsibility was merely to safeguard his members' interests.[975]

As we shall see below, the achievement of this common ground regarding issues of sales policy, technological innovation, and innovative management styles only went so far, and did not extend to the perceived need for pit closures and steps to ameliorate their negative impact on mining communities.

The Robens Era at Fryston

The Robens vision of employing fewer miners in a more highly mechanised and productive environment was wholeheartedly endorsed by Edgar Williams. From 1960 onwards, Williams embraced the new business ethos by overseeing the mechanisation of Fryston Pit. According to him,

> I modernised the system of work there from that of the old system to a modern type of delayed-action firing, special boring machines, compressed air and water applications to keep the dust down and disperse the dirt, which was mechanically filled onto a belt. This helped them to make rapid progress and we got some very good results. The first face we turned out in the Flockton Seam we had the help of a trepanner. As soon as we opened the face out in the Beeston Seam, we were fortunate

enough to have some very good conditions and we also used a trepanner there. The trepanner really put Fryston on the map. It exceeded anything in the Area. In one case, we advanced 28 yards in a week. Naturally, we couldn't keep this up, but it was an example of what could be done with modern mining. (Interview, 1986)

An invaluable insight into the nature and impact of this modernisation process was provided in an article, entitled 'Here Are the Men of Fryston', appearing in the *Yorkshire Evening News* (9 May 1963). This essay explained how a £1,250,000 reconstruction scheme had resulted in the modernisation of surface and underground transport, the greater efficiency and cohesion of underground working systems, and the complete electrification of the mine.

The article also noted that output had been increased to 3,000 tons a day, compared with the 1,500 being achieved before the advent of modernisation. Its authors noted that: 'Fryston stands high in the Board's efficiency league, where output per manshift (O.M.S.) has doubled to 50 cwt (O.M.S.) since the reconstruction work began.' These levels of improvement had been achieved with a reduced manpower of 1,240 (down by 360 since 1960). This shrinkage had been achieved by processes of 'natural wastage' and retirement, combined with a 'regulated recruitment' programme.

The same authors quoted Edgar Williams, who expressed his gratitude to Fryston miners for helping him create one of the NCB's local success stories. 'They have given every machine a fair chance and have even increased production during this period,' he said, 'but the Fryston miners have adapted themselves and mastered the new machinery very quickly.' Williams emphasised that technological innovation was already requiring the acquisition of new skills:

The future miner will need a mechanical aptitude because brain is replacing brawn. At the moment half our lads serving apprenticeships are electricians and fitters – the electrical and mechanical engineers of the future.

One of these authors dispelled any supposition that mechanisation had removed the extreme discomfort traditionally associated with mining. This man graphically described the 'eerie sensation' he had experienced while descending 1,500 feet into the 'inky blackness' underground. He also referred to the claustrophobic feeling involved in travelling three miles under the River Aire by 'paddy train', before 'scrambling under and over conveyors and tubs to get to the coal face', which was only four-feet high. Here,

> The miners on the coal-face were stripped to the waist, clad only in shorts, kneepads, helmet and boots. And their bodies were caked in coal and sweat. The sound of the machines and the rumble of the conveyors is almost deafening and the rising coal dust gets into your nostrils, your eyes, your mouth, and covers every exposed part of your body. You can't escape the heat or the dust and you're grateful for the constantly circulating air which travels along the 280-yard long four feet high 'face,' and for the water sprays which suppress the dust on all working machinery. Normal conversation is impossible. Every instruction and request is made by bawling. Identification is not easy with every man almost blackened from head to foot with the whites of his eyes looking whiter than white and lips made pink and clean by jaws champing on tobacco – thick twist to keep the taste of dust away.

The major difference now was that, according to the article, massive, 'whirring, steel-toothed machines' were displacing the emphasis on physically exacting manual work. The article quoted one miner, a 28-year-old father of two, who maintained that, prior to modernisation, he had been too tired to dig his garden once his shift was over, but things were different now. 'More machines and better machines are making life easier and giving us more security,' he said. Meanwhile, weekly earnings had risen exponentially.

The article concluded that this new-found sense of security was undoubtedly related to Fryston's improved market position. Some 62% of coal produced at Fryston was feeding Ferrybridge Power Station, with another 32% going to industrial and domestic clients in Yorkshire and Lancashire, and the remainder to local miners as part of the NCB's 'home scheme'. Extra capacity was also due to come on stream at the nearby Ferrybridge and Eggborough power stations, each of which would soon be capable of digesting five million tons of coal per annum.

This was sure to provide ample custom for the 27 million tons of underground reserves at Fryston — enough to extend the colliery's lifespan by another 50 years.

The Transformation of Fryston Village
During Edgar Williams's tenure as manager, Fryston also experienced a transformation of its housing stock, and local welfare and leisure amenities. This had corresponding implications for its demographic structure and sense of community cohesion.

The viability of this now-decaying village came under review in 1955, when local authority planners agreed to allocate housing grants in support of a planned Coal Board part-clearance and modernisation programme in Fryston. Of the village's 251 houses, 108 were earmarked for removal. The three rows of back-to-back houses in Oxford Street, Castle Street and Wellington Street were demolished forthwith. Later that decade, further houses were demolished in Hope Street, while 20 more of the village's back-to-backs were converted into 'through' houses, equipped with full modern amenities. Other rows of terraces comprising School Street and Wheldon Road were removed in the early 1960s, leaving a total housing stock of 137 properties. In 1963, the project entered its final phase with the upgrading of properties in Brook Street and South View.[976]

Many of those born and raised in Fryston chose to leave the village, due either to the decreasing availability of local housing, or the allure of newly-built council houses in Ferry Fryston or NCB homes on the specially commissioned 'Shepherd's Estate' (a complex of 312 properties built by Shepherd and Sons of York), located in nearby Townville.[977] This had obvious consequences for the age and occupational structures of the remaining population:

> I think that folk, especially the younger end of Fryston, had started to think that, whilst a 'two up, two down' might have been ok for their parents, they wanted summat a bit more comfortable and modern for their own kids. Some of those houses were pretty basic and you'd hardly call 'em ideal. Not by today's standards. I think we were conditioned that bit different to our mams and dads. (Ex-Fryston woman, 1986)

Anecdotal evidence appearing in the aforementioned *Yorkshire Evening News* article (9 May 1963), indicates that the colliery workforce was becoming increasingly cosmopolitan. The essay reported that 'Almost one in three of the Fryston miners drives to work.' Of the 41 miners photographed or otherwise referred to in the article, only seven were Fryston residents. The majority came from Airedale (eleven) or Ferry Fryston (sixteen), with three more living in Townville, and one each in Redhill, Glasshoughton, central Castleford, Featherstone, Pontefract and Silverwood (Rotherham).

A similar transformation had occurred in relation to the village leisure and welfare facilities. This posed a similar threat to social cohesion:

> I'd say the first nail in Fryston's coffin was when they took the allotments off us in 1954. Everybody had been entitled to an allotment before then and they'd been a meeting place for all the blokes in the village. That, and when they started demolishing the back-to-backs, near enough the same time. That's when the village started to lose its stride, and it wasn't long afterwards — 1960, 1961 — that we had our final carnival. (Fryston man, 1987)

As early as 1956, the future viability of the Fryston welfare hall and sports stadium had already become uncertain. A visiting local newspaper reporter had spoken eulogistically of the club: 'Imagine miners, just off the shift, drinking at a bar which would do credit to many a Mayfair club,' he stated, 'and there you have a daily setting in Fryston Welfare Hall and Institute — the place which brought new life to a dead-end Castleford district.'[978] It was evident that local miners retained great pride in having built this place from scratch.

> Yet, although nearly 800 people enjoy Sunday night concerts in the Fryston Hall, everything in the adjoining stadium is not lovely. It seems that when the popular Mr Bullock left the area last August, he took with him the driving spirit which caused the miners to work so hard for this excellent centre. Several schemes for the stadium are, as yet, incomplete. 'The fellows seemed to lose interest when he left,' one retired miner told me, 'but they are willing lads and if they get a good leader they will finish the job.'[979]

These final sentences proved telling. It was no secret that Jim Bullock was disliked by Edgar Williams, though this is not the reason the latter gave for his eventual decision to close the club, section by section, and discontinue the creation of the stadium – much to the chagrin of local people and the press:

> One section, which was supposed to be for drama, and art and dancing, I closed down during my early stages at the colliery – much to the dislike of the local authorities – and had to give the reason, which was that, after the Saturday night dancing, Fryston was getting a very bad name. So, I had no option other than to close it down. The other hut was for the benefit of gymnasts and the band. But when I asked about the band, I discovered they'd no instruments, so I thought, 'Well, that club's being closed down as well.' So, in the early stages, I was not only having trouble in the pit, but I was discarding the so-called social effects and closing them down to save me annoyance. This was talked about in the press, condemning my attitude towards running a mine, but I did weather it through. Eventually, I looked around a bit and decided with the help of the union to get a change of club. I thought that the miners of Fryston were worthy of something better than a Nissan hut. I got the union secretary to agree to deduct a payment of tuppence per week to build a new club. (Edgar Williams, 1986)

In due course, a 'spacious, plushy' Fryston Miners' Welfare Club was erected in August 1962, up in Ferry Fryston, at an overall cost of £30,000. This new building and its surrounding football pitches, tennis courts and bowling greens was reputed to be 'the best of its kind in the country', and its facilities were extended to miners and their families from neighbouring collieries.[980] Its design and ethos were created in recognition of the fact that 'The modern miner enjoys much more social life and their wives are taking a much bigger part in the life of the club.'[981]

My Cup Runneth Over

It has already been established that Edgar Williams was frequently at loggerheads with members of the colliery football team, whom he sought to make an example of to other sections of the workforce. It was therefore ironic that, by winning the WRCC Cup in the 1962-63 season, the colliery football team was surpassing the exploits of the more fancied predecessors, who had benefitted from the greater encouragement and patronage bestowed on them by previous colliery managers.

This Fryston team of the early 1960s had been languishing in the Second Division of the West Yorkshire league. Under the canny guidance of head coach and Fryston stalwart, Dick Foulkes, the inspirational captaincy of Pete Waddington, and steadying influence of ex-professionals like Jackie Sharp and Harold ('Agga') Mattison, the team was already on the brink of promotion to the First Division, and had unexpectedly but deservedly progressed to a final tie against the much-vaunted Bradford team, Thackley. A previously unbeaten and seemingly invincible member of the upper tier of the West Yorkshire Amateur League, Thackley exuded a professional ethos which permeated their on-field demeanour and pre-match preparation. A Fryston victory in the final at East End Park (Leeds) seemed too far-fetched to contemplate.[982]

Shortly before this match, Dick Foulkes pulled off a masterstroke by recalling to the side the iconic Freddie Howard, a free-scoring Fryston centre-forward of the 1950s, who was concluding his career by playing occasional games for the reserves. Foulkes was willing to gamble on Howard's well-known 'big match temperament' and it proved a risk worth taking. The Fryston defence, in which Mattison and, especially, Sharp were outstanding, withstood relentless waves of Thackley pressure. In a rare Fryston foray into the Thackley penalty area, Howard proved himself the hero of the hour by scoring an admittedly fortuitous winning goal, a miss-hit shot which bamboozled the hapless opposition goalkeeper.[983]

Post-match celebration was unrestrained; but a feeling of bitterness arose when, as Jack Sharp explained, the trophy was taken from the dressing room back to Fryston Miners' Welfare Club, in advance of the players responsible for winning it:

> Edgar Williams were there and he didn't have any interest in football. In fact, there was hell on that day because after we'd been presented with t' cup, he took it back in his car to Fryston club, so we were deprived of the cup in the dressing room! And there was a big to-do about that, even though we were re-introduced to t' cup when we all arrived at t' club an hour or two later.[984]

In the course of the next few days, Fryston managed, as a result of Freddie Howard's continuing goal-scoring exploits, to secure sufficient points from their remaining five league games to land the Second Division title. Edgar Williams temporarily redeemed himself by belatedly organising a reception in their honour. He blotted his copy book, however, by opening the proceedings at a Darrington hotel with the stipulation that, whilst each player could have his first drink 'on the Welfare', anything further would have to be paid for from their own pocket. As one Fryston miner, the 'first-aid man', Brian Wood, recalled,

> T' bosses carried on drinking and, because we were sure they weren't paying out of their own pockets, we decided that neither were we. So we kept calling t' waitresses over: 'We'll have another bottle of Blue Nun apiece and we'll each have another beer and cigar!' That went on all night! On Monday morning, t' phone rang in t' medical centre and it was only Edgar Williams for Christ's sake! He said, 'Have you got anybody in with you just now? No? Well get thissen over here!' He says to me: 'What were you doing on Friday?' I said, 'What do you mean, Mr Williams?' and he chucked this bill over to me and says, 'What the bleeding hell were you playing at? I don't know what it was you were drinking but you'll never do it again!'[985]

This Fryston 'class of '63' had gone one further than any of their arguably more prestigious forebears. In previous eras, managers like Soar, Purcell and Bullock had used sport to mollify conflict, enhance managerial authority and promote co-operation. Under Williams, it had become a site of opposition.

Having tasted such satisfaction, the Fryston players were determined to repeat the feat next year. There was something almost preordained about the outcome of the following year, when Fryston and Thackley met once again in the final. This time round, Thackley exacted revenge for the previous season's defeat. The final, played on Bradford Park Avenue's ground, was largely one-sided, with Thackley deservedly prevailing, 3-1.[986]

The Fryston victory of 1963 was never subsequently emulated. What made the cup-winning team so distinctive from those of previous eras was that they 'regarded themselves as playing on behalf of the "village"', rather than the local colliery. Even those players still working down the mine 'were far too alienated from the industry and its management for [the latter] sort of identification to have existed in reality'.[987]

Henceforward, the team would be made up of players drawn from outside of Fryston village and the neighbouring streets of places like Airedale and Ferry Fryston. The majority of such players did not even work at the colliery. This and other trends referred to in this chapter, such as the clearance of village streets, the outmigration of younger people, the breakdown and geographical distancing of welfare and leisure facilities, and the transformation of workplace culture, were bound to detract from the once powerful sense of community identity.

BACM'S New Set of Teeth

As the 1960s progressed, signs of growing workforce alienation and unrest permeated the British coalfields. Relations between Bullock and Robens always remained amicable; but, whilst they agreed on some aspects of NCB policy, they could not see eye-to-eye on others.

Robens continued to attract plaudits from Bullock and his BACM colleagues in terms of his commitment to defending or cultivating new markets. When the Labour Prime minister, Harold Wilson, stated a preference for running down the coal industry in favour of nuclear power, the NCB Chair 'defied ministers by winning a coal contract with the Canadian multinational Alcan for its Lynemouth smelter in preference to electricity from the new generation Advanced Gas-Cooled Reactors (AGR), subsidized by government.'[988] This bold act of defiance 'won Robens few friends among his erstwhile Labour colleagues but [...] it won him admiration from managers and BACM'.[989]

Against this, BACM, under Bullock's presidency, adopted a progressively more oppositional stance in relation to a wide range of political issues:

> Bullock and Tyler forged a distinct and independent agenda for BACM; one that they argued was in keeping with their role as trade-unionists. [...] Breaking with Walton-Brown and Anderson they were vocal in criticizing the failure of governments to alleviate the distress from the industry's contraction and to develop a robust national fuel policy, and they worked with the NUM and NACODS to lobby against closures in the 1960s.

This strategy found favour, coinciding with a 39% growth in BACM membership from around 12,000 in 1956 to a peak of 16,700 in 1964.[990]

BACM was already collaborating with other mining unions in a concerted campaign against pit closures when Bullock and Tyler began mooting the possibility of becoming affiliated to the TUC. A vote to this effect occurred in September 1964; but, amidst 'robust opposition' from places like Durham and Northumberland, only 37% voted in favour.[991] One year later, Bullock and Tyler tried again to persuade their members, arguing for example that TUC membership would give them access to such bodies as the National Economic Development Council, and therefore greater influence over the future of the coal industry. Opponents counter-argued 'that affiliation would embroil them in debates about Rhodesia and Britain's potential involvement in the Vietnam war'.[992] It was apparent, however, that, even by this stage, Bullock and Tyler had transformed the Association into a highly proactive and less inward-looking institution than had hitherto been the case.

Chapter Twenty-Four

A Chip Off the Old Block

'Rebellious By Nature'

Quentin Crewe was, variously, a writer, bon viveur, raconteur, society host, dandy, philanthropist, traveller, champion of the socially marginalised, and intimate friend of royalty. These descriptors had previously been applicable, of course, to his great grandfather, Richard Monckton Milnes. The following chapter will emphasise that, just as Milnes had cut a ubiquitous and influential presence in the social, cultural and political milieux of the mid-to-late Victorian era, so did his great grandson feature prominently in the 'swinging sixties' of a century later.

A compelling insight into the nature of this charismatic, though often controversial, individual is helpfully provided by his daughter, Candida (an author in her own right), who observed that her father 'was a naturally spirited character and never one to toe lines'.[993] Candida expended much energy in contemplating 'what it was about his character that enabled him to step away from the prevailing view and judge that these prejudices were wrong'.[994] Perhaps, she concluded, it was a sense of vulnerability, resulting from a lifelong disability, which not only enhanced his ability to empathise with others, but also equipped him with 'an enlightened courage and defiance born of a quick wit, a keen inquisitiveness and optimism about the world'.[995] Candida maintained that such traits were already evident in Quentin's school years, when he was beaten for breaking or scoffing at rules he considered 'as unimaginative as they were daft'.[996]

Candida also emphasised that her father's nonconformist orientation was reinforced by the fact that he harboured 'little sense of belonging', least of all to the aristocratic class he ostensibly formed part of:

> The way Pop saw it, his association with the aristocracy was part of him but not all. It did not preclude a relish of all that

was new and imaginative – in terms of people from different backgrounds, of unpredictable political opinion, of innovative arts and ideas.[997]

This is not to pretend that Quentin ever renounced his aristocratic origins, for he relished living expensively and was, most fundamentally, a 'shocker of a snob'. Rather, he was imbued with a spirit of independence, a fascination and respect for the different and unconventional, which earmarked him as 'rebellious by nature but not a revolutionary'.[998]

Like his great grandfather before him, Quentin's personality was reflected in his dress sense and unflagging sociability: according to Candida, 'Sombre pinstripes were not for him. One suit was brown with gold threads and, according to my mother, made him look like a comedian at the Palladium.'[999] The 60 or so cigarettes he smoked daily (with the help of lengthy black or amber holders) were not the only things making him so conspicuous:

> I was proud of his indomitable charm and a charisma which seemed to emanate from the fixed point of his wheelchair and sweep like dry ice across a room to touch people even in the furthest corners. At parties people would literally queue up to talk to him. He was a consummate raconteur and would tell the same anecdote a hundred times to different audiences and each telling would sound like a fresh telling.[1000]

This vividness of appearance, personality and conduct in public was, as we shall now see, the key to Quentin's tremendous influence on British cultural life of the 1960s and beyond, which corresponded in many ways to the impact achieved a century earlier by Richard Monckton Milnes.

Into the 'Swinging Sixties'

Quentin's career had rapidly unfolded in the wake of his doomed liaison with Sarah Macmillan. Having finally accepted that this relationship was over, he travelled in September 1952 to Lerici in Italy, where he spent most of his time reading out loud to the author and literary critic, Percy Lubbock, whose eyesight was rapidly fading. It was Lubbock who inspired and encouraged Quentin to become a writer – by 'subcontracting' the younger man to write reviews for the *Times Literary Supplement*. On returning home for the Queen's Coronation in 1953, Quentin was taken to lunch by Bob Boothby and the deputy editor of the *Evening Standard*, who invited him to write a freelance article on rumours that Prince Rainier intended to sell off Monaco to the Greek shipping magnate Aristotle Onassis. This rumour proved unfounded, but the commissioned article was captivating enough to gain Quentin a permanent job as Leader writer on the *Standard*.[1001]

His journalistic career now on track, Quentin expanded his range by becoming 'society correspondent' for the same paper. In 1956, he was engaged to the tall and beautiful, Columbia University-educated American, Martha Sharp, whom he had met while staying with friends in Oxfordshire. The couple threw a lavish engagement party at Londonderry House in Park Lane. Among the scores of guests was Harold Macmillan. The jazz band they hired was fronted by the Scottish jazz singer, Annie Ross, and contained members of the American Stan Kenton Band.[1002]

Following their eventual marriage, Quentin and Martha spent the next twelve months touring the United States and Caribbean. The former was now dependent on a wheelchair. This did not deter him from spending the remainder of the decade in Kyoto, an experience he recounted in *A Curse of Blossom* (1960). On returning from Japan, he became an assistant director of *Queen* magazine, where, due to an unexpected turn of events, he embarked on a much-lauded career as a restaurant critic:

> Someone had forgotten to make the usual listings and an empty half-page was filled with Crewe's account of lunching at Wiltons a restaurant in St James's, where he described how the aristocracy were served nursery food by waitresses dressed as nannies. He ended by saying that the prices, as befitted the clientele, were like death duties, aimed at capital rather than income. He thus started a new and lasting trend whereby restaurant reviews were as much about style and entertainment as about food.[1003]

Sometime in 1959, Quentin Crewe was introduced to a newly arrived junior colleague on *Queen*. The ambitious Angela Huth had studied art in France and Italy, and spent a year exploring the United States, before returning to Britain, where she worked on a variety of newspapers and magazines. She was now employed by *Queen* to refashion articles for colleagues who, according to her, 'knew a lot about their stuff, but weren't writers'.[1004] Angela soon learned that Quentin Crewe was 'both loved and somewhat feared for his sharp tongue' by his colleagues.[1005] Asked to write a short article on the wedding of an old friend, she bucked up the courage to ask 'Q', as she eventually called him, to comment on an early draft. Quentin's constructive criticism was also rich with encouragement. 'So,' Angela added, 'my immediate feeling about [him] was gratitude for such a precise, helpful lesson.'[1006]

Though still capable, at this stage, of walking a few steps unaided, Quentin invariably fell over in the process, and spent most of the time in his wheelchair. He nonetheless possessed a 'beautiful voice, exquisite handwriting, an acerbic sense both of humour and of language, and gave absolutely no sense of being a "cripple", as he called himself'.[1007] Huth regarded Quentin as 'unconventionally handsome', while he rated her in turn as 'gaspingly beautiful'.[1008] Soon after she had established herself as a feature writer at *Queen* (and completed a year-long stint on the Woman's Page at the *Sunday Express*), a mutual attraction developed, despite the thirteen-year age difference between them.[1009]

Following Quentin's divorce from Martha, he and Angela were married at a registry office in August 1961. He had been determined not to turn up in his wheelchair. He somehow managed to walk down the aisle by propping himself up with his hand on his best man's shoulder and stayed upright throughout the service. He then walked unsteadily out to an awaiting car, which drove him to the reception. 'It was the last time he ever walked for more than a few yards,' Angela soberly reflected.[1010]

The Sage of Chelsea

If Richard Monckton Milnes was the 'Cool of the Evening', his great grandson was unarguably the 'Sage of Chelsea'. Quentin Crewe began to solidify his reputation as societal host *par excellence* after he and Angela had moved from the former's 'agreeable but rather dull' house in

Chelsea into a ground floor-with-basement flat in Wilton Crescent.[1011] The couple had developed a wide network of friends and acquaintances in the arts by now, and their new property was ideally suited to entertaining them in large numbers: 'There were good rooms and a terrace garden downstairs, a large dining room and a magnificent drawing room on the ground floor. Just the place for giving parties, and the 1960s were beginning to unfold.'[1012]

In no time at all, Wilton Crescent became the focal point of after-dinner parties, or a place where friends simply turned up unannounced. As Angela pointed out, her husband was ideally suited to the role of host: 'Quentin was regarded as a kind of sage. People liked to sit at his feet and listen to him. He was marvelous at giving both advice and encouragement.'[1013] Among the regular visitors were rock musicians like Bill Wyman and Keith Richards of the Rolling Stones; jazz musicians such as Dudley Moore and George Melly; actresses of the calibre of Shirley MacLaine; and authors and playwrights, such as Edna O'Brien and Kenneth Tynan. These gatherings were reminiscent of those held a century before by Quentin's great grandfather: 'Some of the parties produced bemused or indignant juxtapositions such as Peter Sellers with Arthur Koestler, or Jocelyn Stevens becoming purple with rage in discussion with Bernard Levin about Karl Marx and even more so with Kenneth Tynan about Cuba, offering to send him there to see for himself what sort of hell it was.'[1014]

Tynan and his wife, Kathleen, were among the numerous couples who regularly swapped invitations with the Crewes. Quentin recollected how, at one such party, hosted by the Tynans,

> Edna O'Brien sat on a sofa at his house, chatting to Paul McCartney. Ken, in his role as host, worried that the young Beatle might not know how to extricate himself if he wanted to, and asked me if I thought he should rescue him. My view was that he looked happy and that, if he had achieved the sophistication of being invited to one of Ken's parties, I should have thought he could look after himself. At that moment, Edna and McCartney stood up and left the house together. Ken was transformed, weaving fantasies about a romance. What actually happened was that Edna took McCartney home to Putney where he innocently made up songs for her children.[1015]

The Crewes were invited to a subsequent dinner party, thrown by the editor of *Queen*, Jocelyn Stevens, and his wife, Jane — one-time Lady-in-Waiting to Princess Margaret. The princess had also been invited to this party, along with her husband, Lord Snowdon (originally, Antony Armstrong Jones). Snowdon had previously worked alongside Quentin Crewe at *Queen*. According to Angela, Quentin 'shared with Tony Snowdon an insatiable curiosity, the quality of being totally honest, and the more dubious characteristic of enjoying jokes at other people's expense'.[1016] Not surprisingly, they had forged a lasting friendship.

The dinner party to which the Crewes and royal couple had been invited was an extremely enjoyable occasion in which Princess Margaret 'was in sparkling form — beautiful, lively, always questing to learn about disparate things. In those days she and Tony sparked each other off — stories, mimicry — brilliantly. There was much laughter.'[1017] More memorable still was the subsequent occasion, a few days later, when Quentin and Angela were invited by Princess Margaret to a luncheon engagement at Kensington Palace. Also included among a guest-list of 20 were the actor/playwright, Noel Coward, and future poet laureate, John Betjeman. 'There was a slight feeling of nervous tension, guests wondering how to behave,' Huth recalls. 'But the princess and Tony were good and lively hosts, making people laugh and putting everyone at ease.'[1018]

Royal Connections

Quentin and Angela dared to return the compliment by inviting the princess and Lord Snowdon to one of their own parties. Much to their delight,

> The princess accepted at once. She was naturally drawn to writers, artists, dancers, actors — the arts world — so was delighted to find a lot of people to whom she could talk about the things that most interested her. And she danced and danced. We judged that first invitation to have been a success, because they did not leave till 7 a.m. After that, we became close friends until she died some forty years later.[1019]

It was a testament to their strengthening relationship that the Crewes were invited to 'the wedding of the decade' in 1960, when the princess and Lord Snowdon were married at Westminster Abbey.[1020]

Afterwards, Angela and Margaret were highly supportive of each other during the later stages of their pregnancies. In 1963, Margaret was pregnant with Sarah, while Angela was expecting Candida. Angela had suffered an earlier miscarriage and was therefore required to stay in bed for six months. The bedroom was located in the dreary basement of Wilton Crescent – a 'dark and dismal' affair, containing little to stimulate her interest. Princess Margaret came to the rescue by visiting most weekends, with a film projector and trays of food in tow.[1021] 'I was allowed up, finally, a month before Candida was born,' Angela explained. 'By then Princess Margaret was in bed, waiting for the birth of Sarah. It was our turn to be invited for picnic suppers in her bedroom.'[1022]

Following Candida's birth, Angela Huth stepped into the role of TV reporter for two years on Desmond Wilcox's BBC documentary series, *Man Alive*. She combined this for a short time as presenter of a weekly live arts programme called *How It Is*, on which she famously interviewed John Lennon and Yoko Ono. Angela soon sensed, however, that she was spending too much time away from the family home. This became a major factor in the Crewes' decision to move (in 1967) to Wootton House in the Bedfordshire countryside. This relocation kept them within reasonably close range of London and placed them within a stone's throw of their new-found friends, the jazz musicians, Cleo Laine and John Dankworth.

A mere two days after they had been 'chaotically installed' in their new home, the Crewes were pleasantly surprised by the arrival by helicopter of Princess Margaret, Lord Snowdon and Jocelyn and Jane Stevens. Within minutes of their landing, the visiting party was enthusiastically stripping wallpaper off the drawing-room walls.[1023]

Quentin and Angela enjoyed an extremely luxurious lifestyle at Wootton. She continued her career as TV interviewer and he busily wrote columns for the *Sunday Mirror, Queen* magazine and, later still, the *Evening Standard*. They continued to lavishly entertain; and, as ever, Quentin 'enjoyed his role as a host and took great care in choosing the right people together'.[1024] For example,

> One weekend, when the Snowdons were staying, John and
> Cleo Dankworth came over bringing Dudley Moore. He was
> dressed in a handsome dark green jacket with silver buttons.

Not unreasonably, Candida thought he was the postman. After dinner there was music and carousing: Dudley played the piano in his extraordinary fashion, and hilariously imitated various singers. John played his clarinet, Cleo's singing swerved from melancholy to cheerful jazz, Princess Margaret sang numbers from Guys and Dolls – she knew every word by heart. Suddenly we noticed sun in the drawing room: it was 7 a.m. We had eggs and bacon in the kitchen [...] before we finally went to bed.[1025]

Voyages of Discovery

Quentin Crewe also shared his great grandfather's fascination for 'otherness', and his great desire to understand and empathise with geographically, socially or psychologically discrepant cultures. This was exemplified by Quentin's decision in 1966 to accompany the inventor and entrepreneur, Jeremy Fry, on an expedition to Saudi Arabia. Like Quentin, Fry was a well-known bon viveur and close friend of the Snowdons. Both he and Quentin had been inspired to undertake the expedition on reading *Arabian Sands*, a book written by the explorer and military hero, Wilfred Thesiger. 'I was determined to see the tribes that he had written about while their pattern of living was still unchanged,' Quentin wrote.[1026]

The two men had scarcely begun their expedition when, recalling the much-publicised experience of Richard Monckton Milnes, Quentin accepted an invitation to attend a public execution. He confessed that he 'had always disapproved vaguely' of his great grandfather's response to the public hanging of the young Swiss man, Courvoisier, at Newgate in 1840. Milnes had witnessed the execution in the company of the writer, W.M. Thackeray; but, whereas Thackeray was clearly revulsed by what he saw and ashamed at the 'brutal curiosity' which had led him there,

> Monckton Milnes had obviously not been so affected, as he afterwards collected autographs and woodcuts of Courvoisier, of Calcraft the common hangman and other notorieties connected with crime and its punishment. Perhaps I shared with him the feeling that one should have almost any experience, with the obvious provisos of excluding cruelty, criminality and the corruption of others. In any event we went.[1027]

A huge crowd had gathered for the spectacle. Having caught sight of Quentin in his wheelchair, the officer in charge of the firing squad had him transferred to the top of a short flight of stairs where he could claim a better view. Three brightly coloured vans rolled in and three prisoners stepped out of them. Quentin's eyes briefly met with of one of these three, who had all been convicted of raping and killing a 15-year-old girl. Quentin considered this charge irrelevant: no-one had a right to kill another, no matter how heinous the crime committed:

> In our society, if we are to be shot, we stand and face the firing squad – blindfold as a rule, for whose greater comfort I am not sure. This was different. The three men crouched down facing the wall, their backs to the three firing squads. The order snapped. The two further men fell first. The man in white just began to turn his head to see if it had happened, then he too fell. They threw the bodies on to the trucks like rubbish and drove away.[1028]

With an elaborate entourage of guides, cooks and drivers in tow, Quentin and Fry succeeded in crossing into the East Aden Protectorate before encountering territory described as 'unexplored' on contemporary atlases. On the way back home, one of the party's interpreters suddenly became unbalanced, attacked some of his co-travellers, and had to be restrained from cutting his own throat. The self-harming colleague was calmed down with a shot of morphine and had his wounds stitched up by Quentin. Things then returned to normal.[1029]

It was also evident that Quentin shared his grandfather's distaste for oppression and an unwavering sympathy for the outcast and underdog. This became apparent in 1968, when he was commissioned to go to South Africa and report for the *Sunday Mirror* on the various ways that – according to Sir Alec Douglas-Home – the lives of blacks and coloureds were markedly improving.

> It did not take long to discover that far from being better the plight of the blacks in South Africa was becoming worse. Sir Alec Douglas-Home had evidently not noticed that the previous few years had seen more and more oppressive new laws, passed in the vain hope of giving substance to the preposterous and inhumane fantasy that was apartheid.[1030]

Quentin rated the four once-weekly articles he produced for the *Sunday Mirror* 'the most worthwhile pieces of journalism I ever wrote'.[1031] He felt especially satisfied when the South African authorities began resorting to 'personally vicious' comments in an attempt to discredit him. One especially distasteful phrase – 'Crippled in body means crippled in mind' – was cruelly levelled at him.[1032] Other discrediting tactics were employed. Two supposedly English men – later revealed to have come from the South African Embassy – turned up at the *Sunday Mirror* offices, purporting to have proof that every member of the South African cabinet had 'black blood' in their ancestry. Had Quentin fallen for it, the story would have been used to undermine his credibility.

Quentin resigned soon afterwards from a corresponding job at *Queen*, when he discovered that its new owners were hatching plans for a 20-page supplement on South Africa (with the backing of a lavish advertising campaign), encouraging people to go there on holiday. Quentin protested that he could not countenance working for a magazine which was implicitly 'bolstering the lies' being propagated by an avowedly racist society.[1033] This adds credence to Candida's claim that, 'Long before the vocabulary and practice of racism became unacceptable, he was with quiet dedication championing the cause against it.'[1034]

Another instance of the campaigning spirit occurred when a member of the British travelling community (a 'Gipsy', according to Quentin's misspelling) wrote to ask him why, given that he was always writing about oppressed minorities abroad, he had never addressed the plight of travellers in his own country. Quentin therefore rented a caravan and latched onto a traveller community in Oxfordshire, with whom he stayed for several weeks. The travellers were never turned away from any place they visited. On one occasion, however,

> Freedom took a knock when the police came at two in the morning, angry in their shame, to thump on the roof of each caravan telling us to move, waking babies and frightening the old. There was a moment of farce when I protested and the police were startled by the unexpected accent, but the Connors family in the next caravan told me not to make a fuss. They were used to it, and I was to become so.[1035]

This attitude of resignation endured even when one of Quentin's co-travellers had his head banged against a caravan window by the police, having been suspected of stealing some copper. Two days later, the police returned to apologise, having tracked down the actual perpetrator.[1036]

Quentin eventually realised that what most distinguished the 'gipsies' from mainstream society was their 'stalwart independence and a determination to maintain the way of life that they have chosen, no matter how much it affronts the set of rules of our society and brings down on them the hatred and contempt of half the population'.[1037] The gipsies admitted to occasional acts of theft, adding that this typically involved 'something nobody will miss much', such as the odd chicken or an old, discarded bicycle. To be a gipsy was to belong to a rather exclusive 'club' – an aristocratic elite who tend 'to intermarry and have cousins all over the country'.[1038] While the 'prejudice and cruelty' Quentin witnessed first-hand made him feel ashamed, he was nonetheless 'excited by the courage, simplicity and the camaraderie of Gipsy life'.[1039]

The Snowdon 'Chairmobile'

In the summer of 1968, Lord Snowdon set about designing Quentin an innovative type of wheelchair, ideally suited to his domestic and professional needs. The pair were already members of the Polio Research Fund, a disease which Snowdon had contracted in his childhood. By now, Quentin's muscular dystrophy was becoming increasingly debilitating.

This project was given considerable impetus when Snowdon asked Quentin to accompany him to the London Olympia, where the former was exhibiting photographs. As they were entering the building, a steward refused Quentin access because his wheelchair was deemed too large and unwieldly. 'Tony couldn't believe what was happening,' Quentin recalled, 'and he determined that it would not be repeated. So, he set about designing a new wheelchair for me that would be more convenient for everyone.'[1040] With his customary enthusiasm, Snowdon bypassed conventional protocols governing wheelchair design:

> What he came up with was, in essence, a motorised chair-base
> on which seating of different types and heights could be fitted,

and which was small enough to pass through a standard door and fit into a small bathroom. [...] With a high stool on the chair platform, Crewe could be at the same height as other people, making conversations both easier and socially more equitable. Other seats could be for sitting and reading, or for moving from one place to another. The prototype Chairmobile, with its adjustable steering column, was powered by a battery removed from one of his children's toys.[1041]

The chair proved resoundingly successful – to the extent that Snowdon soon persuaded the head of an engineering firm to manufacture it. The *Mirror* (Newspaper) Group then purchased 2,500 chairs, which they passed on at a heavily discounted price to readers of the *Sunday Mirror*. The Chairmobile received further publicity when Scotland Yard acquired one on behalf of a disabled police officer, and the wealthy textile manufacturer, Sir Joseph Kagan, presented six models to the Parliamentary All-Party Disablement Group. Insofar as Quentin was concerned,

> It was a wonderful little machine and it served me well for fifteen years. But it served an additional purpose. In having to promote the chair by writing about it and even publishing pictures of myself using it, I learned that my inhibitions about mentioning my disability were absurd. [...] It was no longer a thing to be hidden; it might even be a benefit rather than a handicap.[1042]

Falling Apart

As early as 1967, the marriage between Princess Margaret and Lord Snowdon was allegedly already unravelling. A major rift had occurred towards the end of 1966, when Snowdon heard from an associate that Margaret had begun an affair with an old friend, the Earl of Home. This had inevitable repercussions for Tony's relationship with the Crewes:

> Invited to stay with Quentin Crewe and his wife Angela Huth, Tony told Margaret at the last minute on Friday afternoon that he was not going to come with her. She went by herself, putting as brave a face on it as possible. The only sign of her inner distress was her request to Angela (an Italian-speaker) to translate

some Italian articles for her to see what they were saying about her marriage and the Douglas-Home affair.[1043]

A separation soon followed, at which point Snowdon threatened Angela: 'If you ever do anything against Princess Margaret I'd kill you.'[1044] Ironically, the Crewes' marriage was also coming to an end. Since moving to Wootton, Angela had begun writing her first novel, the eventual best seller, *Nowhere Girl*, and spent the remainder of her time with Candida or working in the garden; but she and Quentin were slowly drifting apart. Their subsequent divorce was entirely devoid of rancour – undertaken, in Quentin's words, 'in sorrow, certainly not in anger'.[1045] Angela would later say of her continuing friendship with Princess Margaret:

> Our divorces, like our daughters, more or less coincided. I don't remember much soul-baring: we both come from the stiff upper lip school in which deflection seems a better option than agonising. There's much to be said for recognising a friend's plight but not dwelling on it.[1046]

Angela moved out of Wootton into a Wiltshire cottage, which Margaret and her daughter, Sarah, regularly dropped in on. The friendship between the two women extended beyond Angela's remarriage, when she and her second husband, James, frequently met up with her. Even when the princess grew older and her health started to decline, Angela often went to stay with her at Buckingham Palace, took her out swimming, or escorted her to the ballet.[1047]

Out of the Ashes?
In the meantime, Quentin had remarried in 1970 to the beautiful and 'tempestuous' Sue Cavendish, a second cousin of Sarah Macmillan. Three years earlier, his life had altered course following the death on 13 March of Peggy, Marchioness of Crewe, who was buried alongside her husband at Barthomley, Cheshire. A tribute appearing in the following day's edition of *The Times* characterised Peggy as a 'unique personality, whose charm fascinated her friends drawn from the widest circle, which includes all ages and interests, political, literary and artistic'. Quentin inherited from his step-grandmother land surrounding his family home of Madeley Manor, located close to the Cheshire/

Staffordshire border. This small estate incorporated three tenanted farms, one of which, Netherset Hey, he and Sue decided to occupy, with a view to working the land.[1048]

Quentin entered the role of gentleman-farmer with much enthusiasm, utilising a golf buggy to get around the fields. He and Sue were gradually integrated into the surrounding community. Their son, Nathaniel, had been born in London, but the christening took place in the local village. Church bells rang out in the presence of scores of local well-wishers.[1049]

On one occasion, Quentin was accompanied by a friend of Sue's, the architect, Hugh Geddes, as they went to observe some cattle which were grazing on fields at Lycett, near Madeley. This was the mining village once patronised by Lord Crewe, and still fondly regarded by his grandson. 'As a boy,' Quentin recalled, 'I had been down the mine, crawling for the last yards to the workface, both excited and horrified by the life of the miners.'[1050] He had often gazed across the lake at the 'whirring wheel and high spoil heap' of Lycett Colliery from the vantage point of the old house.

> Now the wheel was still and the mine-shafts capped; thin grass and stunted trees tried to establish themselves on the sterile slopes of the slag heap. The Coal Board had closed the mine in 1968 and torn down all the buildings, including the pithead baths [...] as well as the three streets of houses built by my great-great-uncle. Only his school still stood, determinedly kept open by the displaced villagers, who had great faith in it.[1051]

Quentin and Hugh begun asking out loud what could possibly be done to regenerate the neglected village and three hundred acres of derelict mining land. They soon committed themselves to revitalising this environment. A consortium was established (comprising Quentin, Colin, Hugh and two more business partners) which spent several months deciding what kind of village to recreate. A plan was drafted, with the aim of constructing 450 houses – half to be built by housing associations for people on local authority housing lists, and the remainder for private buyers. Provision was also made for old folks' homes, and accommodation for students attending a local teacher-training college and Keele University, situated three miles away.[1052]

The partners also stipulated that several shops be dotted about the new village, to give people more opportunity for interaction. Just as crucially,

> To give the village a purpose, we felt it should have an industry of some sort, although we expected many of its inhabitants to work in the Pottery towns seven miles away. It was Colin who suggested that we make an equestrian centre, partly because it was a very rural and English interest and partly because nearly all horsey activities took place in the South, and we thought the North needed some share in this national pleasure.[1053]

The planners' basic objective was to devote 25 acres each to the actual village and adjoining equestrian centre and allocate the remaining 250 acres to picturesque parkland skirting a central lake. With the oil crisis of the early 1970s now looming, the planners had the novel idea of using methane gas, generated by horse manure, to fuel the village lighting, and of employing the deep mine shafts still in the vicinity to operate heat-exchangers.[1054]

A major problem arose, however, when the partners discussed their proposal with a County Planning Officer, based in Stafford. The CPO objected to the fact that Lycett was located within a Green Belt area; and was impervious to the argument 'that derelict land topped with a slag heap did not add to the beauty of a Green Belt region'.[1055] Quentin and his colleagues were left with the impression that the CPO was more eager to promote a rival scheme, hatched by a huge private corporation, to build a Disneyland-style theme park in the region.[1056]

Not Forgetting the Rest

For the rest of his life, Quentin remained incorrigibly committed to new adventure. In 1981, he embarked on an eighteen-month trek across the Sahara, in search of fast-disappearing, unfamiliar ways of life, but the voyage was poorly organised. When an impromptu decision was made to travel from the capital of Mauritania to a particularly well-regarded restaurant in southern Morocco, the expeditionary party encountered a lethal minefield: Quentin's truck was blown up and he was thrown from the vehicle, lucky to survive unscathed. His subsequent account of this misadventure, *In Search of the Sahara* (1983), was one of the several books he continued to write – on subjects ranging from food and travel to a non-fiction account of his family seat, *Crewe House: The Royal Embassy of The Kingdom of Saudi Arabia* (1995). He also produced a candidly entertaining autobiography, *Well, I Forget the Rest: The Autobiography of an Optimist* (1991).

Quentin Crewe's second wife, Angela, and their daughter also wrote prolifically in this period. Following the success of *Nowhere Girl*, Angela Huth wrote ten more novels and three collections of short stories. One of these books, *Land Girls* (1995), was adapted into a feature film. Meanwhile, Candida Crewe produced six critically acclaimed novels and numerous high-profile newspaper and magazine columns for a variety of publications, notably, the *Evening Standard*, *The Times* and the *Times* magazine, the *Daily Telegraph*, and *The Spectator*. A boldly revealing memoir (*Eating Myself*, 2007) dealt openly, as the name suggests, with her own eating disorder.

Angela and Quentin stayed close throughout the remainder of his lifetime. The former paid him regular visits along with her husband, and he often reciprocated. 'He and James held many views in common and joined in teasing me', she amusedly explained.[1057] When Quentin's death drew near in 1998, he was visited by all three ex-wives 'as frequently as geography would allow'. Angela Huth was exceptional in visiting him three times a week, 'bearing baskets of books, snowdrops and marmalades as well as an enduring willingness to help him sort out his financial perils'.[1058]

It was a fitting testament to the high regard in which Quentin was now held that, in 2003, on the 25th anniversary of the publication of his most celebrated work (*Great Chefs of France: The Masters of Haute Cuisine and their Secrets*), the muscular dystrophy campaign group, Q Trust, arranged a celebratory dinner in his honour. Ten leading chefs needed little persuading to cook a five-course meal for 450 people at the Savoy Hotel in London. As Quentin's daughter proudly explained, 'It was both to celebrate the book, which in chefly circles has become something of a classic, and to raise money for research into the disease which killed Pop and continues mercilessly to beleaguer many others.'[1059]

Chapter Twenty-Five
The Troubles of Terence O'Neill

Chip Off Another Old Block

The 'chip off another old block' referred to in this chapter is Terence Marne O'Neill (later, Baron of the Maine), whose personality and political career bore close similarities to those of his grandfather, Lord Crewe. Each of these men spent notable periods of their political careers embroiled in Irish affairs: Crewe as Viceroy of Ireland (from 1892 to 1895) and O'Neill as the fourth Prime Minister of Northern Ireland (1963-69). Having already described and evaluated the contribution to Irish history of Lord Crewe in Volume 1, we now present a similar overview of his grandson's political career and significance.

O'Neill undoubtedly shared with his ancestor a reputation for aloofness, and was equally deemed unsuitable for such high office by Irish Catholics and Protestants alike. This overview begins with a brief explanation of the origins of the Northern Irish state and of O'Neill's ascension to the office of Prime Minister. It provides the foundation for discussing the impact of his leadership style and policies on the onset of the 'Troubles' – the highly conflictual epoch in Northern Irish affairs, commencing in the late 1960s.

Northern Ireland: Inception and Division

The nationally autonomous northern Irish state was conceived by the Government of Ireland Act 1921, which provided for two general elections – one in the six counties of the north, and the other for a Home Rule parliament in the south (the so-called Republic of Ireland). The northern election resulted in 40 seats for the Unionists, and six each for Sinn Féin and other Nationalist parties. On 22 June 1921, the King opened a new parliament, based on a huge Protestant majority, and Northern Ireland officially materialised.[1060]

Shortly afterwards, the Constabulary Act (NI) 1922 was passed, heralding the formation of a Protestant-dominated Royal Ulster Constabulary (RUC), which was immediately regarded as biased and repressive by the minority Catholic community. The predominantly Protestant 'B Specials' (a part-time adjunct of the RUC) were retained under the Act to provide supplementary assistance wherever necessary. The activities of the police were underscored by a panoply of powers contained in the Civil Authorities (Special Powers) Act Northern Ireland 1922. Among its innumerable provisions were powers invested in the police to search, arrest and detain individuals arbitrarily (for the purpose of interrogation), and to disperse gatherings of three or more people to prevent possible breaches of the peace. Moreover, 'Under authority invested in the Minister for Home Affairs, the Act also provided for internment without trial, the imposition of curfews, the serving of exclusion orders against named persons, the prohibition and distribution of certain forms of literature, the banning of various associations and the death penalty for causing or attempting to cause an explosion likely to lead to injury.'[1061]

The contested nature of this state (which was considered illegitimate by large sections of the population of southern Ireland and by Catholics in the north), and grievances arising from the political and economic subjugation of Northern Irish Catholics, produced intermittent conflict between the IRA and the authorities in the 1920s, around WWII, and the period from 1956 to 1962. The most recent wave of the 'Troubles' in Northern Ireland, which emerged and escalated during Terence O'Neill's tenure, was closely related to the style, substance and objectives associated with his period as Prime Minister – all set against the tension created by his attempts at economic reform versus its implications for civil rights.

Prime Minister O'Neill

O'Neill's progression to the premiership of Northern Ireland had proven a tortuous process from the moment he first started his lengthy political apprenticeship in the Ministry of Health. In 1953, he became Chairman of Ways and Means; and, two years later, he was moved into the role of parliamentary secretary to the Minister of Home Affairs. O'Neill eventually joined the Cabinet as Minister of Home Affairs in 1956, becoming Minister of Finance six months later. The impression he made was favourable. Virtually unique in having no outside business interests or need to supplement his ministerial salary, O'Neill soon became renowned for his unusually strong work ethic, though it was equally acknowledged there were inherent flaws in his character. Like his grandfather before him, 'Here was a meticulous and conscientious politician, but not a relaxed party "boss", easy with small talk, idle socialising and patronage.'[1062]

The rising politician's role as Minister of Finance proved exceptionally challenging. In 1958, unemployment rose by 10%, affecting the staple textile and shipbuilding industries, in particular. This was epitomised by events in July 1961, when 8,000 of the shipbuilder, Harland & Wolff's 21,000 workers were made redundant, followed by 2,000 more in the next twelve months.[1063] The Northern Irish Government, led by the Prime Minister, Lord Brookeborough, responded to this problem by asking Britain to prop up these ailing traditional industries. For his part,

> O'Neill at first had little idea how to approach the crisis. However, the Northern Ireland civil service autonomously developed a scheme of infrastructural development, concentrating on road building and the promotion of new towns. The Matthew plan, published in February 1963, thus made a more positive case for British subvention. O'Neill was quick to realize the significance of this new approach. It chimed in with his familiar refrain [...] that Northern Ireland should rely upon self-help. Now he argued, notably in a speech to the Pottinger Unionist Association, Belfast, in February 1963, for generous pump-priming with British funds.[1064]

It became increasingly apparent that Brookeborough's policy of 'relying on charm, contacts and special pleading to win resources from the exchequer' was destined for failure.[1065] The Prime Minister was spared the humiliation of overthrowal by his own colleagues by the emergence of a duodenal ulcer that forced him into retirement. As Mulholland points out, O'Neill was 'well placed to don the mantle of technocratic modernization'.[1066] Controversy and disgruntlement arose, however, when, following a private meeting between the Prime Minister and the Governor, Lord Wakeham, O'Neill was *directly appointed* Prime Minister, rather than being elected by the parliamentary Unionist Party at Stormont.

It was therefore inarguable that, 'From the outset O'Neill lacked legitimacy.'[1067] His predecessor, Lord Brookeborough, had always insisted that any successor would be elected by the Parliamentary Party.

As it turned out O'Neill was selected by the Governor. In October 1963 an unsigned letter was delivered to 33 Unionist Members of Parliament at Stormont protesting at the lack of consultation in the party on O'Neill's appointment as Prime Minister. It soon emerged that Edmund Warnock, a veteran MP now on the backbench, was the author. Though he claimed that O'Neill himself was not being criticized it was an inauspicious beginning.[1068]

True to his word, O'Neill single-mindedly embarked on a policy to secure the industrialisation and modernisation of Northern Ireland: 'A series of schemes to rationalize railways, build motorways, encourage growth points, clear slums, reorganize ministries, establish a new university, create a new city, and reach a concordat with the trade unions to facilitate quasi-corporate planning were all designed to wring funds from Britain.'[1069] O'Neill's approach was superficially non-sectarian in style and delivery — in essence, non-divisive and apolitical, in such a way as to engage and co-opt the Catholic minority:

In fact, O'Neill did not see the problem of communal relations as being directly amenable to governmental action or even rhetoric. He was rigorously laissez faire in the religio-political sphere, if not in the economic, and firmly believed that intervention from above could only aggravate sectarian tensions, never ameliorate them. Catholics, he believed, would come in time to accept the economic sense of the Union, and until then all that could profitably be done was to 'think and speak of each other with clarity and understanding.' 'If you wish to spend your time talking about discrimination,' he once astonished hecklers, 'then you can be sure that relations in Northern Ireland will get worse and worse. If you wish them to improve, then for a time the discussion must be put to one side. In that way relations will slowly improve.' Here was O'Neillism in a nutshell.[1070]

Huge amounts of public finance were invested in the building of extra housing, road infrastructure and education and training, but it was evident that a lingering commitment to declining traditional industries was holding the economy back and perpetuating Northern Irish dependency on Great Britain. Also problematic for O'Neill were growing Catholic perceptions that many key decisions within the 'modernising' framework blatantly favoured the Protestant community. This was true, for example, of the decision to build a new university in Protestant-dominated Coleraine, rather than Londonderry where a Catholic majority held sway.[1071]

A serious dilemma was created for O'Neill by the election of a British Labour government in October 1964, whose pre-electoral rhetoric spoke of the need for reforms in Northern Ireland. The British Prime Minister, Harold Wilson, was likely to make any extension of already costly subsidies conditional on a more egalitarian economic modus operandi: 'As Britain would eventually make very clear, if Northern Ireland failed to deal with these problems, the faucet of discretionary funding could easily be turned off again.'[1072]

O'Neill was conscious that any substantive reforms ran the risk of provoking hard-line Protestants, notably the faction led by the firebrand clerical politician, the Reverend Ian Paisley, whose 'roots were in Ulster's long tradition of turbulent street preachers'.[1073] A portent of things to come had arisen in 1963, when Paisley publicly objected to the flying of the Union flag at half-mast over Belfast city hall to commemorate the death of the Pope. Then, in the build-up to the Westminster general election in September 1964, he protested about the flying of the Republican flag over their election headquarters in the West Belfast constituency. Twice, the RUC broke in to tear down the flag. On the second of these occasions, their action provoked the worst night of rioting for 30 years.[1074]

O'Neill reacted by blaming the Republicans. He nonetheless restated a principal objective of his administration – 'to build bridges between the two traditions within the community'.[1075] O'Neill adopted a campaign based on 'carefully symbolic gestures' in relation to Catholic disaffection, such as visiting a Catholic school, where he was photographed in front of a crucifix, enjoying a good-natured conversation with nuns. He then made a point of crossing the floor in Stormont to congratulate the ultra-Nationalist politician, Cahir Healy, on his 87th birthday, and commiserating with another Nationalist MP, Patrick Gormley, regarding injuries sustained in a car crash.[1076]

More daring still was a staged meeting with the taoiseach (political leader) of the Irish Republic, Sean Lemass, at Stormont on 14 January 1965. This dramatic development occurred without any prior consultation by O'Neill of his Cabinet colleagues. Almost predictably, Ian Paisley was there to greet the taoiseach's arrival. He and his colleagues threw snowballs at Lemass's car and, along with three of his followers, Paisley drove laps round Stormont with a Union flag trailing from their car.

> Later, at a meeting in the Ulster Hall, where he launched his 'O'Neill Must Go' campaign, Paisley announced that 'Captain O'Neill has forfeited the right to be our Prime Minister. [...] He is a bridge builder he tells us. A traitor and a bridge are very much alike for they both go over to the other side.' From this point on, Paisley harassed O'Neill remorselessly. For the rest of his premiership, O'Neill could rarely make a public appearance without enduring the attentions of a shouting crowd of Paisleyite protestors.[1077]

Undeterred, O'Neill subsequently returned the compliment by visiting Lemass in Dublin.

Mulholland makes the point that O'Neill's poor interpersonal skills and attitude of aloofness towards his close political colleagues compounded the difficulties he experienced in office.

> Personally shy and awkward, he had little inclination to mix with those with whom he had little in common, and to whom he certainly felt superior. Despite urgings from his lieutenants, O'Neill rarely visited the Chief Whip's room in Stormont, where backbenchers tended to congregate. Lord Brookeborough had always been careful to mix informally even with those backbenchers critical of his leadership. In Stormont O'Neill would dine only with his civil servants and even had a private WC built adjoining his office to avoid crossing through the Members' room.[1078]

In the next few years, O'Neill continued his uphill struggle to appease both sides of the sectarian divide. Nationalist parades to commemorate the fiftieth anniversary of the Easter Rising of 1916 were allowed to go ahead (even though they were technically illegal), giving rise to Protestant accusations that their Prime Minister was legalistically negligent. It was in this context that, in June 1966, the Ulster Volunteer Force (UVF) suddenly rose to prominence, their modus operandi being to perpetrate acts of violence but attribute them to the IRA in such a way as to undermine O'Neill's bridge-building agenda.[1079] However, as Purdie points out,

> The most horrifying aspect of the violence of 1966 was the responsibility of the UVF. A Protestant widow died in a blaze caused by a misdirected petrol bomb, an innocent Catholic was shot dead as he drunkenly sang republican songs and three Catholic barmen were shot, one of them fatally. The killings were shocking not only because they were brutal and unjustified but also because they were so arbitrary.[1080]

Later in 1966, O'Neill was forced to endure an embarrassing situation which arose when one-third of the 36 Union backbenchers at Stormont raised a petition calling for his resignation. The pressure on him was incessant. On 2 August 1966, Harold Wilson summoned O'Neill to Downing Street to emphasise, along with Home Secretary, Roy Jenkins, that the Labour Government was coming under increasing pressure from its own backbenchers, and that reform measures were necessary, otherwise 'Westminster would be forced to act'.[1081]

This message was repeated even more stridently in a similar meeting on 12 January 1967. Meanwhile, the snail pace at which civil rights reforms were taking place had prompted the emergence of the Catholic Northern Ireland Civil Rights Association (NICRA), which formed on 30 March 1966.[1082] Mulholland reports that, by 1967, O'Neill had become 'notably weary of the burdens of office and ill at ease with his party'; but this was only the 'lull before the storm', in which Catholic demands for improved civil rights were already becoming more strikingly insistent.[1083]

Troubles and Strife

The difficulties now confronting Terence O'Neill in the late 1960s were due, in part, to the impossible political dilemma in which he found himself; but they were also partly of his own making. As Purdie points out, 'Paisleyism' not only 'limited the room for manoeuvre of

O'Neill and his supporters in the Unionist government and party, but it also undermined trust in O'Neill among civil rights supporters.'[1084] In Purdie's view, the left-wing faction of the civil rights movement was apt to interpret any 'hesitations and evasions' by O'Neill as 'concessions to extreme loyalism'.[1085] Purdie has no doubt that this basic lack of trust was further attributable to the way that O'Neill had succeeded in alienating the Catholic community.[1086]

This community was being asked, in Purdie's words, 'to swallow part of a tradition that was alien to them'.[1087] This argument is more forcibly restated by Mulholland, who maintains:

> The civil rights movement developed a tremendous forward momentum. For years Irish nationalism had been a declining, archaic force. Unionism, under O'Neill, had seized the mantle of modernism, liberalism and progressiveness. Catholics felt their old certitudes disintegrating and feared a loss of identity. Ironically, O'Neillism, which attempted to absorb them into a uniform, essentially unionist body politic, was much more corrosive to catholic communal self-respect than the hard-nosed repressiveness of old-style unionism. The catholic community, in many respects, preferred to be feared and hated than to be patronized and dismissed. The civil rights movement came as a festival of liberation and vengeance for the minority.[1088]

Central to the impending violence were a host of Catholic grievances, which had existed since the inception of the Northern Ireland state but were now growing in salience:

> To begin with, Catholics objected to religious discrimination reflected in the unfair allocation of jobs, housing and industrial investment. A second serious cause of complaint concerned the heavy restrictions on the local election franchise which was not available to lodgers, sub-tenants and children under 21 living with their parents. This cut out a quarter of people otherwise eligible to vote, the majority of whom were Catholics. Moreover, the Representation of the People Bill 1922 entitled limited companies to up to six votes in local elections, depending on their rateable value. This, too, operated to the advantage of Protestants. A similar complaint surrounded the deliberate manipulation of ward boundaries (i.e. 'gerrymandering') to ensure the greatest possible representation of Protestant politicians.

Finally, there was popular Catholic resistance to the implementation of the Civil Authorities (Special Powers) Act, and resentment at the retention of the B Specials, who were seen as drawn from, and biased towards, the Unionists.[1089]

The increasing prominence of these issues, and the establishment of a protest movement committed to their resolution, has been attributed to a variety of factors, such as: the evolution of a better-educated Catholic middle class, less willing to accept conditions of subjugation than previous generations; the precedent set by the US African-American Civil Rights movement; the election of a Labour Party apparently in favour of reform; disaffection towards the 'toothless' policies of the Catholic National Party; and the growing impoverishment and de-skilling of the Catholic working class amidst escalating unemployment.[1090]

The civil rights movement was given major impetus by the 'Caledon squatting incident' of 20 June 1968, in which a local Member of Parliament occupied a council house in a small village in the Dungannon Rural District, in protest at the eviction of a Catholic family and reallocation of their house to a Protestant woman who was not rated a priority. The resulting protest march of 2,500 people, going from Coalisland to Dungannon on 24 August 1968, was the first ever organised by NICRA. It passed off without incident.[1091]

This was not the case of a subsequent march in Londonderry (known to the Catholic population as 'Derry') on 5 October 1968, which was chiefly instigated by left-wing groups and Republican activists, with NICRA only choosing to participate at the last moment. Two days before the scheduled march, the Minister of Home Affairs banned all processions occurring within the city walls. Police expectations of trouble were reinforced by the fact that demonstrators took a different route to the one notified to them by organisers. The police responded aggressively: two MPs at the head of the march were batoned, 'apparently without instruction from the senior officer', and whilst NICRA leaders appealed for crowd restraint, some activists threw stones and placards. The police broke ranks and 'used their batons indiscriminately'.[1092] Other officers hemmed demonstrators into a confined space and used water cannons against them. The crowd eventually dispersed but some were chased into the Catholic Bogside area, where barricades were erected in defiance and petrol bombs hurled at the police.[1093]

In the wake of massive media publicity, the People's Democracy (PD) group was formed around a 'Young Socialist hard core' from Queen's University, Belfast. Henceforward, they would be at the forefront of civil rights marches across the country, many of which were attacked by Protestant counter marchers: 'Derry, in particular, seemed to be in a state of constant turmoil as marchers broke the government's ban on processions several times a day. Something clearly had to be done.'[1094]

Terence O'Neill urgently stepped forward. He was acting hot on the heels of a meeting with Harold Wilson, on 4 November 1968, characterised by 'a roasting for the Stormont delegation' who were also threatened with the 'complete liquidation of all financial arrangements with Northern Ireland'.[1095] On 22 November, O'Neill outlined a package of reforms which went some way to ameliorating the principal Catholic grievances. These included: encouraging local authorities to devise a points system for the allocation of housing; abolishing the company vote for local elections; and repealing sections of the Special Powers Act.

He consolidated this with a famous broadcast on 9 December, in which he issued the dire prophecy that Northern Ireland stood 'at the crossroads'. It was time, he insisted, for Unionist colleagues to stop defying the British Government's pro-reform measures and for street demonstrations to cease forthwith.[1096] However, as Farrell points out,

> It was too little too late. It was enough to outrage the Loyalists without satisfying the Civil Rights movement at all. The whole campaign began to centre around 'One Man, One Vote'. [...] O'Neill wouldn't concede it − it would have split the Unionist Party. The Civil Rights movement wouldn't be satisfied without it.[1097]

The upshot was a series of marches throughout the province. The most significant and monumental of these was the four-day march from Belfast to Londonderry (modelled on the famous Selma-Montgomery march of the US Civil Rights era), which took place on 1-4 January 1969. Aside from constantly being harassed by Loyalists, the marchers were led, on the final day, into an ambush by the RUC, in which demonstrators were attacked by cudgel-wielding assailants, many reputed to be off-duty B Specials. Barricades were erected across the Bogside later that night to deter further incursions by the RUC.[1098] Such conflict then reoccurred on a nightly basis.

Following a spate of ministerial resignations and calls by twelve hard-line Unionist MPs for him to relinquish his leadership, O'Neill unexpectedly called a general election for 24 February.[1099] He pointedly refused to canvass on behalf of candidates opposed to his objectives, while lending his support to more favourably disposed independent counterparts. This proved a far from successful strategy, which left O'Neill without an elected majority of MPs in favour of his reforms, and saw him come within a whisker of losing his Bannside seat to Ian Paisley. Moreover,

> The resounding election victory of 21-year-old Bernadette Devlin, a student member of PD who stood as an anti-Unionist candidate, in the Mid-Ulster by-election on 17 April, was taken as affirmation of the minority's support for the Civil Rights movement. Confronted with this reality, O'Neill conceded the principle of 'one man, one vote', and the full parliamentary party voted it in on 22 April. That night, two major water pipes were blown up, depriving Belfast of its water supplies. This was allegedly perpetrated by Protestants intent on panicking the Unionist Party into bringing O'Neill down. If this was their intention, they succeeded – by precipitating his resignation.[1100]

Soon thereafter, O'Neill 'melted into the shadows of obscurity', leaving no prospect of Catholics being subsumed into a non-sectarian 'New Ulster'. Any progress could only now be achieved in conditions of intense duress:

> A cycle of sectarian escalation was virtually unstoppable. Politics was now an affair of the streets, led by suspicion, fear and a desperate, frenzied excitement. Both communities prepared for the showdown that came with shuddering force in the August riots. In doing so they cast barely a backward glance at the high hopes and expectations of the O'Neill years.[1101]

'The First Decent Prime Minister'?

It was the 'chip off the old block' referred to in our previous chapter (i.e. Quentin Crewe) who explained how the question of politics rarely came up in his *Sunday Mirror* column, unless he was given the opportunity to dwell light-heartedly on the 'absurdities of politicians'. The one exception to this rule was 'when those repulsive Ulster Orangemen betrayed my half-brother Terence O'Neill, who, as the first decent Prime Minister they had ever had, introduced "one man one vote" to the Province, I did express some views, but it was a rare event for me to take politicians seriously.'[1102]

Whatever the merits or otherwise of his tenure as Prime Minister, Terence O'Neill quickly faded from public view. Having resigned his seat in January 1970, he was elevated to life peerage as Baron O'Neill of the Maine. Somewhat ignominiously for him, his Bannside seat was taken over by his old nemesis, Ian Paisley, in the resulting by-election. As if to make a clean break, O'Neill took up residence away from Northern Ireland in Lisle Court, Lymington, Hampshire, though he continued to speak up on the problems of Northern Ireland in the House of Lords, and was otherwise 'studiedly moderate [in] rejecting the New Right of Thatcherism'.[1103]

In a final, penetrating assessment of O'Neill's period in high office, Mulholland speaks critically, both of his subject's ideological perspective and of his political approach. Noting that O'Neill was happier when working alongside civil servants than in the company of politicians, Mulholland comments that:

> His attempts to reform Northern Irish politics depended upon administrative reform and quasi-presidential rhetoric rather than refashioning the party he led. Himself distinctly Anglo-Irish, he underestimated the fierce identity politics of both Catholic and Protestant communities. He viewed popular Protestant opinion warily, suspecting it of atavistic sectarianism, and regarded Catholics patronizingly as degraded with a slave mentality. He assumed that his natural supporters were the middle classes and thought them capable of pioneering enlightened public opinion. [...] His efforts to subsume ethnic passions within a constructive civic society were gratingly patrician, though decent in motivation and sincere.[1104]

Terence O'Neill was 75 years old when he died of cancer at his Hampshire home on 12 June 1990. An IRA bomb had exploded only one day earlier at the nearby Hampshire home of the Tory, Lord McAlpine. The Northern Irish Nationalist politician and leader of the Social Democratic and Labour Party (SDLP), John Hume, responded to O'Neill's passing by observing that the Province could have been spared great pain had his fellow Unionists only supported O'Neill's objectives. The Reverend Ian Paisley took the predictably countervailing view that O'Neill had de-stabilised Northern Ireland by catapulting it into 'the turmoil of the civil rights movement'. Thus, as Mulholland points out, 'The acrimony of the Northern Ireland conflict, both literal and rhetorical, had followed O'Neill to his last rest.'[1105]

Chapter Twenty-Six
Comings and Goings

A Period of Transition

This chapter focuses on a crucial, fifteen-year period, from the late 1960s up to the early 1980s, in which a host of crucial transformations occurred – all of which are relevant to the forthcoming analysis of the 1984-85 miners' strike, appearing in Chapter 27.

One such transformation concerns the death of Dr George Sloan and his eventual succession as GP in Fryston and Airedale by his son, Dr Richard Sloan. The latter would later bear witness to the mental and physical impact of the strike on local people, both during the dispute itself and in its socially problematic aftermath.

The chapter also describes the late careers and subsequent entries into retirement of Jim Bullock and Lord Robens. Such detail is central to our understanding of mounting trade union opposition to pit closures, and of the growing militancy of the National Union of Mineworkers (NUM), in particular.

Finally, we chart the occupational and political progress of Geoffrey Lofthouse, erstwhile personnel manager at Fryston Colliery and Member of Parliament for Pontefract and Castleford. It was as a newcomer to Westminster that he first came across the newly elected leader of the Conservative Party and future Prime Minister, Margaret Thatcher – someone now regarded as the mining industry's political nemesis.

A 'Servant of Mankind'

Dr George Sloan died unexpectedly at home on 6 January 1967, by which time he was 69 years old. The universal affection he commanded was reflected in a local newspaper obituary. Poignantly headlined 'Doctor who was dedicated to serving mankind', this tribute appeared in the 12 January edition of the *Pontefract and Castleford Express*. It noted that he was the 'first doctor to become a resident practitioner at Airedale' and had practiced there for 42 years. This piece drew heavily on a moving testimonial from the social worker and local magistrate, Mrs W. Wheeldon, who was one of Sloan's friends and former patients. 'This generous man was dedicated to his mission at Airedale — it was his life,' she touchingly asserted, while adding that:

> He believed that no-one should serve the public unless it was their desire to serve mankind. A local minister once said that he was 'a seeker' — a Christian man seeking for the good of the people. He was a great believer and this was reflected in his entire life — in his desire to serve mankind. We people of Airedale owe him a debt of gratitude which can never be repaid. His wonderful care of the human being, and his great sense of humanity, gave him his greatness. We were fortunate to know him.

Sloan's funeral was also something special. His wife, Gerda, did not attend the service, having felt too distraught to do so;[1106] but, as Richard Sloan recalled, 'The funeral was amazing to me and my family. Fryston and Airedale did him proud that day.' George's youngest son had returned home from medical school to attend the service, along with his half-siblings and their uncle:

> We went down the bottom of the drive and the blokes were all out from their houses. They'd come up from Fryston and were standing at the bottom of that drive; and then, all the way up Fryston Road, there were fellas with their flat hats and they were raising them to the coffin. Really marvellous. I don't think that will ever happen to anybody again. (Interview, 1987)

'Miner Extraordinary'
The working life of a second iconic local figure was celebrated two-and-a-half years later. On 22 July 1969, Yorkshire Television screened a documentary, *Miner Extraordinary*, reviewing the career history of Jim Bullock, following his recent retirement as National President of BACM. The documentary had been preceded by a four-part series of conversations with Bullock on Radio 4 in December 1968, one month before he was awarded the Order of the British Empire (OBE) for services to mining.[1107]

The YTV documentary commenced by showing Bullock, contentedly walking round his Swillington estate, shotgun in hand and with his ten-year-old son, James, beside him. Following a brief tour of Bullock's converted stables, the focus shifted onto his native village of Bowers Row. Scenes were shown of children playing hopscotch in the street; of washing lines stretching from one pavement to the other; and, most poignantly of all, of Bullock stood watching the pit in the process of being dismantled. At this point, he ruefully reflected how:

> Closing a pit doesn't just mean closing a pit and losing that output. It destroys a whole community [...] What touches a lot of us in mining families is that this has destroyed something that I don't think'll ever be built up again.[1108]

A camera crew then accompanied Bullock around the streets of Fryston, where he reflected on his rise from pony boy to eventual occupant of the 'house on the hill'. Bullock spoke nostalgically when visiting the miners' welfare hall and sports stadium he had nurtured to fruition.

The hall was now dilapidated, and the interior grown dusty through disuse. 'Well, I think it were a wonderful place,' Bullock poignantly recollected. 'When I look at it now,' he observed, 'it's very, very painful.'[1109] He looked on with similar dismay when he and the interviewer, Austin Mitchell, stood alongside the site of the former sports stadium, which was now being flattened by mechanical diggers. Bullock snapped back defiantly when Mitchell dared to suggest that the stadium might be described in hindsight as 'Bullock's folly'. 'Is it hell described as Bullock's folly!' he scorchingly replied.

> I mean, if every time anybody tries an experiment, or sees a vision or dreams a dream, it's going to be counted as a folly, I mean where the bloody hell are you gonna get to? I mean, the thing is that the first aeroplane crashed. I expect the first balloon never came down or something. I mean, everybody who's ever tried to do anything and failed in the first experiment. But I haven't failed. I completed the stadium![1110]

Asked what he felt about the project in retrospect, Bullock admitted to feeling thoroughly dejected:

> Well I'm disappointed. I'm hurt — I wish I hadn't come, because I've never seen it like this, you see. I'd seen it, last time I saw

it, it was a stadium: the football field was here, the running track was here, so I could, if I were a less[er] man, be heartbroken but I'm not because I've enough knowledge now, at my age, to realise that human nature has its weaknesses.[1111]

He referred diplomatically to the contrast between his own attitude to social welfare and that of Edgar Williams, his successor as colliery manager:

> And t' bloke that followed me wasn't as interested in this sort of thing as I am. He were more interested in other aspects of welfare. I don't blame him – I don't blame anybody. It's just that it was my dream, and if I'd have stopped here it would have been a dream fulfilled. And the dream, as I saw it, was fulfilled.[1112]

Williams had long since retired by now; but another individual of great relevance to Fryston's history of the 1970s and 1980s was about to join the colliery's management team.

From Stewpot Row to Fryston

Geoffrey Lofthouse had been born into a mining family in Featherstone, West Yorkshire, in December 1925. His maternal grandfather had moved up from Staffordshire around 1890 and was one of the initial shaft sinkers of Ackworth Colliery. Lofthouse's father died when he was only four years old. The family lived until he was nine in the memorably christened 'Stewpot Row'. At this point, the terrace was condemned as a slum, obliging the family to move to Little Lane in nearby Purston. Lofthouse's mother also died prematurely, forcing his older sister, Daisy, to assume responsibility for looking after young Geoffrey, his brother and two sisters.[1113]

Lofthouse was fourteen when he started work at Ackton Hall Colliery, one of two local mines (along with Featherstone Main) and focal point of the infamous 'Featherstone Massacre' of 1893. He left Ackton Hall for Methley Junction in the 1950s because he could not get on with the Undermanager, but returned to Featherstone only six months later.[1114] One year afterwards, he was elected onto the pit's branch committee; and, in 1958, he became both NUM Branch President and workmen's safety inspector.

During the 1960s, Lofthouse attended the miners' Day Release Course at Leeds University, where, in his own words, he acquired a 'theoretical basis' for his socialist philosophy. Other knowledge was derived from direct experience:

> Looking back at this period, I recognise that moderation in union leadership brought few advantages to the industry, but then it is easy to see mistakes by hindsight. The years of the sixties were years with reasonably full employment, and this made any resistance to the erosion of the industry which was taking place when Alf Robens was Chairman of the NCB, quite impossible. Throughout the period, the NUM acted like gentlemen but they were gentlemen out of their depth. Not politically organised, they accepted their fate and put no pressure on MPs to improve the situation.[1115]

The politically ambitious Lofthouse also became a Labour councillor; but, in 1964, he opted for a surprising change of career, employing the rationale that:

> I have always been impressed by Joe Hall's statement that the miners could not have a central place in their industry until they took power and created, from out of their own ranks, a new breed of Managers. I decided that I would try my hand, applied and got appointed as Deputy Manpower Officer at the NCB's Castleford Area Headquarters.[1116]

Lofthouse discovered to his dismay that management was not prepared to encourage a more co-operative relationship with its workforce. There was only one aspect of his role which afforded him the legroom to exercise creativity and initiative.

The 'Pick Your Pit' scheme had been devised in 1965 under the chairmanship of Lord Robens, to enable miners in those areas affected by pit closure to transfer to other coalfields where alternative work was still plentiful.[1117] Lofthouse was charged with mounting a recruitment drive to attract miners to the relatively newly established Kellingley Colliery 'super pit', where hundreds of vacancies existed.

Lofthouse and his colleagues therefore set about visiting the declining coalfields of Scotland and County Durham. Slide shows were presented and interviews conducted in these areas. These presentations deliberately highlighted local sporting attractions. Post-interview visits were arranged, enabling the prospective workers and their families to see for themselves the pits, town centres, education facilities and relevant housing estates on offer.[1118]

Having now served for five years on the local council, Lofthouse was elected in 1967 as Mayor of Pontefract. He was the youngest ever occupant of that role. Ironically, this development proved detrimental to Lofthouse's managerial career, insofar as his line manager at Allerton Bywater disapproved of his foray into local politics.

> We disagreed on a number of things. His way of getting back at me was to put as many restrictions as he could on my progress. For instance, when I was Mayor of Pontefract, he insisted that I take all of my holiday in half days. In the end he kicked me down the ladder to be in charge of personnel at Fryston Colliery.[1119]

The move to Fryston provided a 'breath of fresh air' for Lofthouse, who had now entered a role to which he felt temperamentally well-suited. Lofthouse considered that it was his combined experience as union negotiator and member of management which enabled him to empathise with both sides. He also had the advantage of having attended Day Release courses, on which he formed a close friendship with the senior Fryston NUM branch official, Eric Maskill. Lofthouse's modus operandi as personnel manager was worthy of Jim Bullock in his prime:

> Early on I called in the officials of the NUM and NACODS, the Deputies' Union, for some straight talking. I put it on the line. 'The only way you'll get owt is through me. If you don't keep the negotiations on any issue close inside this pit, but go to a second stage meeting at Area, they'll go by the book, and you'll invariably get less. I have more room for manoeuvre than they have. Always remember that I've done your job and although I might be a bit raw, you've never done mine. I don't say I've nothing to learn, but I won't fall for fairy stories like some might. I can smell genuineness.' This was the type of talk which went down well.[1120]

It was partly due to the undoubted charm and charisma at his disposal that Lord Robens was able to cultivate a generally harmonious relationship with his NCB workforce and their trade union representatives. He was also fortunate in commanding the support of the highly influential Will Paynter, leader of the South Wales Area NUM:

> However, the improved labour relations that these two men built up between the NCB and its workers (which ironically facilitated pit closures) rapidly dissipated towards the end of Robens's tenure. He had always been tough on wage demands and had little time for the militant fringes of trade unionism (once urging the government to take action on unofficial strikes and secondary picketing). After the mid-1960s, when Labour plans for the contraction of the coal industry intensified, Robens became increasingly unpopular and the NUM began to shed its attitude of meek compliance. The scene was set for future strikes.[1121]

This growing militancy was reflected in an unofficial strike in 1969 (involving workers throughout Yorkshire and at most pits within Scotland, South Wales and the Midlands) concerning the poor pay and working conditions of surface workers. A return to work took place only when the TUC General Secretary, Vic Feather, promised to help set up an independent inquiry into the relevant issues.[1122] Robens attributed the strike action to the sinister influence of communist agitators.[1123]

Strike action also occurred in 1970, when the NUM Annual Conference passed a resolution calling for a £20 per week minimum for surface workers, £22 for underground men, and £30 for faceworkers. After negotiations had broken down, a national ballot of NUM members achieved 55 per cent in favour of a strike. This was less than the two-thirds required for the strike to become official, but miners at all South Wales and Doncaster-based collieries, and in all but eight in Scotland, unofficially downed tools.

When Robens visited the NCB Area HQ in Doncaster in November 1970, he was met by a cordon of pickets (a 'yarling mob', as he described them). Had it not been for the presence of the police, he alleged, 'they would cheerfully have murdered me'.[1124] Robens's subsequent assertion on radio and television that these men were subversives, intent on wrecking, not merely the mining industry, but the country at large, provoked 80 MPs into signing a petition calling for his resignation. Robens dismissed these out of hand as 'the super-democrats, the lefties, the softies and the constituency band-wagoners – a poor lot'.[1125]

The NCB supremo briefly continued in his role even after the Labour Government had been ousted at the 1970 general election by the Conservatives under Edward Heath; but he felt increasingly marginalised, and it was not long before he tendered his resignation. Robens had presided, during his 'ten-year stint', over the massive rundown of the mining industry. The number of pits had been reduced in this period from 698 to 292, and the workforce more than halved, from 583,000 to 283,000. Tweedale points out, in Robens's defence, that he advocated a 'social policy' designed to offset the impact of pit closures by providing replacement industries; and, according to those closest to him, exhibited a genuine concern regarding the hardship endured by mining communities.[1126]

In common with Geoffrey Lofthouse, many academics and trade unionists speak more disapprovingly of the Robens legacy. Allen represents both of these parties in maintaining that 'Robens was of enormous value to Governments for he diligently executed their policies whilst maintaining a profile of an aggressive, independent critic who was in some ways closer to the interest of miners than their own officials.'[1127]

'Blunt, Frank, Fresh as a Daisy'

In 1972, Jim Bullock and Alfred Robens each published memoirs of their careers in the mining industry. These two books, *Them and Us*,[1128] and *Ten-Year Stint*,[1129] contained glowing testimonials by each man in reference to the other.

Bullock's tribute to Robens was predictably warm and full of admiration. It was nonetheless suffused with implicit recognition of the characteristics for which the former NCB Chairman often drew criticism: 'Sometimes he appeared to fight a lonely battle,' Bullock studiously observed:

The man at the top is lonely, but Alf Robens made enemies out of powerful friends. He did not do this for himself, but for the sake of the industry he had been *asked* to lead. He worried about the social and moral consequences of pit closures. He fought against the destruction of mining communities. He was tolerant at times; but intolerant of pig-headedness and inefficiency. He could talk a dog's hind leg off! He accepted no case without argument.[1130]

'The Last Word' in *Them and Us* constitutes a correspondingly heartfelt tribute to Bullock from Lord Robens, commencing with an ornate and moving dedication:

There will never be another Jim Bullock, he was as much hewn out of the solid earth as the mineral he spent a lifetime in winning. He could never be anything but himself. Blunt, frank, fresh as a daisy with an immense streak of good humour that flashed out like the gleam of gold in the gold prospector's pan, he was never humble but nevertheless always respectful.[1131]

Robens also emphasises that, while Bullock invariably argued 'with great vigour and clarity of argument' for improvements in his members' wages and conditions, he was equally prepared to discuss such contentious issues as pit closures as constructively and co-operatively as his position might allow.[1132]

An equally impassioned tribute to Bullock subsequently appeared in Robens's own memoirs. 'A Yorkshireman, he was outspoken to the point of offending people who did not know him and mistook his frank, vigorous approach for rudeness,' said Robens of his friend. One reason for their mutual affection and respect was the frankness and openness they exhibited towards each other:

His word was never broken and if he was sometimes hard-hitting in discussion, I knew that he was only doing it in the interest of his members and of what he thought was right. There was no trace of any personal animosity in him, though he never left any room for misunderstanding his position on a particular issue.[1133]

Robens concluded by deriving pleasure from the fact that Bullock had 'lovingly and carefully restored' the Georgian stables once forming part of Sir Charles Lowther's magnificent Swillington Hall: 'I reckon he gets a deal of quiet satisfaction as he, the ex-pit boy, ruminatively pulls on his pipe and thinks of the aristocratic predecessors who first created the graceful surroundings in which he now lives, enjoying his richly earned retirement.'[1134]

Two Striking Successes

Bullock and Robens had each left the industry just as trade union power was proliferating. On 9 January 1972, the NUM embarked on a seven-week stoppage of work which produced a complete shutdown of the nation's 269 collieries. The union was demanding a £9 a week rise on their average pay of £25. In pursuing this claim, they innovatively deployed travelling 'flying pickets' to prevent coal being transported into key industrial targets, especially power stations. An extremely pivotal event occurred on 10 February when hundreds of miners under the direction of the future NUM National President, Arthur Scargill, succeeded with the help of thousands of sympathetic trade unionists in forcing the closure of the huge Saltley coking plant near Birmingham, which harboured, at this time, the nation's last major stockpile of fuel.[1135]

Faced with this disturbing reality, the Conservative Government under Edward ('Ted') Heath designated the miners a 'special case' and accorded them a pay rise way beyond the parameters of their strict incomes policy. The lessons of the Saltley debacle had not been lost, however, on the right of the Conservative Party, including Heath's Secretary of State for Education, Margaret Thatcher, who now saw 'that the struggle to bring trade unions properly within the rule of law would be decided not in the debating chamber of the House of Commons [...] but in and around the pits and factories where intimidation had been allowed to prevail'.[1136]

A further trauma followed: towards the end of January 1974, the NUM membership voted, with 81% in favour of striking in defiance of a pay limit imposed under 'Stage Three' of the Government's statutory incomes policy. Eager to avoid another disastrous showdown with the miners, Heath pre-emptively called a general election based on the slogan 'Firm Action for a Fair Britain'. This strategy backfired when the election produced a 'hung parliament'. Heath's resignation as Prime Minister paved the way for Labour, under the leadership of Harold Wilson, to form a minority government.[1137]

A subsequent general election the following October earned Labour a slim outright majority of three seats. This was enough to trigger a leadership contest within the Tory Party (in February 1975) in which Heath was defeated by Margaret Thatcher. It subsequently became evident that, following her election as leader, Thatcher began contemplating ways of handling a possible future confrontation with the NUM.[1138]

Geoffrey Lofthouse believes that it was the way he conducted himself during the strikes of 1972 and 1974 which helped consolidate his credibility and endeared him to the Fryston workforce. He emphasised his solidarity with local miners by deciding that, for the duration of each dispute, he would continue to draw his salary but then donate it in equal measure to the NUM strike fund and the local Labour Party.[1139]

On one particular occasion, Lofthouse went on the picket line to deter a possible confrontation between striking Fryston miners and the police. 'It's to no one's advantage if conditions underground become intolerable and this is understood by both sides,' Lofthouse stated of this incident:

> There is, however, a point in any coal strike when the men, because they are frustrated, want to put pressure on the Board to negotiate and one way to do this is to prevent the deputies getting in. They, therefore, threaten safety procedures. One morning this point had been reached, and I had gone down on the picket line to ease tension. The men were not letting the deputies through.[1140]

A Police Support Unit (PSU) looked on as the men continued to obstruct the colliery officials. Unaware that Lofthouse was a member of the management, a police officer inadvisably manhandled him. This prompted one picket to protest: 'You've just pushed over a Justice of the Peace, a local councillor, an ex-Mayor of Pontefract and the Personnel Manager of this colliery.' Seemingly undeterred, the officer replied: 'Our job is to get these men into work,' to which Lofthouse argued back: 'Yes, and I can do it a damn sight better than you.'[1141] The pickets dutifully parted and the deputies walked through, unmolested.

In 1976, Jim Bullock published a second book of memoirs, called
Bowers Row: Recollections of a Mining Village.[1142] An accompanying
television documentary, *The Boy from Bowers Row*, appeared on BBC
North in June 1977, having been previewed as follows in the relevant
issue of the *Radio Times*

> Bowers Row was a tiny mining village near Castleford in
> Yorkshire. Today it no longer exists – and with its disappearance,
> a whole lifestyle has vanished. Tonight Jim Bullock, OBE, talks
> about his childhood in Bowers Row. He describes what it was
> like to be the youngest of 12 children in a four-roomed miner's
> cottage – and to start work down the pit at 13.[1143]

Bullock continued in retirement to farm and develop his land,
while occasionally taking time off to extend hospitality and offer
wise counsel and career advice to visiting friends and associates, such
as the former Leeds United and England World Cup-winning
centre-half, Jack Charlton. 'Big Jack' had become a regular visitor
to Swillington in the 1970s, where he and Bullock often went out
fishing and shooting on the estate. By this stage, Charlton had entered
football management, and he seized every opportunity to draw on
Bullock's mentorship. The Leeds favourite enjoyed early managerial
success by guiding Middlesbrough to the Second Division
Championship in 1973-74. After two promising seasons in the First
Division, however, Charlton was already sensing that his team's
development was starting to stagnate:

> And then I got to thinking about some advice my trusted friend
> Jim Bullock had given me. Jim was a big Labour man, an ex-pit
> manager who chaired the first mine manager's union. He was
> also a bit of a philosopher, one of the shrewdest men I've known,
> and I valued what he said. One of his theories held that four
> years was the optimum with any bunch of players. At the end
> of that period, they get to know how you think, to anticipate
> what you're going to say and, frankly, they switch off.[1144]

Bullock's advice to Charlton was to quit while the going was good.
'Another mediocre season and I might be asked to leave,' said Charlton,

'and that was unacceptable to me.'[1145] He therefore left the club in February 1977.

The mentor's guiding hand was also present when Charlton re-entered management at struggling Sheffield Wednesday in the autumn of 1977. The 'Owls' had been five points adrift at the bottom of the Third Division when Charlton joined them, but he succeeded in saving them from relegation. On one occasion, Big Jack saw fit to angrily rebuke the club Chairman for having had the temerity to mete out a dressing down to Charlton's friend and Assistant Manager, Maurice Setters, and another member of the coaching staff. 'One of the gems of wisdom which Jim Bullock imparted,' Charlton explained, 'was that you are never stronger in any managerial job than in the first few months of taking it. If you don't assert your authority in that period, you're living with a time bomb.'[1146]

'Wednesday' achieved promotion from the Third Division in the third season of Charlton's managerial tenure. Two years later, they missed out on promotion to the First Division by a single point. The next season, Wednesday reached the semi-finals of the FA Cup, losing 2-1 to Brighton, but failed, once more, in their bid to achieve promotion. Charlton's decision to leave the club at this point was influenced, yet again, by Bullock: 'Each of the club directors in turn came to my house, asking me to stay, but all to no avail,' Charlton stated in his memoirs. 'Jim Bullock's advice was to leave while they still want you – and, for all the happy times I had experienced in Sheffield, I knew this was the time to go.'[1147]

Return of the Prodigal Son
In the same year that Jack Charlton helped rescue Sheffield Wednesday from relegation to the Fourth Division, a prodigal son returned to Fryston. Richard Sloan had experienced an extremely varied career since enrolling as a medical student at University College London in 1963. Once qualified as a doctor, he had taken on 'house jobs' at two London hospitals, but then obtained a lectureship in physiology and undertook a PhD. Sloan then entered his next post, as a partner in a general practice in Cheltenham. It was at this point (in 1970) that he married his first wife, Felicity. The young couple bought a three-storey town house in Cheltenham, and his mother, Gerda Sloan, moved

down south in order to be near to them.[1148] This marriage eventually failed seven years later, whereupon Richard returned briefly to his physiology lectureship in London but felt sufficiently disillusioned after only one week to tender his resignation.

The course of Richard's life changed irrevocably when, soon after divorcing Felicity, he re-established contact with Kath Sanders, whom he had first courted, albeit unsuccessfully, in his student days. The couple moved into a flat in Roehampton, London, owned by a former school friend of Gerda's. This flat was close to a surgery run by a close friend of the Sloans, who offered Richard the post of assistant medic with a view to eventually awarding him a partnership. Increasingly frustrated by their inability to afford London house prices, Richard and Kath's thoughts turned to the fact that Tieve Tara had lain empty since Gerda's retirement in 1975:

> One day, on impulse, we decided to approach my mother and offer to buy her house and surgery and set up a general practice there. I had decided working in Roehampton was not for me. My mother sold us the house at a generously low price, and Kath was willing to give up her really good consultancy job in London. This was a really big sacrifice for Kath for which I am eternally grateful.[1149]

Determined to stay within close range of her son, Gerda also returned north and settled down in a bungalow in Airedale. Kath took on the role of practice manager and Richard saw his first patient on 1 November 1978. This Dr Sloan quickly became unpopular with other GPs in the district once their patients began transferring to his practice in their droves. The greater workload involved also pushed Richard to the brink of a nervous breakdown. His own GP insisted that he and Kath take a complete break from medicine and was kind enough to start seeing Richard's patients as a short-term goodwill gesture.[1150]

The longer-term solution was for Gerda to temporarily come out of retirement. Unfortunately, her partnership agreement prohibited her from working in Castleford and district for the next five years. A relevant injunction was served by Gerda's ex-medical partner (whose practice was leaking patients to Tieve Tara); the surgery was temporarily suspended and Gerda received a fine. Richard feared at this stage that 'the closure of the practice for three days would have a deleterious effect, but actually it had the reverse. More patients changed GP to us than ever after that.'[1151]

In preparation for this new venture, Richard paid a brief visit underground.

> Our neighbour, Martin Raftery, was a retired miner from Fryston, and he organised a gang of us from the surgery to go down Fryston Colliery. It was seven miles to the place where coal was cut (the coalface), and we travelled part of the way on a coal belt and the rest on a small railway. It was very hot, and when I emerged, I was incredibly thirsty, the dirtiest I had ever been, and with backache from bending so much. I could empathise with the miners who were unable to work for periods of time because of what might be perceived as minor illnesses. I could also understand why they quenched their thirst after work in the Fryston Hotel.[1152]

This first-hand experience promoted a lasting empathy towards local miners and their families. Henceforward, Sloan was more inclined than other GPs to dispense 'medical certificates of unfitness to work' to miners. He also worked closely with the chest unit at Pontefract General Infirmary to raise awareness of emphysema and pneumoconiosis among colliers, and helped lobby for such ailments to be recognised as mining diseases warranting appropriate compensation.[1153]

George Sloan would undoubtedly have applauded his son's decision to return to Fryston. 'I know he always wanted me to come back,' said Richard. He conceded that, whilst he would always feel daunted by his parents' reputations, he was extremely fortunate in other respects:

> I don't think I'll ever follow in my mother and father's footsteps. I haven't got a thing about it, but I admit I don't think there will ever be a doctor like him around here again. I've learned a lot about doctoring from his example. All you've got to do in Airedale and Fryston is to treat people with respect and not look down on them. I think that good name [...] anyone with the name 'Sloan' could come here and be a doctor for the next two hundred years. (Interview, 1987)

Another important handover occurred during the same year (1978), when the longstanding Labour MP for Pontefract and Castleford, Joe Harper, died suddenly of a heart-related illness, thus triggering a local by-election. Geoff Lofthouse allowed his name to go forward as potential Labour candidate, even though he privately doubted his chances of success, due to the fact that 'this was an NUM seat, and I was no friend of the leadership of the NUM'.[1154] Despite intense lobbying in favour of his rival candidate (by the Yorkshire Area NUM President, Arthur Scargill, in particular), Lofthouse secured the Labour nomination, and eventually won the seat, polling 19,508 votes – 8,080 more than the Conservative runner up.

Lofthouse's entrance into parliamentary politics coincided with the death throes of Labour's most recent period in office (1974-79). The Prime Minister of the day was James Callaghan, who had taken over from the recently retired Harold Wilson. Ted Heath had already been deposed as Tory leader, of course, by Margaret Thatcher. Lofthouse was initially unimpressed by the so-called Iron Lady: 'When I first got to Westminster, I was amazed and could not understand how such an average run-of-the-mill politician had come to lead the Conservatives,' he confided.[1155] This was a difficult period for Labour: the strike-ridden 'Winter of Discontent' in 1978-79 had shifted popular support in favour of Mrs Thatcher's pre-election pledge to 'tame' the trade union movement and was undoubtedly key to her party's electoral success of 1979.

Lofthouse was eventually forced into conceding that Thatcher had gradually been transformed into a 'formidable performer who takes some beating'.[1156] He attributed her characteristically indomitable style of leadership to the fact that she was the first woman to become a British Prime Minister:

> Anxious to show that a woman could do the job, she has developed for her protection a granite stubbornness which presents itself as intolerance. Although pleasant enough to talk to, you soon realise that she is not listening to what you are saying, but rather is concerned with what she might say next. On the surface, at least, she has no self doubt, but believes that what she is doing is right. Seemingly, there is no insight into other people's difficulties.[1157]

True to their manifesto promise, the Conservative government took on and defeated key groups of striking public sector workers – most notably, in BL Cars (formerly British Leyland) and the steel industry in 1979 and 1980, respectively – in a bid to downsize the relevant workforces and disempower the trade unions involved. Speculation grew that the mining industry was next in turn on the Government's reformist agenda.[1158]

In the preceding six years, Fryston Colliery had been technologically upgraded. A recently installed washery and blending plant now provided for 70% of Wheldale (as well as Fryston) coal to be prepared for distribution to markets. A state-of-the-art surface control room now guided the transportation of coal – power-loaded by shearers – to the surface via a remotely controlled conveyor network. In January 1978, a further system was introduced enabling freshly won coal to be pneumatically blown to ground level via a 39-inch diameter pipe. NCB returns for the financial year ending March 1978 showed that 600,000 tons of coal per annum were now being produced by 979 employees, compared with the 407,000 achieved by 933 reported in March 1971.[1159]

Optimism regarding the perceived security of local employment was tempered by fears that the increased dilapidation of village housing might culminate in its wholesale demolition. NUM branch officials were leading a campaign to prevent the serving of 'time and place' notices, requiring tenants to vacate all properties deemed substandard by local authority assessors. Village prospects improved when a joint undertaking was reached by the NCB and Wakefield District Council to suspend any major redevelopment of the land currently occupied by village housing for the next fifteen years.[1160]

Morale was further boosted in the wake of the twelve-week steel strike. The *Pontefract and Castleford Express* reported in its 15 May 1980 edition that some 90 Fryston properties earmarked for demotion had been formally reprieved following discussions between the NCB and District Council. The council's 'deputy director of demolition' explained that both parties regarded the houses as 'reasonably long life' and that he would therefore be encouraging local residents to purchase their homes at a generous rate of discount and take up home improvement grants for which they would automatically become eligible. Less positively, the same article confirmed that the village school was due for imminent closure and its 40 pupils set to be relocated elsewhere in the locality. It remained to be seen whether the village and/or its mine could now withstand the confrontation with the Conservative Government that now seemed increasingly inevitable.

Chapter Twenty-Seven

One Strike and You're Out

An Overview of the 1984-85 Miners' Strike

The year-long miners' strike of 1984-85 was even more protracted and bitterly contested than the General Strike and Lockout of 1926. In this chapter, we focus on the experience of the strike from the perspective of Fryston residents and workers at the colliery, and note its implications for the future of the village and its mine. While local experience was consistent with that of many other coalfield communities, one particular episode of violence achieved national prominence and became central to the National Coal Board's propaganda campaign. Detailed overviews of the strike are available in earlier publications.[1161] The following summary, drawn from these accounts, is sufficient for our purposes.

According to most relevant narratives, the Conservative Government under Margaret Thatcher is alleged to have engaged in extensive preparation for the strike in order to avoid – or, possibly, better still, *avenge* – the humiliating setbacks of the 1970s. Following recommendations drafted by her colleague, Nicholas Ridley MP, one year prior to the Tories' election victory in 1979, her party purportedly steeled itself for possible confrontation by: 'stockpiling coal at the power stations; having a contingency plan for importing coal; introducing dual oil- and coal-fired burning in power stations; curtailing social security relief for those on strike; establishing mobile police units to deal with flying pickets; and enlisting non-union drivers who were willing to cross picket lines'.[1162]

Once elected, the Thatcher administration started to fulfil its stated intention to overpower militant trade unionism by taking on and defeating the steel unions in 1980. Attention then turned to the mining industry, when, in February 1981, the NCB submitted a proposal to the NUM for the 'accelerated closure' of 23 collieries. The Government quickly backed off when faced with a plethora of unofficial strikes; but this was only a tactical retreat, which Mrs Thatcher later attributed to a lack of forward planning and poor stockpiling of power station coal.

A possible sign of more earnest intent emerged with the appointment (in 1983) of Ian MacGregor as the NCB Chair. MacGregor had already prevailed in earlier confrontations with the transport and steel unions at BL Cars and the British Steel Corporation, respectively. During his brief tenure at the latter, he succeeded in halving the workforce from 166,000 to 85,000. Convinced that he had been appointed with a similar remit to 'butcher' the coal industry and 'emasculate' the mining unions, the NUM embarked on an overtime ban (in October 1983), intended to run down stocks of coal in readiness for an eventual strike. Also symptomatic of growing rank-and-file agitation was a wave of unofficial strikes in Scotland and South Yorkshire, relating to allegations of managerial heavy-handedness.

It was in this increasingly discordant environment that the NCB announced (without any prior consultation with the NUM) its intention to close the Cortonwood Colliery in South Yorkshire, and Bullcliffe Wood, near Wakefield. Unlike its West Yorkshire counterpart, Cortonwood had not previously been earmarked for possible closure. Given its location in the union's 'militant heartland' and the fact that the closure announcement was made in the spring (when demand for coal was at its lowest ebb), the NCB's decision was widely perceived as a deliberate 'tactical provocation'. With unofficial action now proliferating, especially throughout South Yorkshire, the NUM received further notification, on 6 March, of the Board's intention to shut down an additional nineteen mines. The union's National Executive responded, two days later, by authorising its Scottish and Yorkshire Areas to undertake official action under Rule 41 of its constitution, thus obviating the need for a national ballot.

This tactical ploy backfired. Expectations that invoking Rule 41 would induce miners in other Areas to join the strike proved tragically unfounded. Most workers in the strategically important Nottinghamshire coalfield pointed to the 'bully boy tactics' of flying pickets and the NUM's failure to hold a national ballot as justification for carrying on working. The impression was propagated by a largely unsympathetic mass media that the strike was therefore both 'violent' and 'undemocratic'.

Such definitions helped legitimise the strike-breaking activities of the police. As expected, scores of mobile police units, centrally co-ordinated by the National Reporting Centre in Scotland Yard, were uncompromising in their handling of the strike. Elaborate systems of police roadblocks were used to deter flying picketing. Those miners able to circumvent these obstacles were invariably contained, often roughed up, and their efforts rendered ineffectual by resolute police units. Anyone unfortunate enough to be arrested was liable to find himself sentenced to some form of detention, and/or subjected to curfew by an equally unyielding legal system. In due course, the police operation was diverted away from picket lines to become focused on escorting so-called scabs back into hitherto strike-bound collieries. The strike was further undermined as pit villages became transformed into violently contested areas.

As in 1926, mining villages depended heavily on their much-vaunted reserves of community spirit, mutuality and resilience. Women, in particular, proved the 'backbone of the strike', setting up soup kitchens and forming Women's Support or Action Groups, which engaged in fund-raising, attended picket lines or participated in demonstrations. Mining communities enjoyed the unwavering financial, practical and moral support of wide sections of the general public and other trade unions. The NUM nevertheless failed to gain the support of other strategically important unions. A sympathetic strike by the National Association of Colliery Overmen, Deputies and Shotfirers (NACODS) would have succeeded in bringing the industry to a standstill. They were mollified, however, by an NCB assurance that future proposed pit closures would be subjected to the binding assessment of an Independent Colliery Review Procedure. Not long afterwards,

> The final blow to the NUM was delivered on 25 February 1985 when the Nottinghamshire NUM Area executive voted to call off their overtime ban, adding another 100,000 tonnes of coal per week to the national stockpiles. With the NUM apparently facing defeat, the South Wales Area proposed an orderly return to work of all miners. [...] Eventually, on 3 March, the NUM's national executive narrowly voted for an organized return of its members without settlement of the strike.[1163]

Some academics, journalists and political commentators reject any notion that the strike was consciously engineered by Margaret Thatcher and her government.[1164] Without disputing that the Thatcher administration engaged in extensive preliminary preparation with a view to resisting a miners' strike, they argue that the dispute was precipitated somewhat calamitously and unwittingly: that the decision to close Cortonwood was communicated prematurely and in error by the Director of the NCB's South Yorkshire Area, much to the consternation of government ministers and other senior NCB officials.

Local Political and Trade Union Reaction

This alternative version was rarely subscribed to by individuals currently or formerly associated with Fryston Colliery. Geoffrey Lofthouse referred, by way of interpretation, to an occasion in 1981 when he and Mrs Thatcher were standing, side-by-side in the Houses of Parliament, digesting the news headlines electronically printing out before their eyes.

> We were being told that the NCB had withdrawn its pit closure programme. With great bitterness she replied, 'They've got themselves into a right mess.' I now know what she meant. She meant that the Board had been presumptuous and had sprung the trap too early. The police had not undergone riot training in sufficient numbers, the trade union legislation to prevent secondary picketing was not perfected, the strategies for bringing continental coal were not detailed and she had not got anyone sufficiently bloody minded to hack at our communities with little or no thought of the social consequences.[1165]

Lofthouse maintained that this was an early sign of Mrs Thatcher's determination to confront the miners, but only when appropriate preparations were put in place. As he told the House of Commons in July 1984, Margaret Thatcher had already promised in her pre-election speeches to 'take on' the trade union movement. The NUM was the 'prize' she coveted most of all. According to Lofthouse, the Prime Minister was 'almost tempted' to confront the miners over pit closures in 1981; but, as indicated above, coal stocks were too low, the police were not adequately prepared, and the man she most wanted to help her fulfil her main objective – namely, Ian MacGregor – was currently unavailable. By 1984, however, all preparations had been made in readiness.[1166]

Of all the pits in Lofthouse's constituency, Fryston was arguably the most 'militant' and battle-hardened. According to the colliery's Personnel Manager of the time, the local branch was resolutely supportive of the policies and methods associated with Arthur Scargill:

> He was looked upon with great respect and great loyalty by the majority of Fryston workers and Fryston always seemed to be one of the first collieries to come out on strike if it was an Area or National strike and took great pride in being among the last to return to work. It didn't matter what ballot was taking place, if the recommendation was for 'x' type of action, Fryston would give a resounding vote in support of it. Sharlston, Glasshoughton and several other collieries could register fifty-fifty, or one totally opposite to the Area recommendation, but Fryston took great pride in having a majority vote – and the highest percentage vote at that. (Interview, 1986)

Any suggestion that local men had been 'led by their noses' by the NUM President were indignantly rejected by a Fryston branch official interviewed for television late in the stoppage:

> I mean, it annoys me, as well, when they get on and say, 'It's Scargill leading this.' Scargill can't lead 240,000 men out for eleven months. They're out because they're on *a principle*. They're out because they *actually believe* in something. That's why they're out. I mean, they get on about 'Scargill started this strike.' *Yorkshire* started this strike when t' threatened closure of Cortonwood and Bullcliffe Wood Colliery became imminent.[1167]

It was precisely this ethos that would underpin branch and village solidarity for the duration of the year-long stoppage.

Digging in Deep

The strength of local resolve was powerfully conveyed in a *Pontefract and Castleford Express* article ('Why pit families are still digging in'), appearing on 27 March 1984 during the fourth week of the strike. 'Fryston, the dead-end pit village with the 30s look,' it said, 'is very much alive in community spirit – unified by men and women striving for a common cause.'

Local residents were unanimous in their determination to remain on strike for however long it might take to safeguard jobs and preserve the fabric of community. One 37-year-old divorcee who lived on Brook Street explained in the article how he was surviving on holiday savings in the absence of any other income, while two married couples with small families on William Street were totally reliant on family allowance payments. Angrily dismissing the suggestion that miners' spouses were eager for their menfolk to return to work, one of these latter two wives maintained that:

> It is utter rubbish. I am wholeheartedly behind my husband and every woman here feels the same about her man. The future of the trade union movement and the country depends on the miners winning this dispute, and we are prepared to see it go on for as long as it takes to win the battle. We will survive on what bit we've got until the strike succeeds.

The article boldly asserted that: 'Few pits supporting the strike call can be showing more militancy,' whether in the form of the '24-hour stranglehold' men were exerting on their own colliery, or the cars and busloads departing each day 'to carry the struggle into other coalfields'. Local miners were predictably well-represented from the outset in groups of 'flying pickets' seeking to dissuade colleagues elsewhere from going into work.

The Fryston NUM Branch President, Roy Wright, was among a handful of such men appearing on the BBC late evening news bulletin on 10 April 1984, as they congregated outside the entrance of the Agecroft mine in Lancashire. Wright reacted defiantly to the suggestion that the Government might serve a legal injunction to prevent further picketing. Miners like him were prepared to go to jail if necessary, he bullishly declared, adding that, once all the pits had been halted, 'we're gonna get stuck back into t' power stations', along with 'all these blacklegs' who were providing them with lorry-loads of coke.[1168]

Geoffrey Lofthouse subsequently explained that it would be misleading to characterise the miners' strike primarily in terms of the picket-line violence ceaselessly highlighted in media reports. This coverage, he claimed, distracted attention from the enduring instances of community solidarity and mutual support, and the generosity of wider sections of society, which helped sustain the dispute. This was exemplified by the efforts of the five Women's Support Groups, scattered throughout his constituency – including one at Airedale Church House.[1169]

Here, local women set up soup kitchens, attended picket lines and demonstrations, and helped raise vital funds for food supplies. On one particularly salient occasion, two hundred Fryston women responded collectively to threats that their electricity was about to be cut off due to their inability to pay their bills: 'So they organised a demonstration and picket of their local Electricity Board offices, demanding that no miner's electricity was cut off during the strike. The manager met their delegation and agreed to their demands.'[1170]

These women were, by and large, 'Practical, down to earth, good providers, people who knew how to combat hardship.'[1171] They were dependent in their efforts on public donations and goodwill. As one such benefactor subsequently recalled:

> My wife Sally, and two friends, Audrey and Matthew, came from Leeds to the picket line at [Fryston] pit in 1984. We brought a boot-load of foodstuffs and a sum of money collected in Leeds, mainly round the University. We returned often and were introduced to the women organising the kitchen throughout the strike. I have forgotten its location. I think a lady called Betty was a dynamic organiser, but I may have the name wrong. She struck up a friendship with our comrade, Audrey, another dynamo.[1172]

The fund-raising activities required to sustain the strike (notably, by helping to stave off hunger and hardship) ranged from street collections to overseas campaigns. Typical of this was a three-week lecture tour of Canada by the 44-year-old Fryston NUM Branch Delegate, Brian Dakin, and his wife, Irene. The tour was organised by the Ontario director of the Canadian Steelworkers, with air fares and accommodation being paid for by a host of other unions. By the first week of the tour, Dakin had addressed union members in six major cities and appeared on three nationwide television networks. The tour organiser confidently predicted that an eventual sum of $1 million would be achieved via Dakin's efforts.[1173]

Adding to the hardship of the strike was the fear, frustration and insecurity inevitably associated with such a lengthy stoppage. Richard Sloan witnessed the medical consequences of this reality:

> The miners' strike [...] created some specific medical problems. There were more children to see in the surgery because the fathers panicked somewhat and would not let the mothers leave things for a while to see whether there was an improvement with time. Lots of miners came to us with symptoms of depression and other conditions, and we gave out lots of sickness certificates. This helped with their finances. I had one miner who had lost weight because he could not chew properly because of a terrible toothache.[1174]

Sloan built up a healthy rapport with local pickets, who set up a hut and brazier at the entrance to the village with a view to deterring potential strike-breakers. On one occasion, he presented them with a sustaining bottle of whisky and lost no opportunity to share a joke and laugh.[1175] Sloan's experience was a testament to the characteristically peaceful picketing at Fryston during the first seven months of the strike.

Tragedy had nonetheless occurred away from the local picket line when, on 15 June, Fryston miners were assigned to the entrance of nearby Ferrybridge Power Station on the day that a 55-year-old Kellingley miner, Joe Green, was run over and killed while endeavouring to speak to the driver of a delivery lorry.[1176] Addressing the Home Secretary, Leon Brittan, in the House of Commons, Geoffrey Lofthouse pointed out that no police were present at the time and that Mr Green had been acting well within the law.[1177]

Fryston miners suffered another body blow, two months later, when a spontaneous underground fire erupted in the important Beeston Seam. The Coal Board decided to sink a borehole at nearby Brotherton with the intention of flooding all roadways leading to the fire and using this 'water seal' to prevent any further spreading.[1178] The NCB North Yorkshire Director, Michael Eaton, maintained that the six-year supply of workable coal remaining in the mine had 'now been drastically reduced' due to the conflagration.[1179]

This prognosis was stridently rejected by the local NUM branch, who promised to resist any attempt to close down their colliery. 'We do not intend being another Cortonwood,' maintained the Fryston NUM President. 'There are only Selby and Kellingley in North Yorkshire which have more coal reserves than Fryston and we intend to do everything we can to ensure that these reserves are mined.'[1180]

This perturbing development had no overtly discernible effect on relations between pickets and their local colliery management. As Fryston's Personnel Manager later confirmed:

> The pickets, initially, were good-humoured, though many in number. There was the usual amount of leg-pulling and name-calling, but nothing that you'd describe as malicious or vindictive towards management. Management had to come through in order to keep the colliery safe. The men realised that. It was a well-known fact that Fryston – the Beeston Seam – was very prone to spontaneous combustion. It was a very hot pit. We'd had fires in the past: we'd lost, just prior to the strike, a district which had cost thousands upon thousands of pounds to get ready through a fire. The men understood our position and were, therefore, tolerant. But this good humour changed as events wore on and the strike grew more serious. (Interview, 1986)

By the autumn of 1984, picket-line confrontations were becoming more commonplace at neighbouring pits. At Kellingley Colliery on 7 September, for example, Geoffrey Lofthouse was knocked to the ground when police in riot gear unaccountably waded into two hundred peacefully dispersing pickets.[1181] A corresponding shift in picket-line behaviour occurred at Fryston soon after police began escorting strike-breakers into the mine. According to the NUM Branch Delegate:

> Fryston, when people started to return to work, was just similar to every other mining village in Great Britain. It was excessively policed the same as any other mine and, although the police said they took an independent view and were just there to make sure that anyone who wanted to attend work could get in, they were fetching them from home in special vehicles and transporting them in. As many are aware, they took a political stance and policed Fryston in line with the Tory philosophy. (Interview, 1986)

Making matters worse was the fact that strikers and their partners walking through the village at night were being stopped by unfamiliar police officers and asked where they were going or coming from. Even the time-honoured custom of coal-picking during strikes was allegedly deterred by a prohibitive police presence.[1182] All such developments stoked up the propensity for violence.

The Fryston Riots

The elderly Fryston resident, Jack Hulme (who was aged 78 at the time), could vividly recollect the precise moment at which picket-line violence first occurred in Fryston – in the early hours of Monday 19 November. 'One o'clock it was,' Hulme recalled in our 1987 interview. 'I know because I happened to go to the toilet – the pickets were running up and down all the streets. I don't know what they were doing, but they had big pick-shafts with them, and they went in the pit yard.' A sleeping Richard Sloan and his wife, Kath, were also woken up by the sound of ongoing confrontation, which was comparable, so they were told, to anything witnessed locally during World War II.[1183]

Trouble arose when a handful of miners returning to work in a transit van were escorted onto the colliery premises by police vehicles, having spent several hours previously in the protective custody of a local police station.[1184] The Fryston Personnel Manager maintained that it had been 'a matter of great pride' to local activists that no potential strike-breakers had, so far, tried to return to work. The sudden appearance of these 'blacklegs' was therefore taken as a particular affront. Thus, as the manager put it, 'Tempers overflowed and what followed was truly unbelievable' (interview, 1986).

Battle commenced as soon as this van entered the colliery yard. The police were unexpectedly outnumbered and powerless to prevent the pickets from pursuing the working miners.[1185] Most of the management team took refuge in the colliery control room, where they wrongly assumed that strikers would not dare to damage such vital mechanisms as ventilation monitoring equipment, fire warning alarms and gas detection devices.[1186]

Unfortunately, two other members of management were left, still exposed to possible attack. This hapless pair had been sent out with instructions to escort the working miners and their van driver into a nearby electricians' surface workshop. The managers appeared to have succeeded in their mission, but the door they had fastened behind them was uncompromisingly smashed open by a 'gang of pickets, led by a union official'.[1187]

The striking miners were now face-to-face with their non-striking counterparts. They singled out one strike-breaker, Michael Fletcher, as the primary focus of their displeasure: 'They told him: "You, you bastard, owe this union more than any individual. You, more than anyone, should never have returned to work and, if you come through that picket line once more, you'll live to regret the day"' (Personnel Manager, 1986).

Fletcher was spared from further harm by a sudden explosion, which caused the pickets to disperse.

> When the two management personnel dashed after them to the door, they were amazed to see that the Ford Transit van that had brought the working miners had been physically turned on its side, a pick-shaft driven through its petrol tank and the whole thing set fire to. It was an unbelievable sight. Certainly, on that particular morning, with police and pickets fighting hand-to-hand on the colliery premises, the van overturned and exploded, windows smashed through and missiles being thrown from all directions, we honestly believed we were on the streets of Belfast, not Fryston. (Personnel Manager, 1986).

The strikers had now ceded the vital element of surprise. On the following day, police with Perspex riot shields proved more than a match for the 200 pickets entering the village. Pickets responded to this strategic disadvantage by hauling a tractor from a nearby scrapyard, positioning it at the entrance of the bridge, and pouring oil across the road to discourage further strike-breaking activity. The police eventually succeeded in clearing the entrance, forcing the strikers to adopt an alternative deterrence strategy.[1188]

The Michael Fletcher Incident

On 23 November 1984, Fryston Colliery became the focal point of national news coverage when it emerged that the above-mentioned strike-breaking miner, 24-year-old Michael Fletcher, had been attacked at home in the presence of his family. Robert Hall's bulletin for ITV's *News At One* was typical of this coverage:

> This morning, Mr Fletcher, who is a married man with two children, left his home in the nearby village of Airedale en route

for the pit. But on the way, he was attacked by twenty men who began hitting him with their fists. Mr Fletcher managed to break away and run home, but he was pursued by six of the group, wearing Balaclava helmets. As his wife and children listened, terrified, Mr Fletcher was given what the police described as a 'severe beating with baseball bats'. It left him with a broken shoulder blade and suspected broken ribs.[1189]

Asked to explain why he had returned to work, Fletcher contended that, following the breakdown of talks, and in the absence of 'any help from the union', he had decided that this was his only way of paying off his mounting bills. He confessed that he had not expected to provoke such an extreme and violent reaction:

> I expected, you know, probably a couple of windows in the house getting broke, things like that. But for 'em to do this, it isn't classed as picketing, not when they're out and round your house. If I had the decision now, I wouldn't be in the NUM. But [it's a] closed shop, so I've got no choice.[1190]

Pressed into saying who he held responsible for the attack, Fletcher blamed the NUM *as an institution*: 'The union,' he replied. 'I think the union is behind it all. [...] Well, when they're on the picket line, they don't condemn violence or anything.'[1191] Fletcher was determined to return to work, for, in failing to do so, he would be exposing other working miners to the possibility of a similar attack: 'Well, if I don't go back, I'll feel as though I'm letting a lot more down who have gone back, because the pickets'll think, if they've done it once – got a person not to go back – they can do it again.'[1192]

The Fletcher case was quickly used as NCB propaganda. Speaking on a BBC documentary, Fletcher disclosed how 'a lot' had written to him, stating that they were 'dead frightened' of returning to work in case of what might happen to themselves or their families. He restated his intention to return to work as soon as possible, but doubted whether he would be accepted back by colleagues currently on strike.[1193] The programme's narrator, Robert Kee, explained how Fletcher had received a letter of commiseration and bunch of flowers from the NCB's North Yorkshire Area Director, and been visited in hospital by Ian MacGregor.[1194]

Writing in his subsequent memoirs, the NCB Chairman referred generically to the Fletcher incident and the case of the Welsh taxi driver, David Wilkie, who was killed when pickets dropped a huge slab of stone onto his vehicle from a motorway bridge as he was driving a miner to work. In MacGregor's estimation, 'neither of these stupid, mindless acts would have taken place were it not for the constant emotional and extreme oratory that Scargill had been keeping up for the duration of the strike'.[1195]

At local level, though, NUM *and* NCB officials were unanimous in their alternative interpretation of events. The Fryston Personnel Manager certainly conceded that:

> Fletcher could never be described as the ideal worker. He had, on several occasions, been disciplined for absenteeism and other acts of misconduct. On occasions prior to the strike, the union had presented good arguments and a united front in fighting for Fletcher to keep his job. They'd assisted Fletcher on several other occasions, e.g. to gain Coal Board housing, which means of course that his rent was subsidised. In many respects, it's got to be admitted that Fletcher owed a great deal of thanks to the union at Fryston Colliery. This was well-known and was probably the main cause of outrage. (Interview, 1986)

Without condoning the violence that occurred, the NUM Branch Delegate, maintained that Fletcher would have been sacked well before the strike had it not been for the union's intervention. 'We felt that we'd given him of our best,' Brian Dakin explained, 'but people who knew him said that he'd started to aggravate the men by boasting that he was going into work and that the Coal Board were going to "look after him"' (interview, 1986). Callinicos and Simons maintain that such indignation was compounded by the fact that Fletcher had been receiving parcels from a nearby food kitchen just before returning to work.[1196] These mitigating factors proved irrelevant once the police started rounding up Fryston pickets suspected of having participated in the attack.

Geoffrey Lofthouse was adamant that Michael Fletcher should never have been subjected to such a beating, 'even if he was breaking ranks'; but the MP also knew from his time spent at Fryston that those arrested 'were not thugs but men who in the normal course of events would never have put a foot wrong'.[1197] Lofthouse had first heard of the mass arrests when his wife, Sarah, phoned the House of Commons to inform him that several 'distraught women' had been in touch to say that their menfolk had been taken to various police stations in Pontefract, Normanton, Castleford and Wakefield. Mrs Lofthouse had already ensured that as many individuals as possible were being legally represented.[1198] Their cases unfolded very rapidly:

> The prisoners came up before the court on Monday, most got remand, and I went to see them in Leeds prison the following Saturday. It was a harrowing experience. In the end many did not come up for a trial for many months. The constant grind of court and recommittal was wearying especially when many could have been out on bail. I had been only one Saturday, some of those honest women went every Saturday.[1199]

Callinicos and Simons interpret the charge brought against the NUM's Roy Wright especially as evidence of a sinister police strategy. Wright was initially remanded for four weeks in Armley jail (Leeds) and subjected to curfew for seven more.[1200] When his case eventually came to court, the charge brought against him ('causing grievous bodily harm on the basis of inciting, aiding or abetting') was dropped due to an absence of incriminating evidence. These authors maintain that the Fletcher case therefore represented 'one of the starkest illustrations in the whole strike' of the police usage of the legal system to neutralise industrial action. More specifically,

> The arrests in Fryston after the attack on Fletcher had just the purpose the police intended. They removed one of the best officials in the North Yorkshire area from the action and the best militants in the branch from the picket line. As a result the atmosphere on the Fryston picket line was more demoralised and depressed by the mass arrests than the return of the first scab to the pit.[1201]

Endgame

There is no evidence to suggest that Fletcher's return to work induced any further copycat behaviour. On 11 February 1985, a group of

Fryston miners interviewed as part of Channel 4's *Here We Go!* documentary strove to put the small trickle of strike-breakers (nine so far out of a total workforce of 1,100) into proper perspective. As one of them explained,

> Out of them nine, there's five young and four older NUM members going into that pit. The four older men *wanted* redundancy before this strike even started. They're the ones that's gone in now to *make sure* they get redundancy. They hadn't gone in there to side with Ian MacGregor or Margaret Thatcher; they'd gone in there for their own ends, for their own gains. They've forsaken their [fellow] workmen, they've forsaken their union that fought for them. The five young men that's in there, they're lads whose union has *saved their jobs* several times.[1202]

A second picket added that such people were 'making the rod' that was breaking the strikers' backs. There was no way, he held, that the Board would be willing to negotiate while strike-breakers like these maintained the possibility of a mass return to work.[1203]

It was widely acknowledged by now that Mrs Thatcher's government had no intention of trying to achieve a settlement. This would be detrimental to their wider ambition of fragmenting and selling off the nationalised industry to private investors. The NUM's priority now was to ensure that, as part of any return-to-work settlement, all miners jailed or sacked during the strike were given back their jobs as part of a general amnesty.

By the end of February, the number of men returning to work at Fryston had swollen to fifteen – still insufficient to suggest any fatal depletion of resilience and solidarity. A nationwide 'drift back' was nonetheless occurring, in response to which the NUM Executive sanctioned an 'orderly return to work without settlement'. Fryston miners marched back into the colliery yard on 3 March 1985, their branch banner proudly held high.

Aftermath

In the immediate post-strike period, NCB managers devised imaginative ways of reincorporating strike-breaking employees back into the mainstream. There was scant possibility of this happening at Fryston. As a means of resolving this problem, management resorted to horse-trading measures. At Savile Colliery (Methley), for example, sacked strikers were reinstated, conditional on local NUM officials agreeing to take on 'scabs' from Fryston and Wheldale.[1204]

The end came all too soon for Fryston. In a pithead ballot of 26 November 1985, the workforce voted by a majority of 79 (308 for and 229 against) for the closure of the colliery, thus terminating 111 years of mining in the village. While a handful of employees would stay on as 'salvage workers', the remainder had already volunteered to accept redundancy or agreed to transfer to other collieries in the locality, or as far afield as Selby.[1205]

NUM officials accused the NCB of treachery. Brian Dakin maintained in interview that the previous Area Director had devised a plan in June 1985 to reduce the workforce from just over 950 to 650 men, pull out of the Beeston Seam altogether, and concentrate production on the Flockton Seam instead. This would have extended the colliery's lifespan by an extra seven to ten years. Fryston miners had already started to implement this plan following the post-strike resumption of work:

> We went into the Flockton Seam, we changed shift patterns — we asked men to do shifts they didn't normally do — we set about driveages diligently, doing a hundred metres a week with new machines, all in the hope of a future of some seven to nine years. However, when they changed the Area Director, it was obvious from Day One that the political will wasn't there to keep Fryston open. (NUM Branch Delegate, 1986)

Seasoned campaigners with expert knowledge of Fryston spoke of the wider act of betrayal perpetrated by the NCB. Both Jim Bullock and Geoffrey Lofthouse had been consistently scornful of many of Arthur Scargill's prophesies and tactics during the strike, but now conceded that, in numerous important respects, the NUM President's judgement had proven superior to theirs. Thus, as Bullock pointed out,

> It amazes me: I thought when the strike first started that Scargill was just completely exaggerating; that there'd only be fifteen pits shut — and everybody knows you can't run a pit when it's exhausted. I thought he was going too far. But as the strike

progressed to its bitter finale and then to its aftermath, a lot of things that Scargill said would happen have happened. Now, I'm no supporter of Scargill's methods, but his foresight about what would happen was better than mine was – because I never thought that this would happen. (Interview, 1987)

Geoffrey Lofthouse steadfastly maintained that the NUM President had been wrong in refusing to call a ballot and in his failure to condemn all picket-line violence. The MP was prepared to admit, however, that in one major respect Scargill's judgement had been infallible:

I thought that we should have accepted the olive branch settlement which the deputies accepted. With the Bates Colliery decision behind us, where an eminent Queen's Counsel chairing an independent review procedure ruled that a pit should not be closed, and then saw it overruled; I have learned a lesson, the Board under MacGregor cannot be trusted. […] The NCB would not listen. Many of the men, all of the Deputies Union leadership, and I believed that the Board would honour the finding of the Independent Review Procedure. Scargill didn't. He was right.[1206]

What made Mr Lofthouse so unique in comparison to all other individuals mentioned in this study was the fact that, having lived and worked for the first five decades of his life alongside the 'pit-folk' of Featherstone, Pontefract and Castleford, he would eventually 'rise' into the peerage system once occupied by Lord Crewe and Richard Monckton Milnes. Having continued to serve as MP for Pontefract and Castleford until retiring in April 1997 (and also been Deputy Speaker of the House from 1992 onwards), Lofthouse was made a life peer in the Dissolution Honours List of 1997. He therefore became known as Baron Lofthouse of Pontefract, the title he held until his death on 1 November 2012.[1207]

Chapter Twenty-Eight
Representing the People

'Capturing the Essence'

Shortly after Fryston Colliery formally ceased producing coal, a headline appearing in the 12 December issue of the *Pontefract and Castleford Express* gloomily inquired: 'Is closure of pit village death knell?' Three months later (on 17 March 1986), the *Yorkshire Evening Post*'s Frank Metcalfe likened the place to an 'abandoned ghost town', already ravaged by change and neglect occurring years before the colliery's ultimate demise:

> A skyline sprawl of pithead winding gear, red-bricked pithead baths, coal-dusted long-arm conveyors and snaking railway sidings is set against the curve of the Aire. Half-a-dozen rows of pit houses, some with windows boarded up or broken, some with For Sale notices, form a straggling ribbed pattern amid the bulldozed area. [...] That is Fryston today. Not a soul in sight. Just the odd dog or cat nosing around abandoned pigeon huts. Hardly a sound other than clunks and clanks from the pithead area.

Central to this article were the moving recollections of a community stalwart, Jack Hulme, who was now in his 80th year. 'Fryston has some marvellous memories for me,' Hulme reflected. 'It was a wonderful place, just one big, happy family.' Life was hard, he said, but the people were kind and honest, and the community close-knit. Metcalfe consolingly disclosed that Hulme's modest North Street terrace was already evolving into an unofficial museum of 'memories, photographs and records', documenting several decades of life in a village seemingly destined for extinction.

Throughout his adult life, Hulme had gradually stored up thousands of negatives of the photographs he had taken of everyday life in Fryston. These were haphazardly preserved in scores of wallets, toffee tins, suitcases and boxes, then seemingly abandoned. It was only when the Castleford-based Yorkshire Art Circus (YAC) appealed for people to come forward with photographs to help illustrate a book on 'local voices' that Hulme sent in half a dozen such images, so striking and evocative that they instantly prompted a follow-up inquiry.[1208] 'I remember asking Jack if he had any negatives,' said Brian Lewis, founder-director of the YAC, 'and he led me into a cluttered back room where there were about ten thousand of them, mainly bungled in an old tea chest.'[1209]

This 'treasure trove' of images[1210] became the focal point of an exhibition at Pontefract Museum in 1986, attended by no fewer than 10,000 visitors. Hulme's photographs have since been exhibited all over Britain, Europe and Australia, attracting unremitting media interest in the process. One notable example was the television feature, 'Photographing Fryston', which appeared on the BBC North *Northern Lights* arts programme (13 February 1987). The YAC has also produced two separate anthologies of Hulme's photograph's.[1211] His life's work reached a rare pinnacle of acclaim when it was included alongside the paintings of L.S. Lowry in a 'Myth of the North' exhibition, staged at the Lowry Galleries in Salford Quays in July 2007.

A similar stroke of good fortune also kick-started the career of another ex-Fryston miner, Harry Malkin. Since leaving Fryston in December 1985, Malkin had been rediscovering an artistic ability which first blossomed during childhood, when he began producing charcoal sketches of miners toiling underground. Like Hulme, Malkin responded to a YAC call for anyone, 'however ordinary', to step forward with literary, artistic or photographic examples of their work.[1212] Malkin duly brought a portfolio of eight drawings to the attention of Brian Lewis, who felt sufficiently impressed to set about organising a modest preliminary exhibition in a small restaurant in nearby Pontefract. So enthusiastic was the reaction that the YAC, in partnership with the NUM, decided to exhibit a collection of Malkin's charcoal drawings ('Fryston, Above and Below Ground'), alongside Hulme's photographs at London's Royal Festival Hall.[1213]

The public response was unbelievable. Each one of Malkin's pieces was purchased instantly. Subsequent exhibitions were staged at places like the National Mining Museum and The Ridings (both Wakefield), and the Dean Clough and McGee Galleries in Halifax and York, respectively. Malkin has also exhibited his work in other countries, such as Wales, Russia and Switzerland. During one of his larger exhibitions – at the South Bank in London – a 'city gent' purchased a job lot of five Malkin paintings, with the aim of providing his daughter with an insight into working-class life.[1214]

Here, we focus in close detail on the artistic exploits of Jack Hulme and Harry Malkin. Emphasis is placed on the special significance of their work in capturing the essence of rapidly disappearing industrial and community-oriented ways of life.

Renaissance Man

Jack Hulme will always be remembered, according to Fryston folklore, not only as a renowned photographer but also a gifted entertainer. The first inklings of these talents occurred when Hulme's parents presented him with a 'magic lantern' one Christmas when he was still a Fryston schoolboy. This paraffin-fuelled device, capable of projecting cartoon images onto a screen, was a huge draw, attracting up to 20 other village children at a time, all of whom assembled every Friday night in the cellar of Hulme's house to witness slide shows of Robin Hood, Red Riding Hood and countless other characters. 'Then, at a later date,' Hulme explained, 'I bought some real good slides: some that you could pull a lever and show the actions, such as a little boy in an apple tree pinching apples and the farmer thrashing him when you lifted your hand up and down' (interview, 1987).

Equally, if not even more pivotal, was an accident occurring in the Fryston school playground when the nine-year-old Hulme was trapped under a heap of over-exuberant playmates and permanently injured his knee. 'First my patella had to come off,' he recollected, 'then they took a cheese joint out and gave me an aluminium support.'[1215] His outlook on life was suddenly transformed. Realising that his career prospects had been heavily circumscribed, Hulme quickly developed a more resilient, self-sufficient and, arguably, entrepreneurial outlook.[1216]

It was less than one year later that, while casually wandering around Castleford Market, Hulme stumbled across a box of hair-cutting instruments, comprising a comb, shears and pair of scissors.

So, I went home as fussy as owt and had a practice on my old man! He was half-bald to begin with, so I didn't really spoil owt! I was interested in training to be a hairdresser because I had a lame leg and I never knew what my future was going to be. Anyway, that got me started and, before very long, they used to all call round and ask me to cut their hair. (Interview, 1987)

Three years later, Hulme started working on 'the screens' at Fryston Colliery. This job — involving picking out stone and other unwanted materials from coal trundling past on a conveyor belt — was a form of 'surface work' allocated to recent recruits and older, injured or disabled miners. Though he subsequently worked in the blacksmith's shop and, for a short time, in the ambulance and first-aid room, Hulme always remained conscious of the need to have other career strings in his bow.[1217]

This was at the back of Hulme's mind when, at the age of fourteen, he bought his first camera, a second-hand Box Brownie. His enthusiasm for photography had already been ignited by the sight of a man who occasionally came into Fryston village, taking pictures via a big camera on a tripod with a hood over his head:

I thought, 'Right, I'm going to have a go at that job!' So, one day when I was in Castleford, looking round the second-hand stalls, I saw a camera in a box — a plate camera it was — and I bought it, and there were instructions and everything to dissolve and develop. So, I thought to myself, 'Take your own photo, Jack, through a mirror, and take a good 'un!' which I did. I took two, but one was better than the other because I timed them differently. In them days you'd to guess the timing of the exposure. That was the beginning of my photography. I always printed and developed my own film. I never took any to the chemist. (Interview, 1987)

Much to his delight, Hulme found himself pestered by local young women who were prepared to pay sixpence a time to have their photos taken. His talents improved immeasurably as he progressed onto a film camera which he bought on the strength of savings stamps from the *John Bull* magazine.

It was not long after he acquired his first camera that Hulme also began learning how to play the violin. Here, too, he was partially driven by a pecuniary motive: 'I was realistic about the limp,' he explained, 'and thought that if the pit ever made me redundant I could get a job in one of those orchestras in the cinema.'[1218] Hulme's musical tutor was one of the Fryston chapel organists – a man who greatly improved his musical proficiency.

In due course, Jack Hulme would go on to make the most of his musicianship and new-found hairdressing skills. The only resident barber in Fryston was someone whose instruments were so blunt that most village men were prepared to pay the novice Hulme tuppence a time to cut their hair. By the late 1930s, he was able to supplement his pit income by charging local people one shilling for a haircut and sixpence for a shave. Among his regular customers were Oscar Fisher (who always gave Hulme a three-shilling tip) and Jim Bullock, who invariably fell asleep in the chair. During World War II, Hulme took over the running of a barber's shop in Castleford for a man who had enlisted in the army.[1219]

By this time, Hulme had also become a musician of great local renown. It was back in the mid-1930s that he had first been approached by three young Fryston men to see whether he would be willing to act as a conductor for the harmonica team they were about to put together. Hulme went one step further by arranging the purchase of two sets of harmonicas costing 12s 6d each from Germany. Eventually, the number of band members increased, and they engaged in a mixture of paid and charitable performances:

> There were twelve people in the band. We never had trouble getting bookings because we would play anywhere. First off we called ourselves *Jack Hulme's Serenaders* but I felt that was a bit strong. I didn't want my name up front, so we changed it to the *Fryston Harmonica Band*. We would do about twelve to fourteen tunes a session starting off with 'Here we are again, happy as can be, all good pals and jolly good company'. Another tune we did was *Tiger Rag*. You'll know it, 'Hold that Tiger, hold that tiger'. We would play all over; Pontefract Workhouse, all over. At Christmas we would go to Carleton Children's Home and play by candlelight.[1220]

Hulme was the consummate exhibitionist. On one occasion, he was arrested, over in nearby Brotherton, and fined for causing an obstruction while impersonating Charlie Chaplin to an audience of local young men and women. He had a knack of making people happy. He claimed that Cuddy Bateson sometimes gave him a shilling just to make him laugh.[1221] In addition, he became a stalwart of the community, co-organising the annual Fryston Gala or trips to Roundhay Park in Leeds.

The Camera Never Lied

It was in the guise of 'village photographer', however, that Jack Hulme produced such a lasting and significant legacy. Having started out with the second-hand Box Brownie, he graduated onto the film camera, referred to above, and then an even more sophisticated *Ensign*, which he purchased from a pawnbroker in Pontefract. Hulme met his first wife, Lydia, while at the local cinema, and they were married in 1936. It was Lydia who bought her husband a vastly expensive Leica camera for £91 in 1941. After the war, Hulme invested another £12 in purchasing a flash from Germany. 'I never regretted the money I spent on that camera,' he later explained. 'It was in a class of its own.'[1222] It was only in later life when his eyesight began to fade that Hulme began using an automatic.

From the 1920s onwards, he became, in his words, 'the village's semi-official photographer', providing passport photographs or turning up on request at marriages and christenings. The special significance of Hulme's photography lies in the fact that:

> Most photographs of working-class life are taken by outsiders — voyeuristic intruders who poke around with their lenses and move onto the next project. Jack lived the way of life he photographed. With rare insight, sympathy and humour, his pictures show a warm, vigorous, tightly-knit community typical of industrial Northern England. He photographed the big village events — the VE Day and Coronation celebrations, the annual charabanc trips, retirements, football teams. He photographed the annual Fryston Carnival and pinned up his pictures in the draper's window, for sale for a few pence. He followed the expansion and decline of the pit — through the opening of the pit head baths in 1932, nationalisation in 1948, and the building of the Miners' Welfare in 1952 — though even during the pit's decline there was no strong political dimension to his work. He

preserved the memory of a dying community, but to the end retained an unshakeable conviction in the justice of 'the circumstances of the moving world'.[1223]

It is precisely this unselfconscious and uncontrived nature of Hulme's work which makes it so invaluable. As he, himself, put it,

> I took a lot of pictures others wouldn't bother with because they wouldn't think the subjects were important enough. There's not many pictures about of women using a dolly tub, hanging out washing, blacking grates, cleaning windows, pea pulling or scrubbing a pavement. I've got one picture of a long line of people looking into a camera, but what makes it is the woman in the corner washing the step. That's unusual.[1224]

According to Bill Longshaw, the curator of the 'Myth of the North' exhibition, the significance of Hulme's work resides in the authenticity it lends to popular conceptions of the 'true' nature of the industrial North:

> The interesting thing about Jack is that you get quite a lot of images of domestic interiors. For a lot of other photographers the Northern home would have been one step too far. There's a lot of images taken outside [...] but to get inside the house is unusual. [...] Jack's photos are very naturalistic and I think it's the ability to just seem not to be there which is part of the skill of taking great photos.[1225]

This point is reinforced by Stephen McClarence, who observes that Hulme was familiar enough to those around him for his camera to be virtually unnoticed, thus ensuring that his pictures were 'for the most part intimate, unposed and unselfconscious', rather than appearing as if they might have been 'posed for posterity'.[1226] Hulme possessed, as McClarence put it, 'an uncanny instinct for making the ordinary memorable'. His photographs therefore constitute 'a precious document, holding a key to their community's identity. They have given the people of Fryston a sense of place, a sense of belonging, a context.'[1227]

Harry Malkin's enthusiasm for art was first aroused in early childhood. Like Jack Hulme's father, Malkin's grandfather had arrived in Fryston (in 1904, in his case) as part of the influx of miners from Staffordshire. The next generation of seven sons, including Harry's father, were all employed in Castleford collieries, where they each received the promise of 'a job for life'.[1228] Malkin was born and initially raised as part of a family of two boys and one girl in a small terrace house in central Castleford. When he was ten years old, the family moved into newly-built Airedale. 'For the very first time we had hot and cold running water,' he remembered. 'We had gas and electricity and a smart new range oven, but there still wasn't spare money around for drawing paper.'[1229]

Malkin remained undeterred, however, and soon discovered an alternative 'sketch pad and easel' on which to express himself:

> That's why I ended up using my old dad's back as a canvas. When I was a kid he used to come home from work, sit in front of that roaring fire and take his shirt off. He was a pretty big bloke, so there was a lot of space and I'd spend hours drawing on him with a biro. When you're going to spend 10 hours the next day at the coal face there's no point washing too carefully in the morning, so all his colleagues used to see the efforts of my labours.[1230]

Young Harry began by drawing 'tattoos' and portraits of such exotic creatures as eagles and dragons. He would also create caricatures for the amusement of his father and other miners. 'He used Biro at first, then pencil,' Arnot explains, 'But it was the switch to charcoal that imbued his work with the depth and tone that best suited his subject matter.'[1231]

Seemingly predestined for a career down the mine, Malkin regarded his school career and subsequent training as unwelcome, but necessary prerequisites to taking on a job. His apprenticeship as a fitter required him to attend classes at Whitwood Technical College. While there, he experienced a growing desire to broaden his basic knowledge and express himself creatively. 'Our English teacher was a Cambridge graduate,' he later revealed. 'He really looked the part with a tweed jacket and he opened me up to a whole world of books and literature.'[1232]

Malkin had begun working as a fitter at Fryston Colliery, two weeks after leaving school (aged fifteen) in 1966. His passion for art remained dormant thereafter but was never fully extinguished. Indeed, during the year-long miners' strike, he won first prize in a CISWO-sponsored art competition and succeeded in selling off the winning painting.[1233] His career as a professional artist was now destined to gain even more momentum – albeit in the most ironic and unpredictable of circumstances.

Malkin and his fellow Fryston miners had returned to work in early March 1985, still convinced that the local colliery had a minimum of seven more years of productive life; but this optimism was destroyed following its closure ten months later. Malkin later acknowledged with the benefit of hindsight how: 'That was a big turning point for me because the pit closures gave me the time and impetus to carve out another way of making a living.'[1234]

His initial response to having been made redundant was to search for similar work as a fitter. This proved repeatedly demoralising. He was one of 10,000 applicants who applied without success for three jobs being advertised at Ferrybridge Power Station. Eventually, he did land a job – a local authority position requiring him to draw pencil sketches of items unearthed as part of an archaeological excavation on the outskirts of Pontefract Castle.[1235] Aside from repositioning Malkin in a stable working routine, this job helped to rekindle the enthusiasm for art he had felt so powerfully as a child.[1236]

It was in this context that the closure of Fryston Pit proved particularly catalytic and, ironically, liberating:

> For the first time since I was a kid I had spare time and I decided to fill it by going to art classes. I guess I'd never really stopped drawing, but after I left the pit it took on a whole new meaning.[1237]

Malkin began drawing charcoal sketches of underground scenes he had committed to recent memory. These were the ones he showed to Brian Lewis, who, as we have seen, was sufficiently impressed to organise an exhibition of the novice artist's work 'between the toilet and the serving hatch' in the passageway of an Italian bistro, deep in the basement of Pontefract Market.[1238]

The second, more prestigious, exhibition (at the Royal Festival Hall), also referred to above, ran for three months, rather than three weeks, as originally intended. This showcasing of Malkin's charcoal drawings was facilitated by one of Arthur Scargill's administrative assistants, who 'managed to get hold of someone in London who was interested enough to ask to see examples of Harry's and Jack's work'.[1239] The exhibition was a 'media sensation', with each of Malkin's drawings being sold on the night. It was estimated that he could have sold five times more sketches than he actually did.[1240]

Paint It Black

Following the success of the Festival Hall exhibition, Malkin soon found himself working in a studio space provided by the YAC, overlooking the former Glasshoughton coal mine. The paintings and drawings he has since produced comprise 'intense, energetic images that reveal not just the claustrophobia of working in dark, confined spaces, but also the sheer unremitting effort required to tear a living out of the bowels of the earth'.[1241] A more technically adept appreciation was proffered by the curator of the York-based gallery which exhibited his work:

> Cheeks and eye sockets are ink black, shoulders are slick crescents, and amidst the trembling chiaroscuro the figures quicken and bristle in their brutal work. Their poise and movements are perfectly calibrated with the instinct and knowledge hewn from many decades' worth of witnessing and working more than one mile deep underground.[1242]

Malkin rejects the view of many of his erstwhile Fryston colleagues that the Thatcher Government was solely responsible for the demise of the coal industry. In his opinion, the year-long confrontation merely accelerated an already gradual, but ultimately inevitable, phasing out of coal.[1243] It was in this context that Malkin developed a huge sense of personal responsibility: 'The slag heaps are now grassy hills and nature reserves have replaced the old pit heads, but it's important to remember what went before.'[1244] Local people already had no conception of what it was like to work down a mine, and Malkin was afraid that such a rich legacy would be increasingly forgotten with each passing generation:

> 'Not only do they destroy the industry but try to wipe away all traces of it,' says Malkin. 'We've got all these museums for the

late and great but not museums for the little people. In two or three generations, we might be forgotten completely.'[1245]

His paintings therefore represented 'a way of passing on memories from a world that has all but disappeared'.[1246] He recognised that the wider world could not stand still, 'but while the Yorkshire I grew up in may no longer exist, it remains in my heart and in my art'.[1247]

Subsequently, Malkin accepted an invitation by the Castleford Women's Centre to run a series of art classes on Wesley Street. Though lacking any prior experience other than that of practitioner, he began teaching a roomful of people who had only previously painted as a hobby and not shared their work with anyone else. 'I decided very quickly that it wouldn't just be drawing and painting,' he said.

> We tried all sorts of techniques, many of which were things I had learned how to do myself just weeks before. We did marbling, painting on glass, lino-cutting and sculpture work with wire and plaster of Paris, as well as painting techniques.[1248]

The class was quickly transformed into an even more exciting 'art club', in which the women came together in a spirit of mutual supportiveness and, using artistic materials bought on their behalf by Malkin, began drawing and painting still-life images. Malkin not only provided the students with 'sitters', but also taught them how to mount and frame their works and find places in which to exhibit them.[1249] The ex-fitter was embarking in this environment on his own 'voyage of discovery', soon realising that he had become a very accomplished sculptor – a natural talent first evident in his boyhood days, when he once sculpted a greyhound out of snow.[1250] As we shall see in Chapter 29, this new-found capability would eventually be employed in creating a lasting memorial for Fryston village.

Every Picture Tells a Story
In the two-year period following the closure of Fryston Pit, it seemed accurate to assume that a 'village death knell' had, indeed, been sounded. An article appearing in the 19 March 1987 edition of the *Pontefract and Castleford Express* was tantamount to an obituary. 'Pictures that tell sad tale: Death of pit marked death of village', its sombre headline

maintained. Amidst the illustrative photographs of a colliery in rubble, of its now derelict pithead baths, the wasteland of a former school, and an overgrown graveyard, there appeared a sad written eulogy:

> Perhaps in a few years' time there will be little of Fryston to suggest it was ever a village. Already, just two years after its ailing pit gave up the ghost, the houses, roads, school and the pit are turning inexorably to dust. Where once children played there is rubble. Streets have been razed, houses boarded up. There are still a few people who live at Fryston, still a few children, too. But they live in a dead village.

An air of decay and imminent demise — even of *extinction* — permeated what remained of a village which, according to the same article, now 'lies twitching at the end of Wheldon Road'. Our interview respondents of the time dolefully endorsed this sad prognosis. One ex-Fryston man described the situation as:

> Terrible. I go down every week nearly and, to see it, it's sad. To see just odd houses and the rest boarded up [...] There isn't a shop, there isn't a bus and nearly the biggest part of 'em's old folks. They've got to come to the top of Airedale or go into Castleford to shop, so they walk to the bottom of Airedale for a bus and find they can't even get on 'cos it's full. (Interview, 1987)

A Different Kind of Swan Song

Such appearances eventually proved unfounded. Possibly buoyed up by the work of Jack Hulme and the publicity it generated, local people and town planners were starting to rediscover the value and significance of this once iconic community. Interviews with existing village residents already suggested a growing restoration of self-worth, optimism and defiance. Such people talked of the village eventually transforming into a beautiful green landscape, 'like Fairburn, Ledston or Brotherton', and of 'the swans returning to Fryston'.[1251] Those remaining in the village were diehards in the main: 'The people who are left know me and I know them,' was how one interviewee put it. 'They're all "old faithfuls" and, perhaps like me, they wouldn't leave Fryston if you paid them' (Fryston man, 1987).

This attitude was shared, not surprisingly, by Jack Hulme, who confessed that he had once wavered in his determination to stay in Fryston:

> Not so long ago. I put in to go live in an old folks' house up in Airedale. I felt all ready to leave the village. But when they sent me a letter to tell me I could have a bungalow, I thought, 'Oh, Jack, you can't leave your house. If you go live somewhere else, you'll desert the village that brought you up; you'd be deserting Fryston.' Then I began to think of all the times I've spent in this house, where I've lived since 1944, and this very room where my wife died in my arms, and I thought, 'If I left Fryston, I'd be deserting her as well.' So, I stayed. And I'm right glad I did because things are looking up for the village again. People were down in the dumps, but they're starting to look to the future again. (Interview, 1987)

Hulme explained how it would be one of the saddest days of his life when the pit wheels at Fryston were finally taken down. 'To me,' he maintained, that'll be like taking the crown off a king or queen's head' (interview, 1987). Typically, the octogenarian was present among a huddled group of fellow observers, intent on taking a photograph at the vital moment when – at approximately 1pm on Sunday, 11 October 1987 – the colliery's head-gear was toppled to the ground.[1252] Yet another important image had therefore been preserved – a further testament to Fryston's remarkable history. As Stephen McClarence pertinently explained:

> Jack Hulme enjoyed four years of this celebrity before he died in January 1990 at the age of 83. At his funeral service, mourners in the corrugated iron village chapel heard him described simply as 'Mr Fryston.'[1253]

Chapter Twenty-Nine
Martha's Finger

Keeper of the Faith

The 1990s was a decade in which two iconic individuals passed away, the memories of whom remain solidly preserved in the folklore of Fryston and the surrounding area.

An important link with the village's post-war past was severed on 23 February 1990 with the passing of 77-year-old Gerda Sloan. 'Dr Gerda' had lived alone since the death of her husband in 1966. According to her son, Richard, she had continued to lead an active life, playing bridge, travelling with her friend (Nurse Box's daughter-in-law, Edna) and regularly betting on the horses.[1254] Her ashes were laid to rest in a shared grave with her husband in London's Putney Vale Cemetery. Richard Sloan reflected on how Gerda's stoicism had helped shape his own outlook on life:

> I have learned a lot from my mother and others about how to cope with bereavement and living alone. Towards the end of her life, I sat with her in her nursing home. She could not communicate. On the TV in her room, footage was being shown of the Berlin Wall coming down. How she would have loved to see that momentous event.[1255]

The termination of an even longer era in Fryston's history occurred in April 1995 with the death of the now legendary Jim Bullock. The headline accompanying his obituary in the 13 April edition of the *Pontefract and Castleford Express* ('"Only socialist pit manager" dies at 92') echoed the compliment first paid to Bullock by the Yorkshire NUM President, Joe Hall. 'He was a staunch Labour Party supporter and pit manager,' the article explained, 'and in his later years he became a writer and a renowned public speaker at conferences and on the after-dinner circuit.' A public funeral service was held at Bullock's native Bowers Row Mission in the morning of 13 April, followed by a private cremation immediately afterwards. Among the dozens of mourners was Bullock's friend and protégé, Jack Charlton.

Richard Sloan subsequently recalled how both of his parents had 'never really "clicked" with Mr Bullock'. The reason was nothing personal, he added; it was just that neither of them was 'a manager's sort' of person:

> They both worked primarily for the blokes and helped them with their compensation claims and so forth. It must have made their work a bit more difficult, having the managers as neighbours, but they got round that somehow. (Interview, 1987)

'Dr Gerda's' passing made it contingent upon Richard to uphold the family tradition. He observed how the first half of the 1990s was economically 'grim' in Castleford, following the closure of Fryston and other, neighbouring collieries. Unemployment was high and heroin addiction rife. The Tieve Tara practice cared medically for some 60 users and their families, following a treatment regime which combined intensive counselling (largely conducted by a specially trained colleague) with prescribed doses of the heroin substitute, methadone.

This was an immensely challenging period. The practice received no extra funding for this work. On two occasions, the Sloan family home was burgled while they slept, and various items, such as a video player and camera, stolen to help fund the perpetrator's habit. Reception and medical staff were relentlessly overwhelmed.

> The behaviour of some of these patients was sometimes bad. Sitting on the floor in the corridor and sleeping in the waiting room was common. I made the mistake of leaving one such patient in my consulting room while I went to reception to get something. On my return, I noticed a large bulge under his pullover. I stared at it and he burst into tears, producing our video camera he was intending to steal. He genuinely apologised to me and asked me to forgive him. I said I would do nothing about this and continued with the consultation.[1256]

This first-hand experience reinforced Sloan's professional faith in the effectiveness of methadone 'maintenance therapy'. It succeeded, as he saw it, in reducing crime and offsetting police and medical costs.[1257]

The social and medical problems confronting Richard Sloan and his colleagues were not the only overt manifestations of industrial decline. Smith observes that the loss of 3,000 mining jobs in Castleford, due to pit closures occurring between 1985 and 2002, greatly affected the local economy and had 'immeasurable consequence for community pride and security'.[1258] She qualifies this point by observing that conspicuous forms of regeneration have been achieved in the meantime, like the Freeport Outlet Village and the XSCAPE leisure complex (which incorporates an impressive artificial ski-slope).[1259]

A corresponding attempt to 'resurrect [the] community pride' which 'took a severe bashing' during and after the strike[1260] has been undertaken by the Castleford Heritage Trust (CHT), a registered charity and limited company 'which aims to promote the community's heritage and culture to build a strong, successful community'.[1261] Here, we focus on the work of the CHT, placing particular emphasis on a controversial scheme for the regeneration of Fryston village, which was also supported financially by Channel 4 and featured in a TV documentary.

In Heritage We Trust

Established in 2000 under the leadership of a Castleford-born, former school headmistress, Alison Drake, the CHT has sought since then to complement and build on the town's well-publicised links to the Roman era by emphasising the family, class and community values associated with its more recent industrial heritage.[1262] Among the Roman remains uncovered by archaeologists in and around Castleford (or Legeolium or Lagentium, as it was known at the time) were those of a fort, bathhouse and milestone.

As Smith maintains in her case study of the CHT, many of the town residents and Trust workers she interviewed are eager to see the bathhouse (which was covered over following its excavation in 1978) exposed again and put on public display; and for many of the artefacts housed in museums in Wakefield and Leeds to be 'repatriated' back to Castleford. At first sight,

> The concern for the bathhouse and the significance of the Roman period generally to the residents of Castleford may seem to contradict the emphasis placed on intangible notions of

identity based around a sense of 'community', class and family. However, as the above extract reveals, the Romans provide a sense of pride in demonstrating not only the long history of the Castleford community, but that the community and its achievements are anchored or linked to wider narratives of national history.[1263]

This emphasis on Castleford's Roman past has worked at one level 'to attract the attention of external heritage agencies which have tended to dismiss the town as having any heritage of value'.[1264] Its secondary function has been to buttress a complementary emphasis on Castleford's industrial heritage – i.e. it has been 'used unconsciously by local residents [...] to legitimize a local sense that Castleford's industrial and recent heritage matters'.[1265] In contrast to the evidencing of the Roman connection in the form of physical artefacts, Castleford's industrial heritage has been highlighted via processes of ritualised performance and re-enactment.[1266]

Fundamental to these processes is the annual Castleford Festival, a 'week-long community event in which things are done and children learn, amongst other things [...] what coal is and the meanings that coal has had and continues to have for different generations in Castleford'.[1267] Old pit banners feature strongly on these occasions; but alongside these more familiar touchstones are a host of new banners, designed by the CHT, which incorporate symbols of Castleford's Roman past. Generally speaking,

> The festival and exhibitions that the CHT mount are very much interactive, nobody comes to gaze dispassionately at art works or exhibitions, but rather they come and are encouraged to engage and experience. Exhibitions on mining, for instance, require children to crawl through dark tunnels while ex-miners hide and squirt them with water to simulate the dark, hot and wet conditions of the mines, pottery exhibitions encourage you to don an apron and try your hand at decorating and so forth. Not only are memories being jogged for older residents, but they are also being created for younger people as they are engaged in acts of collective remembering of not only past events but the community values that they generated.[1268]

In 2002, Castleford's Roman heritage was given prominence in an episode of the popular Channel 4 *Team Time* programme in which their 'team of archaeologists' excavated part of the Roman Fort.[1269] This focus was consistent with an 'authorized heritage discourse', subscribed to by everyone from funding agencies to documentary makers, which grants priority to the antiquated and physically tangible. Such a discourse 'cannot readily recognize that Castleford has any "heritage" left, as memory alone is untrustworthy without the material evidence'.[1270] It is a testament to the great progress made by the CHT that they were able to lobby successfully, five years later, for Castleford to become the focal point of a four-part Channel 4 series on neighbourhood regeneration. One of the places visited with a view to receiving a revitalising 'make-over' was the former mining village of Fryston.

The Big Town Plan

Conceived of in 2003, the 'Castleford Project' referred to a programme of renewal in which a team of design experts, members of regeneration agencies (notably, English Partnerships, Groundwork UK, the Coalfields Regeneration Trust and Yorkshire Forward) and representatives of Wakefield Metropolitan District Council consulted with participating community groups with an ambition to 'improve the area on behalf of those who live there […] and to "regenerate" it, in order to attract new investment and new housing'.[1271] The project was the brainchild of the Channel 4 television company, which, in keeping with its public-service remit, commissioned Talkback Productions to make 'a series of television programmes that would document the process of the regeneration of a town and share it with the viewing public'.[1272]

The production team considered several towns and cities for possible inclusion before eventually deciding on Castleford.[1273] One team member reported that, when first visiting the town in 2001, he came across 'a wounded place', suffering some of the highest unemployment in the UK, with one ward in particular (Ferry Fryston) ranking among the top five per cent of England's most deprived. Thus, 'if ever a place was worthy of regeneration, Castleford was it'.[1274] Alison Drake has maintained that her own brother 'died aged 37 of a broken heart after they closed the pit,' adding how: 'Those things increase the fight in the rest of you.'[1275] The Chair of the CHT thus played a pivotal role in coaxing Channel 4 to Castleford:

> More could have been done to support Castleford when the pits went. We're still a proud town full of the sort of people who get stuck in and try to do things for ourselves, and that's what Channel 4 spotted. I first heard about the project when Yorkshire Forward, the regional regeneration organisation, asked me to meet a young man from Channel 4, show him around and explain our regeneration strategy. What I didn't know was that he was looking for a town to make a programme in. I did my best to sell him the town and tell him why we wanted better. I think we needed that push from outside the district. I don't think we would have been so successful so quickly without it. You put a camera in front of funders and local authorities and they're not going to be as negative as they might have been.[1276]

A seed-corn grant of £100,000 from Channel 4 provided the initial platform for an investment package of over £14.5 million, donated by other partners.[1277] It has been asserted that, during the project's five-year lifetime, relevant partners succeeded, not only in transforming several targeted public spaces, but also in leveraging £250 million of additional investment into Castleford.[1278] As planned, a four-part television series, *Kevin McCloud's Big Town Plan*, first aired in August 2008, 'tests the theory that good design can help to kickstart regeneration. But crucially, that design would be led not by the council, or for that matter Channel 4, but rather by the residents of Castleford.'[1279]

Filming by Channel 4 covered the project's lifetime from 2003-2008, during which a handful of local initiatives were developed in consultation with relevant community and civic groups. These included a new footbridge across the River Aire, a town square development, and the redesign and refashioning of three recreational areas – in Cutsyke, Ferry Fryston and, most crucially for our purposes, New Fryston.[1280] All three initiatives were featured in the 18 August 2008 edition of the series, which traced their development from the initial process of public consultation to the third year of their existence.

It became apparent in this programme that, unlike the two play areas for local children, established in consultation with 'community activists' in Cutsyke and Ferry Fryston, a 'prestigious sculpture park' designed by the 'prize winning' American architect, Martha Schwartz (at a cost of £1 million) was developed on the basis of only 'token consultation' with the residents of Fryston.[1281]

'Queen of Landscape Design'

The Philadelphia-born Schwartz was the founder of her own internationally renowned firm of architects, Martha Schwartz Partners (MSP), which has offices in London, New York and Shanghai. In recognition of her ground-breaking approach to modern architectural design, Schwartz was appointed Professor in Practice of Landscape Architecture at the Harvard University Graduate School of Design. Kevin McCloud referred to her in his series as 'the International Queen of Landscape Design'.[1282] She once described her personal philosophy and professional approach to landscape design as follows:

> What's important is that there is enough visual content so that people can bring their own interpretation to a public space. There has to be a visual coherence that people 'get' that there is a narrative of some sort; it needs to be able to be described and memorable. But it must also be open-ended so it is not prescribed or didactic. A space doesn't work if you feel that the viewer must think and feel the same way you do or to 'get' the story. I am not interested in those types of spaces and, frankly, I don't think most people find them particularly interesting either. People like a mystery or riddle.[1283]

Schwartz arrived in Fryston having previously engaged in the re-landscaping of Geraldton, a very small former gold-mining town, in North-West Ontario (Canada), which had been transformed by pit closure into a 'devastated [and] environmentally toxic landscape'. Schwartz and her associates set about converting the unsightly local 'tailings' (piles of mine waste or 'slag heaps') into sculpted examples of 'land art'.[1284] As predicted, people previously apt to speed past Geraldton on the Trans-Canadian Highway now tended to pause along their journeys to explore the more intriguing landscape. Local planners also responded to the town's fresh image by establishing a new golf course, thereby boosting the local economy.[1285]

Schwartz would now set about applying this 'incredibly robust model' in the regeneration of Fryston village. Having informed viewers of the 18 August episode that the 'top American designer' had 'flown in' to 're-vamp' Fryston's village green, Kevin McCloud further explained that what distinguished this venture from its counterparts in Cutsyke and Ferry Fryston was that 'this is *Martha's* project: *she* decides what happens'. Viewers were told that, whilst Schwartz 'doesn't usually consult the community […] she is willing to have a go'.[1286] Footage was then shown of the American walking along North Street with two female residents, in whose presence she maintained:

> Well, you feel like you're kinda coming into this magic little kingdom, the kinda place that time forgot! […] There is a scraggly kind of quality about it, but there's certainly no kind of narrative or kind of interpretation about what it's about. There's no other *higher meaning* to it.[1287]

The programme revealed that, in nearby Ferry Fryston, another landscape designer, Paul Heaton, had striven to involve local people, including children, in the design of a new park on 'The Green'. Heaton had transformed an old toilet block into a 'suggestion box', on the walls of which residents scribbled their ideas. This approach clearly contrasted with what went on in Fryston, where one section of the programme showed Martha Schwartz outlining three possible ideas for the transformation of village green to a small audience of residents. Two of these proposed ways forward harboured the shared objective of using stone blocks to form a village amphitheatre, while a third would employ 'a very sculptural earth-mound', based on the premise that 'It's gotta function at a spiritual level, too, it's gotta make you *feel good*.'[1288]

Schwartz was given a very uncomfortable ride by those present. When trying to explain, for example, how her idea for an amphitheatre involved making the design 'more curved and embracing, [so that] if you ever had concerts or plays, or whatever you wanted to do out here, this could happen here',[1289] she was greeted with derisive laughter. Villagers had set their sights on the more mundane objective of securing a community hub to replace the ramshackle tin hut they were currently dependent on. A local woman protested that, 'We asked for a community centre for t' older kids and all that, but nowt's been mentioned about all this,'[1290] to which Schwartz helplessly responded, 'Well, I don't know what to say about all that.'[1291]

The strength of Schwartz's continuing resolve became apparent when McCloud suggested to her that 'putting design into the community and getting their input' was 'a good thing'. The American was obviously unconvinced:

> It's impossible to come out with anything of excellence if you have, like, a hundred people holding onto the same pencil, trying to kind of draw out a design. You know, the artist and designer, those are the experts. Just because everybody has an opinion doesn't mean that their opinion is a good or informed opinion. Now, I know that's an unpopular thing to say, but it's true.[1292]

Schwartz proceeded in line with this philosophy by discounting local appeals for a new community centre and opting, instead, for an amphitheatre design (also incorporating the earth mound) which, she maintained, would prove attractive and alluring to potential new residents and investors. Asked by McCloud for her response to the accusation that 'you play God', Schwartz uncompromisingly retorted: 'That's just not what these people want right now, but that's what artists are supposed to be doing: we're supposed to visualise a new world.'[1293] McCloud then presented the additional observation that many local people regarded the project as entirely for the benefit of the potential new arrivals and that it was of no value to existing residents. 'They don't?', Schwartz defiantly retorted. 'Well then, I actually feel sorry for them.'[1294]

At this preliminary stage of the proceedings, Kevin McCloud could not avoid offering a sobering summary of progress made so far. 'The million-pound sculpture park,' he insisted, 'will probably do exactly what English Partnerships want and attract new housing developers to New Fryston, but almost all the villagers are unhappy.'[1295] Schwartz, meanwhile, remained obdurate in her response: 'I guess the world really can't and *won't* leave them alone,' she said. 'Change is going to happen. It's coming, one way or the other.'[1296]

In a subsequent promotional anthology of the various projects they have completed, MPS set out a comprehensive and illuminating discussion of the nature of, and underlying rationale for, their 're-vamping' of Fryston's village green.[1297] When the company was first commissioned, Fryston constituted, in their words, a 'dying village' with 'two aging rows of terraced housing, crumbling, poorly drained roads, decaying sidewalks, and an overgrown vacant field [the Village Green] with rusty play equipment in one corner'.[1298] What this small, tightly-knit community required was 'a powerful symbol for change to help them grow toward a sustainable future'.[1299]

A resulting masterplan was therefore hatched in conjunction with English Partnerships which envisaged the restoration of surrounding former mining lands into a picturesque country park, replete with cycle and bridle paths and a woodland comprising 40,000 trees; and the provision on the former pit site of 150 new homes, served by an appropriate civic infrastructure of shops, transport, etc.[1300] The first component of this scheme was the development of the Village Green, which 'would signal a new image for Fryston to attract a future population, and offer hope and commitment to the current community for whom change from the outside had not always been positive'.[1301] It was deemed essential that the green would prove engaging to the existing community, both reconnecting them to their mining heritage while 'setting the stage' for the arrival of a future population.[1302]

In keeping with these principles, the amphitheatre design incorporated a terraced series of steps, taking residents down from street level into the belly of the park. This was a throwback to traditional patterns of community sociability:

> The front steps of Fryston's terraced houses have always been the primary public space of the village. Every morning, people sit out on their stoops to drink their tea, to catch up with their neighbors [sic], and to watch their children play. The stairs are the threshold between people's private lives and the community. To fully connect the new Green into this existing model of village life, MSP's first design move extends the front steps of the terraces out into the park. A series of smooth concrete benches stack up to connect the park to street grade and are essentially a series of

front steps, inviting people to come out of their homes and into the new community. The old, crumbling front steps and inadequate sidewalks are replaced with new ones to match the material of the benches, extending the threshold of people's homes down the steps, across the street, and into the park.[1303]

The tradition of coal mining itself is manifested in a 'deep gauge' in the earth, whose black, rubberised surface (reminiscent of a coal seam) forms the basis of a children's play area.[1304] On the western periphery of the green, Schwartz has retained from the original playground the red colliery wheel, regarded as 'an eternal monument to the town's mining heritage and the legacy of Fryston Pit. No matter what the future holds for Fryston, the colliery and its mining legacy will always be present in the community.'[1305]

The contemporary preoccupations of Fryston villagers were also duly recognised in Schwartz's design. The recent tradition of horse-riding is accommodated, for example, by a sand bridle path, skirting the entire length of the green, which enables horses and their riders to maintain a safe distance from the road. Cast-iron bollards designed by the acclaimed sculptor, Antony Gormley, provide a series of illuminated markers for the 'horse path'.[1306] With its novel lighting scheme, the green aimed to provide 'a safe and welcoming environment' for existing and incoming community members: 'The playground and recreation area invite endless opportunities for play, and an informal outdoor theater [sic] is ready for public performances and community gatherings.'[1307]

Most unusual and controversial of all the artefacts included in this design is a solid structure (a 'cairn'), comprising three pieces of stone, mounted on top of one another to give the appearance of a large, crooked finger. As Waugh explains, this abstract feature has an inherent — if not immediately apparent — symbolic significance:

> The cairn, a form created from stacked rocks, rises from the center [sic] of the stage to provide a signifier of growth and change. The spiral mound of cut stone gradually tapers to a series of glass bricks that are lit to provide a beacon for Fryston, day and night.[1308]

MSP's overview of the Fryston project acknowledges that 'It was not easy at first to engage the people of Fryston in the process', a state of affairs the company attributed to the fact that: 'They had already been through so much with the aggressive mine closures, and they had heard so many broken promises before.'[1309] Once the village green had become 'welcomed as a member of the community', however, and the prospect of new housing grew more tangible, residents started to look upon Martha Schwartz's design 'as a constant reminder that this upheaval and change will yield positive results'.[1310] This overview is endorsed in a featured comment by Alison Drake:

> Since the green has been done, the fact that the residents were proud of the center [sic] of their village made them better able to cope with the fact that for three years, developers have been churning up the land around them, cleaning it up, dragging cars out of the basin where the coal barges used to be. The fact that they could have something immediately that they could be proud of while all this work was going on around their village [...] they knew that good things were going to happen because that had already happened with the square.[1311]

This optimistic note did not chime with other, more critical assessments of the project. Returning to Fryston in 2008, Kevin McLoud let slip his own feelings by asking one local resident whether there was anyone in the village who *actually liked* the Martha Schwartz initiative. The man in question described himself as 'probably one of the more pro' local individuals; but he was decidedly lukewarm in his appraisal. 'It's *interesting*,' he diplomatically conceded, while adding: I don't think it's quite what everybody expected [...] It just seems a little bit back to front in the way it's been designed, because it's more for the people that will be *coming into* the village.'[1312]

Local disaffection focused on the fact that the old tin hut had disappeared but not been replaced, in keeping with community wishes, by an alternative meeting centre. Standing amidst the tall grass and weed-strewn concrete of a neglected parkland, McLoud pointedly wiped animal excrement off his shoe. 'As for Martha's unloved monument,' he concluded. 'no-one's looking after it, so it isn't looking so good.'[1313]

This view was more forcibly and comprehensively reiterated in two contrasting evaluative reports on the scheme, one journalistic,[1314] the other formal.[1315] In the first of these, the reporter, Stephen McClarence, spoke to one woman – a former resident whose mother still lived in Fryston – who was puzzled by the fact that the new design was not looked upon more favourably. The overriding consensus, though, was that the green, 'though tidy and attractive when lit-up at night, looks alien and irrelevant by day. Designers might see it as stylish and radical; locals see it as out of context.'[1316]

One local man maintained that the whole initiative was more suitable for a city location where people might sit down and casually eat their lunches. His front room overlooked the green, which he regarded as a total waste of money. 'Nobody in their wildest dreams thought it would be like this,' he emphasised. 'There's nowhere to park now and nowhere for the kids to play football. We'd have preferred a new community centre.'[1317]

The corresponding report by Brian Lewis (which was commissioned by Wakefield Metropolitan District Council) contains the telling disclosure that the official opening of the green on 22 July 2005 by Yvette Cooper, the Labour MP for Normanton, Pontefract and Castleford, was boycotted by most Fryston residents. Martha Schwartz also chose not to attend the ceremony. The report generally echoes the view that considerable expenditure had been wasted, and that the money involved should have been more wisely invested in line with local preferences:

> The architect brief for Fryston as set out by Channel 4 says clearly that the provision of a community centre is paramount. That instruction was ignored. [...] The root cause of the problems lies here – the village wanted a community centre and it got an obelisk.[1318]

Similar resentment focused on the fact that the process of consultation between villagers and Martha Schwartz had been merely 'tokenistic' and that she was intent on pursuing her own agenda, regardless of local wishes.[1319]

Certain aspects of the MSP design rankled in particular. The small play area for local children was unfavourably compared with its counterpart in Ferry Fryston: 'What they've got there is *outstanding*, and the rumour is, it wasn't [anywhere] near as much as what ours cost', one respondent argued. 'All the money for ours went on bricks, Martha and "Martha's Finger,"' he added.[1320]

Here was a direct allusion to one of several artefacts whose symbolic significance was lost on local people. The four small statues, or 'bollards' ('Oval', 'Snowman', 'Penis' and 'Peg'), designed by Antony Gormley, were universally derided as 'anal plugs': 'They point out that since they are cast iron, the way that they stain the limestone might be symbolic,' said Lewis, but no-one was able to decode any underlying meaning.[1321] This was nothing compared to the opprobrium directed at the highly conspicuous cairn now protruding from the earth:

> That's what she's left us as a present from Boston, a 'stuck up middle finger facing right at us', saying stick that up your – well you know where. We've yet got to hear just how much those three stones cost. Rumours say £15,000 per stone.[1322]

Like many of his co-residents, this man appreciated that there was a need to attract new housing stock into the village itself or, at least, on its periphery, as this would undoubtedly improve the sustainability of what was left of Fryston. He nonetheless shared a wider concern that the village's surrounding landscape (currently dominated by 'green space, horses and trees') might well be undesirably sacrificed in favour of housing re-development.[1323]

One District Council officer interviewed by Lewis acknowledged how 'The feeling that this is an imposed scheme is very evident.'[1324] Martha Schwartz had been assigned to this development, based on the expectation that 'the work of an iconic American landscape architect' would kindle local enthusiasm and raise their aspirations. 'Where the operation fell down,' he now conceded, 'was that it didn't have much of a community involvement process. There was no local choice, it was Martha Schwartz or no-one.'[1325]

'Fryston, Above and Below Ground'
Two related initiatives – each meeting the approval of local residents – achieved fruition shortly afterwards. Strategically linked to the

regeneration of the village green was the Fryston Country Trails project, based on an £18 million investment by the Homes and Communities Agency. This project involved transforming the 98-hectare landscape surrounding Fryston and nearby Wheldale into an eight-kilometre network of footpaths, bridleways and cycleways. In addition, 40,000 trees had been planted and two river basins dredged clean. The scheme also provided for a new gas supply into the village, an improved sewage drainage system, and better access into Fryston via a new road bridge across the railway line.[1326]

A community event was staged on 20 March 2010 to celebrate the project's completion. This incorporated boat trips on the River Aire, archery and canoeing demonstrations, a treasure hunt, and guided country walks. At this stage, plans were being drafted for a new 150-home housing development to occupy the former pit site.[1327]

More in keeping with local preferences than 'Martha's Finger' was the three-dimensional sculpture – or 'wall mural' – commissioned by CHT and funded from the outset by English Partnerships. Consultations with local residents produced the idea of having the wall underneath the railway bridge (facing South View) symbolically decorated. This task was entrusted to Harry Malkin, who by this stage had already produced a similar artefact in the form of a wall sculpture in Castleford town centre.[1328]

Following the difficult preliminary task of attaching a 20-by-8-foot wooden panel (capable of supporting three tons of clay) onto the bridge wall, the actual shaping of the clay sculpture was undertaken in formerly abandoned shop premises in Castleford town centre. This resulted in the familiar sounding 'Fryston Above and Below Ground', a mural juxtaposing two images: one of a small group of miners at the coalface, the second depicting three well-known local male characters, leaning on a brick wall, on which a greyhound is also standing.[1329] As one observer explained,

> The stone mural was chiseled into being using one of Jack Hulme's photographs from the late 1930s as the inspiration. Holding on to the dog is a character known locally as 'Clinker' Steel. Always in and out of jail apparently. He's leaning on a wall with the local butcher and a character called Les Oxtoby, who was fourteen at the time but looks a lot older, perhaps

because he's flat-capped and mufflered. Teenage 'gear' was still a long way in the future when Jack took that shot.[1330]

Oxtoby's inclusion in Malkin's mural partly reflected the fact that, having worked down Fryston Pit for 41 years, he remained alive and well, and still living in the village. It was also undoubtedly related to the notorious sense of mischief which made him so universally popular. One of five brothers, Oxtoby had just commenced working at Fryston when Hulme took his famous photograph. His nascent career was quickly terminated when, true to form, he was summarily dismissed for fighting underground. A spell of National Service followed, during which he became a regular boxer in the Army.

Once discharged, Oxtoby was taken back on at Fryston by Jim Bullock, who immediately recruited him into the colliery boxing team. Thereafter, he spent more time training than working underground. Oxtoby and his colleagues competed against other teams of boxers elsewhere in Yorkshire and its neighbouring counties. His appetite for a good fight was superseded, though, by his passion for training and racing greyhounds. The success he enjoyed on the track was soon noted by Bullock's successor, Edgar Williams, who regularly took Oxtoby 'off shift' to exercise and train up his dogs.[1331] Thanks to Harry Malkin's efforts, this perennially popular Fryston man had now become immortalised.

Chapter Thirty
'The Past We Inherit – The Future We Build'

Going Down in History

Themes of 'death', 'rejuvenation' and 'legacy' predominate in this, our concluding chapter. On 8 April 2013, it was announced that the former British Prime Minister, Margaret Thatcher, had died, aged 87, following a stroke. Mrs Thatcher had suffered a series of 'mini strokes' since 2002 and recently been affected by dementia. Among the scores of widely quoted reactions to her death was that of a former Fryston Colliery electrician, 47-year-old Mick Dickinson, who had been a stalwart of the picket line during the 1984-85 miners' strike. Dickinson undoubtedly spoke for many ex-miners in asserting that:

> [Thatcher] will go down in history as one of the greatest post-war prime ministers thanks to the privatisation she was driving the country into, and some of the nationalised industries did need to change. But I think she took the miners' strike too personally and it became a personal crusade. We went into a battle with our unions and we never won. She devastated the industry and devastated people's lives.[1332]

Another 'death' of sorts occurred on 18 December 2015, when Kellingley Colliery – located roughly 6.5 miles south-east of Fryston – finally ceased production, thus terminating a centuries-long tradition of deep coal mining in Britain. According to one national newspaper, the industry and its 'workplace culture of hard graft, comradeship and danger' had been 'killed off by a mixture of cheap imports, low-carbon alternatives and government indifference'.[1333]

The passing of 'Big K' was commemorated by a 'funeral march' involving thousands of miners and their families, at the head of which was a brass band and a hooded man masquerading as the Grim Reaper.[1334] These theatrics were hardly inappropriate, for, as the journalist and broadcaster, Jeremy Paxman, states in his *Black Gold: The History of How Coal Made Britain*:

Britain has decided that its coal days are over and the future belongs to a cleaner energy. A way of life has vanished, and those who might otherwise have had to spend their working lives toiling in the mines, breathing the dust which would send them coughing to their graves, are better off: I never met a miner who wanted the same life for his children. A filthy, dangerous occupation is finished. *But a part of our history has gone, and something happens to a people when they lose a sense not only of the origins of the place they live in but of how their politics and identities developed.*[1335]

Paxman captivatingly juxtaposes the traditionally exacting roles and lifestyles of British miners and their families with the more comfortable existence of the mine- and land-owning elite, and painstakingly explores the profoundly oppositional and exploitative nature of their relationship. While generally endorsing Paxman's blunt characterisation of this dichotomy, the present, two-part history of Fryston has advanced the more nuanced proposition that there is much to be lauded and admired about the life stories of *both* the pit-folk and peers referred to here, and that the remarkable history of *each party* contributes to a rich and, arguably, unrivalled local heritage.

The Milnes-Crewe Legacy

The 'peers' referred to in the title of this book and that of its companion volume are figures of paramount historical significance. In Volume 1, we focused primarily on the outstanding social, cultural, political and philanthropic achievements of Richard Monckton Milnes (the first Lord Houghton), whose Fryston Hall was the hub of Victorian high society, and he one of the most renowned (and often controversial) societal hosts and benefactors of his age.

Our attention has shifted in this second volume onto the outstanding political career of his more introverted but equally famous son, the second Lord Houghton (better known as Lord Crewe, in whose honour Crewe Road was named). We have observed how, like his father before him, Crewe was a poet and biographer of distinction, although he did not rival the former in terms of literary reputation or critical acclaim. Within the political sphere, however, Crewe unambiguously outshone his illustrious forebear.

It was Crewe's second wife, Peggy, who dwelled authoritatively on some of the marked similarities and differences between her husband and father-in-law. Each man, she observed, was materially extravagant, harboured a tremendous fondness for literature and pageantry, and was extraordinarily charitable towards the poor and needy.[1336] What mostly distinguished them, though, was Milnes's highly gregarious nature: he 'would rather see anybody than be alone,' she said, while adding: 'That was not so with his son.'[1337] Peggy maintained that it was primarily due to Milnes's flamboyant and outspoken nature that he never became a politician of similar standing to Lord Crewe. Unlike the latter, she elaborated, Milnes 'was noted for his indiscretion which, in those times, made him an impossible candidate for office'.[1338]

Other commentators have concluded that Lord Crewe was also a political underachiever. Johnson asserts, for example, that Crewe's chances of achieving any of the highest governmental positions were fatally undermined by 'a natural rigidity of manner and personal diffidence that conveyed an unfortunate impression of aloofness and dryness'.[1339] He was further handicapped, she insists, in possessing a hesitant and extremely monotonous speech-making style, which was not helped by the presence of a stammer.[1340] Against this, 'Crewe nevertheless obtained and sustained a reputation for sound judgement, solidity and trustworthiness.'[1341] Little wonder, then, that he figures so conspicuously in any serious discussion of twentieth-century British political affairs.

We saw in preceding chapters how Crewe's brief stint as Colonial Secretary proved an extremely challenging and often chastening experience. It was a period in which his ministerial attempts to suppress the hostile and expansionist activities of the 'Mad Mullah of Somaliland', and to implement a 'Concubine Circular' discouraging British military and civil servants from consorting with women indigenous to the colonies, unwittingly aggravated the situations they were intended to resolve. It was also Crewe's unsympathetic response, as Minister for India, to sustained lobbying by Mahatma Gandhi, concerning the rights and living conditions of Indian migrant labour in South Africa, which consolidated the latter's ultimately successful commitment to overthrowing British colonial rule. It is unquestionable that Crewe's stances on all these political issues – and, indeed, his initially unaccommodating attitude to women's suffrage – would have been anathema to the first Lord Houghton. They were all undoubtedly indicative of a more conservative, pro-colonial and Establishment-oriented political predilection.

The second Lord Houghton's wartime involvement in government also attracted much controversy. He had sensibly urged caution in relation to the proposed British incursion into Mesopotamia; but evidence suggests that he failed to intervene with sufficient assertiveness to prevent ensuing catastrophe. He and other members of the War Council were similarly taken to task for not pressing Naval Advisers for their views in advance of Churchill's ultimately disastrous Dardanelles campaign. While he and Peggy helped broker what became known as the 'Balfour Declaration' – heralding a 'homeland' for the Jews – this intervention was arguably to the long-term detriment of Middle Eastern peace prospects, which remain dangerously volatile.

Crewe fared better when his astute backstage manoeuvring of fellow politicians, religious leaders, and even the reigning monarch helped secure House of Lords reform. Similar organisational and diplomatic acumen was skilfully exercised when, as Minister for India, he was pivotal to the creation of the ostentatious Durbar of 1911, which (in addition to symbolically strengthening British rule over its colonial subjects) reversed the earlier partitioning of Bengal and saw Delhi upgraded as the nation's capital.

During the early inter-war period, Crewe settled into the more comfortable diplomatic role of British Ambassador in France. We saw how, in relation to crises concerning the Franco-Belgian occupation of the Ruhr and Mussolini's invasion of Corfu, he had a steadying and, ultimately, positive influence on his Foreign Office colleagues. He demonstrated further strength of character in facing down the Italians (Mussolini and all) at the Conference of Ambassadors. The adroit diplomacy he exercised in relation to the Locarno Agreement proved vital in achieving a harmonious relationship between potentially conflictual European states, which only unravelled following the emergence of Adolf Hitler.

These accomplishments reinforce the theory posited by Crewe's daughter, Cynthia Colville, that it was his unflagging capacity to remain patient and conduct a 'temperate assessment of people' which undoubtedly carried 'the hallmark of a statesman though not by any means always of a politician'.[1342] Had he possessed his father's considerably bolder temperament, Crewe might well have shaped numerous political developments for the better, and become more widely and justifiably regarded as an individual of great strategic insight. Based on his actual record alone, he still ranks as one of the more sincere, nobly intentioned, and influential politicians of his day – 'a perpetual fountain of good sense', as Lord Samuel famously described him.

Crewe was not the only member of his much-celebrated family to leave a significant mark on British twentieth-century history. We saw, for example, how both his wife, Peggy, and his daughter, Cynthia, engaged in charitable, committee and public service work of estimable social impact.

The former is chiefly remembered for her patronage and support of female factory workers (especially those threatened with wartime unemployment), a role she carried out in conjunction with Queen Mary. Her stepdaughter is similarly associated with efforts on behalf of the downcast and impoverished of London's East End – its women and infants, in particular. At an important crossroads in her career, Cynthia Colville might well have accepted the nomination to stand as Liberal MP for Shoreditch, but responded, instead, to a 'higher calling' by becoming Queen Mary's Woman of the Bedchamber and trusted confidant at times of national and personal crisis. Both Cynthia and Peggy were also at the forefront of initiatives which saw women entering previously inhospitable realms of the male-dominated legal profession.

It was the youngest of Cynthia's three sons, 'Jock' Colville, who made a separate, highly significant contribution to twentieth-century British political history by dint of the calculated discretion and subterfuge he employed in ensuring that the debilitating stroke experienced by the ageing Winston Churchill during his second term as Prime Minister was concealed from the wider British polity.

Colville's highly personable and gregarious manner was ideally suited to this task. The infinitely more reserved, methodical and circumspect personality traits associated with Lord Crewe were visibly embodied in the second of his grandsons to make a telling impact on British political life. The socially aloof and highly introspective Terence O'Neill was the youngest of five children belonging to Crewe's eldest daughter, Annabel, and her husband, Arthur O'Neill (the first Member of

Parliament to be killed in action during World War 1). As Prime Minister of Northern Ireland, Terence managed (like Crewe had done during his stint as Viceroy of Ireland) to alienate both sides of the sectarian divide, thus tipping the province into arguably the most vicious and deadly phase of its recurring 'Troubles'.

Far different in character from his grandfather was Annabel's younger son from her second marriage, Quentin Crewe (formerly Dodds), who more closely resembled his *great grandfather*, Richard Monckton Milnes. Like Milnes, Quentin was an inveterate bon viveur, socialite, traveller, and writer and critic of distinction. He, too, moved comfortably in royal circles, and shared with his great grandfather a lifelong distaste of oppression (being openly critical, for example, of the British attitude to gypsies and of the South African Apartheid system). Family and professional connections gave him the opportunity to witness an adulteress affair involving the wife of a future prime minister (Harold Macmillan) and the deterioration of the marriage of his close friend, Lord Snowdon, and Princess Margaret.

Marital discord and scandal afflicted the life of the final member of the Milnes-Crewe dynasty highlighted in this book: Mary, Duchess of Roxburghe, the daughter of Lord and Peggy Crewe. In common with most of her father's descendants, she benefited from his immense (and largely inherited) personal wealth and endless social capital by gaining access to royal circles (she was a goddaughter of Queen Mary and helped carry the bridal train at the wedding of Queen Elizabeth II). This youngest of all Lord Crewe's children is primarily remembered, however, for having successfully resisted her husband's attempts to have her evicted from their mansion. Despite otherwise maintaining a relatively low historical profile, it was Mary who, as we shall now discover, helped determine the current resting places of literary and cultural artefacts formerly associated with Fryston Hall.

'So Many Treasures'

On 23 March 2015, the famous auction house, Sotheby's of London, issued a press release, announcing that, in two months' time, they would be throwing open the doors of the 'quintessentially English red-brick 16th century Mansion and 400-acre Leatherhead [West Horsley] estate', comprising the erstwhile country retreat of Mary, Duchess of Roxburghe.

Here was an opportunity, they enthused, for the general public to acquire any of the 700 lots of 'exquisite objects' up for sale (including furniture, paintings, jewellery and other precious items).[1343]

Each of these exhibits was certain to be imbued with 'the extraordinary provenance and history, outstanding taste and sense of ceremony particular to the lifestyle of the British Aristocracy over the last century'. Collectively, they constituted 'a portrait of an England that no longer exists but was preserved, untouched for almost half a century', and formed part of a story 'that unites two of the most powerful British dynasties of the last century and is interlinked with the British Royal family throughout the 20th century'.[1344]

Following her death (aged 99) one year earlier, Mary had unexpectedly bequeathed the mansion to her great-nephew and godson, the television presenter, broadcaster and historian, Bamber Gascoigne, who was best known as the affable and erudite presenter of the popular TV quiz game, *University Challenge*, from 1962 to 1987.[1345] Since childhood, Gascoigne had been a regular luncheon and dinner guest at the mansion, but had never ventured into its labyrinthine outer reaches where untold treasures now lay neglected.

Among the 700 lots were reminders of key events in the lives of the Duchess and her forebears. These included: the gown she had worn when bearing Queen Elizabeth's canopy at the coronation of King George VI in 1937; a set of 39 photographs of native Americans and scenes of the American West, presented to Lord Crewe by General William Tecumseh Sherman in 1875; ceremonial jewels worn by Crewe while he was Viceroy of Ireland; suites of monogrammed glasses, silver and China that once catered for up to 50 people from Crewe's days as Ambassador to Paris; and a rare 18th-century Axminster carpet from Fryston Hall.[1346]

Gascoigne had inherited a property in need of extensive repair. Far from balking at this prospect, he and his wife, Christina, resolved to see it restored to full health for the benefit of the nation. The Sotheby's auction was vital to securing this ambition. 'It was completely unexpected by me that I would be heir to [the Duchess's] estate,' Gascoigne readily conceded.

> She had expressed that, given the work required to restore the house, she expected I would sell it. But having spent many memorable times with my aunt here, and knowing how special

the house was to her and her family, together with my wife I decided to take up the challenge of carrying out the essential work to the house to ensure that it can withstand what may lie ahead over the course of its future, and continue to stand as a monument of its remarkable past.[1347]

Not part of Gascoigne's inheritance was a separate bequest by the Duchess – this time to the Wren Library of Trinity College, Cambridge, where her father, Lord Crewe, and grandfather, Richard Monckton Milnes, had each studied as undergraduates. The Trinity Librarian, Dr Nicolas Bell, described this 'Crewe Collection', amassed by the Marquess and his father between the 1830s and early twentieth century, as 'one of the most important private collections in Britain'.[1348]

The bulk of it once resided, of course, in the library of Fryston Hall. Included in this trove were first editions, bearing the signatures of such legendary figures as Byron, Shelley and Wordsworth. These literary treasures sat alongside previously unknown manuscripts written by Napoleon Bonaparte, George Washington, Florence Nightingale and Charles Dickens. As Dr Bell explained,

> Richard Monckton Milnes was a fastidious collector of unusual books. As well as major works of English and French literature, his library included transcripts of notorious trials for murder, forgery and witchcraft, rare political pamphlets on the French Revolution and the American Civil War, and several shelves of unpublished literary manuscripts.[1349]

A visit to West Horsley Place by Bell and Trinity's Sub-Librarian, Sandy Paul, confirmed the presence of many thousands of precious volumes, often arranged in free-standing piles reaching up to the ceiling. It was in a cupboard located in the Duchess's bedroom that the pair came across a suitcase containing what they excitedly described as 'the holy of holies': 'Opening the suitcase was an exciting moment: it contained some exceptionally rare first editions of Shelley's poems, books inscribed by William Beckford and Oscar Wilde, a pristine first edition of Walt Whitman's "Leaves of Grass", and some bizarre curiosities such as a fragment of Voltaire's dressing gown.'[1350]

The significance of the Duchess's bequest was put in true

perspective by Gascoigne himself, who maintained with undisguised satisfaction:

> It is a delight for me, and would be for my aunt who left her library to Trinity, that the books from now on have a secure and lasting home as the Crewe Collection. And it is thrilling that the team at the Wren Library are discovering so many treasures and rarities unknown to anyone since the death of her father in 1945, and that they will from now on be available to everyone.[1351]

Redevelopment Schemes

The corresponding rejuvenation of faraway (New) Fryston appeared to have been fully realised in January 2019, when the most recently built of the 150 new homes comprising the 'River Meadows' estate, situated on the former Fryston pit site, came up for sale. The Meadows project had commenced in November 2016, after the housing construction company, Kier Living, was granted permission by Wakefield Council to start building a range of two-, three-, four- and five-bedroom homes.[1352]

In its press release, the company underlined the relevance of the recently upgraded local environment and its proximity to a celebrated Royal Society for the Protection of Birds (RSPB) nature reserve at Fairburn Ings. 'Riverside Meadows,' it said, 'is located in a beautiful countryside setting and on the banks of the River Aire with direct access to scenic trails and a wonderful area preserved for nature lovers.'[1353] This sales pitch lacked any corresponding reference to the symbolic significance of Martha Schwartz's 'grand design'; or, for that matter, any mention of the area's rich mining heritage. There was, indeed, an obvious cultural, as well as proximal, no-man's-land between the 'old' and 'new' physical manifestations of Fryston.

Another relevant development in the property market occurred in the spring of 2019 when it was reported that Swillington House, the mansion-style home of Jim Bullock, its stables and the surrounding nine acres of land, had been listed for sale at an asking price of £1,595,000.[1354] This marked the settlement of an acrimonious two-year dispute between the two children from Bullock's second marriage. The house itself had been inherited by Jim's son, James, with 160 acres of adjoining farmland and the former gardener's cottage allocated to his daughter, Josephine. For the previous two decades the latter had been producing prize-winning examples of organic and ethical farming with the help of her husband and their son.[1355]

A bitter dispute ensued, however, when Josephine and her family added to their herd of beef cattle and began sheltering them all during winter months in a nearby barn, where the additional noise they allegedly created was found intolerable by James. The case was referred to Leeds City Council, who ordered noise levels to be monitored for a twelve-month period.[1356] The protracted dispute was ultimately resolved by the eventual sale of the property. A more harmonious atmosphere thus prevailed when, on 21 May 2020 at the height of the COVID pandemic, a small, socially distancing ceremony took place on the site of the former mining village of Bowers Row.

This ceremony represented the latest instalment of the 'Historic Plaques Scheme', instigated in 1987 by the Leeds Civic Trust to promote public awareness of the city's heritage. The blue plaque, which was erected on the non-denominational chapel – the only remaining building in Bowers Row – commemorated the life and accomplishments of Jim Bullock. The plaque was proudly unveiled by James. Its simple inscription read:

> The youngest of twelve children lived here in Bowers Row pit village. He left school at thirteen and went down the pit as a pony driver, rising through the mining hierarchy to become National President of the British Association of Colliery Management. 1903-1995.[1357]

This monument is similar in design to the small plaque located beside the front door of the terraced house in North Street, Fryston, once occupied by the celebrated photographer, Jack Hulme. These modest tributes to significant individuals associated with Fryston stand alongside Harry Malkin's wall mural and the much-derided 'Martha's Finger' as increasingly tenuous reminders of the 'remarkable history' of the pit-folk referred to in this volume.

Following the civic ceremony in honour of Jim Bullock, a more elaborate tribute appeared in the Leeds Civic Trust annual review magazine, reminding readers that:

> The story of Jim Bullock really is one of rags to riches. Born in 1903 the youngest of 12 children, he started working at the age of 13 as a pony driver. He became a pit deputy at the age of 25 and ten years later was a pit manager at Fryston Colliery. Having seen life quite literally 'on the coalface', he was particularly keen on miners' welfare. His colliery was one of the first to have a pithead bath installed, and later he constructed the Fryston Welfare Hall for his workers. His life on both sides of the tracks was recorded in his book 'Them and Us.'[1358]

The Trust's list could easily be extended to include other important milestones, such as: the construction of the Holy Cross Church from the remnants of Fryston Hall; the provision of motorised carriages for paraplegic miners; charitable events featuring famous Bevin Boys like Len Shackleton and Johnny Downie; the creation of a sports stadium; and, of course, the daring 'Lister Addy rescue'.

Details of Bullock's life 'on both side of the tracks' highlight (as does the biography of Richard Monckton Milnes) the need to acknowledge a more fluid and nuanced definition of the class dichotomy outlined by Jeremy Paxman.

The first Lord Houghton's existence was characterised by enduring privilege and hedonism, and yet his largely inherited fortune became depleted as he pursued one philanthropic commitment after another. He was a tireless social reformer who campaigned for better industrial working conditions, Irish Home Rule, the provision of free libraries, the abolition of slavery, the introduction of the female suffrage, and countless other humanitarian issues.

Jim Bullock clearly never forgot 'the rock from which he was hewn' in the process of striving to improve the working and domestic lives of people in mining communities like Fryston. He was, in his own words, a latter-day Robin Hood, using Coal Board money in the interests of mining families. Despite being (according to Joe Hall) Britain's 'only socialist manager', Bullock was not averse to employing the type of cunning and deception he so deplored in others to gain the compliance of his workers. It was, indeed, this 'elasticity of conscience' he acquired which enabled him to seek out 'a bit of heaven below', as he progressed from a terraced house in Airedale, via the managerial 'house on the hill' to the converted remains of property once belonging to the mine- and land-owning aristocracy of Swillington.

While Bullock's ambition and inspiration were crucial to the many feats accomplished while he was colliery manager, it was the collective efforts of the people of Fryston which brought them to fruition. These conspicuous highlights of the 'Bullock era' must not obscure the significance of those less salient or dramatic features of everyday community existence, described in earlier chapters, which also made village life so laudable and worthy of admiration.

It is imperative that any discussion of these qualities should also carry the disclaimer that, throughout most of its existence, Fryston was, by contemporary standards, an *imperfect* 'Shangri-la'. Previous chapters have emphasised how local colliers and their womenfolk adapted to the historically arduous, dangerous and austere conditions they endured by creating a culture which prioritised the man's working and domestic requirements, and extolled 'the virtue of obedience to [his] wishes, [and] of subordination to his needs'.[1359] Consequently,

> Women [were] denied participation in those activities whereby men achieve success or reputation. They definitely [tried] to assert their individual worth among other women by doing the job of motherhood as well or better than their neighbours.[1360]

Such women were unwittingly complicit in a process of 'social reproduction' – i.e. 'producing a labour force of the kind, in the quantities that capitalism requires'.[1361] They transmitted, via their own attitudes and conduct, norms of appropriate masculinity and femininity. A young woman learned via her mother's example that 'she [would] be praised for "looking after" her husband well, making a pleasant and easy-going homestead as a contrast to his arduous toil at the pit'.[1362] Young men quickly grasped in turn that they were expected to serve as 'good husbands' and family providers, by working with due punctuality, diligence and loyalty to fellow workers, and by showing mental and physical resilience towards the occupational hazards of danger, injury and industrial disease.

'Only those who grow up in the environment of mining, for whom the costs are an everyday feature, become immune to them,' Allen maintains. 'The mining family, therefore, serves to perpetuate the mining industry.'[1363] A way of life had rapidly evolved whereby female prospects were especially circumscribed, but in which a lack of scholastic ambition or attainment was the wider norm.

The highly insular and parochial nature of places like Fryston also encouraged a devout cynicism towards external perspectives, and a failure to understand, let alone *celebrate*, social diversity. Finally, few contemporary observers are liable to bemoan the passing of such a dangerous, health-impairing and polluting industrial reality.

There nonetheless remains a great deal to praise about a type of culture that evolved within a context of physical and economic adversity. British society has long acknowledged its great indebtedness to mining communities like Fryston for providing the mineral lifeblood which enabled it to survive and prosper both in peacetime and during episodes of global conflict. The chapters of this book comprise a compelling testament to the noble and enduring values of mutuality, emotional resilience, courage and resourcefulness characterising village life in the face of a battery of industrial and domestic hardships seldom, if ever, experienced elsewhere in society.

Not Forgetting 'The Dark Beneath Our Feet'
On 8 February 2022, Bamber Gascoigne died, aged 87, following a brief illness. Since the Sotheby's sale, which succeeded in achieving the £10 million required for the total renovation of the manor, Gascoigne and his wife had transformed West Horsley Place into a community arts centre, the centrepiece of which was a 700-seater opera house. Fittingly enough, the Duchess of Roxburghe's ashes were interred beneath the orchestra pit. The house itself was used for conferences and as a location for the filming of historical dramas. These developments validated Christina Gascoigne's claim that her husband was 'an incredibly generous man and everything he did was pointed towards sharing the gifts of his own life with others'.[1364]

Within one week of Gascoigne's passing, Fryston's oldest surviving ex-resident, Dora Lunn, celebrated her hundredth birthday. An article anticipating this milestone appeared in the 10 February edition of the *Pontefract and Castleford Express*. It recalled a life spent in Fryston from the early 1920s to the mid-1960s, at which point, she moved, like many other villagers, to her marital home in neighbouring Ferry Fryston. Readers learned that Mrs Lunn had been employed as housekeeper by Jim Bullock and his wife from 1955 until his eventual passing almost 40 years later. Dora reminisced that the Fryston she grew up in was a 'superbly friendly, self-sufficient and mutually supportive place in which to live'. She explained that, in the inter-war years of her youth, 'The people of the village looked out for one another, laughed together, and took collective pride in our honest, hard-working way of life.'

Mrs Lunn died at a Normanton care home in January 2023 – a few months short of the 150th anniversary of the sinking of the local mineshaft. Her funeral service took place before a large congregation at the iconic Holy Cross Church on 15 February (two days on from her birthday). A similar service was staged at the same venue several weeks later, following the death, aged 92, of a second Fryston stalwart, Les Oxtoby. Like Bamber Gascoigne's passing, these deaths highlighted the progressive unravelling of the tenuous link between present-day Fryston and its truly incredible past.

Jeremy Paxman observes that deep coal mining has lamentably become 'a part of our history we no longer need to know about'.[1365] He soberly insists that: 'Much of what went on in the dark beneath our feet is already almost forgotten,' and that, 'One day, it may be impossible to imagine.'[1366] With this type of prognosis in mind, the present study has endeavoured to document and preserve Fryston's rich mining tradition. By extolling the nature and importance of the area's accompanying aristocratic past, it has further emphasised that Castleford's historical significance reaches far beyond its celebrated links to the Roman era.

Beynon and Hudson refer to the inscription on one now obsolete miners' banner, which read: 'The past we inherit – the future we build.'[1367] It is conceivable that the remarkable history of Fryston, retold in these two volumes, might prove a stimulus for further cultural and emotional regeneration, not only in Castleford per se, but also in similar localities where precious black diamonds were so courageously hewn amidst the 'dark beneath our feet'.

Acknowledgements

I feel greatly indebted to the following people and organisations for granting me permission to employ the photographs used in illustration of this text:

Alamy
Bridgeman Images
The City of Wakefield Metropolitan District Libraries
The Daily Mail
The Daily Telegraph
The History of Parliament Blog
The Holy Cross Church, Airedale, Castleford
Trevor Hulme
Harry Malkin
Harold Mattison
The McNeillstown True Blues Orange Loyal Lodge Institution
The National War Museum
Pontefract and Castleford Express
Shutterstock
Richard Sloan
Marcus Soar
Bill and Frances Spedding
The Times
Liz Wheeldon
Yorkshire Post
Yorkshire Evening Post

I am also extremely grateful to a wide range of individuals and institutions whose support and encouragement helped make this publication possible.
I would like to begin by thanking the staff of Castleford Library

(especially their Customer Service Assistant, Lucy Bellwood) for helping me to trawl through relevant archives. I am similarly indebted to the Reverend Angela Brownridge (a former resident of Fryston), who granted me access to scores of photographs belonging to the Holy Cross Church, Airedale.

Being a born technophobe, I have good reason to feel thankful for the technical support I received from Eva Alamurova and Kiril Alamurov (without an 'a'!) at various stages of this project. I am equally grateful to Parissa Motamedi-Mousavi, who helped in the construction of the Milnes-Crewe 'family tree' and the summary table appearing in Chapters 1 and 4, respectively.

I considered myself a very lucky man when Dr Richard Sloan accepted my invitation to write the foreword to this book. The Sloan family name still commands great reverence and affection in Fryston, where Richard and his parents before him acted as general practitioners from 1923 to 2005. I would like to thank him wholeheartedly for his fond references to the village and kind comments on my work.

As ever, the magnificent editorial support I have received from Ian Daley and Isabel Galán of Route has been invaluable. I have benefited greatly from their combined wisdom and expertise. It has been a great pleasure and privilege to work with them once again.

Finally, it is true to say that this book would never have reached fruition had it not been for the practical and emotional support volunteered by my brother, Paul, my cousin Janet and her husband, Graham, and my partner in life, Rayna. The same could be said, before her passing in January 2023 (one month short of her 101st birthday) of my beloved auntie, Dora Lunn. During our nightly telephone conversations amidst the COVID pandemic, she captivated me with her constant reminiscences of a life spent primarily in Fryston. She was my lifelong teacher and inspiration.

Notes

1 Wassell (2009)
2 Waddington (2020)
3 Page Arnot (1953, p. 16 and p. 17)
4 Kimber (2018a and 2018b)
5 *Pontefract and Castleford Express*, 7 August 1914
6 See 'Lord Privy Seal': https:www.gov.uk/government/ministers/lord-privy-seal. Crewe would occupy this position for two finite periods: October 1908 to October 1911; and February 1912 to May 1915
7 quoted in Hardy and Pinion (1972, p. 133)
8 *Scientific American* (1853, p. 285)
9 quoted in Raynes (1928, p. 57)
10 *Yorkshire Post*, 17 October 2005
11 ibid.
12 e.g. High (2003), Neumann (2016, Salford (2009)
13 'The urban ghosts', *The Economist*, 12 October 2013
14 *Yorkshire Post*, 17 October 2005
15 ibid.
16 ibid.
17 ibid.
18 Manning (1977)
19 See Allen (1981); Hall (1981)
20 See Waddington 2020, pp. 19-21)
21 Stephenson and Wray, (2005); Wray (2011)
22 Wray (2011, p. 111)
23 ibid.
24 quoted in ibid., p. 116
25 ibid, p. 117
26 Waddington (2020, p. 21)
27 Pope-Hennessy (1955, p. 67)
28 ibid., p. 68
29 ibid.
30 ibid., p. 107
31 ibid., p. 111
32 Huttenback (1966, p. 275)
33 ibid., p. 276
34 ibid., p. 273
35 ibid., p. 281
36 ibid., p. 277
37 ibid., p. 285
38 ibid., pp. 286-287
39 Vahed (2019, p. 668)
40 Herman (2010, p. 171)
41 quoted in Desai and Vahed (2015, p. 138)
42 ibid.
43 Vahed (2019, p. 669)
44 Herman (2010, p. 171)
45 quoted in Vahed (2019, p. 670)
46 Vahed (2019, p. 670)
47 quoted in Vahed (2019, p. 670)
48 All quoted in Guha (2013, p. 43)
49 Guha (2013, p. 43)
50 Desai and Vahed (2015, p. 144)
51 Hiralal (2014, p. 227)
52 Reed (2017, p. 184)
53 Hess (1964, p. 415)
54 ibid., p. 429
55 ibid.
56 ibid., p. 421
57 ibid., p. 422
58 ibid., p. 423
59 ibid.
60 Irons (2013, p. 97)
61 quoted in ibid., p. 106
62 quoted in ibid., p. 107
63 ibid., p. 115
64 quoted in ibid., p. 116
65 ibid., p. 116
66 ibid., p. 118
67 quoted in ibid., p. 119
68 ibid., p. 121
69 Hess (1964, p. 425)
70 Callaway (1993, pp. 45-46)
71 Paxman (2012, p. 144)
72 Hyman (2010, p. 423)
73 ibid.
74 ibid., p. 424
75 Ray (2015, p. 103)
76 quoted in ibid., p. 116
77 ibid.
78 quoted in ibid., p. 107 .
79 ibid.
80 Ray (2015, p. 131)
81 ibid.
82 Pope-Hennessy (1955, p. 72)
83 ibid.
84 ibid.
85 Lloyd George (1910, p. 143)
86 Dorey and Kelso (2011, chapter 1)
87 Colville (1963, p. 50)
88 Pope-Hennessy (1955, p. 112)
89 quoted in ibid., p. 113
90 ibid., p. 114
91 ibid., p. 115
92 ibid., p. 79
93 Pope-Hennessy (1955, p. 79)
94 ibid., p. 82
95 ibid., p. 83
96 Ballinger (2012, p. 277)
97 Ibid., pp. 116-117
98 Pope-Hennessy (1955, p. 122)
99 Crewe (1995, p. 57)
100 Crewe (1955, p. xii)
101 quoted in Pope-Hennessy (1955, p. 92)
102 Pope-Hennessy (1955, p. 92)
103 Crewe (1955, p. xii)
104 Pope-Hennessy (1955, p. 90)
105 ibid., p. 91
106 Ballinger (2012, p. 28)
107 Pope-Hennessy (1955, p. 123)
108 ibid.
109 ibid., p. 125
110 ibid., p. 126
111 Weston and Kelvin (1994)
112 Pope-Hennessy (1955, p. 130)
113 quoted in ibid., p. 137

114 Pope-Hennessy (1955, footnote p. 135)
115 Pope-Hennessy (1959, pp. 446-447)
116 ibid., p. 447
117 Johnson (2015, p. 22)
118 Broomfield (1968, pp. 39-40)
119 Eustis, F.A. II and Zaidi, Z.H. (1964, p. 174)
120 Broomfield (1968, p. 40)
121 Eustis, F.A. II and Zaidi, Z.H. (1964, pp. 179-180)
122 Pope-Hennessy (1959, p. 449)
123 ibid., p. 50
124 ibid.
125 ibid., p. 451
126 Brendon (2008, p. 245)
127 quoted in Pope-Hennessy (1959, p. 462)
128 Pope-Hennessy (1955, p. 98)
129 ibid., p. 103
130 ibid., p. 99
131 ibid., p. 103
132 ibid., p. 53
133 Edwards (1984, p. 257)
134 Pope-Hennessy (1955, pp. 138-139)
135 Edwards (1984, p. 257)
136 Pope-Hennessy (1959, p. 470)
137 Edwards (1984, p. 257)
138 Pope-Hennessy (1959, p. 472)
139 Pope-Hennessy (1955, p. 141)
140 quoted in ibid.
141 Pope-Hennessy (1955, p. 141)
142 Huttenback (1966, p. 289)
143 ibid., 289-290
144 ibid.
145 *Hansard*, House of Lords, 30 July 1913
146 ibid.
147 quoted in Verma (2009/2010, p. 866)
148 Corder and Plaut (2014, p. 32)
149 quoted in ibid.
150 Corder and Plaut (2014, p. 32)
151 Anand (2015, p. 287)
152 quoted in ibid.
153 quoted in ibid., p. 289
154 Anand (2015, p. 290)
155 quoted in Pope-Hennessy (1955, p. 138)
156 Pope-Hennessy (1955, p. 138)
157 Colville (1963, p. 96)
158 ibid.
159 ibid., p. 102
160 Hardy (1984, p. 384)
161 Pinion (1990, p. 149)
162 Henniker (1912)
163 ibid., p. 58
164 Anglessey (1994, p. 2)
165 Pope-Hennessy (1955, pp. 139-140)
166 ibid., p. 140
167 *Hansard*, House of Lords, 27 January 1913
168 *Belfast Evening Telegraph*, 25 April 1914
169 Howie (1986, p. 217)
170 McEwan (1972, p. 111)
171 Wray (2011, p. 109)
172 ibid., p. 107
173 ibid., p. 109
174 Bulmer (1975)
175 Waddington et al. (2001, p. 71)
176 *Yorkshire Post*, 17 October 2005
177 *Yorkshire Evening Post*, 17 March 1986
178 Downes (2016, pp. 221-223)
179 ibid., p. 221
180 ibid., p. 222
181 Kimber (2018)
182 Waddington (2015; 2020)
183 Pelsall History Society (no date)
184 *Pontefract and Castleford Express*, 17 February 1884
185 *Pontefract and Castleford Express*, 18 April 1891
186 *Pontefract and Castleford Express*, 24 August 1901
187 ibid.
188 Kelly's West Riding of Yorkshire Directory (1908)
189 *Pontefract and Castleford Express*, 7 April 1911
190 quoted in Van Riel at al. (1990, no page)
191 *Pontefract and Castleford Express*, 9 April 1903
192 Waddington (2013)
193 ibid., pp. 41-43
194 *Pontefract and Castleford Express*, 17 April 1914
195 Lynch (2016)
196 ibid, pp. 17-19
197 Pope-Hennessy (1955, p. 144)
198 ibid.
199 ibid., p. 145
200 Woodward (1929, p. 180)
201 ibid., p. 181
202 Pope-Hennessy (1959, p. 492)
203 ibid., p. 493
204 Woodward (1929, p. 181)
205 ibid., pp. 182-183
206 ibid., p. 183
207 Pope-Hennessy (1959, p. 493)
208 ibid.
209 Woodward (1929, p. 185)
210 Pope-Hennessy (1959, p. 492)
211 Woodward (1929, p. 191)
212 ibid., p. 190
213 Colville (1963, p. 92)
214 http://www.rte.ie/centuryireland/index.php/articles/the-irish-mp-the-democract-of-death
215 Thornton (2017)
216 ibid., p. 95
217 ibid., p. 96
218 Murland (2010, p. 18)
219 quoted in Thornton (2017, p. 97)
220 Pope-Hennessy (1955, p. 147)
221 quoted in ibid., pp. 147-148
222 ibid., p. 148
223 O'Neill (1972, p. 1)
224 ibid., p. 5
225 ibid., p. 9
226 Colville (1976, pp. 19-20)
227 ibid., p. 21
228 ibid.
229 O'Neill (1972, p. 10)
230 Hardy and Pinion (1972, pp. 159-160)
231 Pite (2006, p. 430)
232 quoted in ibid.
233 quoted in ibid., p. 431
234 Pite (2006, p. 431)
235 quoted in Hardy and Pinion (1972, p. 178)

236 ibid., p. 178, footnote 563
237 Pope-Hennessy (1955, p. 147)
238 Thornton (2017, p. 100)
239 quoted in ibid., p. 102
240 Adams (1986)
241 Brock and Brock (2014)
242 quoted in ibid., p. 182 (underlining in original)
243 quoted in ibid., p. 227 (underlining in original)
244 quoted in Desai and Vahed (2015, p. 281)
245 quoted in Herman (2010, p. 200)
246 Goold (1976, p. 925)
247 ibid.
248 ibid., p. 924
249 ibid., p. 926
250 Ulrichsen (2007, p. 350)
251 ibid., p. 354
252 quoted in Goold (1976, p. 297)
253 ibid.
254 ibid.
255 ibid.
256 quoted in Skelly (2009, p. x)
257 Skelly (2009, p. x)
258 quoted in Barker (2009, p. 61)
259 ibid., p. 58
260 ibid., p. 61
261 Pope-Hennessy (1955, p. 149)
262 Crowley (2004, p. 335)
263 Skelly (2009, p. xiv)
264 Adelson (1995, p. 101)
265 quoted in Adelson (1995, p. 101)
266 Adelson (1995, p. 103)
267 Curran (2011, p. 18)
268 quoted in ibid., p. 19
269 Adelson (1995, p. 112)
270 Curran (2011, p. 20)
271 ibid., p. 23
272 Adelson (1995)
273 Lambert (2012, p. 320)
274 ibid., p. 417
275 quoted in Stationery Office (2000, p. 25)
276 Bell (2017, p. 267)
277 quoted in Curran (2011, p. 22)
278 Bell (2017, p. 268)
279 quoted in Stationery Office (2000, p. 31)
280 ibid.
281 ibid., p. 73
282 Stationery Office (2000, p. 157)
283 ibid., pp. 157-158
284 Mathew (2011); Scepanovic (2018)
285 Mathew (2013, p. 236)
286 ibid., p. 237
287 Veréet (1970)
288 Mathew (2011, p. 31)
289 ibid., p. 32
290 Livingstone (2021, p. 262)
291 Schneer (2011, p. 129)
292 quoted in Livingstone (2021, p. 263)
293 Livingstone (2021, p. 265)
294 Schneer (2011, p. 135)
295 Livingstone (2021, p. 266)
296 ibid.
297 Schneer (2011, p. 120)
298 quoted in ibid., p. 158
299 ibid.
300 Schneer (2011, p. 160)
301 Pope-Hennessy (1955, p. 150)
302 quoted in Livingstone (2021, p. 269)
303 quoted in Sokolow (1919, p. 114)
304 Pope-Hennessy (1955, p. 151)
305 Crewe (1995, p. 63)
306 Taylor (1980)
307 Crewe (1995, p. 65)
308 Baylies (1993, p. 398)
309 quoted in Baylies (1993, p. 398)
310 Baylies (1993, p. 398)
311 ibid.
312 ibid., p. 399
313 Ede England (2017)
314 ibid., pp. xvii-xviii
315 Lynch (2016, pp. 19-33)
316 ibid., pp. 109-110
317 ibid., p. 62
318 ibid., p. 66
319 ibid.
320 ibid., p. 103
321 ibid., p. 105
322 Waddington (2013, pp. 51-52)
323 ibid., pp. 53-54
324 *Pontefract and Castleford Express*, 23 April 1915
325 Waddington (2013, pp. 54-55)
326 *Pontefract and Castleford Express*, 11 June 1915
327 ibid.
328 ibid.
329 ibid.
330 quoted in ibid.
331 ibid.
332 *Pontefract and Castleford Express*, 11 June 1915
333 quoted in ibid.
334 ibid.
335 *Pontefract and Castleford Express*, 3 December 1915
336 Ede England (2017, pp. 94-95)
337 *London Gazette [Supplement]*, 3 June 1918
338 *Daily Mail*, 15 May 2009
339 ibid.
340 Wakefield Library (no date)
341 ibid.
342 Franks (2004; 2005)
343 Franks (2005, p. 6)
344 quoted in ibid., p. 11
345 Franks (2005)
346 Franks (2004, p. 46)
347 quoted in ibid., p. 29
348 ibid., p. 31
349 quoted in ibid., p 32
350 ibid., p. 48
351 quoted in ibid., pp. 50-51
352 Taylor (1996, p. 226)
353 Ives (2016, p. 276)
354 Lynch (2016, pp. 146-147)
355 Ives (2016, p. 279)
356 ibid., p. 291
357 ibid., p. 296
358 ibid., p. 295
359 *Yorkshire Illustrated*, October 1952, p. 29
360 Bullock (1972, p. 20)
361 ibid.

362 ibid., p. 22
363 ibid.
364 ibid.
365 ibid., pp. 21-22
366 ibid., p. 22
367 Bullock (1976, p. 179)
368 Bullock (1972, p. 23)
369 Bullock (1976, p. 178)
370 Bullock (1972, p. 23)
371 Bullock (1972, p. 34)
372 ibid., pp. 33-34
373 Bullock (1976, p. 184)
374 ibid.
375 Bullock (1972, pp. 36-37)
376 Bullock (1976, p. 185)
377 Bullock (1972, p. 39)
378 ibid., p. 40
379 ibid., p. 41
380 ibid.
381 ibid., p. 43
382 ibid., p. 52
383 ibid.
384 ibid., pp. 52-53
385 ibid., p. 54
386 ibid., p. 57
387 ibid., p. 58
388 ibid., p.59
389 Downes (2016, p. 222)
390 Waddington (1988, p. 19)
391 Bullock (1972, p. 63)
392 ibid., p. 64
393 ibid., p. 63
394 Winterton (1985)
395 McLynn (2015, p. 369)
396 Morris (1976, p. 124)
397 Bullock (1972, p. 59)
398 Waddington (1988, p. 30)
399 Bullock (1972, p. 59)
400 Waddington (2013, p. 59)
401 ibid., p. 60
402 ibid., p. 62
403 *Pontefract and Castleford Express*, 12 October 1923
404 Waddington (2013, pp. 64-65)
405 Sloan (2020)
406 Sloan (2012, p. 16)
407 Pope-Hennessy (1955, p. 153)
408 See: https:www.westhorsleyplace.org/mar-garet-crewe-milnes-marchioness-of-crewe
409 Crewe (1991, p. 3)
410 ibid., p. 9
411 Colville (1963, p. 104)
412 ibid.
413 ibid., p. 107
414 ibid., p. 108
415 ibid., p. 109
416 ibid., p. 110
417 ibid., p. 116
418 ibid., p. 117
419 ibid., p. 119
420 ibid., p. 123
421 Colville (1976, p. 311)
422 quoted in Hardy and Pinion (1972, p. xxvii)
423 Tomalin (2007, p. 46)
424 quoted in ibid.
425 Hardy and Pinion (1972, p. 201, footnote 632)
426 quoted in ibid., p. 201
427 Tomalin (2007, pp. 460-461)
428 Pinion (1990, p. 15)
429 Millgate (2004, p. 505)
430 ibid.
431 ibid.
432 Hardy and Pinion (1972, pp. xxvi-xxvii)
433 quoted in Pite (2006, p. 456)
434 ibid.
435 Pite (2006, p. 456)
436 See Hardy and Pinion (1972)
437 ibid., pp. 204-205
438 quoted in ibid., p. 207
439 Hardy and Pinion (1972, p. 208)
440 Pope-Hennessy (1955, p. 153)
441 Crewe (1995, p. 62)
442 See: https://westcheshiremuseums.co.uk/wp-content/updates/2018/12/deLaszio.pdf
443 Pope-Hennessy (1955, p. 154v)
444 quoted in Johnson (2011a. p. 53)
445 quoted in Pope-Hennessy, 1955, pp. 156-157)
446 Pope-Hennessy (1955, p. 157)
447 ibid., pp. 161-162
448 ibid., pp. 160-161
449 Gladwyn (1976, p. 200)
450 ibid.
451 Pope-Hennessy (1955, p. 171)
452 Johnson (2011a, p, 52)
453 ibid., p. 53
454 Johnson (2011b, p. 229)
455 Pope-Hennessy (1955, p. 153)
456 ibid.
457 Johnson (2011b, p. 227)
458 ibid.
459 ibid., pp. 229 and 240
460 Johnson (2011a, p. 49)
461 ibid., p. 60
462 O'Riordan (2001; 2004)
463 O'Riordan (2001, p. 1)
464 Gilbert (1926); Sterrett (1927)
465 O'Riordan (2001, pp. 130-141)
466 quoted in ibid., p. 140
467 O'Riordan (2001, p, 162)
468 ibid., pp. 162-163
469 Pope-Hennessy (1955, p. 165)
470 ibid.
471 Cassels (1970, p. 100)
472 ibid., pp. 100-101 (italics in original)
473 Yearwood (1986, p. 559)
474 Barros (1965, p. 122_
475 ibid., pp. 156157
476 ibid., p. 201
477 ibid., p. 221
478 ibid., p. 222
479 ibid., pp. 230-231
480 ibid., p. 249
481 ibid., p. 269
482 Cassels (1970, p. 123)
483 Barros (1965, p. 282)
484 ibid., p. 287
485 quoted in ibid.

486 Jacobsen (1972, p. 3)
487 ibid.
488 Johnson (2006, p. 755)
489 Jacobsen (1972, p. 4)
490 ibid., p. 18
491 Johnson (2006, pp. 758-759)
492 Johnson (2011a, p. 55)
493 ibid., pp. 54-55
494 quoted in ibid., p. 55
495 Johnson (2011a, p. 60)
496 quoted in ibid., p. 61
497 Waddington (2013)
498 ibid.
499 Winterton (1985)
500 See Farman (1972, pp. 36-37) for a fuller explanation
501 Winterton (1985)
502 quoted in ibid., p. 54
503 McLynn (2013, p. 377)
504 quoted in Farman (1972, p. 68)
505 Winterton (1985)
506 Waddington (2013)
507 Farman (1972, pp. 78-79)
508 quoted in Brendon (2000, p. 46)
509 Citrine (1964, p. 171)
510 Brendon (2000, p. 51)
511 ibid., p. 52
512 Waddington (2020, chapter 29)
513 McLynn (2013, p. 392)
514 Griffin (1962, p. 241)
515 ibid., p. 209
516 ibid., p. 220
517 Winterton (1985, p. 54)
518 McLynn (2013, p. 468)
519 Farman (1972, p. 320)
520 Bullock (1972, p. 74)
521 ibid., p. 75
522 ibid., p. 78
523 ibid., p. 80
524 *Pontefract and Castleford Express*, 18 January 1963
525 ibid.
526 Bullock (1972, p. 82)
527 'Miner Extraordinary', *Yorkshire Television*, 22 July 1969
528 Bullock (1972, p. 82)
529 Daly (1985)
530 ibid.
531 ibid., p. 12
532 Bullock (1972, p. 81)
533 quoted in 'Miner Extraordinary', *Yorkshire Television*, 22 July 1969
534 Davies (1987, p. 123)
535 ibid.
536 Lawson (1947, pp. 219-220)
537 Waddington (2013)
538 Daly (1985, p. 15)
539 Pope-Hennessy (1955, p. 171)
540 quoted in ibid., p. 172
541 Crewe (1931a, p. vii)
542 ibid.
543 Crewe (1991)
544 *New York Times*, 1 December 1998
545 Crewe (2007, p. 29)
546 Crewe (1991, p. 2)
547 ibid., p. 8
548 ibid., p. 9
549 ibid., pp. 12-13
550 ibid., p. 16
551 ibid., p. 19
552 Colville (1963, pp. 149-150)
553 ibid., pp. 151-158
554 Bradley (2017, p. 21)
555 ibid., p. 22
556 ibid., p. 20
557 quoted in Crewe (1931a, p. 93)
558 Crewe (1931b, p. 633)
559 quoted in ibid., pp. 656-657
560 Pole (1932, p. 86)
561 Phelps Hall (1972, p. 117)
562 Marriott (1932, p. 121)
563 Crewe (1995, p. 70)
564 Pope-Hennessy (1955, pp. 176-177)
565 https://westhorsleyplace.org/margaret-crewe-milnes-marchioness-of-crewe
566 ibid.
567 Crewe (1995, pp. 70-71)
568 ibid., p. 67
569 Crewe (1991, p. 23)
570 ibid., p. 24
571 ibid., pp. 23-24
572 ibid., p. 24
573 Bullock (1972, p. 83)
574 ibid., p. 84
575 ibid., pp. 84-85
576 ibid., p. 85
577 ibid., p. 89
578 ibid., p. 106
579 ibid., p. 108
580 ibid.
581 ibid., p. 108)
582 Daly (1985, p. 15)
583 ibid.
584 ibid., p. 16
585 Bullock (1972, p. 87)
586 Daly (1985, p, 21)
587 Bullock (1972, p.p. 87-88)
588 Ibid., p. 158
589 Airedale Collieries (1932, p. 2)
590 Bullock (1972, pp. 158-159)
591 ibid., p. 159
592 ibid., p. 160
593 ibid.
594 Downes (2016, p. 222)
595 *Pontefract and Castleford Express*, 22 January 1932
596 quoted in ibid.
597 *Pontefract and Castleford Express*, 22 January 1932
598 ibid.
599 ibid.
600 Daly (1985, p. 16)
601 Wassell (2009, p. 16)
602 Bullock (1972, p. 89)
603 Daly (1985, p. 16)
604 Bullock (1972, p. 88)
605 ibid., pp. 87-88
606 Wassell (2009, p. 17)
607 Bullock (1972, p. 88)

608 *Pontefract and Castleford Express*, 24 March 1933
609 ibid.
610 ibid.
611 ibid.
612 ibid.
613 ibid.
614 ibid.
615 Wassell (2009, p. 18)
616 Daly (1985, p. 17)
617 ibid., p. 22
618 Wassell (2009, p. 35)
619 Bullock (1972, p. 89)
620 Bellamy and Savile (1975, p. 349)
621 Lawson (1949, p. 254)
622 ibid., p. 250
623 ibid., p. 252
624 ibid., pp. 253-254
625 Waddington (2013, pp. 73-74)
626 ibid., p. 73
627 ibid.
628 See Waddington (2013, pp. 72-73) for a fuller account
629 Bullock (1972, p. 89)
630 ibid., p. 90
631 ibid., p. 106
632 ibid., p. 108
633 ibid., p. 106
634 'Miner Extraordinary', *Yorkshire Television*, 22 July 1969
635 *The Herald*, 12 July 2014
636 *The Telegraph*, 9 July 2014
637 ibid.
638 Crewe (1995, pp' 67-71)
639 Pope-Hennessy (1955, p. 173)
640 quoted in ibid.
641 Bloch (1991, p. 102)
642 ibid.
643 *Hansard*, House of Lords, 14 December 1936
644 ibid.
645 ibid.
646 *The Herald*, 12 July 2014
647 Colville (1963, p. 133)
648 Colville (1976, pp. 45-46)
649 ibid., p. 47
650 ibid.
651 ibid.
652 ibid., p. 48
653 ibid.
654 ibid., p. 49
655 ibid., p. 51
656 ibid., pp. 50-51
657 ibid., p. 51
658 O'Neill (1972, pp. 18-19)
659 ibid., p. 19
660 ibid., p. 17
661 Mulholland (2013, p. 6)
662 O'Neill (1972, p. 19)
663 Mulholland (2013, p. 6)
664 O'Neill (1972, p. 18)
665 Sloan (2020, p. 35)
666 ibid., pp. 35-36
667 ibid., p. 36
668 ibid., p. 38
669 Colville (1985, pp. 15-16)
670 Colville (1963, p. 200)
671 Colville (1985)
672 Colville (1963); Colville (1976); Mulholland (2013)
673 Colville (1985, p. 36)
674 ibid., p. 35
675 Ibid., pp. 28-29
676 *The Telegraph*, 8 July 2014
677 ibid.
678 Colville (1985, pp. 39-40)
679 ibid., p. 40
680 ibid., p. 122
681 ibid., p. 123
682 ibid., p. 125
683 ibid.
684 ibid.
685 ibid., p. 126
686 ibid.
687 ibid., p. 128
688 ibid.
689 ibid.
690 ibid., p. 223
691 Colville (1976, p. 90)
692 Colville (1985, p. 73)
693 Colville (1963, pp. 130-131)
694 ibid., p. 131
695 ibid., p. 199
696 ibid.
697 ibid., p. 202
698 ibid., p. 199
699 ibid.
700 quoted in ibid., p. 200
701 quoted in Colville (1985, p. 424)
702 Colville (1985, p. 446)
703 ibid., p. 452
704 ibid.
705 Colville (1976, p. 159)
706 ibid.
707 Colville (1976, p. 160)
708 ibid., p. 161
709 Colville (1986, p. 492)
710 ibid., p. 493
711 ibid., p. 495
712 ibid., pp. 495-496
713 ibid., p. 501
714 ibid., p. 500
715 ibid.
716 Mulholland (2013, p. 7)
717 ibid., p. 8
718 Waddington (2013, p. 79)
719 Bullock (1972, p. 96)
720 ibid., p. 113
721 ibid., p. 103
722 ibid., p. 102
723 ibid., p. 93
724 ibid., p. 94
725 quoted in ibid., p. 94
726 ibid., p. 95
727 ibid.
728 Bullock (1972, p. 96)
729 ibid., p. 112
730 ibid., p. 113
731 Waddington (2013, pp. 80-83)

732 quoted in Malam (2004, pp. 48-49)
733 Waddington (2013, p. 83)
734 *Pontefract and Castleford Express*, 27 April 1945
735 ibid.
736 Waddington (2013, p. 92)
737 Sloan (2012, p. 51)
738 quoted in ibid., p. 38
739 Sloan (2012, pp. 39-40)
740 ibid., p. 40
741 ibid., p. 38
742 ibid., p. 40
743 *Daily Mail*, 15 May 2009
744 Whetton and Ogden (2004, p.2)
745 ibid., p. 9
746 ibid., p. 5
747 Horrocks (2004, p. v)
748 ibid.
749 bid.
750 Whetton and Ogden (2004, p. 101)
751 Crewe (1991, p. 28)
752 ibid., pp. 28-29
753 ibid., p. 29
754 ibid., p. 32
755 ibid., p. 33
756 ibid., p. 34
757 Colville (1985, pp. 133-134)
758 Crewe (1991, p. 34)
759 ibid., p. 35
760 ibid., p. 36
761 ibid., p. 44
762 ibid., pp. 39-40
763 ibid., p. 40
764 Pope-Hennessy (1955, pp. 177-178)
765 Colville (1985, p. 257)
766 ibid.
767 Crewe (1991, p. 39)
768 Colville (1985, p. 354)
769 ibid.
770 ibid.
771 Crewe (1991, p. 39)
772 Colville (1985, p. 502)
773 ibid., p. 527
774 Colville (1963, p. 198)
775 Crewe (1991, p. 44)
776 Colville (1963, p. 198)
777 ibid.
778 Crewe (1991, p. 44)
779 Colville (1963, p. 202)
780 Crewe (1955, p. xv)
781 ibid.
782 Colville (1985, p. 467)
783 ibid., p. 489
784 ibid., p. 571
785 Pope-Hennessy (1955, p. 178)
786 Colville (1985, p. 609)
787 *Hansard*, House of Lords, 22 August 1945
788 ibid.
789 ibid.
790 See Colville (1985, 609-611)
791 Colville (1976, p. 81)
792 Mulholland (2013, p. 9)
793 Mulholland (2000, pp. 13-14)
794 Crewe (1991, p. 46)
795 ibid., p. 47
796 ibid., pp. 47-51
797 Downes (2016, p. 223)
798 Fishman (1976, p. 274)
799 ibid., p. 284
800 Bullock (1972, p. 115)
801 ibid.
802 ibid.
803 ibid., p. 116
804 Waddington (2013, p. 93)
805 ibid., p. 96
806 Shackleton (1955, p. 61)
807 ibid., p. 62
808 quoted in Malam (2004, p. 49)
809 Shackleton (1955, pp. 60-61)
810 quoted in Malam (2004, p. 49)
811 *Pontefract and Castleford Express*, 29 November 1946
812 quoted in Malam (2004, p. 50)
813 Shackleton (1955, p. 62)
814 Bullock (1972, p. 133)
815 'Miner Extraordinary', *Yorkshire Television*, 22 July 1969
816 Bullock (1972, p. 135)
817 ibid.
818 Downes (2016, p. 224)
819 Bullock (1972, p. 148)
820 Bellamy and Saville (1974)
821 ibid.
822 Bullock (1972, pp. 148-149)
823 'Miner Extraordinary', *Yorkshire Television*, 22 July 1969
824 Bullock (1972, p. 149)
825 'Miner Extraordinary', *Yorkshire Television*, 22 July 1969
826 Bullock (1972, p. 149)
827 quoted in ibid.
828 Bullock (1972, p. 150)
829 'Miner Extraordinary', *Yorkshire Television*, 22 July 1969
830 Bullock (1972, pp. 151 and 153)
831 Sloan (2020, p. 56)
832 ibid.
833 Sloan (2012, p. 22)
834 ibid., p. 23
835 Sloan (2020, p. 56)
836 Sloan (2012, p. 19)
837 ibid.
838 Sloan (2020, p. 21)
839 Sloan (2012, pp. 17-18)
840 Sloan (2020, p. 41)
841 ibid.
842 ibid.
843 Mulholland (2000, pp. 13-14)
844 ibid., p. 10
845 ibid., p. 9
846 ibid., p. 14
847 ibid
848 ibid., pp. 14-15
849 Bradford (1996, pp. 137-138)
850 Colville (1985, p. 618)
851 Colville (1976, pp. 218-219)
852 ibid., p. 219
853 *The Scotsman*, 12 May 2004

854 Bradford (1996, p. 138)
855 Colville (1985, p. 620)
856 ibid., p. 623
857 ibid.
858 ibid., p. 626
859 Colville (1981, p. 151)
860 Crewe (1991, pp. 57-60)
861 ibid., p. 69
862 ibid., p. 70
863 Rhodes-James (1991, pp. 112-113)
864 Parris (1997, p. 96)
865 Rhodes-James (1991, p. 114)
866 Parris (1997, p. 101)
867 ibid.
868 Ibid., p. 102
869 Crewe (1991, p. 75)
870 ibid., p. 76
871 ibid., p. 77
872 ibid.
873 quoted in ibid., p. 77
874 Crewe (1991, p. 79)
875 ibid., p. 80
876 ibid., pp. 80-81
877 ibid., p. 81
878 ibid., p. 82
879 ibid., p. 83
880 Colville (1986, p. 631)
881 ibid., p. 632
882 ibid.
883 ibid., p. 633
884 ibid., p. 634
885 Dockter (2017, p. 24)
886 ibid.
887 Colville (1963, p. 131)
888 ibid.
889 ibid., p. 132
890 Edwards (1984, p. 467)
891 Colville (1985, p. 655)
892 ibid., p. 713
893 ibid.
894 ibid., p. 714
895 Colville (1963, p. 133)
896 Colville (1985, p. 651)
897 ibid., p. 654
898 ibid., p. 668
899 Dockter (2017, p. 26)
900 Colville (1985, pp. 668-699)
901 ibid., p. 669
902 Dockter (2017, p. 26)
903 Colville (1985, p. 669)
904 ibid.
905 Dockter (2017, p. 27)
906 Colville (1985, p. 669)
907 ibid., p. 670
908 ibid.
909 *The Telegraph*, 8 July 2014
910 Ewing (2015, no page number)
911 *The Herald*, 12 July 2014
912 *The Telegraph*, 8 July 2014
913 *The Herald*, 12 July 2014
914 Morris (2015, p. 121)
915 *The Herald*, 12 July 2014
916 *Yorkshire Illustrated*, October 1952, p. 29

917 Bullock (1972, p. 125)
918 ibid., p. 124
919 ibid., p. 125
920 ibid., pp. 125-126
921 ibid.
922 ibid., p. 126
923 ibid., p. 128
924 'Miner Extraordinary', *Yorkshire Television*, 22 July 1969
925 ibid.
926 *Daily Mail*, 10 October 1950
927 *Daily Express*, 5 March 2016
928 ibid.
929 'Miner Extraordinary', *Yorkshire Television*, 22 July 1969
930 Bullock (1972, p. 130)
931 ibid., p. 113
932 ibid., p. 167
933 ibid.
934 ibid., pp. 167-168
935 ibid., p. 169
936 ibid.
937 ibid., p. 170
938 *Yorkshire Evening Post*, 6 May 1952
939 quoted in ibid.
940 quoted in Bullock (1972, p. 171)
941 ibid., p. 176
942 *Look and Learn*, Issue 256, 10 December 1966
943 Bullock (1972, p. 145)
944 ibid.
945 ibid.
946 ibid., pp 147-148
947 ibid., p. 205
948 quoted in ibid., p. 207
949 ibid.
950 ibid., pp. 207-208
951 Bullock (1972, p. 219)
952 quoted in ibid., p. 221
953 Bullock (1972, pp. 223-224)
954 ibid., p. 228
955 Perchard (2006)
956 ibid.
957 quoted in Perchard and Gildart (2018, p. 91)
958 Perchard and Gildart (2018, p. 89)
959 Bullock (1972, p. 192)
960 ibid., p. 193
961 ibid., p. 194 (italics in original)
962 Robens (1972, p. 7)
963 quoted in ibid., p. 3
964 Robens (1972, p. 12)
965 ibid.
966 ibid.
967 Hall (1981, p. 111)
968 ibid.
969 ibid.
970 ibid., p. 110
971 ibid., p. 111
972 Bullock (1972, p. 195)
973 ibid.
974 ibid., p. 196
975 quoted in ibid., p. 253
976 See *Pontefract and Castleford Express*, 30 March 1961; Waddington (1988, p. 87)

977 Downes (2016, p. 224)
978 *Yorkshire Evening News*, 27 January 1956
979 ibid.
980 *Yorkshire Evening News*, 9 May 1963
981 ibid.
982 See Waddington, 2013, chapter 11)
983 ibid.
984 quoted in Waddington (2013, p. 204)
985 ibid., p. 205
986 See Waddington (2013, pp. 217-219) for a
fuller account of the match
987 ibid., p. 248
988 Perchard and Gildart (2018, p. 93)
989 ibid.
990 ibid., pp. 91-92
991 ibid., p. 100
992 ibid., p. 101
993 Crewe (2007, p. 29)
994 ibid., pp. 29-30
995 ibid., p. 30
996 ibid.
997 ibid., p. 32
998 ibid., p. 31
999 ibid., p. 34
1000 ibid.
1001 *Independent*, 16 November 1998
1002 Crewe (1991)
1003 *The Independent*, 16 November 1998
1004 Huth (2018, p. 177)
1005 ibid.
1006 ibid., p. 178
1007 ibid., p. 177
1008 Crewe (2007, p. 36)
1009 Huth (2018, p. 177)
1010 ibid., p. 195
1011 ibid., p. 209
1012 ibid.
1013 ibid., p. 217
1014 Crewe (1991, p. 170)
1015 ibid., pp. 169-170
1016 Hoey (2008, p. 206)
1017 Huth (2018, p. 218)
1018 ibid., p. 219
1019 ibid.
1020 ibid.
1021 Crewe (1991, p. 185)
1022 Huth (2018, p. 221)
1023 ibid., p. 235
1024 ibid., p. 240
1025 ibid.
1026 Crewe (1991, p. 195)
1027 ibid., p. 200
1028 ibid., p. 201
1029 Huth (2018, p. 224)
1030 Crewe (1991, p. 222)
1031 ibid., p. 225
1032 ibid.
1033 ibid., p. 226
1034 Crewe (2007, p. 32)
1035 Crewe (1991, p. 232)
1036 ibid.
1037 ibid.
1038 ibid., p. 233
1039 ibid., p. 238
1040 quoted in Hoey (2005, p. 175)
1041 De Courcy (2008, p. 175)
1042 Crewe (1991, p. 227)
1043 De Courcy (2008, pp. 156-157)
1044 ibid., p. 148
1045 Crewe (1991, p. 228)
1046 *Daily Telegraph*, 19 January 2001
1047 Huth (2018, p. 280)
1048 Crewe (1991, pp. 240-242)
1049 ibid., p. 245
1050 ibid., p. 255
1051 ibid.
1052 ibid., p. 256
1053 ibid.
1054 ibid., p. 257
1055 ibid., p. 258
1056 ibid.
1057 Huth (2018, p. 287)
1058 Crewe (2007, p. 197)
1059 ibid., p. 225
1060 Waddington (1992, p. 143)
1061 ibid.
1062 Mulholland (2013, p. 16)
1063 Bew et al. (1996, p. 128)
1064 Mulholland (2004, no page number)
1065 Mulholland (2000, p. 22)
1066 Mulholland (2004, no page number)
1067 Mulholland (2000, p. 69)
1068 ibid.
1069 Mulholland (2004, no page number)
1070 Mulholland (2000, pp. 62-63)
1071 Mulholland (2004)
1072 Mulholland (2013, p. 36)
1073 Purdie (1990, p. 25)
1074 Mulholland (2013, p. 38)
1075 quoted in ibid.
1076 Purdie (1990, p. 14)
1077 Mulholland (2013, p. 40-41)
1078 Mulholland (2000, p. 69)
1079 ibid., p. 101
1080 Purdie (1990, p. 32)
1081 Mulholland (2000, p. 147)
1082 ibid., p. 159
1083 Mulholland (2004, no page number)
1084 Purdie (1990, p. 34)
1085 ibid.
1086 ibid.
1087 ibid., p. 36
1088 Mulholland, 2000, pp. 161-162)
1089 Waddington (1992, p. 144)
1090 ibid., pp. 144-145
1091 ibid., p. 147
1092 ibid., p. 146
1093 ibid., p. 147
1094 ibid.
1095 Mulholland (2000, p. 164)
1096 Mulholland (2004, no page number)
1097 Farrell (1980, p. 248)
1098 Waddington (1992, p.147)
1099 Warner (2005, p. 25)
1100 Waddington (1992, p. 148)
1101 Mulholland (2000, p. 198)

1102 Crewe (1991, p. 215)
1103 Mulholland (2004, no page number)
1104 ibid.
1105 Mulholland (2013, p. 96)
1106 Sloan (2020, p. 58)
1107 See *Supplement to the London Gazette*, 1 January 1969
1108 'Miner Extraordinary', *Yorkshire Television*, 22 July 1969
1109 ibid.
1110 ibid.
1111 ibid.
1112 ibid.
1113 Lofthouse (1986)
1114 ibid., p. 41
1115 ibid., p. 54
1116 ibid., p. 61
1117 Robens (1972, p. 104)
1118 Lofthouse (1986, p. 64)
1119 ibid., p. 91
1120 ibid.
1121 Tweedale (2008, no page number)
1122 Hall (1981, pp. 152-157)
1123 Robens (1972, p. 19)
1124 ibid., p. 32
1125 ibid., p. 33
1126 Tweedale (2008)
1127 Allen (1981, p. 66)
1128 Bullock (1972)
1129 Robens (1972)
1130 Bullock (1972, p. 196)
1131 ibid., p. 251
1132 ibid., p. 253
1133 Robens (1972, p. 290)
1134 ibid.
1135 Waddington (2011, p. 311)
1136 Thatcher (1995a, p. 218)
1137 See Hall (1981)
1138 Thatcher (1985b)
1139 Lofthouse (1986, p. 91)
1140 ibid., pp. 91-92
1141 quoted in ibid., p. 92
1142 Bullock (1976)
1143 *Radio Times*, Issue 2797, 18 June 1977
1144 Charlton (1998, p. 153)
1145 ibid.
1146 ibid., p. 162
1147 ibid., p. 170
1148 Sloan (2020, p. 41)
1149 Sloan (2012, p. 123)
1150 Sloan (2020, pp. 88-89)
1151 Sloan (2012, p. 136)
1152 ibid., p. 137
1153 ibid.
1154 Lofthouse (1986, p. 93)
1155 ibid., p. 116
1156 ibid.
1157 ibid., pp. 116-117
1158 Waddington et al. (1991)
1159 Downes (2016)
1160 *Pontefract and Castleford Express*, 24 January 1980
1161 e.g. Waddington (2017); Waddington et al. (1991); Waddington et al. (2001)
1162 Waddington et al. (2001, p. 14)

1163 Waddington et al. (1991, p. 8)
1164 See Waddington (2017) for a summary of these standpoints
1165 Lofthouse (1986, p. 117)
1166 ibid., p. 118
1167 NUM activist, quoted in 'Here We Go!', *Channel 4*, 11 February 1985
1168 News At Ten, *BBC 1*, 10 April 1984
1169 Lofthouse (1986, p. 125)
1170 *Wildcat*, Issue 1, September 1984, p. 2
1171 Lofthouse (1986, pp. 125-126)
1172 quoted in Barbara's website blog: https://barstew:wordpress.com/fryston-colliery-village-from-1903/
1173 *Daily Telegraph*, 19 November 1984
1174 Sloan (2012, p. 137)
1175 ibid.
1176 Watters (1992)
1177 *Hansard*, House of Commons, 19 June 1984
1178 *Yorkshire Post*, 14 August 1984
1179 *Pontefract and Castleford Express*, 16 August 1984
1180 ibid.
1181 Lofthouse (1986, p. 125)
1182 Waddington (1988, pp. 85-86)
1183 Sloan (2012, p. 138)
1184 *Pontefract and Castleford Express*, 22 November 1984
1185 Waddington (1988, p. 85)
1186 ibid.
1187 ibid.
1188 ibid., p. 84
1189 News At One, *Independent Television News*, 23 November 1984
1190 quoted in ibid.
1191 ibid.
1192 ibid.
1193 *Panorama*, BBC1, 2 December 1984
1194 ibid.
1195 MacGregor (1986, p. 334)
1196 Callinicos and Simons (1985, p. 193)
1197 Lofthouse (1986, pp. 123-124)
1198 ibid., p. 124
1199 ibid.
1200 Callinicos and Simons (1985, p. 193)
1201 ibid.
1202 'Here We Go!', *Channel 4*, 11 February 1985
1203 ibid.
1204 Winterton and Winterton (1989, pp. 218-219)
1205 *Pontefract and Castleford Express*, 5 December 1985
1206 Lofthouse (1986, p. 124)
1207 See UK Parliament: 'Lord Lofthouse of Pontefract' at https://members.parliament.uk/member/905/career
1208 McClarence (1990)
1209 quoted in Arnot (2013, p. 152)
1210 McClarence (1990)
1211 Hulme (1986); Van Riel et al. (1990)
1212 *Yorkshire Post*, 18 April 2007
1213 ibid.
1214 'Harry Malkin: From Pit to Paintbrush', *In These Times*, 19 November 2012:https://inthesetimes.com/article/harry-malkin-from-pit-to-paintbrush
1215 Hulme (1986, p. 5)

1216 ibid.
1217 ibid., p. 6
1218 ibid., p. 7
1219 ibid., p. 9
1220 ibid., p. 10
1221 ibid., p. 9
1222 ibid., p. 11
1223 McClarence (1990, p. v)
1224 Hulme (1986, p. 14)
1225 Verguson (2007, no page number)
1226 McClarence (1990, p. vi)
1227 ibid., p. vii
1228 *Yorkshire Post*, 18 April 2007
1229 quoted in 'My Town: Miner turned artist, Harry Malkin, on Castleford', 5 January 2016: URL lapsed
1230 ibid.
1231 Arnot (2013, p. 151)
1232 ibid.
1233 Clayton and Handforth, 2015, p. 117)
1234 quoted in *Yorkshire Post*, 4 March 2011
1235 Clayton and Handforth (2015, p. 117)
1236 *Yorkshire Post*, 18 April 2007
1237 quoted in 'My Town: Miner turned artist, Harry Malkin, on Castleford', 5 January 2016: URL lapsed
1238 *Yorkshire Post*, 18 April 2007
1239 Arnot (2013, p. 152)
1240 *Yorkshire Post*, 18 April 2007
1241 ibid.
1242 *Yorkshire Post*, 4 March 2011
1243 'Harry Malkin: From Pit to Paintbrush', *In These Times*, 19 November 2012:https://inthese-times.com/article/harry-malkin-from-pit-to-paint-brush
1244 quoted in 'My Town: Miner turned artist, Harry Malkin, on Castleford', 5 January 2016: URL lapsed
1245 quoted in 'Harry Malkin: From Pit to Paint-brush', *In These Times*, 19 November 2012:https://inthesetimes.com/article/harry-malkin-from-pit-to-paintbrush
1246 *Yorkshire Post*, 4 March 2011
1247 quoted in 'My Town: Miner turned artist, Harry Malkin, on Castleford', 5 January 2016: URL lapsed
1248 Clayton and Handforth, 2015, p. 117)
1249 ibid.
1250 *Yorkshire Post*, 4 March 2011
1251 Waddington (1988, p. 91)
1252 ibid., p. 92
1253 McClarence (1990, p. 1v)
1254 Sloan (2020, p. 46)
1255 ibid., p. 57
1256 Sloan (2012, p. 139)
1257 ibid.
1258 Smith (2006, p. 241)
1259 See also *The Guardian*, 10 February 2006
1260 Smith (2006, p. 241)
1261 Castleford Heritage Trust Homepage: https://www.castlefordheritagetrust.org.uk/
1262 Smith (2006); Smith and Campbell (2011)
1263 Smith (2006, p. 254)
1264 Smith and Campbell (2011, p. 22)
1265 ibid.
1266 Smith (2006, p. 258)
1267 ibid., p. 265
1268 Smith and Campbell (2011, p. 25)
1269 Smith (2006, p. 240)
1270 ibid., p. 237
1271 Holland (2009, p. 115)
1272 Barrie (2009, p. 80)
1273 ibid.
1274 *The Independent*, 3 August 2008
1275 *The Guardian*, 10 February 2006
1276 quoted in *The Independent*, 3 August 2008
1277 Barrie (2009, p. 80)
1278 ibid.
1279 *The Independent*, 3 August 2008
1280 Bailey and Popple (2011, p. 24)
1281 Holland (2009, p. 115)
1282 *Channel 4* episode, 'The Big Town Plan', 18 August 2008
1283 Green (no date, no page number)
1284 ibid.
1285 ibid.
1286 *Channel 4* episode, 'The Big Town Plan', 18 August 2008
1287 quoted in ibid.
1288 ibid.
1289 ibid.
1290 ibid.
1291 ibid.
1292 ibid.
1293 ibid.
1294 ibid.
1295 ibid.
1296 ibid.
1297 Waugh (2012)
1298 ibid., p. 94
1299 ibid., p. 91
1300 ibid., p. 94
1301 ibid., p. 96
1302 ibid., pp. 96-97
1303 ibid., p. 99
1304 ibid., pp. 100-101
1305 ibid., p. 101
1306 ibid., p. 99
1307 bid., p. 105
1308 ibid.
1309 ibid., p. 96
1310 ibid., p. 107
1311 quoted in ibid., p. 103
1312 quoted in *Channel 4* episode, 'The Big Town Plan', 18 August 2008
1313 ibid.
1314 *Yorkshire Post*, 17 October 2005
1315 Lewis (2009)
1316 *Yorkshire Post*, 17 October 2005
1317 quoted in ibid.
1318 Lewis (2009, p. 106)
1319 ibid., p. 103
1320 quoted in ibid., p. 105
1321 Lewis (2009, p. 106)
1322 Male resident, quoted in ibid., p. 103)
1323 Lewis (2009, p. 108)

1324 quoted in ibid., p. 109
1325 ibid.
1326 See, for example, *Pontefract and Castleford Express*, 23 July 2009; *Yorkshire Post*, 16 March 2019
1327 *Yorkshire Post*, 16 March 2010
1328 Castleford Heritage Trust homepage: http://www.castlefordheritagetrust.org.uk/
1329 *Pontefract and Castleford Express*, 18 March 2010 and 7 September 2010
1330 Arnot (2013, p. 154)
1331 Personal communication with Les Oxtoby
1332 *The Independent*, online edition, 8 April 2013: https://www.independent.ie/world-news/europe/margaret-thatcher-death-a-great-day-for-coal-miners-29182097.html
1333 *The Guardian*, 18 December 2015
1334 Parry (2023)
1335 Paxman (2022, p. 26) (italics added)
1336 Crewe (1955, p. x)
1337 ibid.
1338 ibid.
1339 Johnson (2011, p. 52)
1340 ibid.
1341 ibid.
1342 Colville (1963, p. 203)
1343 Sotheby's Press Release, 23 March 2015
1344 ibid.
1345 *The Guardian*, 8 February 2022
1346 *Evening Standard*, 20 May 2015; Morris (2015)
1347 quoted in Sotheby's Press Release, 23 March 2015
1348 BBC News, 16 December 2015: https://www.bbc.co.uk/news/av/uk-england-cambridgeshire-38341609
1349 quoted in *Trinity College*, Cambridge, 15 December 2016:https://www.cambridge-news.co.uk/news/cambridge-news/one-most-important-private-collections-12324769
1350 ibid.
1351 ibid.
1352 *Wakefield Express*, 20 May 2016; *Yorkshire Evening Post*, 20 May 2016
1353 Keir Living Press Release, 30 November 2016:https://www.tiliahomes.co.uk/news/fryston-scheme-offers-move-in-package-for-first-time-buyers-220
1354 *Leeds Live*, 4 May 2019:https://www.leeds-live.co.uk/news/leeds-news/look-around-incredible-16m-hidden-16209269
1355 *Farmers Weekly*, 11 July 2018
1356 *Daily Mail*, 13 July 2018
1357 Leeds Civic Trust: https://openplaques.org/plaques/53704
1358 Leeds Civic Trust (2020) Annual Review. Leeds: Leeds Civic Trust, p. 20
1359 Allen (1981, p. 79)
1360 Dennis et al. (1969, p. 238)
1361 Allen (1981, p. 75)
1362 Dennis et al. (1969, p. 240)
1363 Allen (1981, p. 84)
1364 *The Guardian*, 8 February 2022
1365 Paxman (2022, p. 352)
1366 ibid., p. 353
1367 Beynon and Hudson (2021, p. 341)

List of Interview Respondents, 1986-87

Albert Addy
Colin Addy
Annie Aplin
Les Aplin
Asher Astbury
Bill Astbury
Colin Betteridge
George Box
Bill Bradley
Ivy Bradley
Jim Bullock, OBE
Carol Chilton
Jean Chilton
Harry Copley
Marion Copley
Charles Crossland
Sylvia Crossland
Brian Dakin
Bishop John Daly
Beth Firth
Reg Firth
Jabie Foulkes
Ronnie Foulkes
Hettie Griffiths
Elsie Heaps
Jack Hepton
Jack Hulme
Wilf Hunter
Mary Jones
Tom Jones
John Lofthouse
Dora Lunn
Claude Middleton
Arthur Milner
Minnie Milner
Rose Moss
Les Oxtoby
Nancy Oxtoby
Frances Payne

Joe Payne
Madge Payne
Margaret Perry
Mabel Platt
Maude Raftery
Gertie Renton
Jean Renton
David Rutherforth
Edna Schofield
Frank Schofield
Dr Richard Sloan
Joe Smith
Bill Spedding
Florrie Spedding
Frances Spedding
Christine Stevens
Fred Stevens
Ethel Templeman
Terry Templeman
Tommy Templeman
Alan Town
Mary Waddington
Melvin Waddington
Peter Waddington
Olive Walters
Joan Watson
Dot Weatherill
Harry Weatherill
Edgar Williams
Winnifred Wilson
Jim Winterbottom

References

Ackers, P. and Payne, J. (2002) 'Before the storm: the experience of nationalization and the prospects for industrial relations partnership in the British coal industry, 1947-1972 – rethinking the militant narrative', *Social History*, 27(2): 184-209.

Adams, J. (1985) *Rockerfeller Centre Designation Report*. City of New York: New York City Landmarks Preservation Commission.

Adams, R.J.Q. (1986) 'The May coalition and the coming of conscription, 1915-1916', *Journal of British Studies*, 25(3): 243-263.

Adelson, R. (1995) *London and the Invention of the Middle East: Money, Power, and War, 1902-1922*. London: Yale University Press.

Airedale Collieries Ltd. (1932) *Fryston Colliery Pit Head Baths*. Castleford: Airedale Collieries Ltd.

Allen, V.L. (1981) *The Militancy of the British Miners*. Shipley: The Moor Press.

Anand, A. (2015) *Sophia: Princess, Suffragette, Revolutionary*. London: Bloomsbury.

Anglessey, Lord (1994) *A History of the British Cavalry: Volume 7, 1816-1919 – The Curragh Incident and the Western Front, 1914*. Barnsley: Pen & Sword.

Arnot, C. (2013) *Britain's Lost Mines: The Vanished Kingdom of the Men Who Carved Out the Nation's Wealth*. London: Aurum Press Limited.

Bailey, C. (2008) *Black Diamonds: The Rise and Fall of an English Dynasty*. Harmondsworth: Penguin.

Bailey, M. and Popple, S. (2011) 'The 1984/85 Miners' Strike: re-claiming cultural heritage', in L. Smith, P.A. Shakel and G. Campbell (eds) *Heritage, Labour and the Working Classes*. London: Routledge.

Ballinger, C. (2012) *The House of Lords, 1911-2011: A Century of Non-Reform*. Portland, Oregon: Hart Publishing.

Barker A.J. (ed.) (2009) *The First Iraq War – 1914-18: Britain's Mesopotamian Campaign*. New York: Enigma Books.

Barrie, D. (2009) 'Regeneration as social innovation, not a war game', *Journal of Urban Regeneration and Renewal*, 3(1): 77-91.

Barros, J. (1965) *The Corfu Incident of 1923: Mussolini and the League of Nations*. Princeton, New Jersey: Princeton University Press.

Baylies, C. (1993) *The History of the Yorkshire Miners, 1881-1918*. London: Routledge.

Bell, C.M. (2017) *Churchill and the Dardanelles*. Oxford: Oxford University Press.

Bellamy, J.M. and Saville, J. (1975) *Dictionary of Labour Biography*, Volume I. London: The Macmillan Press. 2nd Edition.

Bellamy, J.M. and Saville, J. (1978) *Dictionary of Labour Biography*, Volume II. London: The Macmillan Press. 2nd. Edition.

Benson, J. (1993) *The Miners of Staffordshire, 1840-1914*. Keele: Centre for Local History, Keele University.

Berlinski, C. (2011) *'There Is No Alternative': Why Margaret Thatcher Matters*. New York: Basic Books.

Berthoud, R. (2003) *The Life of Henry Moore*. London: Giles de la Mare.

Bew, P., Gibbon, P. and Patterson, H. (1996) *Northern Ireland, 1921-1996: Political Forces and Social Classes*. London: Serif.

Beynon, H. and Hudson, R. (2021) *The Shadow of the Mine: Coal and the End of Industrial Britain*. London: Verso.

Bhagavan, M. (2001) 'Demystifying the "Ideal Progressive": resistance through Mimicked Modernity in Princely Baroda, 1900–1913', *Modern Asian Studies*, 35(2): 385-409.

Bloch, M. (2012) *The Reign and Abdication of Edward VIII*. London: Black Swan.

Bond, R.C. (2009) *History of The King's Own Yorkshire Light Infantry in the Great War, 1914-1918*. Uckfield: The Naval & Military Press.

Bowman, T. (2007) *Carson's Army: The Ulster Volunteer Force, 1910-22*. Manchester: Manchester University Press.

Box, E.C. (no date) *The Box Family*. Published by the Author.

Bradford, S. (1996) *Elizabeth: A Biography of Her Majesty the Queen*. London: Heinemann.

Bradley, K. (2017) 'Saving the children of Shoreditch: Lady Cynthia Colville and needy families in East London, c.1900-1960', *Law, Crime and History*, 7(1): 145-163.

Brendon, P. (2000) *The Dark Valley: A Panorama of the 1930s*. London: Pimlico.

Brendon, P. (2008) *The Decline and Fall of the British Empire, 1781-1997*. London: Vintage Books.

Brock, M. and Brock, E. (eds) (2014) *Margot Asquith's Great War Diary, 1914-1916: The View from Downing Street*. Oxford: Oxford University Press.

Bromet, Group Captain G.R. (2009) 'Formation and early days in France', in Capt. E.G. Johnstone, (ed.) *Naval Eight: A History of No. 8 Squadron R.N.A.S. – Afterwards No. 208 Squadron R.A.F. – From its Formation in 1916 Until the Armistice in 1918*. Uckfield: The Naval & Military Press.

Brooker, W. (2016) 'Alice's evidence: examining the cultural afterlife of Lewis Carroll in 1932', *Cultural History*, 5(1): 1-25.

Broomfield, J.H. (1968) *Elite Conflict in a Plural Society: Twentieth-Century Bengal*. Berkeley and Los Angeles: University of California Press.

Bullen, J.B. (2013) *Thomas Hardy: The World of His Novels*. London: Frances Lincoln.

Bullock, A. (1960) *The Life and Times of Ernest Bevin, Volume 1: Trade Union Leader, 1881-1940*. London: Heinemann.

Bullock, J. (1972) *Them and Us*. London: Souvenir Press.

Bullock, J. (1976) *Bowers Row: Recollections of a Mining Village*. Wakefield: EP Publishing.

Bulmer, M.I.A. (1975) 'Sociological models of the mining community', The Sociological Review, 23(1): 61-92.

Burgoyne, M. (2008) 'Conrad's last letter to Sir Sidney Colvin', *The Conradian*, 33(2): 102-117.

Callaway, H. (1993) 'Purity and exotica in legitimating the Empire: cultural constructions of gender, sexuality and race', in T. Ranger and O. Vaughan (eds) *Legitimacy and the State in Twentieth-Century Africa*. London: Springer.

Callinicos, A. and Simons, M. (1985) *The Great Strike: The Miners' Strike of 1984-5 and Its Lessons*. London: Socialist Worker.

Cassels, A. (1970) *Mussolini's Early Diplomacy*. Princeton, New Jersey: Princeton University Press.

Castleford Public Libraries (no date) *The Fryston Estate*. Unpublished Factsheet. Castleford: Castleford Public Libraries.

Charlton, J. (1996) *Jack Charlton: The Autobiography*. London: Partridge Press.

Citrine, Lord (1964) *Man and Work. An Autobiography*. London, Hutchinson.

Clayton, I. and Handforth, M.R. (2015) (eds) *Wisdom of Our Own: Living and Learning Since the Miners' Strike*. Castleford: Castleford Community Learning Centre.

Colville, C. (1963) *Crowded Life: The Autobiography of Lady Cynthia Colville*. London: Evans Brothers Limited.

Colville, J. (1976) *Footprints in Time: Memories*. London: Collins.

Colville, J. (1981) *Winston Churchill and His Inner Circle*. New York: Wyndham Books.

Colville, J. (1985) *The Fringes of Power: Downing Street Diaries, 1939-1955*. London: Hodder and Stoughton.

Corder, C. and Plaut, M. (2014) 'Gandhi's decisive South African 1913 campaign: a personal perspective from the letters of Betty Molteno', *South African Historical Journal*, 66(1): 22-54.

Cowan, T. (2011) *Labour of Love: The Story of Robert Smillie*. Glasgow: Neil Wilson Publishing.

Cowles, V. (1973) *The Rothschilds: A Family of Fortune*. London: Weidenfeld & Nicolson.

Crang, J.A. (2020) *Sisters in Arms: Women in the British Armed Forces During the Second World War*. Cambridge: Cambridge University Press.

Crewe, C. (2007) *Eating Myself*. London: Bloomsbury.

Crewe, Q. (1991) *Well, I Forget the Rest: The Autobiography of an Optimist*. London: Hutchinson.

Crewe, Q. (1995) *Crewe House: The Royal Embassy of the Kingdom of Saudi Arabia*. London: Stacey International.

Crewe, M. (1955) 'Preface', in J. Pope-Hennessy (1955) *Lord Crewe: The Likeness of a Liberal*. London: Constable & Co. Limited.

Crewe, Marquess of (1920) 'Lord Houghton', in T.H. Ward (ed.) *The English Poets: Selections with Critical Introductions*. New York: The Macmillan Company.

Crewe, Marquess of (1929) 'Lord Houghton and his circle', in H. Granville-Barker (ed.) *The Eighteen-Seventies: Essays by Fellows of the Royal Society of Literature*. Cambridge: Cambridge University Press.

Crewe, Marquess of (1931a and b) *Lord Rosebery* (2 Vols.). London: John Murray.

Crowley, P.T. (2004) 'Operational lessons of the Mesopotamia Campaign, 1914–18', *Defence Studies*, 4(3): 335-360.

Curran, T. (2011) 'Who was responsible for the Dardanelles naval fiasco?', *Australian Journal of Politics and History*, 57(1): 17-33.

Curran, T. (2015) *Grand Deception: Churchill and the Dardanelles*. Newport, New South Wales: Big Sky Publishing.

Daly, J. (1985) *Four Mitres: Reminiscences of an Irrepressible Bishop*. Published by the Author.

Dalziel, P. (ed.) (1992) *Thomas Hardy: The Excluded and Collaborative Stories*. Oxford: Clarendon Press.

Davies, J (2008) 'Milnes, Robert Offley Ashburton Crewe, Marquess of Crewe (1958-1945)', *Oxford Dictionary of National Biography*. Oxford: Oxford University Press. http:www.oxforddnb.com/view/article/32628

Davies, P. (1987) *A.J. Cook*. Manchester: Manchester University Press.

De Courcy, A. (2008*) Snowdon: The Biography*. London: Phoenix.

Desai, A. and Vahed, G. (2015) *The South African Gandhi: Stretcher-Bearer of Empire*. Stanford, California: University of Stanford Press.

Dockter, W. (2017) 'Managing a giant: Jock Colville and Winston Churchill', in A. Holt and W. Dockter (eds) *Private Secretaries to the Prime Minister: Foreign Affairs from Churchill to Thatcher*. London: Routledge.

Dorey, P., Kelso, A. (2011) *House of Lords Reform Since 1911: Must the Lords Go?* Palgrave Macmillan, London.

Downes, E. (2016) *Yorkshire Collieries: 1947-1994*. London: Think Pit Publications.

Ebbatson, R. (1993) *Hardy: The Margin of the Unexpressed*. Sheffield: Sheffield Academic Press.

Ede England, R. (2017) *Miners' Battalion; A History of the 12th (Pioneers) King's Own Yorkshire Light Infantry, 1914-1918*. Barnsley: Pen & Sword. (Edited by Malcolm K. Johnson.)

Edwards, A. (1984) *Matriarch: Queen Mary and the House of Windsor*. New York: William Morrow and Co.

Ellmann, M.J. (1950) 'Tennyson: Unpublished Letters,1833-36', *Modern Language Notes*, 65(4): 222-238.

Emery, J, (2019) '"That once romantic now utterly disheartening (former) colliery town": the affective politics of heritage, memory, place and regeneration in Mansfield, UK', *Journal of Urban Cultural Studies*, 6(2/3): 219-240.

Eustis, F.A. II and Zaidi, Z.H. (1964) 'King, viceroy and cabinet: the modification of the partition of Bengal', *History*, 49(166): 171-184.

Farman, C. (1972) *The General Strike, May 1926: Britain's Aborted Revolution?* St Albans: Panther.

Farrell, M. (1980) *Northern Ireland: The Orange State*. London: Pluto Press. Second Edition.

Feaver, W. (1988) *The Pitmen Painters — The Ashington Group, 1934-1984*. London: Chatto & Windus.

Fee, E. (2016) *Disease and Discovery: A History of the Johns Hopkins School of Hygiene & Public Health, 1916-1939*. Baltimore, Maryland: John Hopkins University Press.

Fishman, N. (1996) 'The beginning of the beginning: the National Union of Mineworkers and nationalisation', in A. Campbell, N. Fishman and D. Howell (eds) *Miners, Unions and Politics, 1910-47*. Aldershot: Scolar Press.

Flynn, N. and Taylor, A.P. (1986) 'Inside the rust belt: an analysis of the decline of the West Midlands economy. 1: International and national economic conditions', *Environment and Planning A*, 18: 865-900.

Franks, N (2004) *Sopwith Triplane Aces of World War 1*. Oxford: Osprey Publishing.

Franks, N. (2005) *Sopwith Pup Aces of World War 1*. Oxford: Osprey Publishing.

Fraser, P. (1982) 'British war policy and the Crisis of Liberalism in May 1915', *The Journal of Modern History*, 54(1): 1-26.

Friedman, I. (1973) *The Question of Palestine, 1914-1918: British-Jewish-Arab Relations*. London: Routledge & Kegan Paul.

Geary, R. (1985) *Policing Industrial Disputes: 1893 to 1985*. Cambridge: Cambridge University Press.

Gibson, J. (1996) *Thomas Hardy: A Literary Life*. London: Macmillan Press Ltd.

Gilbert, S.P. (1926) 'The meaning of the "Dawes Plan"', *Foreign Affairs*, 4(3): i-xii.

Gladwyn, C. (1976) *The Paris Embassy*. London: Collins.

Goold, D. (1976) 'Lord Hardinge and the Mesopotamia Expedition and Inquiry, 1914-1917', *The Historical Journal*, 19(4): 919-945.

Green, J. (no date) 'Interview with Martha Schwartz FASLA', American Society of Landscape Architects. https://www.asla.org/ContentDetail.aspx?id=33801

Griffin, A.R. (1962) *The Miners of Nottinghamshire, 1914-1944: A History of the Nottinghamshire Miners' Unions*. London: George Allen & Unwin.

Griffin, A.R. (2005) *Mining in the East Midlands, 1550-1947*. London: Routledge.

Guha, R. (2013) *Gandhi Before India*. London: Allen Lane.

Hall, T. (1981) *King Coal: Miners, Coal and Britain's Industrial Future*. Harmondsworth: Penguin.

Hardy, E. and Pinion, F.B. (eds) (1972) *One Rare Fair Woman: Thomas Hardy's Letters to Florence Henniker, 1893-1922*. London: Macmillan.

Hardy, T. (1984) *The Life and Work of Thomas Hardy*. London: Macmillan.

Hartley, S. (1987) *The Irish Question as a Problem in British Foreign Policy*. New York: St Martin's Press.

Hartwell, Lord (1992) *William Camrose: Giant of Fleet Street*. London: Weidenfeld and Nicolson.

Harvey, S.C. (2016) *Transatlantic Transcendentalism: Coleridge, Emerson and Nature*. Edinburgh: Edinburgh University Press.

Henniker, F.E.H. (1912) *Arthur Henniker: A Little Book for His Friends*. London: A.L. Humphreys.

Herman, A. (2010) *Gandhi and Churchill: The Rivalry that Forged an Empire and Forged Our Age*. London: Random House.

Hess, R.L. (1964) 'The "Mad Mullah" and Northern Somalia', *The Journal of African History*, 5(3): 415-433.

High, S. (2003) *Industrial Sunset: The Making of North America's Rust Belt, 1969-1984*. Toronto: University of Toronto Press.

Hiralal, K. (2014) 'India's voice in the Satyagraha Campaigns in South Africa', *Journal of Sociology and Social Anthropology*, 4: 19-30.

Hoey, B. (2005) *Snowdon: Public Figure, Private Man*. Gloucester: Sutton Publishing.

Holland, P. (2009) 'The after-memory: documentary films and the aftermath of the miners' strike', in G. Williams (ed.) *Shafted: The Media, The Miners' Strike & the Aftermath*. London: Campaign for Press and Broadcasting Freedom.

Horrocks, Lt. Gen. Sir B.G. (2004) 'Foreword' in Lt. Col. J.T. Whetton and Lt. Col. R.H. Ogden (authors) *Z Location or Survey in War: The Story of the 4th Durham Survey Regiment, R.A., T.A.* Swansea: Jim Whetton (Second Edition).

Howie, J. (1986) 'Militarising a society: the Ulster Volunteer Force, 1913-1914', in Y. Alexander and A, O'Day (eds) *Ireland's Terrorist Dilemma*. Lancaster: Martinus Nijhoff.

Hulme, J. (1986) *A Photographic Memory*. Pontefract: Yorkshire Art Circus.

Huth, A. (2018) *Not the Whole Story: A Memoir*. London: Constable.

Huttenback, R.A. (1966) 'Indians in South Africa, 1860-1914: the British imperial philosophy on trial', *The English Historical Review*, 81(319): 273-291.

Hyman, R. (1968) *Elgin and Churchill at the Colonial Office, 1905-1908: The Watershed of the Empire-Commonwealth*. London: Macmillan.

Hyman, R. (2010) *Understanding the British Empire*. Cambridge: Cambridge University Press.

Irons, R. (2013) *Churchill and the Mad Mullah of Somaliland: Betrayal and Redemption, 1899-1921*. Barnsley: Pen & Sword.

Ives, M. (2016) *Reform, Revolution and Direct Action among British Miners: The Struggle for the Charter in 1919*. Chicago, Illinois: Haymarket Books.

Jacobsen, J. (1972) *Locarno Diplomacy: Germany and the West, 1925-29*. Princeton, New Jersey: Princeton University Press.

Jancovich, L. (2016) 'Building local capacity in the arts', *Journal of Policy Research in Tourism, Leisure and Events*, 8(3): 289-306.

Jardine, D. (1927) *The Mad Mullah of Somaliland*. London: Herbert Jenkins Limited.

Johnson, D.A. (2015*) New Delhi: The Last Imperial City*. London: Palgrave Macmillan.

Johnson, G. (2000) 'Lord D'Abernon, Austen Chamberlain and the origin of the Treaty of Locarno', *Electronic Journal of International History*, Article 2: 1-9. https://sas-space.sas.ac.uk/3386/1/Journal_of_International_History_2000_n2_-_Johnson.pdf

Johnson, G. (2006) 'Austen Chamberlain and Britain's relations with France, 1924–1929', *Diplomacy and Statecraft*, 17(4): 753-769.

Johnson, G. (2011a) 'Sir Austen Chamberlain, the Marquess of Crewe and Anglo-French relations, 1924-1928', *Contemporary British History*, 25(1): 49-64.

Johnson, G. (2011b) '"Diplomatic light and shade": Sir Eric Phipps and Anglo-French relations, 1922-1928', in J. Fisher and A. Best (eds) *On the Fringes of Diplomacy: Influences on British Foreign Policy, 1800-1945*. Aldershot: Avebury.

Johnstone, Capt. E.G. (ed.) (2009) *Naval Eight: A History of No. 8 Squadron R.N.A.S. – Afterwards No. 208 Squadron R.A.F. – From its Formation in 1916 Until the Armistice in 1918*. Uckfield: The Naval & Military Press.

Kaplan, F. (1993) *Thomas Carlyle: A Biography*. Berkeley, California: University of California Press.

Kavanagh, D, and Seldon, A. (1999) *The Powers Behind the Prime Minister: The Hidden Influence of Number Ten*. London: HarperCollins.

King, K.R. and Morgan, W.W. (1979) 'Hardy and the Boer War: the public poet in spite of himself', *Victorian Poetry*, 17(1/2): 66-83.

Lambert, N.A. (2012) *Planning Armageddon: British Economic Warfare and the First World War*. Cambridge, Massachusetts: Harvard University Press.

Lawson, J. (1941) *The Man in the Cap: The Life of Herbert Smith*. London: Methuen and Co.

Laybourn, K. (1993) *The General Strike of 1926*. Manchester: Manchester University Press.

Leeds Civic Trust (2020) *Annual Review 2020*. Leeds: Leeds Civic Trust.

Lewis, B. (2009) *Castleford on Aire: The Regeneration of a Yorkshire Town, 1990-2008*. Pontefract: Pontefract Press.

Livingstone, N. (2021) *The Women of Rothschild: The Untold Story of the World's Most Famous Dynasty*. London: John Murray.

Lloyd George, David (1910) *The People's Budget: Better Times*. London: Hodder & Stoughton.

Lofthouse, G. (1986) *A Very Miner MP*. Pontefract: Yorkshire Art Circus.

Lumsdon, J. (no date) 'Pithead Baths Researched by John Lumsdon'. http://btckstorage.blob.core.windows.net › site559

Lynch, T. (2016) *Pontefract & Castleford in the Great War*. Barnsley: Pen & Sword.

Lyon, L. (1922) *The Pomp of Power*. New York: George H. Doran.

MacGregor, I. (1986) *The Enemies Within: The Story of the Miners' Strike: 1984-5*. London: Collins.

Magee, F. (1995) '"Limited liability": Britain and the Treaty of Locarno', *Twentieth Century British History*, 6(1): 1-22.

Malam, C. (2004) *Clown Prince of Soccer? The Len Shackleton Story*. Compton, Newbury, Berkshire: Highdown.

Manning, P. (1977) *Police Work: The Social Organization of Policing*. Cambridge, Massachusetts: MIT Press.

Marriott, Sir J. (1932) 'Lord Rosebery', *Fortnightly Review*, 131 (January, 1932): 121-122.

Mathew, W.M. (2011) 'War-time contingency and the Balfour Declaration of 1917: an improbable regression', *Journal of Palestine Studies*, 40(2): 26-42.

Mathew, W.M. (2013) 'The Balfour Declaration and the Palestine Mandate, 1917–1923: British imperialist imperatives', *British Journal of Middle Eastern Studies*, 40(3): 231-250.

McClarence, S. (1990) 'Introduction' in R. Van Riel, O. Fowler and H. Malkin (eds) *World Famous Round Here: The Photographs of Jack Hulme*. Pontefract: Yorkshire Art Circus.

McEwan, J.M. (1972) 'The Liberal Party and the Irish Question during the First World War', *Journal of British Studies*, 12(1): 109-131.

McIlheney, C.J. '(1985) 'Arbiters of Ulster's destiny? The military role of the Protestant paramilitaries in Northern Ireland', *Conflict Quarterly*, 5(2): 33-40.

McIlroy, J. (2009) 'Nottinghamshire', in J. McIlroy, A. Campbell and K. Gildart (eds) *Industrial Politics and the 1926 Mining Lockout: The Struggle for Dignity*. Cardiff: University of Wales Press.

McKinstry, L. (2006) *Rosebery: Statesman in Turmoil*. London: John Murray.

McLynn, F. (2013) *The Road Not Taken: How Britain Narrowly Missed a Revolution, 1381-1926*. London: Vintage Books.

Millgate, M. (ed.) (1984) *The Life and Work of Thomas Hardy by Thomas Hardy*. London: Macmillan Press Ltd.

Millgate, M. (2004) *Thomas Hardy: A Biography Revisited*. Oxford: Oxford University Press.

Milnes, R.O.A. (2nd Lord Houghton) (1891) *Stray Verses, 1889-1890*. London: John Murray.

Moore, H. and Hedgecoe, J. (1986) *Henry Moore: My Ideas, Inspiration and Life as an Artist*. London: Ebury Press.

Morris, M. (1973) *The British General Strike 1926*. London: The Historical Society.

Morris, M. (1976) *The General Strike*. Penguin: Harmondsworth.

Morris, R. (2015) 'Treasures of a Duchess', *Homes and Antique Magazine*, June 2015: 127.

Mulholland, M. (2000) *Northern Ireland at the Crossroads: Ulster Unionism and the O'Neill Years, 1960-9*. London: Macmillan Press.

Mulholland, M. (2004) 'O'Neill, Terence, Marne, Baron O'Neill of the Maine (1914-1990)', *Oxford Dictionary of National Biography, Vol. 1* (online edition). Oxford University Press. https://www.oxforddnb.com/display/10.1093/ref:odnb/9780198614128.001.0001/odnb-9780198614128-e-39857?docPos=1

Mulholland, M. (2013) *Terence O'Neill*. Dublin; University College Dublin Press.

Neumann, T. (2016) *Remaking the Rust Belt: The Postindustrial Transformation of North America*. Philadelphia, Pennsylvania: University of Pennsylvania Press.

O'Day, A. and Stevenson, J. (1992) 'Ulster's Solemn League and Covenant, Saturday, 28 September 1912', in A. O'Day and J. Stevenson (eds) *Irish Historical Documents Since 1800*. Dublin: Gill and Macmillan.

O'Neill, T. (1972) *The Autobiography of Terence O'Neill – Prime Minister of Northern Ireland 1963-1969*. London: Rupert Hart-Davis.

O'Riordan, E.Y. (2001) *Britain and the Ruhr Crisis*. London: Palgrave.

O'Riordan, E.Y. (2004) 'British policy and the Ruhr Crisis, 1922-24', *Diplomacy & Statecraft*, 15(2): 221-251).

Page, N. (1986) *Thomas Hardy Annual, No. 4*. London: Springer.

Page Arnot, R. (1949) *The Miners: A History of the Miners' Federation of Great Britain, 1889-1910*. London: George Allen & Unwin.

Page Arnot, R. (1953) *The Miners: Years of Struggle – A History of the Miners' Federation of Great Britain (from 1910 onwards)*. London: George Allen & Unwin.

Parris, M. (1997) *Great Parliamentary Scandals: Four Centuries of Calumny, Smear & Innuendo*. London: Robson Books.

Paxman, J. (2012) *Empire: What Ruling the World Did to the British*. London: Viking.

Paxman, J. (2022) *Black Gold: The History of How Coal Made Britain*. London: William Collins.

Penn, G. (1999) *Fisher, Churchill and the Dardanelles*. Barnsley: Leo Cooper.

Perchard, A. (2006) "'Colliers with a collar on": the mine management professions in the Scottish coal mining industry, 1930-1966', *Forschungen und Forschungsberichte*, 36: 85-104.

Perchard, A. and Gildart, K. (2018) "'Run with the fox and hunt with the hounds": managerial trade-unionism and the British Association of Colliery Management, 1947.–1994', *Historical Studies in Industrial Relations*, 39: 79-110.

Pettit, C. (2016) *Reading Thomas Hardy*. London: Springer.

Phelps Hall, W. (1932) 'Rosebery', *The American Historical Review*, 38(1): 117-119.

Phillips, G.A. (1976) *The General Strike: The Politics of Industrial Conflict*. London: Weidenfeld and Nicolson.

Pinion, F.B. (1990) *Hardy the Writer*. London: Palgrave Macmillan.

Pite, R, (2006) *Thomas Hardy: The Guarded Life*. London: Picador

Pole, F. (1932) 'Lord Rosebery', *The Downside Review*, 50(1): 74-86.

Pope-Hennessy, J. (1949) *Monckton-Milnes: The Years of Promise: 1809-1851*. London: Constable.

Pope-Hennessy, J. (1951) *Monckton Milnes: The Flight of Youth, 1851-1885*. London: Constable.

Pope-Hennessy, J. (1955) *Lord Crewe: The Likeness of a Liberal*. London: Constable & Co. Limited.

Pope-Hennessy, J. (1959) *Queen Mary*. London: Unwin Paperbacks.

Purdie, B. (1990) *Politics in the Street: The Origins of the Civil Rights Movement in Northern Ireland*. Belfast: The Blackstaff Press.

Ray, C.E. (2015) *Crossing the Color Line: Race, Sex, and the Contested Politics of Colonialism in Ghana*. Athens, Ohio: Ohio University Press.

Ray, M. (1997) *Thomas Hardy: A Textual Study of the Short Stories*. Aldershot: Ashgate.

Raynes, J.R. (1928) *Coal and Its Conflicts: A Brief Record of the Disputes Between Capital & Labour in the Coal Mining Industry of Great Britain*. London: Ernest Benn Limited.

Reddy, E,S. (2016) *Gandhi and the Chinese in South Africa*. Occasional Paper, 3. Rajghat, New Delhi: National Gandhi Museum.

Reed, C.V. (2017) *Royal Tourists, Colonial Subjects and the Making of a British World, 1860-1911*. Manchester: Manchester University Press.

Reid, S.J. (ed.) (2010) *Memoirs of Sir Wemyss Reid, 1842-1855*. London: Aeterna Press.

Rhodes James, R. (1991) *Bob Boothby: A Portrait*. London: Hodder and Stoughton.

Robens, Lord (1972) *Ten Year Stint*. London: Cassell.

Rockefeller, D. (2003) *Memoirs*. New York: Random House.

Rosebery, Earl of (1955) 'Lord Crewe's interest in racing: a note by the Earl of Rosebery', Appendix 1 in J. Pope-Hennessy (1955) *Lord Crewe: The Likeness of a Liberal*. London: Constable & Co. Limited.

Rothwell, V.H. (1970) 'Mesopotamia in British war aims, 1914-1918', *The Historical Journal*, 13(2): 273-294.

Salford, S. (2009) *Why the Garden Club Couldn't Save Youngstown: The Transformation of the Rust Belt*. Harvard, Connecticut: Harvard University.

Sanderson, E. (1910) *King Edward VII, His Life and Reign: The Record of a Noble Career*. London: Gresham Publishing.

Sangari, K. (2019) 'Who is an Alien?', *Social Scientist*, 47(1–2): 15-36.

Scientific American (1853) 'Coal – Our Black Diamonds', *Scientific American*, 8(36): 285.

Scepanovic, J. (2018) 'David Lloyd George and the Balfour Declaration: assessing the role of Individuals in historic policy making', *Fudan Journal of the Humanities and Social Sciences*, 11: 389–410.

Schneer, J. (2011) *The Balfour Declaration: The Origins of the Arab-Israeli Conflict*. London: Bloomsbury.

Schuyler, R.L. (1932) 'Lord Rosebery by Marquess of Crewe', *Political Science Quarterly*, 47(3): 449-451.

Seldon, A. (2017) 'Conclusion: The prime minister's private office from John Martin to Chris Martin', in A. Holt and W. Dockter (eds) *Private Secretaries to the Prime Minister: Foreign Affairs from Churchill to Thatcher*. London: Routledge.

Sengupta, R. (2007) *Delhi Metropolitan: The Making of an Unlikely City*. London: Penguin.

Shackleton, L. (1955) *Len Shackleton, Clown Prince of Soccer: His Autobiography*. London: Nicholas Kaye.

Skelly, J.M. (2009) 'Introduction: "In Mesopotamia a safe game must be played"', in A.J. Barker (2009) *The First Iraq War – 1914-18: Britain's Mesopotamian Campaign*. New York: Enigma Books.

Sloan, R. (2012) *The English Doctor*. Bloomington, Indiana: Xlibris.

Sloan, R. (2020) *Tieve Tara*. Tolworth: Grosvenor House.

Smith. J. (2015) *Churchill's Secret*. London: Abacus.

Smith, L. (2006) *Uses of Heritage*. London: Routledge.

Smith, L. and Campbell, G. (2011) 'Don't mourn organise: heritage, recognition and memory in Castleford, West Yorkshire', in L. Smith, P. Shakel and G. Campbell (eds) *Heritage, Labour and the Working Classes*. London: Routledge.

Sokolow, N. (1919) *History of Zionism, 1600-1918*. London: Longmans, Green and Co.

Stationery Office, The (2000) *Lord Kitchener and Winston Churchill: The Dardanelles, Commission Part 1, 1914-15*. London: The Stationery Office.

Stephenson, C. and Wray, D. (2005) 'Emotional regeneration through community action in post-industrial mining communities: the New Herrington Miners' Banner Partnership', *Capital and Class*, 25(3): 175-199.

Sterrett, J.E. (1927) 'The Dawes plan in operation', *The Journal of Accountancy*, 43(6): 401-416.

Stewart, J.L.M. (1971) *Thomas Hardy*. London: Longman.

Stokes, W. and Thorne, R.G. (1986) 'Milnes, Robert Pemberton (1784-1858), of Fryston Hall, Yorks', in R.G. Thorne (ed.) *The History of Parliament: The House of Commons 1790-1820*.

https://www.historyofparliamentonline.org/volume/1790-1820/member/milnes-robert-pemberton-1784-1858

Stuart, C. (1921) *Secrets of Crewe House: The Story of a Famous Campaign*. London: Hodder and Stoughton.

Sykes, G. (1986) 'A privilegd eye', *Yorkshire Artscene*, November 1986, 66-68.

Sykes, G (1987) 'All for pleasure', *Amateur Photographer*, Week Ending 10 January 1987: 66.

Taylor, A. (1984) *The Politics of the Yorkshire Miners*. Beckenham: Croom Helm.

Taylor, A. (1996) 'The politics of labourism in the Yorkshire coalfield, 1926-1945', in A. Campbell, N. Fishman and D. Howell (eds) *Miners, Unions and Politics, 1910-47*. Aldershot: Scolar Press.

Taylor, A.J.P. (2001) *English History, 1914-1945*. Oxford: Oxford University Press.

Taylor, P.M. (1980) 'The Foreign Office and British propaganda during the First World War', *The Historical Journal*, 23(4): pp. 875-98.

Thatcher, M. (1995a) *The Path to Power*. London: HarperCollins.

Thatcher, M. (1995b) *The Downing Street Years*. London: HarperCollins.

Thompson, S. (2013) '"But ye de de art, divvint ye?" Authenticity, identity and the historicisation of the Pitmen Painters', *Visual Studies*, 28(3): 207-217.

Thornton, N. (2017) *Led By Lions: MPs and Sons Who Fell in the First World War*. Stroud: Fonthill Media.

Thorpe, D.R. (2011) *Supermac: The Life of Harold Macmillan*. London: Pimlico.

Tomalin, C. (2007) *Thomas Hardy: The Time-Torn Man*. London: Windsor Paragon.

Ulrichsen, K.C. (2007) 'The British occupation of Mesopotamia, 1914–1922', *Journal of Strategic Studies*, 30(2): 349-377.

Vahed, G. (2019) 'An evil thing': Gandhi and Indian indentured labour in South Africa, 1893–1914', *South Asia Journal of South Asian Studies*, 4(4): 654-674.

van der Vat (2009) *The Dardanelles Disaster: Winston Churchill's Greatest Failure*. London: Duckworth Overlook.

Van Riel, R., Fowler, O. and Malkin, H. (eds) *World Famous Round Here: The Photographs of Jack Hulme*. Castleford: Yorkshire Art Circus.

Vereté, M (1970) 'The Balfour Declaration and its makers', *Middle Eastern Studies*, 6(1): 48-76.

Verma, R.S. (2009/2010) 'Gopal Krishna Gokhale and his contribution to struggle of people of Indian origin in South Africa', *Proceedings of the Indian History Congress*, 70: 860-868.

Villiers, K. (no date) *Memoirs of a Maid of Honour*. London: Ivor Nicholson and Watson.

Waddington, D.P. (1988) *One Road In, One Road Out: A People's History of Fryston*. Sheffield: PAVIC Publications.

Waddington, D.P. (1992) *Contemporary Issues in Public Disorder: A Comparative and Historical Approach*. London: Routledge.

Waddington, D.P. (2013) *Coal, Goals and Ashes: Fryston Colliery's Pursuit of the West Riding County FA Challenge Cup*. Pontefract: Route.

Waddington, D.P. (2017) 'An open and shut case? Reappraising "conspiracy" and "cock-up" theories of the strike', in D. Allsop, C. Stephenson and D. Wray (eds) *Justice Denied: Friends, Foes & the Miners' Strike*. London: Merlin.

Waddington, D.P. (2020) *Pit-Folk and Peers: The Remarkable History of the People of Fryston – Volume 1: Echoes of Fryston Hall (1809-1908)*. Pontefract: Route.

Waddington, D.P., Critcher, C., Dicks, B. and Parry, D. (2001) *Out of the Ashes? The Social Impact of Industrial Contraction and Regeneration on Britain's Mining Communities*. London: Routledge.

Waddington, D.P., Wykes, M. and Critcher, C. (1991) *Split at the Seams? Community, Continuity and Change After the 1984-5 Coal Dispute*. Buckingham: Open University Press.

Warner, G. (2005) 'Putting pressure on O'Neill: The Wilson Government and Northern Ireland', *Irish Studies Review*, 13(1): 13-31.

Wassell, J. (2009) *A History of Airedale with Fryston and Guide to the Holy Cross Church*. Ferrybridge: Pen2Print.

Wasserstein, W. (1992) *Herbert Samuel: A Political Life*. Oxford: Clarendon Press.

Watters, F. (1992) *Being Frank: The Memoirs of Frank Watters*. Barnsley: Monkspring Publications.

Waugh, E. (ed.) (2012) *Recycling Spaces: Curating Urban Evolution: The Landscape Design of Martha Schwartz Partners*. London: Thames & Hudson.

Wemyss Reid, T. (1890a) *Life, Letters and Friendships of Richard Monckton Milnes, First Lord Houghton, Volume 1*. London: Cassell & Company Limited.

Wemyss Reid, T. (1890b) *Life, Letters and Friendships of Richard Monckton Milnes, First Lord Houghton, Volume 2*. London: Cassell & Company Limited.

Weston, C.C. and Kelvin, P. (1984) 'The "Judas Group" and the Parliament Bill of 1911', *The English Historical Review*, 99(392), 551-563.

Whetton, Lt. Col. J.T and Ogden, Lt. Col. R.H. (2004) *Z Location or Survey in War: The Story of the 4th Durham Survey Regiment, R.A., T.A.* Swansea: Jim Whetton (Second Edition).

Williamson, B. (1982) *Class, Culture and Community: A Biographical Study of Social Change in Mining*. London: Routledge & Kegan Paul.

Williamson, S. (1999) *Gresford: The Anatomy of a Disaster*. Liverpool: Liverpool University Press.

Winterton, J. (1985) 'The crisis in British coal mining', *Insurgent Sociologist*, 13(1-2): 53-62.

Winterton, J. and Winterton, R. (1989) *Coal, Crisis and Conflict: The 1984-85 Miners' Strike in Yorkshire*. Manchester: Manchester University Press.

Woodward, K. (1929) *Queen Mary: A Life and Intimate Study*. London: Hutchinson and Co.

Wray, D. (2011) 'Images, icons and artefacts: maintaining an industrial culture in a post-industrial environment', in L. Smith, P. Shakel and G. Campbell (eds) *Heritage, Labour and the Working Classes*. London: Routledge.

Yearwood, P.J. (1986) '"Consistency with Honour": Great Britain and the League of Nations and the Corfu Crisis of 1923', *Journal of Contemporary History*, 21: 559-579.

Further Fryston Titles
by David P. Waddington

Pit-folk and Peers: The Remarkable History of the People of Fryston: Volume I — Echoes of Fryston Hall (1809-1908)

The West Riding pit village of Fryston was once famously referred to as 'a mining Shangri-la'. Nestling on one side against the mighty River Aire and hemmed in by colliery buildings on the other, this small, isolated community of twelve terraced streets was only accessible via a narrow railway bridge. No village was more emblematic of the nature of mining tradition and community, and of a once-fabled but now endangered way of life.

The name of the village pub, the 'Milnes Arms', alluded to Fryston's fascinating past, for the local mine and associated village were established in the grounds of the vast Fryston Hall estate, owned by the wealthy cloth-trading Milnes dynasty of Wakefield. Most prominent in this narrative is the name of Richard Monckton Milnes, subsequently Lord Houghton (1809-1885). Best known as the earliest biographer of John Keats and long-time suitor of Florence Nightingale, Milnes was also a poet of great distinction, and an enlightened, charismatic, reformist politician who championed the great humanitarian issues of the day. During his lifetime, Fryston Hall became the most important hub of Victorian society outside of London, attracting the most eminent poets, writers, politicians, adventurers and other celebrities of the era.

He nonetheless cut an extremely controversial figure. Milnes's Fryston Hall library reputedly contained the largest collection of erotic literature and artefacts in Europe, and he is said to have frequented London flagellation brothels as part of a famously libertine lifestyle. Such details cannot detract from the fact that Milnes engaged in countless acts of practical and financial support towards struggling or needy individuals and institutions, thus making him perhaps the foremost philanthropist and patron of the arts of the entire nineteenth century.

This family tradition was continued by two of Milnes's three children. His only son, Robert Offley Ashburton Milnes, became a renowned career politician and close friend and confidant of Edward VII (who visited Fryston in 1896). The younger of Milnes's two daughters, Florence, was a novelist and animal rights activist. She is best remembered as the woman who rejected the amorous advances of Thomas Hardy, but provided the muse for several instances of his work, most notably for the character of Sue Bridehead in *Jude the Obscure*.

The transitional period of the early twentieth century saw a severing of ties between the Milnes family and Fryston Hall estate which triggered its rapid physical deterioration. This was in stark contrast to the ongoing consolidation and development of Fryston village. In this, the first of two volumes tracing the 'remarkable history of the people of Fryston', David Waddington outlines the immense cultural, political, social and humanitarian contributions made to British society by Richard Monckton Milnes and his immediate descendants by focusing our attention on the echoes of Fryston Hall.

Coal, Goals and Ashes: Fryston Colliery's Pursuit of the West Riding County FA Challenge Cup

On 22 May 1963, a group of men representing Fryston Colliery Welfare ran out against the much-vaunted Bradford team, Thackley AFC, to contest the final of the West Riding County FA Challenge Cup, the 'ultimate prize' for local amateur teams. Captaining the Fryston side that day was Pete Waddington.

To mark the fiftieth anniversary of the final, the author, academic and son of The Colliers' captain, Dave Waddington, has produced a book that tells the story of a century of footballing exploits by a team from the heart of the Yorkshire coalfield. This is an account of 'bread and butter' contests, where the slope of the pitch and the strength of the wind are important factors in results, where 'unnecessary roughness' is all part of the game. It is an account of a group of working men from one small village, whose endeavours in pursuit of the 'ultimate prize' are revealed to be just as extraordinary as those of their supposedly more illustrious contemporaries of the professional game.

Armed with three years' worth of research in local archives, and interviews with the surviving players from the final, Waddington has used all the academic discipline he can muster to try and provide an objective and dispassionate account, both of the final and of the wider history of the club. What has emerged, however, is a story of sporting heroism and romance, where the names of heroes like Dick and Jabie Foulkes, Archie Ward, Jack Sharp, Agga Mattison, Cobbo Robinson and Freddie Howard resonate just as loudly as those of the professional icons, such as Clem Stephenson, Len Shackleton, John Charles and Stanley Matthews, who we also encounter along the way.

For more information on these books,
and the full Route list of titles, visit:
www.route-online.com